A-LEVEL
AND AS-LEVEL

LONGMAN
REVISE
GUIDES

ART AND DESIGN

Tom McLean
Bill Read

Longman

LONGMAN A AND AS-LEVEL REVISE GUIDES

Series editors
Geoff Black and Stuart Wall

Titles available
Art and Design
Biology
Chemistry
Computer Science
Economics
English
French
Geography
Mathematics
Modern History
Physics
Sociology

NAMES AND ADDRESSES OF THE EXAM BOARDS

Associated Examining Board (AEB)
Stag Hill House
Guildford
Surrey GU2 5XJ

University of Cambridge Local Examinations Syndicate (UCLES)
Syndicate Buildings
1 Hills Road
Cambridge CB1 1YB

Joint Matriculation Board (JMB)
Devas St
Manchester M15 6EU

University of London Schools Examination Board (ULSEB)
Stewart House
32 Russell Square
London WC1B 5DN

Northern Ireland Schools Examination Council (NISEC)
Beechill House
42 Beechill Road
Belfast BT8 4RS

Oxford and Cambridge Schools Examination Board (OCSEB)
10 Trumpington Street
Cambridge CB2 1QB

Oxford Delegacy of Local Examinations (ODLE)
Ewert Place
Summertown
Oxford OX2 7BX

Scottish Examination Board (SEB)
Ironmills Road
Dalkeith
Midlothian EH22 1BR

Welsh Joint Education Committee (WJEC)
245 Western Avenue
Cardiff CF5 2YX

Longman Group UK Limited,
Longman House, Burnt Mill, Harlow,
Essex CM20 2JE, England
and Associated Companies throughout the world.

First published 1990
Second impression 1991

British Library Cataloguing in Publication Data

McClean, Tom
Art and design. – (Longman A-Level revise guides).
1. England. Secondary schools. Curriculum subjects:
Visual arts. Examinations
I. Title II. Read, Bill
707.6

ISBN 0–582–05780–9

Produced by Longman Singapore Publishers Pte Ltd
Printed in Singapore

CONTENTS

EDITORS' PREFACE

Longman A Level Revise Guides, written by experienced examiners and teachers, aim to give you the best possible foundation for success in your course. Each book in the series encourages thorough study and a full understanding of the concepts involved, and is designed as a subject companion and study aid to be used throughout the course.

Many candidates at A Level fail to achieve the grades which their ability deserves, owing to such problems as the lack of a structured revision strategy, or unsound examination technique. This series aims to remedy such deficiencies, by encouraging a realistic and disciplined approach in preparing for and taking exams.

The largely self-contained nature of the chapters gives the book a flexibility which you can use to your advantage. After starting with the background to the A, AS Level and Scottish Higher Courses and details of the syllabus coverage, you can read all other chapters selectively, in any order appropriate to the stage you have reached in your course.

Geoff Black and Stuart Wall

INTRODUCTION: HOW TO USE THIS BOOK

1. Quotations from known sources are printed in ***bold italics***, with the source acknowledged each time. This is to enable you to follow up references in more detail if you wish.
2. The names of designers, architects, craftspersons and movements in art and design are printed in capital letters when they first appear in a section of the book, to allow you to identify them quickly. This first mention accompanied by a date, where appropriate, so that you can begin to build up a 'time scale' in your mind.
3. Information about examining boards and the practices in art and design, such as drawing, painting, stage design and so on, is carried in individual chapters.
4. Information about those aspects of art and design which will benefit your examination result most, such as 'historical knowledge' or 'contextual knowledge', is carried continuously throughout the book. What is said in each chapter is part of a cumulative build-up of knowledge and understanding. This makes it important for you to read the whole book. Each examining board has more or less the same fundamental beliefs about art and design, whatever the specifications in their syllabus. These beliefs are the foundations of the information given here.
5. This book deals with 'ways of working' towards the best examination results possible. It does not give you lists of *things* you must do, but rather *recommends* approaches you should take in the interests of your overall enjoyment of the subject, and of course, your final examination result.

CHAPTER 1

SYLLABUS CONTENT AND TECHNICAL TERMS

GETTING STARTED

This book is intended to help you to study for any Advanced Level (A-level) or Advanced Supplementary (AS-level) Art and Design examinations offered by any of the examinations boards in England, Wales and Northern Ireland. The Scottish Higher Grade and Certificate of Sixth-Year Studies are also covered.

If you are a full- or part-time student at a school or college, the examination board will normally be chosen for you and this will determine the form your examination will take. If you are a private or external candidate, you will need to decide which syllabus and scheme of examination you prefer, and you will then have to register as a candidate. Syllabuses with a compulsory coursework requirement are not normally available to private candidates.

A number of examination boards set their own version of a syllabus and examination for these courses in art and design. Not all of them call their syllabus and examination 'Art and Design', but for the purpose of this book, we shall refer to each syllabus and the range of study it encourages and examines by that name.

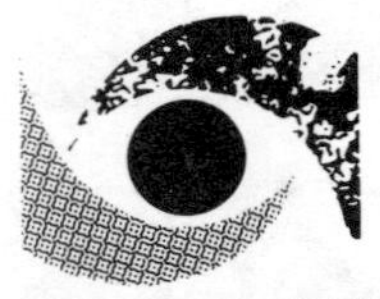

ESSENTIAL PRINCIPLES

EXAMINATION BOARDS AND SYLLABUSES

In Table 1.1 you can see the title each examining board gives its syllabus and examination. This is the title your examination award will have on it.

AS-level art and design examinations

AS-level examinations are intended to broaden the sixth-form curriculum and allow students to study for an examination in a subject different from their main A-level examinations.

The syllabuses in art and design are generally broadly based rather than specialist, but in all cases it is intended that the standard of work should be the equivalent of A-level. For the purposes of university and polytechnic entrance requirements, however, the two-year AS examinations are considered to be worth half an A-level. Chapter 10 will provide details of these syllabuses.

EXAMINING BOARD	SYLLABUS	SYLLABUS No.
Associated Examining Board* (AEB)	Art – Painting	603
	Art and Crafts	605
	Crafts – Printmaking	662
	Crafts – Pottery	663
University of Cambridge Local Examinations Syndicate** (CAMBRIDGE)	Art and Design	9309
Joint Matriculation Board** JMB	Art and Design	
	Craft (Design and Practice)	
Northern Ireland Schools Examinations Council (NISEC)	Art – Syllabus A	
	Art – Syllabus B	
University of Oxford Delegacy of Local Examinations (OXFORD)	Art with Art History	9894
Oxford and Cambridge Schools Examinations Board (OX/CAM)	Art and Design 1991	9642
Scottish Examination Board (SEB)	Art and Design	
University of London School Examinations Board** (ULSEB)	Art and Design	020
	Art and Design – Fine Art	021
	Art and Design – 3D Design	022
	Art and Design – Fashion Textiles	023
	Art and Design – Graphic Design	024
	Art and Design – Photography	025
	Art and Design – Film and Video	026
	Art and Design – Critical and Historical Studies	027
Welsh Joint Education Committee** (WJEC)	Art and Design	

* The abbreviations in brackets after the full names of the examining boards will be used for convenience throughout the book.

** These boards also offer Advanced-Supplementary examinations in Art and Design.

Table 1.1 List of A-level examining boards and their syllabus titles.

Examinations in Scotland

The Scottish equivalent of A-levels is the Scottish Certificate of Education, Higher Grade. In art and design the syllabus and standards required are broadly similar to those of A-level. In addition to the Higher Grade, the Scottish examinations also include the Certificate of Sixth-Year Studies.

A-LEVEL AND THE GCSE MAINSTREAM

"Newly revised syllabuses."

Some of the examining boards have recently rewritten their syllabuses and revised the format and content of their examinations. In most cases this has been done in order to relate what is done at A-level more closely to work for the General Certificate of Secondary Education from the ages of fourteen to sixteen-plus (GCSE Mainstream). In this way a continuity is being established between the various art and design examinations obtainable at the closing stages of secondary education. This pattern of continuity is shown in Table 1.2.

We have singled out the syllabuses which have been rewritten in the way just described, devoting Chapter 10 exclusively to them. Table 3.1. (page 48) indicates which examining boards this involves.

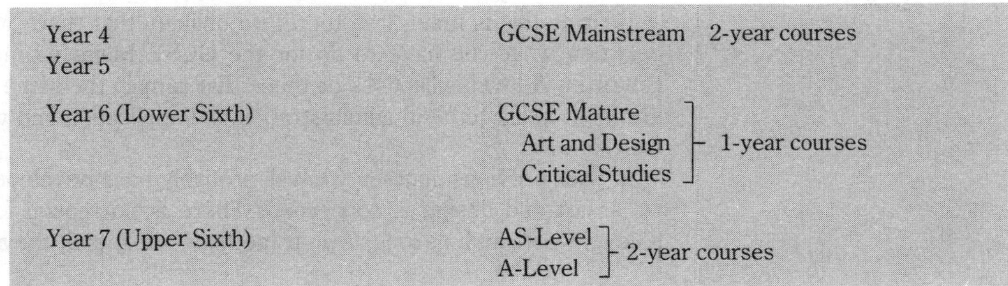

Year	Examination	Course length
Year 4 Year 5	GCSE Mainstream	2-year courses
Year 6 (Lower Sixth)	GCSE Mature Art and Design Critical Studies	1-year courses
Year 7 (Upper Sixth)	AS-Level A-Level	2-year courses

Table 1.2 Relationship of secondary education examinations in art and design.

PRACTICES IN ART AND DESIGN

"Established syllabuses."

Not all the examining boards have rewritten their examination syllabuses and in Chapter 3 we will cover those which are continuing to use their well-established A-level courses, looking at the specific requirements of each particular examination. Then, in Chapters 4 to 9, we will cover what we call the 'practices' of art and design included in their examinations. These chapters are relevant to your work irrespective of your particular syllabus, newly revised or well established.

A **practice** in art and design is intended usually to mean work which fits a particular **genre**, or is based upon a specific art and design **material** and its related techniques and processes. A genre might be, for instance, 'Still life' or 'Plant drawing'. On the other hand, a practice related to a specific material might be 'Lino-printing', or 'Embroidery'.

WHAT IS A-LEVEL ART AND DESIGN?

So far in your education you may have taken GCSE Art and Design. You may even have taken a one-year sixth-form course and examination in the subject, such as GCSE Mature Art and Design or GCSE Mature Critical Studies. It is now necessary to ask yourself what the differences are between your GCSE Mainstream examination, usually taken at the end of your fifth year of secondary education, and the GCE A-level and AS-level examinations. Do you, for instance, have to:

- be better at art and design?
- do more work?
- do a different type of work?
- work differently?

It is, of course, inevitable that you will be expected to be 'better' at art and design in some way. The effects of maturation must be evident in what you do for your A- level (or equivalent) examination. After all, you will be two years older than you were when you took your GCSE Mainstream examination and it would be very odd if your work did not reflect what had happened to you in that time. Teaching and learning are supposed to take you beyond the stage at which you start; if they do not, both teacher and student are wasting their time. So, between the time of GCSE Mainstream and A-level or AS-level, serious students can be expected to have improved in the subjects they are continuing with in their education.

When you received your A-level timetable you will have seen that you have more time available for each subject than you did with your GCSE Mainstream timetable – usually approximately twice as much each week. Therefore, it seems reasonable to expect that you will be required to do more work.

Let us now address the question of whether or not you have to do something different in art and design for your A-level studies and examination. First of all, the format of A-level examinations is often different to that of GCSE Mainstream examinations. Then, the specification of what you actually have to do is often different. You will need to find out details from your particular syllabus.

“Be familiar with your syllabus.”

It cannot be over emphasised that it is vital for you to read closely the particular syllabus *you* are using for your studies and examination, no matter how often we may quote and refer to others in this book. The addresses of the various examining boards are given at the front of this book.

Whether the syllabus you are using has changed recently or continues in its traditional form, remember that art and design is still art and design – that is to say, whatever the stages of development and achievement you have reached, and whatever your examination syllabus says, you are still using the same time-honoured principles and practices as the most experienced and accomplished artists and designers. This holds true for every examination syllabus, whatever its specific detail.

Bearing this is mind, it is therefore unlikely that there will be any startling differences between what you have to do for the GCSE Mainstream, GCSE Mature, the recently rewritten A-level syllabuses or those that remain the same. The differences that do exist are most likely to be in administration and application and will be explained in Chapters 3 and 10.

In your previous courses you will probably have developed a sound working method so far as art and design is concerned. There is no reason for you to change that in your A-level work, and, as long as your methods are sound, they can be developed still further.

A SOUND WORKING HABIT

“Develop a sound working habit.”

The idea of a 'sound working habit' will be stressed throughout this book. As authors, teachers, examiners and artists ourselves, we believe most strongly in its nurturing and development. It might be that you picked up this book expecting to be told *what* to remember and exactly *which* art and design artefacts to produce in order to gain a good examination result. Instead of this, however, we shall try to impress upon you that gimmicks, such as using novelty materials, cramming, learning solutions by heart and so on, cannot replace the advantages that a sound working habit will give you, both in your coursework studies and in your examination.

A sound working habit in studying art and design involves:

“Aspects of a sound working habit.”

- working in depth;
- thinking of and exploring alternatives;
- gaining knowledge of materials;
- learning about, and understanding, historical traditions;
- using the old in a new and exciting way;
- combining old technologies with new technologies.

Working in depth

As it is likely that you have already taken an art and design examination at GCSE Mainstream, GCSE Mature or Scottish Standard level, it will be easier for you if we use an example from those examinations as an illustration of what working in depth means.

For instance, the London and East Anglian (LEAG) GCSE Mature Art and Design syllabus gives you a **theme** (or you can choose your own) at the beginning of your year of study. You are asked to explore the theme in depth, in any way and involving any media you wish, with one year to complete your project. Working in depth does not necessarily mean using one medium only – perhaps clay – developing and expanding your knowledge of it to such a degree that you become say, 'a good potter'. To concentrate on one medium would probably mean that you failed to consider and develop a number of other aspects and skills fundamental to creating worthwhile art and design products. Indeed many aspects and skills are inextricably interwoven when working in any art and design media. We shall expand upon this as the book proceeds, but for the moment bear in mind that working in depth is an important part of a sound working habit but must be viewed in a broad context. Knowing what working in depth means, and working in that way, is part of a sound working habit.

Considering alternatives

Hopefully, your GCSE or Scottish Standard syllabus and examination will have encouraged you to study the full potential of an idea by thinking of, and exploring, as many angles as possible, based upon the original idea. Discovering and considering alternatives is an important aspect of a sound working habit.

Knowledge of materials and skills in using them

All art and design materials have certain qualities, and it is important that you should learn about these and use them, both in a traditional way and also in an original and creative way. Being able to do this will enable you to select materials which are appropriate to your specific needs. Having this knowledge and these skills is part of a sound working habit.

Technical knowledge and technological skills

Part of your knowledge about materials and their properties will come from studying the techniques which famous artists and designers currently use or have used in the past. This will develop your technological skills when it comes to producing practical work of your own. Having this type of knowledge, together with the associated skills, is also part of a sound working habit.

KNOWLEDGE AND INFORMATION IN ART AND DESIGN

“Critical, historical and contextual skills are important in all syllabuses.”

It is clear when you read the various A-level and equivalent syllabuses that the acquisition and use of knowledge and information is becoming an increasingly important part of the examination, in direct contrast to the days when it was acceptable merely to turn out good, practical work in art and design. In the various syllabuses there are many references to the critical, historical, cultural and contextual aspects of art and design. Indeed, a specific section in some of the syllabuses is called critical, or historical, or contextual studies. This usually refers to a written piece of work, often concerned with famous artists, designers or architects, for example, which is examined in its own right. Even where no such specific section exists, the sort of knowledge involved in these studies is of vital importance in any work in art and design, be it written or practical.

Remember, even if your particular syllabus appears not to refer to such studies, they are still an important aspect in the way that you work.

CONTEXTUAL STUDIES

Where a syllabus does specify a section on the critical, historical and contextual aspects of art and design, it is usual for it to state, more or less, that you should work with a view to: developing your understanding of the context in which artists and designers work. Apart from the knowledge and information to be gained (we shall return to this later), never forget that you too are working in a particular context when producing your own work.

Administrative and economic constraints

These might include:

- the constraints of the A-level (or related) examination
  You cannot ignore the constraints and the demands your examination places upon what you do and how you do it.
- the constraints of economics
  What you have to work with is dictated by how much money you and your teachers can afford to spend on materials and equipment.

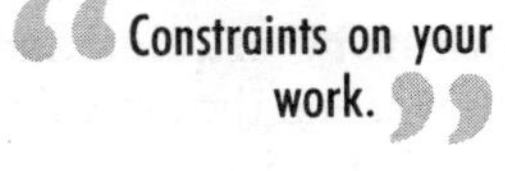

- the constraints of time
  During your course you have only a limited amount of time. This depends not only on the overall duration of your course but also on how your lessons are divided up.
- the constraints of access
  No matter how well equipped your school might be for your art and design lessons, being able to use the equipment when you want to might prove difficult. This could result in your doing something in a different way, or doing it later or earlier than you had intended.

In planning your work – that is to say, what you will do and how you will do it – you need to take these constraints into account. For instance, it will be of little use if you do things which are not asked for in the particular examination you are taking. To set out to make a three-dimensional object in answer to a question which specifies two-dimensional work will mean that you are unlikely to receive much reward for your work, and this will be reflected in your examination result. In the same way, it is foolish to embark upon projects which will be too expensive in terms of materials and equipment for you or your school, or which will take up more time than you have available.

“Be adventurous.”

However, you should ensure that these constraints do not confine you to unadventurous projects. To be too timid and safe will usually result in your work lacking vigour and excitement – qualities which are very important in art and design work.

Even if your school does not have the materials and equipment you need, you might find someone who can provide you with your requirements. For instance, you might wish to include photography in your work. Even if your school has no equipment or dark room, you might be able to make arrangements with a friend, relative or photographic shop in order to do your own processing and printing. You will usually find that your teachers encourage such enterprise and will validate the work you may do, even though it is not carried out within their direct control.

Study constraints

Apart from the particular types of constraint dealt with above, there are others which are to do with the way that you work and with the knowledge and information you might discover in the course of your work.

It is likely that you will have a tendency to think that studies in art and design are about producing good art and design artefacts, and this is certainly true. But if this attitude means that you concentrate upon the productive skills alone, you will be missing out on a lot that is vital to your learning and educational development. Of course, you might produce very good art and design artefacts by concentrating on the productive aspects to the exclusion of all else, but we can say with confidence that you would produce *even better* work if you took into account all the other types of knowledge, information and skills which are really part and parcel of studying art and design.

Working in this well-rounded way involves skills such as:

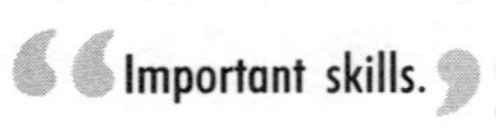

- researching;
- using primary (original) sources of information;
- using secondary (pre-existing) sources of information;
- selecting;
- organising.

All these skills are just as important for producing good practical work in art and design as they are for studying the subject in a theoretical way.

Of course, there could be a danger that working in this well-rounded way leads you to separate one activity from another in your studies. You could, for instance, research, using primary source materials; then make a selection from the information you have; then organise this into one piece of art or design work; and then produce it as you have planned it. You might, in answer to a question about ‘Decay’, go out and find a collapsing building. If so, you would have **researched** the theme and found a **primary source** of information. You might then make drawings of this building; to do so you would have made decisions involving certain **selections** and **organisations**. You would perhaps make even more selections and organisations in coming to a decision about the nature and content of, say a painting you wanted to end up doing. You might then paint your picture.

If you did all this, you could be excused, in our opinion, for believing that this was what was demanded of you by your examination syllabus. This is because it is common in such syllabuses to specify that you should first make some **preparatory studies** and then **realise** (or make) your finished article. But the terms listed above, and the activities they appear to describe, are really no more than useful devices for explaining art and design for purposes of teaching, learning and examining.

Carrying out art and design work as an artist or a designer, or even as a student at school or college, is a different story. You will, we hope, have seen in your studies so far that it is not only possible but also necessary that ‘one thing leads to another’ so far as art and design is concerned. Art and design is an **interwoven activity**, where it is almost impossible to say that one thing comes first or that in one activity you should do only this, whereas in another activity you should do only that.

Even at the time of carrying out your final piece of work, such as the picture portraying your responses to the theme of 'Decay', it would be proper, and indeed better, if you still allowed your decisions to develop as the final picture unfolds. Thus, even as you painted the picture, you might further modify some of your intentions, or introduce new and unexpected elements into your work.

If you are working well and correctly, you will find that what you do in art and design is affected by all the background knowledge and experiences you have acquired over time. If this is so, then it is important that you become more *aware* of just how much background knowledge and experience you are calling on at any time. If you do this you will become increasingly able to *use* this knowledge and experience in a positive and profitable way.

In the same way, if you are studying an activity such as pottery, or ceramics, just think how foolish – even impossible – it would be to restrict all your activities to using and expressing yourself in clay. There would be times in your studies when it would be advantageous to work in paint, or with collage, or with photography, and so on. Because your activity, or practice, is called pottery, does this mean that you should not work in other materials, or use the practices they represent? The only sensible answer must be, 'of course not'.

Using all the study constraints concerned, you will be using *contextual knowledge* and *information*, as well as involving a number of *contextual activities* at any time.

There will, of course, be those who say that working in this 'contextual' way takes away the 'inspirational' aspect of art and design. The usual argument is that 'too much theory and thinking makes the art and design work unimaginative and rather boring'. Well, does it? What such people seem to be saying is that each time any of us does anything in art and design, we not only should but also can ignore all that we have done before and all that we know and have experienced in our lives – except, perhaps, our productive skills and knowledge. We doubt most strongly whether such a situation is possible.

“'Inspirational' does not mean entirely new.”

In trying to come up with an 'inspirational' response to a problem in art and design, we usually call upon all that we know in order to arrive at our solution. Even if the solution seems to come to us from 'out of the blue', it is more likely that our subconscious quickly computed all that we knew in relation to the problem in hand. The solution can still of course, be 'inspirational' to the extent that it is able to present the old in a new way, or to solve the problem concerned more effectively and economically. There is nothing wrong in this. No matter what level of ability you might have in art and design, it is unlikely that you will invent something entirely new. What is more likely is that you will, like most before you, continue to 'reinvent the wheel'.

It is interesting to note that a lot of people who are experts in the field of art and design regard the work of the French artist PAUL CÉZANNE (1839 – 1906) as original and innovative. It is said that he helped to change the face of art. Yet this was not something that 'just happened'. Cézanne was a prolific writer as well as an artist. In his writings we can read that he approached his work with the thought that, ***'art is theory developed and applied in contact with nature'***. Or that in nature there is, ***'the cylinder, the sphere, the cone, everything in proper perspective so that each side of an object is directed towards a central point'***. (Read 1967)

These are hardly the words of someone who does not think things out, does not have a theory, or who researches only art itself! On the contrary, here is someone who is familiar with the theoretical underpinnings of art itself, as well as with other sources of knowledge and information, such as science and mathematics. Look at the illustration of Cézanne's work (Fig. 1.1) and see if you can find evidence of the theories he brought to bear when painting it.

To help ensure that you use this method of working – that is to say, calling upon what you know – to the full, it is best to relate what the syllabuses say about critical studies, historical studies, contextual studies and so on to *everything* you do in your studies, even if you consider your work to be inspirational and original.

This means calling upon the historical background of art and design. It also means referring to matters such as the social and cultural contexts in which work has been, and is, produced. It also means developing, by actively and consciously using, your critical faculties in all that you decide, do and say, so far as your art and design studies are concerned.

“Do not ignore the historical, the critical and the contextual.”

Historical, critical and contextual aspects, and the skills associated with them, are integral to the new approaches in A-level and AS-level Art and Design examinations. They

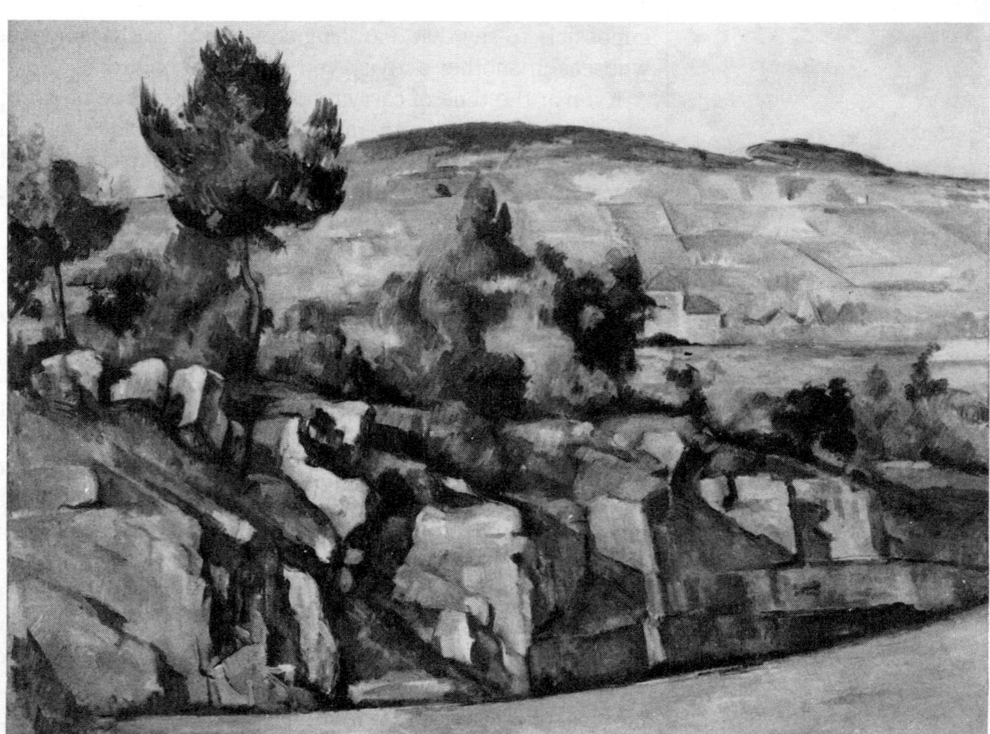

Fig. 1.1 'Rocky Scenery in Provence', Paul Cézanne (reproduced by permission of the Trustees of the National Gallery, London).

are worthwhile skills to cultivate, not only for working in art and design but also for your approach to issues generally.

There are terms for these aspects in the current examination syllabuses, so it is important for you to know and understand them. The glossaries in this book are intended to help you to do this. Do not just swallow our definitions, though. Treat them as starting points, then use your own experience and knowledge to begin to refine the definitions in your own terms. You should do this from time to time and a useful method would be to keep a notebook in which you write the terms as you find them, and try to define them. Then, as time goes by you could rewrite your definitions. Do this as many times as necessary. Thinking about what is asked of you, and what it all means, will influence and develop your art and design work.

We hope you can now see how a 'sound working habit' evolves. In addition to our earlier list of the qualities and activities which lead to its development, you can now add the following:

"Contextual studies."

- contextual studies which include,
  historical knowledge and information;
  cultural knowledge and information;
  social knowledge and information;
  being critical.

"Critical appraisal."

- being critical which includes,
  actively seeking out possible alternatives;
  selecting on the basis of some set of principles;
  organising according to your own principles and the traditions of art and design;
  being able and prepared to justify your decisions;
  being willing to change your mind as you gain more knowledge and information, and your experiences grow,

All we say and advise you to do as this book unfolds is based on the vital principles contained in these lists, and we shall seek to justify them to you whenever we suggest that you work in certain ways.

GLOSSARY OF TERMS USED IN ART AND DESIGN SYLLABUSES

The examining boards use a number of words and phrases to describe what it is each of them expect of you when you are studying for your A-level (or equivalent qualification) in art and design, and what it is the examination will consist of. When you read these words and phrases in the particular syllabus you are using, you will find that they are most often left unexplained. This can be very confusing. What is possibly still more confusing is that the various syllabuses seem to use different words and phrases to describe what seems to be the same thing. Of course, in full-time education, your teachers will ensure that you follow a course which sets out to cover all that is demanded of you by your particular board. However, we believe that it is only by reading and trying to understand the syllabus for yourself that you will be able to fulfil *all* that is asked of you.

There can be no substitute for you yourself *knowing* and *understanding* your syllabus, and being able to express it in your *own terms*.

With this in mind we have compiled a **glossary** of the terms used in all the syllabuses available, to help you come to your own understanding of what is being asked of you. With a clear understanding of the terms involved, you will have a better idea of what is expected of you in your work.

The definitions you arrive at should take into account the fact that although you have to complete specified quantities of work (otherwise you will not pass your examination), you have only limited time in which to work. For instance, there is no sense in deciding that pencil drawing means something that results in a specification which is impossible to meet in the time available.

In this instance it should be clear that the essence of defining 'pencil drawing' is to do so in such a way that it forces you to consider what skills are involved in becoming a good draughtsperson. Once you have done this, you will know what you need to do in order to develop those skills. Developing the skills would include drawing *something*, but that something could be the same subject each time. After all, plenty of highly acclaimed artists have done little more than this. For instance, Cézanne is well known for his studies of Sainte-Victoire mountain, and JAN VAN HUYSUM (1682 – 1749) is well known for his studies of flowers. This is not to say that these artists used no other subjects, but it shows that developing skills in art and design is not connected fundamentally with the range of subjects you manage to cover.

The skills involved in pencil drawing might include, among others:

“Skills involved in pencil drawing.”

- developing your ability to produce fluid lines of varying weight;
- creating a sense of three-dimensional form in a two-dimensional image;
- using tone as well as line as a means of expressing form;
- creating symbols which convey the appearance of textures;
- learning how to translate colours into pencil shades of grey, black and white.

In our opinion your definition in all cases should be based upon the **skills** involved in any particular matter. If this is so, you will find it an easy matter to find things to do in order to practise and develop those skills. The things to do might include not only the choice of subject matter each time but also the type of information which might benefit you in exploring your subject matter. Of course, your definition might also include where and why such sources of information exist, as well as many other things.

“Continually update your definitions.”

The glossary of terms follows now, because we think it vital that you read our definitions before proceeding any further with the book. We suggest that you get into the habit of referring back to the glossary as you come across terms later in the book. As you do so, begin to amend the definitions in terms of *your own* developing level of understanding.

GLOSSARY OF TERMS

Cross-references are given in italics.

Aesthetic

A term which has a specialist meaning about 'artistic beauty' but in art and design education at this level it can usually be regarded as meaning that you are able to understand the design or appearance of the work of others, as well as improve the design or appearance of your own work.

Analyse

Making a careful study of the nature, function and effect of a particular thing, subject or environment in order to prepare a detailed description of it; by implication your description will offer a *critical understanding* of what it is you are studying.

Analytical and written study, written studies

In art and design education it is felt that you should be able to express your understanding of your subject in words as well as being able to produce art and design objects and images.

Book production

Decorated text
Written words and letters adorned with patterns and images, which are quite often designs based upon natural forms such as flowers.

Dust cover
The paper cover which protects a book's cover. This is usually decorated with a design or picture and includes lettering; paperback books usually have the design or picture printed as part of their cover.

Illuminated manuscript
A book or page where the initial letter on a page is embellished with a coloured decoration; or a coloured picture in a manuscript.

Illustration
A drawing or a picture in a book or magazine which usually describes and portrays a passage in that book or magazine.

Canvas

A coarse cloth used for painting upon. Examining boards usually insist that if you use canvas, the wooden frame used to hold it stretched out tautly should be removed before your work is submitted for the examination. See also *Hardboard*.

Composition

The arrangement and organisation of the items within a picture, or the forms within a sculpture.

Conceptual thinking

Thinking about things in a abstract or theoretical way; to do with getting ideas, the imagination and mental creativeness.

Context

Cultural
Usually used to mean the type and degree of civilisation a group has; to do with the intellectual, artistic and social development of a group.

Economic
Can be about the economic state of a society or group, but also to do with the amount of time and money you can spend on your own work.

Historical
That which is influenced by the past and traditions; your knowledge of these influences.

Social
To do with the relationships things have with a society, community or group within which they exist. The social context is about being aware of and taking into account this interdependence in what it is you do, say or think, or in your appreciation of what other artists and designers are doing or have done.

Controlled test

The situation whereby you work under examination conditions; all the material pertaining to the conditions you work under and whatever you may do at that time.

Coursework, internal option (OX/CAM)

The work you do of your own accord and under the guidance of your teachers, rather than in response to an examination question; where this work is taken into account in your examination and its final award, this section is sometimes called the 'internal option', as opposed to the 'controlled test'.

Craft

Term used usually to include what are known as the 'manual arts', eg, pottery, wood carving, etc.

Craftsmanship

Skill and dexterity, as well as sensitive judgement; displayed usually in making an object.

Creative

Ability/Talent
The level of your powers to produce work through your intellectual reasoning and artistic skills.

Expression
The way you give form to your ideas.

Test
Sometimes used to describe your controlled test or the question set in your examination.

Critical

Appraisal
The level of your powers to discriminate between things by weighing up the evidence before you.

Appreciation
The outcomes of your critical judgements; how you express them.

Understanding
The level of your ability to see how to make critical judgements about things; knowing what to look for, and at, in any situation.

Critical and historical studies

A section of your studies and assessment with some examining boards. Here, rather than just knowing that something is historically so, the intention is that you find out why it is so and then express your own critical appraisal of the matter in hand, taking into account all the contexts which you can discover about it.

Decision making

Distinguishing between the alternatives usually present in any situation you may find yourself in during your studies and making justifiable value judgements in order to select from those alternatives and proceed with your work.

Design

Activity
The whole process involved in coming up with, and producing a solution to, a usually, open-ended problem.

and make
A phrase often used to describe what is more properly 'design activity'; designing and producing a solution to a problem is an interwoven activity, not a matter of first 'thinking' and then 'doing'.

and practice
A term used to mean the same as 'design and make', with all the weaknesses of the phrase, as mentioned above.

For a craft
The thinking of and mapping out of your ideas of something to make; again, this term contains the notion that thinking of something to do is an activity which stops when you are doing it.

For living
A popular term usually meaning that the problem is concerned with human considerations, rather than abstract or highly imaginative ones.

Realisation
Making your design ideas into an actual object, form or image; this should not go on without constant reviewing and rethinking of your idea in the light of what it is you are experiencing and learning as you realise it, particularly in the earliest stages.

Drawing (Draughtsmanship)

A term used often in art and design without any apparent real definition. It is fundamentally a system of making marks and inventing images which stand for things seen, planned or imagined. It is important to realise that a drawing can be done in colour, or three-dimensional materials as much as in pencil. It is possible to distinguish between many types of drawing, often made for a variety of specific purposes: eg, architectural drawings, maps, diagrams, plans, illustrations, etc.

Embroidery

A specific alternative and examined practice in some examinations; an activity involved with decorating fabrics in needlecraft designs.

Endorsed syllabus

The University of London is using this term, which comes from GCSE Mainstream examinations, to describe examination syllabuses which each deal with a specific and separate art and design activity. It is essential to study the ULSEB syllabus in detail in order to understand fully the options available, as well as their compulsory elements.

Critical and historical studies
A syllabus which is concerned with a broad study of the History of Art and Design but is concerned equally with a *critical understanding* of the way in which artists, designers, architects, critics and historians work, as well as the contextual conditions they work in. Your studies can be visual as well as literary, and can also be linked closely to any practical studies in art and design you may be carrying out at any time. Critical and historical studies are a compulsory element in any endorsed, or unendorsed, syllabus in art and design from ULSEB, but they should also form part of your work in response to any examining board's syllabus.

Fashion and textiles
A broad-based syllabus covering various aspects of the appearance, nature and uses of textiles and their production. The activity is concerned as much with researching, designing and critical understanding as it is with mechanical production.

Film and video
A syllabus which deals with using the media of film and video as a means of personal inquiry and expression; also covers the social significance and relevance of the media and their popular images.

Fine art
To do with those art and design products which have value in themselves as objects and images, rather than as utilitarian pieces.

Graphic design
Work which usually portrays ideas and messages in a visual form so that they can be publicly communicated and understood; the visual presentation of information; the art and design work which serves to promote a variety of other products, such as, cars, make-up, fashion, food, etc.

Photography
See '*Film and video*'.

Three-dimensional design
Concerned usually with final art and design products which are modelled, carved or constructed. This is not restricted to fine art practices, such as sculpture, mobiles and so on, but can include, among other things, packaging and industrial products.

Environment

Usually used in examinations in art and design to mean the physical locality you live in, or may be studying.

Environmental design

An activity concerned with relating your work in art and design to a known physical reality. Thus you may show by means of painting, drawing, modelling and so on either the actual state of an environment or how one may be developed and possibly improved.

Evaluation, evaluate

The critical measurement of something, whereby you are expected to appraise a phenomenon, a situation or an idea in order to find out something about its value rather than simply observe or produce it uncritically. The term is associated with establishing suitable criteria (standards, values, principles) for making a series of value judgements about things and matters.

Experimentation

Investigating things, such as the values and qualities of materials, in as many ways as possible; being not willing to accept the obvious, or the first thing which comes to hand or to mind, but to explore further by a method of trial and error accompanied closely by a suitable system of evaluation.

Expressive activity

A term used usually to describe that work in art and design which is fine-art based; also a specific activity in the SEB'S syllabus.

Externally-set paper, externally-set assignment, practical external examination

The 'question paper' each board might publish for you to use at the time of a final examination.

Fabric printing

An overall term used to include the various methods available for printing designs on fabrics; also the complete activity of designing and printing fabrics.

Fashioned forms, constructed forms, group of common objects

Those objects and articles which are created and constructed, such as pots, engine parts, garden tools, etc.

Figures (in landscape, interiors/exteriors)

It is often expected that your work will include portrayals of figures even if it is more essentially concerned with another subject. This content was popular in the art of the past.

Finished artefact, finished painting

The object, form or image which is deemed to be the final article, deriving from the process of thinking, reviewing and doing which constitutes art and design practice.

Form of communication

May be taken to be the object, form or image in art and design work; the material(s) from which such objects, forms and images are made and the control they exercise over their appearance.

Form of expression

Refers usually to the decisions taken about the eventual form of communication or the object, form or image concerned.

Formal elements

A term used in art and design to describe the means by which objects, forms and images are visually organised. Each product in art and design can be seen to have a combination of these formal elements in their design and construction:

Balance
The way in which one part of an object, form or image is compensated for by another. The balance need not be one of weight, size or shape; it could be colour or anything.

Colour
Could be the natural colour of a material, or the applied colour used to create an effect.

Decoration
The embellishment or adornment of a form or shape, usually with some type of pattern. William Morris, for instance, often used floral patterns to decorate his work.

Form
The shape of an object or the outline of an image; the shape of ideas.

Harmony
A pleasing relationship, whether colours having a particular relationship, a satisfactory relationship of proportion, the balancing of textures or the careful distribution of light and dark within a picture.

Line
Usually a thin mark used to delineate a shape.

Pattern
Usually an arrangement of repeated parts, but it can be the model, or template, used to cut out a shape in another material, as in dressmaking.

Rhythm
In art and design a visual pattern of movement created usually by the arrangement of the parts of the whole.

Shape
The visual boundary of an object, form or image. Two-dimensional work in art and design is usually a harmonious arrangement of a number and variety of shapes.

Space
An interval of distance or time between two or more things. In art and design the 'spaces in between' are as important as the 'shapes' used to construct an object, form or image, and they contribute equally towards the overall design or appearance of a piece of work.

Structure
The relationship created by the way the parts of a piece of work in art and design are combined into a whole.

Symmetry
A balance created by a harmony of proportion, colour and so on.

Texture
Usually a pattern created on an object or a material, either naturally or by design, which can be felt as well as seen.

Tone
A shade of a colour which makes that colour darker and less intense; the shadowing; the use of a pencil to produce a variety of degrees of blackness.

Volume
The sense of size created by a work or part of it. The work need not be three-dimensional; colour or tone can create a sense of 'volume'.

Graphic design

See *Endorsed syllabus*.

Hardboard

A manufactured material used by artists as an alternative to canvas to paint upon. Examining boards are usually unwilling to accept work on this or on wood-framed canvas if it has to be sent to them and subsequently handled by them.

Historical background

The evidence and information which enables you to understand why and how certain aspects of art and design came about. The historical background need not be exclusively about art and design; cultural, social, scientific and political information can be just as informative.

History of art, history and appreciation

This usually refers to the more formal accounts of art and design, which classify and categorise art and artists, as well as designers, into periods, movements, schools and so on. Even so, it pays if you study this aspect of the subject in a critical way, creating your own views about the particular work, or artist or designer you are studying at any time.

History and technique (of subject)

This deals usually with the more technical aspects of the subject and their historical discovery and development. Of course, while it is possible to study techniques and materials in this semi-scientific way, it pays to study and understand the various qualities different materials and techniques have by analysing the actual work of artists and designers.

Ideas

Formation and development of ideas
You get your ideas from a wide range of sources. Even 'inspirational' ideas can usually be seen to come from real rather than totally abstract sources. It pays to let your responses flow when you are coming up with ideas in answer to a problem, because you can then see more clearly which of them are backed by accessible information and thereby have the most potential for development.

Realisation of ideas
The process whereby you turn your idea into an art and design product. Often mistakenly separated from the 'doing' or 'making' side of your work. It is important for you to understand that this is a false, if not an impossible distinction. You should be continuing to develop your ideas as you are producing the outcome of them.

Identify

The process whereby you recognise and accept the relevance of something to the work you have in hand.

Image making

Apart from using materials to give form to your images, the ideas and their development which led to the decisions about those images.

Imaginative work

A term used to suggest that the sources of your work are entirely spontaneous and even unique. In fact, the likelihood is that your ideas come from things seen or remembered and there is nothing wrong in this. Apart from anything else, if you are in doubt about something, it means you can go to the appropriate original source for information. Being imaginative is more a case of re-presenting the old and the known in fresh and original form and circumstances.

Industrial design

A specialist aspect of design which is concerned with the, usually, bigger and often mechanical products of our society, such as cars, cookers, etc.

Innovation

Usually changing something and presenting it in a fresh situation or set of circumstances.

Interpret, interpretation

The way in which you translate things seen or imaged into an art and design form or image. Even when drawing directly from an object, you are interpreting first what it is you see, and then how you translate that into a series of marks or shapes which represent your original interpretation.

Investigative study

In which you explore and inquire into a phenomenon, an environment, a situation or an idea and present all your work as evidence of what it is you understand and as an explanation of what you have done so far and might do as a result of your investigation. This is a specific part of the WJEC syllabus.

Jewellery

The production of artefacts which might be classed as jewellery, but not usually concerned with precious stones and metals such as gold or silver. In art and design the term tends to mean the decorative use of a variety of materials which might be used for personal adornment; the materials might include metals, plastics or natural objects such as shells, stones, etc.

Knowledge

Any form of knowledge is the basis of the information you work from at any time. Thus knowledge might be established bodies of facts, but it can also be the information you get from experience, perception, awareness and so on. It is natural that some of the facts about art and design should be known to you, but working in art and design is not restricted to that particular body of knowledge alone.

Letraset

A system of transfer lettering which is used particularly in graphic design. Letraset is in fact a trade name, and there are other companies producing similar material.

Lettering and calligraphy

Calligraphy is the art of penmanship and refers usually to handwriting. Lettering is also about style and form; what is written is considered as a design and a piece of artwork.

Life, natural forms

In art and design education these terms refer usually to either the human figure or natural objects, such as animals, birds, fish, flowers, pebbles, seaweed and so on.

Medium, media (plural)

The material you work with to produce objects, forms and images in art and design. Thus pencil is a medium; paint, clay, fabric, photography, etc. are media.

Metalwork, beaten metalwork

In art and design education the work done in this medium is usually more decorative than that done in, say a CDT lesson. The concern is to use the medium to give form to your designs and ideas, rather than to obey specified technical and traditional uses of the materials and the tools which work them.

Methods and materials

In art and design there is a technical and traditional way of using the materials most closely associated with a given activity. Even in original work involving flights of fancy, you should either know of the methods and materials concerned beforehand or investigate them closely once you know what it is you want to achieve. It does not follow that you have then to obey all the historical rules in your work.

Model

Sometimes refers to the human figure used for a drawing class to study; also to make or from in a variety of materials or to give tangible shape to ideas which would otherwise remain in your head.

Monochrome print

A print, or any other art and design image, which is carried out and produced in one colour only; often used in reference to work in black and white.

Objective work (direct observation / objective treatment)

Strictly speaking, this is trying to work in an unemotional and non-selective way, recording or shaping everything before you. In fact, this is an impossibility, because whatever you may try to do, you will end up with some degree of interpretation and a whole system of symbols which have to stand for something else. Sometimes this approach is falsely referred to as 'photographic', but even a photograph is selective, as you choose where to point the camera, and the process translates a variety of light impulses into a more restricted code of tonal or colour marks and shapes. Nevertheless, trying to be as 'objective' as possible is a highly important aspect of some work in art and design.

Observed analysis

An exploration and investigation of an object, situation, environment, etc. which can be seen, handled and experienced personally.

Packaging and display

An aspect of design which is involved with the protective containers for various products and the decoration of those containers. While protection is an essential element of this practice, so, invariably, is promotion of the product.

Painting

Refers usually to coloured work which is hand-painted as opposed to a mechanical process such as printmaking. It is generally used to cover all such coloured work, even that which commonly expresses forms as outlines, but 'being painterly' does have a special meaning: it refers usually to work in which forms are portrayed not as defined outlines but as dabs of colour, light and dark, and in which the shapes merge into each other or into the background.

Paper (A1, A2, A3, A4 usually)

Paper is made in a size called A1; this is a sheet which measures 594 × 841 mm. When it is cut in half (one cut) it is called A2; when these two halves are cut in half again it is called A3; when these pieces are then cut in half, it is called A4.

Personal study

In some syllabuses this term is used to describe work in art history, which, rather than relying upon an examination which tests your historical knowledge and your memory of it, allows you to compile a piece of illustrated written work during your course of study to express your critical reaction to historical facts.

Photographic evidence

Can mean documented accounts in the form of photographs. In some syllabuses it refers specifically to the practice of asking you to take photographs of any large pieces of work you have done during your course of study, or even, in some cases, during your examination, and submitting the photographs as evidence. If you do this, try to include in the photograph some indication of scale (eg, photograph your work against a matchbox, which is a well-known object).

Photographs

Can mean those photographs which you have taken yourself, in which case either they are pieces of art and design work in their own right or they constitute 'primary source' evidence and information. It also refers to photographs which you collect from your family, from magazines and so on, in which case you might use them as part of an actual object, form or image in your work, or you might work from them to help you produce objects, forms or images; in these cases they are 'secondary sources' of evidence and information.

Pictorial composition, picture

Both terms usually mean the two-dimensional image which constitutes your solution to a particular subject, which might, for instance, be a landscape. The key word is *Composition*, which is concerned with arranging the elements of your whole image into a satisfactory visual whole. This involves using the *Formal elements* of art and design.

Plant

Most examinations include one aspect which involves working from actual plants as a source of inspiration.

Portray

Giving character and form to your ideas. The term covers a whole process; the materials and methods connected with the medium used plus'getting a likeness'.

Pose (short, long)

The position and environment a human figure might be in for you to work from. In examinations these usually include a short pose and a long pose, both of which involve different problems of representation and approach.

Pottery, ceramics

The practice of making things from clay; an all-embracing term used to describe anything made from clay.

Practical papers

Some examinations call their end-of-course tests 'practical papers'. In doing so they differentiate between visual work, whether two- or three-dimensional, and written tests.

Preparatory studies (preliminary sketches/supporting work/developmental work)

In examinations these terms include all that you do before you set about making or drawing your 'final' piece of art or design work. We suggest that it is not sensible, even if it were possible, to stop refining and redefining your work, even as the 'final' product is being produced. For instance, when you make a mark on a clean sheet of paper you set up a relationship between that mark and the shape of the paper; when you add a second mark you alter and redefine that relationship. Not to be aware of this and take it into account as part of your working habit is foolish and undesirable.

Primary sources (of information)

It is usual to regard all the information which you create yourself as 'primary'. This could be drawings, photographs, objects, materials, etc. See also *Photographs*.

Printed material

This covers such a wide field that it is best to read your syllabus to see if the term is included in it. It could mean a textile, a book, a lino-print, an examination paper, etc., depending on context.

Printmaking

Reproducing an image, usually by mechanical means, using black or coloured inks. There are three basic methods of producing prints: intaglio, relief and planar. Intaglio involves engraving the image to be printed into the surface of a material; relief involves cutting away parts of the surface of a material to be printed, so that the pieces remaining form the image; planar, or 'surface', printing involves transferring an image from the flat surface of a material to paper. Most printing methods reverse the image to be printed at the printing stage of the particular process and this must be taken into account.

Etching (intaglio process)
A method whereby a metal plate is covered in a substance impervious to acid. An image or design is scratched through this substance to the metal below and when the metal plate is then immersed in a bath of acid, the acid penetrates the metal where the lines of the image or design have been scratched. When this part of the process is finished satisfactorily, the plate is withdrawn from the acid, washed and cleaned of the impervious substance. In order to print the image etched into the metal plate, the surface of the plate is rubbed over with printing ink and then wiped clean. The ink will remain in the lines etched into the plate's surface. By putting paper to the surface of the plate under considerable pressure, the ink in the lines is lifted and transferred to the paper.

Lithography (planar process)
This printing process does not require any engraving. By drawing on a slab of stone, or a zinc plate, with a greasy chalk (which may be mixed into a liquid), an image is produced. When the slab or plate is wetted, water adheres only to those parts of the surface which do not have grease on them. When printing ink is rolled over the surface of the slab or plate, it adheres to the greasy surface only. The slab or plate is then passed through a press with paper on its surface and the printing ink is transferred to the paper. Prints combining many colours can be made in this way.

Screen printing/serigraphy (planar process)
A process involving the use of stencils. Stencils are cut for each colour in an image or design and these are then fixed to a silk screen in turn. When a particular colour is passed over the screen it penetrates the gaps in the stencil, printing on the paper held under the screen. The process is repeated on the same sheet of paper held in the same position for as many colours as are required in the design. This is a process which does not reverse the image as it is printed.

Wood engraving (relief process)
The surface of a block of wood is cut away to leave the image required standing up from the cut-away surface; this pattern of lines and shapes which remain is coated with printing ink and paper pressed against it, so that the image is transferred to the paper.

Wood/lino-block cutting (relief process)
Lino is a cheap and easier cut version of wood. See *Wood engraving*.

Product design

An aspect of design work which deals with the development of a product from its original 'idea' state, through its production and into and including its promotion.

Pure painting

A procedure concerned with 'constructing' forms and images by 'modelling' them in paint rather than 'colouring in' outlined shapes. See also *Painting*.

Realisation (outcome/solution)

Refers usually to whatever is done as the 'final outcome' of all your research and preparation. Again, we argue that things are not as simple as this and the division of your work into two distinct processes is a false one.

Record

The documentation of any evidence you might find, including drawing, photography, modelling, compiling scrapbooks, keeping diaries and work journals, etc.

Research

A term used currently in art and design but borrowed originally from other sources which means *all the activities* you might become involved with in your work. The notion behind its inclusion in art and design education is that the subject is just as involved with knowledge and information, logic and reasoning, and observation and recording, as it is with inspiration, creation and imagination.

Responses

Conceptual
May be explained as 'getting ideas'. We respond originally, most often, by a system of mental creativity. Calling upon what we know already, we begin to conceive of solutions to problems. This is an approach that sometimes calls upon us to connect things not necessarily related in the storage systems of our minds.

Perceptual
Responding to what we can see or know to be, rather than searching around for ideas inside our heads. In this approach we connect things which we can see with a particular problem, and in this sense, the connection is most often obvious, or at least universally understandable.

Personal responses (personal reaction)
Whereby even if what we do is known, or has been done before, we turn it into an original, if not a unique, form. Even a so-called objective, observational drawing is made personal by the way in which we approach it. This is like stamping our own, personal handwriting on objects and ideas.

Sculpture

An object or form created in three dimensions. A variety of materials can be used, following either subtractive (carving), additional (modelling) or constructive (building) principles and methods. Sculpture can be 'in the round' or in 'relief'; 'kinetic' (moving) art can also be classified as sculpture.

Secondary sources (of information)

All the information you use which you did not originate is secondary. How you use it and what you produce from it are the means by which you work creatively and originally. You should always acknowledge your secondary sources of information, stating where they come from and who originated them, if known. Acknowledging your sources in this way enhances the value of your work, as it shows the extent of your research and your ability to use profitably things which exist or are known already. See also *Photographs, Primary sources*.

Set of studies

A term used to describe an indefinite number and types of separate forms of study in pursuit of a response and solution to a particular problem. All these studies should be preserved carefully and presented with your work in response to a particular problem.

Silversmithing

Although there is a specific tradition and history concerning silver and silversmithing, in art and design your involvement with the craft would be as much to do with understanding the design demands which the material and methods of working it put upon you, as with whatever it is you might make and how efficiently you might make it.

Sketch book (visual inquiry notebooks)

Usually a pad of paper in which you record your ideas and your responses to things seen. The notion of 'visual inquiry' notebooks opens up ideas of uses going beyond simple 'drawing' in the pad; collecting scrapbook material, making written notes, finding literary references to your problem and writing these down, taking photographs and mounting them in your notebook, etc., all provide you with much more information to work from and can only benefit your work and your examination result.

Sketches

A term used to describe what an artist or designer does when noting down ideas or things seen in a visual form. We recommend that you think of what is done in this connection usually as 'drawings', because this means that you will include more information, which can then be recalled and used profitably later.

In written papers
In the same way as we explain *Sketches*, when you include visual notes and explanations in your written work, try to look upon them as illustrations, and do them with the care and attention that they deserve. Using the correct materials, such as collage methods, transfer lettering, poster paint and so on, is essential in producing work of this nature and not to do so will most likely result in cockled notepaper and timid results.

Skill

In art and design, the combination of manual dexterity and thinking powers necessary to produce good ideas and finely executed products.

Stage costume

The designs for actors to wear. Ideas will come from a variety of historical and social sources. Constructing stage clothing calls for the ability to understand what detail is necessary for their effect, remembering that lighting alters their appearance and that they are often seen from a distance. Stage clothing does not necessarily require dressmaking skills and knowledge; it is sometimes quite satisfactory to stick, rather than sew, for example.

Stage design (stage scenery/theatre studies)

The designs for the environments in which a specific play takes place. The sources of your designs are historical, social, cultural, fantasy, imagination and so on. Real-life environments and details are important, but so are sources such as books, films, comics, etc.

Still life (group)

A study of an arrangement of objects. Their physical and spatial relationship is a vital part of your study in this respect. Choosing the objects wisely often contributes much to the success of a study.

Synthesis

Synthesis is the putting together of all separate parts. It is a better term than 'realisation', or its alternatives, because it contains and suggests the notion that what has been analysed is put together again in a new, complex whole. As such it more accurately describes the attitude we put forward – namely, work in art and design is not in two distinct and separate parts, preparation and realisation, but is really one, intermeshed activity, combined both at all times.

Tactile
To do with the sense of touch; can be touched. Textures most often convey a 'tactile' quality. In art and design it is usually a matter of portraying visually that which can be touched as well as seen in order to be understood.

Textiles and fashion (printed textiles/constructed textiles)
All to do with designing and producing fabrics in response to certain problems involving often specific requirements. Printed suggests that the surface decoration of the fabric remains two dimensional; constructed suggests that one thing is added to, or built upon, another, giving perhaps a strong tactile quality to the fabric. Fashion calls upon fabrics to be not only designed so far as pattern and decoration is concerned but also planned as potential three-dimensional objects – that is to say, dresses, coats, suits, etc.

Thematic studies
Studies you may do in response to a theme. They may be based around an environment, such as the house or the landscape; or around an object such as a plant; or a manufactured object; or they may be based around an idea or concept, such as movement or juxtaposition.

Theme (compositional theme/subject title/starting points)
The subject set for you to conduct your thematic studies around.

Three-dimensional studies
Those studies which result in three-dimensional outcomes. Not all the set of studies needs to be three dimensional; two-dimensional work is an integral part of the exploratory and investigative studies surrounding and supporting three-dimensional work.

Understanding
The critical judgements you show you possess about things and the decisions you make.

Unendorsed syllabus
In the examination set by ULSEB, a syllabus covering a general approach to art and design studies, as opposed to the *Endorsed Syllabus*.

Value judgement
Not just the decisions you make about things, but the criteria you use to justify such decisions; you are making it clear what it is you value and why you do so.

Analytical
Coming to your decisions by examining your subject minutely, separating it into its component parts and thereby arriving at a critical understanding of it.

Cognitive
Coming to your decisions by perceiving. This involves going beyond simple recognition, seeing that something is what it apparently is – to enter the realm of asking yourself questions about an objects true nature in order to pass value judgements upon it. If this is not done, your decisions will remain as decisions and not be value judgements.

Intuitive
Arriving at your decisions according to your own, in-built truths and ethical code. Such value judgements really require you to explain and justify your own ethical code, rather than the value judgements which come from it.

Visual
Communication
Imparting knowledge and information and your decisions to others by visual means, such as forms and images, plans, diagrams, etc.

Exploration
Enquiring into and investigating something by making and documenting visual responses to it.

Imagery
The outcomes of the visual inquiry you might make, such as drawings, maps, plans, etc.

Research and investigation
A systematic inquiry into something which is analysed and expressed in visual terms. See also *Visual exploration*.

Statement
More that the image you might make when inquiring into something. A coherent form or image which probably contains the means by which it can be understood without any further additions.

Studies
A term used to mean much the same as 'art and design'.

Thinking
Whereby you explore your ideas by tracing your thoughts in a string of visual images, perhaps as you talk to someone.

Written examination
Some examining boards set written examinations at the end of their courses. These are sometimes compulsory, sometimes optional.

Working vocabulary
The terms and their associated knowledge which surround the practice of art and design. Without steadily building up your working vocabulary, it is doubtful if you are following the broadest aspects of the course you are studying, and no matter how good you are 'at art', you are unlikely to be achieving the full potential of an advanced course of study.

CHAPTER

EXAMINATION AND ASSESSMENT TECHNIQUES

HOW TO STUDY

A SOUND WORKING HABIT

PREPARING FOR PRACTICAL EXAMINATIONS IN ART AND DESIGN

WRITTEN EXAMINATIONS IN ART AND DESIGN

EXERCISES

GETTING STARTED

First of all, let us say most emphatically that unless you are taking a History of Art and Design written examination paper at the end of your course of study, you have *no need to revise* in the conventional way for your art and design examination.

This is not to say, of course, that you should go into your end-of-course examinations unprepared, but do bear in mind that how well you do will depend largely upon how well you have learned to study during your course. If you have developed a sound working habit throughout your course of study, and have practised and built on this, then taking the examination will simply be an extension of what you have already been doing.

In this chapter we will deal with what is necessary for you to study effectively. We will also look at a number of helpful suggestions for producing work capable of forming part of your final examination assessment.

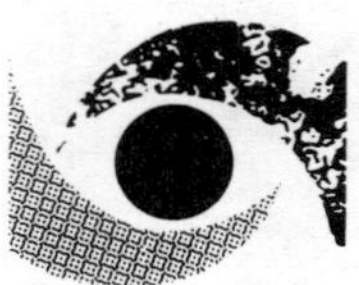

ESSENTIAL PRINCIPLES

HOW TO STUDY

"Study purposes."

Studying fulfils a number of purposes, among them:

- covering the range of knowledge, materials, equipment and techniques considered to be part of the examination curriculum;
- practising and gaining experience in the methods and materials which are taught as part of your course of study;
- learning about the form and content of the examination;
- becoming experienced in, and at ease with, the form and content of the examination;
- developing a sound working habit.

You might well be able to think of more. Try adding to the list on a separate sheet of paper. The more you understand about the nature and purpose of study, the better you are likely to become at studying, and the more likely you are to achieve a good examination result in art and design.

When you have decided what studying is about and the purposes behind it, make certain that you bear these points in mind throughout your course of study. As you work, try to reason out which of the purposes you are covering at any time. In this way you will become clearer in your own mind about what it is you should be doing.

Gaining knowledge

So far as we are concerned the areas of **knowledge** you should cover in your studies are determined by your teachers and yourself. This applies to their actual content also. It would be most inappropriate for us to seek to make selections on your behalf from the great quantities of knowledge which are available. In fact, apart from guiding you towards what is available, or introducing you to information which seems to best suit your needs at any particular time, we believe that what you learn should be guided to a large degree by your own interests and the directions your work seem to be taking.

"Importance of the working habit."

In this sense, the **working habit** you develop is of paramount importance so far as the knowledge you might gain is concerned. It is that working habit which will lead you to need to know certain things, if your work is not to remain superficial and uninformed. So, while we shall cover certain areas of knowledge throughout this book, we are not going to specify to you what it is you *should* know. The knowledge and information we use in making, or illustrating, a particular point, will have been selected for that reason alone.

This is no different to the way you should work in art and design. In order to do what you want to, and to make your point, you should uncover and use all the knowledge and information you can to help in that particular context. If you do this, you will find that the extent of your knowledge, and your ability to interpret and use it, grows as your course unfolds. As this happens you will become better equipped to deal with the examination at the end of your course. At the same time, you will have prepared and produced work during your course which is capable of standing you in good stead when it is used, either in part or full, to determine your final grade.

Gaining experience in methods and materials

What has been said about knowledge applies equally to the methods and materials you might use in your studies. What materials you have available to you will be determined to a large extent by the facilities which have been developed for art and design at your school. These facilities will reflect in part the specialist training your teachers have had, but they will also be controlled by the amount of money your teachers have to spend upon the subject.

With all this in mind, it would be pointless to insist that a good course in art and design should cover clay, photography, printing and paint. In any case, how could we ever hope to justify the suggestion that these materials and methods constituted the perfect art and design course of study? In turn, however, we do not believe that you should allow the sections of the syllabus you select to study to impose a stranglehold upon which materials you use and the methods you employ in their use. That is to say, even if you are going to do your examination in drawing and painting, you would be ill advised (in our opinion) to stick only to drawing materials and painting materials in your course of study.

"Be varied in your approach."

This might sound as if we are saying that a bit of everything makes up the best course, but we are not. We believe that you should choose and use materials according to the job in hand each time you work. Suppose your studies are concerned with representing three-dimensional space in a still-life grouping, or the solidity of the objects in such a group. Even though you are studying drawing and painting, it might still pay you to **model** the group or the objects within it in some three-dimensional and solid material such as clay. Doing this might allow you to come to terms with your problem in a much faster and more informed way that if you had simply waited to come up with a successful method of representation using two-dimensional materials alone. The reason for this, of course, is that the knowledge and understanding gained by modelling in three-dimensional reality are more immediate than what is gained by using materials which lend themselves only to two-dimensional work.

If you let your work dictate which **materials** to use as you proceed, you will find that you gain an accumulation of materials' knowledge. As you do this, because you are trying to find a means to an end, it is also likely that you will explore a wider range of **methods**, through experimentation, as you seek to find an appropriate outcome. As far as developing the **skills** appropriate to the section of the syllabus you are following is concerned, the likelihood is that this will follow naturally, as you will tend to work mainly in the materials and methods the section covers. Even if you do not, your teachers will alert you to any omission in this respect should it begin to occur.

The alternative to all this is to keep repeating the type of work your eventual examination will demand, using the same materials and techniques each time. If you do this, although you can expect gradually to become more proficient at handling your subject and the materials you use, imagine how boring it could be. In addition, if you were to work in this way, just consider how limited your knowledge would be at the end of your course. By working in the wider way we suggest, you will get to know more about the field of art and design. At the same time, our experience suggests that by developing this wider and interactive approach, you will be even better at the specialist work needed for your final examination.

Developing a sound working habit

All of the above makes it obvious and imperative that you should, above all else, develop a sound way of working in your studies. If you do so, you will develop your ability and skills in the subject, call upon specific areas of knowledge and information where needed, and use and experiment with a full range of appropriate materials.

In the last chapter we introduced the suggestion that in art and design there is something which we call 'a sound working habit'. Let us now explore this suggestion a little further.

As far as we are concerned, there are no definite pictures you should paint, drawings you should draw, pots you should make, textiles you should print, fabrics you should embroider, sculptures you should carve, and so on. Even when your examination paper includes a 'title' in a question, setting what appears to be a particular task you must do, we would argue that trying to conjure up in your mind the actual form or image the question seems to impose is *not* the best way of succeeding in your examination. For instance, the following is an extract from a question set by the WJEC.

Q.2 Select from *one* of the following outdoor subjects:

a) Allotments.
b) Scrap yard.
c) Churchyard.
d) Stationary vehicles

(WJEC, specimen question paper, 1988)

Let us imagine that you thought the best subject here was 'Allotments'. Simply by thinking about the problem you could decide that it would be a good idea to do a picture showing the side of a shed with some tools leaning against it and a few cabbages in the foreground. Then, when you went out to an allotment in order to get some first-hand information, you might spend considerable time looking for, and finding, such a scene to draw. This is because you are looking for something in real life which you have already seen in your mind's eye.

If this is a description of the way that you, or anyone, works then there is a danger that by selecting in your mind's eye the picture you want to end up with, you see only what you want to when you actually visit the allotments. What did you *miss* seeing, if this was so? How did you know beforehand that the picture you imagined was the best you could come up with? How confident were you that you knew all there was to know about allotments before you ever visited one?

The composition in Fig. 2.1, because it was conceived beforehand, has become parallel, obvious and boring.

In Fig. 2.2, what actually exists at the allotment site has been seen and recognised. The resulting composition is more complex, invigorating and challenging. Also, the picture begins to contain some sense of drama, or narrative.

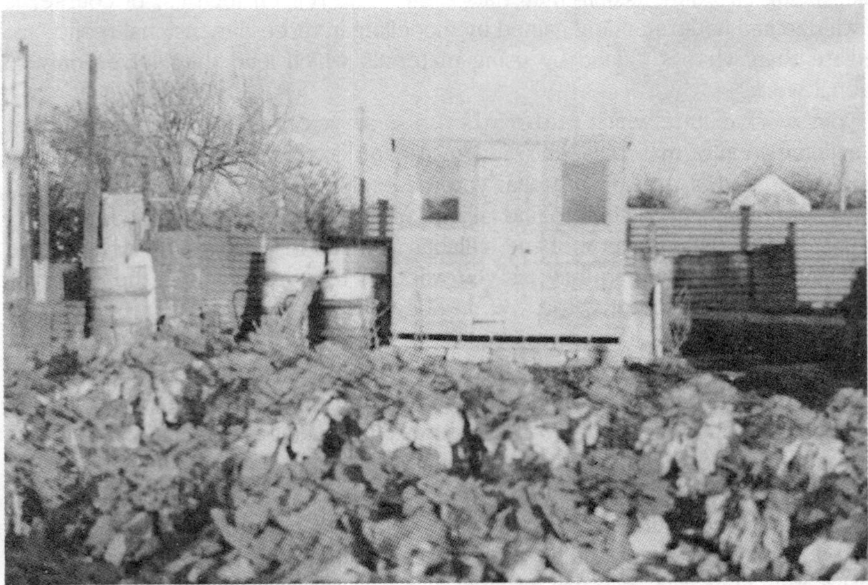

Fig. 2.1 The mind's eye allotment.

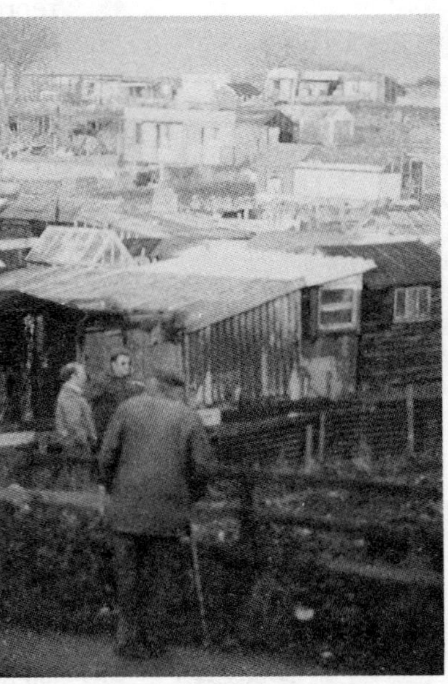

Fig. 2.2 A visually and mentally aware view of an allotment.

Although you may have the picture you want to do in your mind's eye, it is nevertheless essential that you 'go out' and make some studies from real life. This is because the WJEC question continues:

> Study the subjects carefully, then using any medium or combination of media:
> make a finished statement on your chosen topic, *supported by preparatory study sheets*.

We shall return to this particular example a little later on. But for now, let us say that in our opinion, working from your mind's eye alone, or seeking in real life what you have already seen in your mind's eye, is *not* the best way of working in art and design. In fact, we would go further. We are convinced that what you know *and understand* is as instrumental in your choice of what to do as is what you actually see.

Therefore, we are emphatic that you should always concentrate on the way in which you work in your exploration of subject matter, rather than what form or image your work will take in response to the question in hand, and this way of working results in what we call a **sound working habit**.

Your sound working habit will be different to anybody else's even though you and they might both have read this book. We intend that you should respond to our arguments in personal terms, deciding upon *your own* approach. We are confident that if you base it upon the propositions put forward in this book, it will be not only your own but also sound.

A SOUND WORKING HABIT

"Aspects involved in a sound working habit."

In Chapter 1 we drew up lists of things which might constitute a sound working habit. Now let us gather those lists together, and add to them as necessary, before discussing what they mean in terms of art and design. They can be said to fall into five categories:

- materials;
- techniques;
- technologies;
- knowledge and information;
- fundamental skills and concepts.

In all instances these categories refer to art and design, although knowledge and information might be drawn from sources which are not essentially to do with art and design. That is to say, the knowledge and information might be **contextual** as well as subject-specific. By contextual we mean anything which will give you more information on your subject and the circumstances in which it exists. For example, if you were using 'The Railways' as the basis for your work, you would be likely to concentrate upon the visual appearance of your subject matter. On the other hand, if you were an engineering student, you would be more likely to concentrate upon the technical aspects of the railways. Yet in both cases your level of understanding would be most likely to grow if you found out something about the **social** and **economic** factors which surround the railways and their origins. In your case, as a student taking art and design, your insight into the subject would also be improved if you studied the **historical** visual appearance of the railways.

It is probably unnecessary to distinguish too much between **materials**, **techniques** and **technologies**. By grouping them together we end up with just three major headings, and these will best form the basis of our argument here. Using these three major headings, the contents of the lists in Chapter 1 and any new details necessary, let us draw up a table which sets out what working in art and design is really about.

It is essential that you study Table 2.1 closely and begin to try and understand it. It is the basis for our approach throughout this book. We shall explore and explain further the meanings of the terms in it, gradually increasing your understanding of what we mean and intend by them. As your understanding grows, and you begin to act upon the knowledge you are gaining, so your own sound working habit will emerge and develop.

ACQUIRING AND DEVELOPING KNOWLEDGE OF, AND SKILLS IN, MATERIALS, TECHNIQUES AND TECHNOLOGIES

The first section in Table 2.1 deals essentially with what are popularly known as the **productive skills** in art and design.

WAYS OF WORKING	
ACQUIRING AND DEVELOPING KNOWLEDGE OF, AND SKILLS IN, MATERIALS, TECHNIQUES AND TECHNOLOGIES	
Methods of Study	– learning to combine new technologies with old technologies; – doing personal practical work: either work which is creatively original, or which involves analytical copying; – learning about, and understanding, historical traditions; – learning about, and understanding, contemporary practices and innovations.
ACQUIRING KNOWLEDGE AND INFORMATION	
Methods of Study	– acquiring materials and technological knowledge; – acquiring and developing technical skills; – learning about, and understanding, historical traditions; – learning about, and understanding, contemporary practices and innovations; – discovering and connecting contextual knowledge and information with your studies at any time, whether historical knowledge and information, cultural knowledge and information or social knowledge and information, etc.; – discovering and using primary sources of information; – discovering and using secondary sources of information; – establishing and justifying a personal set of principles (criteria) to work to.
ACQUIRING AND DEVELOPING FUNDAMENTAL SKILLS AND CONCEPTS	
Methods of Study	– working in depth; – actively thinking of and exploring possible alternatives; – experimenting and showing inventiveness; – researching; – recording and documenting; – sorting and ordering; – selecting; – organising;

ACQUIRING AND DEVELOPING FUNDAMENTAL SKILLS AND CONCEPTS (cont.)
– presentation; – communicating visually and verbally; – discovering and connecting contextual studies with your work at any time; – being critical which includes analysing and evaluating evidence; interpreting knowledge, the opinions and views of others, what is seen and what is imagined; making value-judgements; and justifying your views and decisions; – establishing a personal set of principles; – being willing and able to justify your principles and the decisions and actions which they lead to; – making selections on the basis of your personal set of principles and the traditions of art and design; – organising your actions and your work according to a personal set of principles and the traditions of art and design; – being willing and able to change your mind as you gain more knowledge and information and your experiences grow.

Table 2.1 Factors fundamental to a sound working habit.

As far as we are concerned, there is a better approach than to base the acquisition and development of the productive skills in art and design upon isolating a particular productive skill, learning about it in theory, practising it, applying it in a piece of work, and then repeating the process with other productive skills one by one. We have already suggested that the selection of many of the materials you use and the methods you employ should be the direct result of your having identified the **needs** which your work requires for further development. Try always to bear this in mind. Nevertheless, we would advocate an approach which is not based upon acquiring productive skills by practical means alone.

Learning about materials and their qualities

You can learn at least as much about materials, their qualities and their uses by visiting an art gallery and studying a successful piece of work as you can from being told what qualities a material has and how to use them, and then practising what you have been told.

What is important is that you should also *understand* what it is you are doing and what it is others before you have done. There can be no better model than the 'others before you' who are recognised as being professional, proficient and highly creative in the field of art and design. While it is not suggested that such people are always represented in a museum or art gallery, there will be many such people in both places. Therefore, you should go to museums and art galleries to study first-hand what it is that successful artists and designers do, how they do it and, if possible, why they do it. For the last question you may have to refer to a selection of **secondary** sources of information, such as books, film-strips, videos, your teachers and so on. Discovering things for yourself in this way usually means that you end up being able to remember what it is you know, and then being able to use the knowledge and information you have gained in a personal and worthwhile way.

“Experiments can help.”

The learning process might well involve you in dealing practically with a material, finding out about its qualities and its possibilities, as you strive to establish how the original artist or designer used it and created the effects which are present in the work you are studying. By **qualities** we mean here the visual appearances a material can produce when used; by **possibilities** we mean the use you might make of those visual effects in your work. Being able to distinguish between qualities and possibilities can only come about if you have some factual knowledge of the properties of materials and some mental awareness of what it is you want to achieve. This means that a series of planned exercises will be necessary in your studies so that you can acquire and develop this knowledge and awareness.

In your own work, no matter how you come about your materials' knowledge, you should be prepared to 'break the mould' as well as to carry on the traditions associated with a particular material. Therefore, it will help, once you have chosen a material, to spend some time exploring its qualities by experimenting with it. By considering a large number of options in its usage and application, you will probably discover *why* there are certain traditions associated with the use of that particular material. You might also discover something new and original for yourself.

At this point, let us return to the examination question, 'Allotments'. No matter what you might intend to draw when you are working at the allotment, it would be a good idea to take along with you some sets of materials which you know possess **different** qualities.

You might know they possess different qualities because of your studies of how other artists and designers have used them in their work. Such knowledge might also have been the result of experiments you conducted beforehand in your classroom studio. Let us say that by a combination of these means you found out that the **water colour** lent itself to portraying atmosphere and the shapes of objects. Studying the work of an artist such as JOHN MIDDLETON (1827 – 56) might have helped you to come to this decision, in addition to your own experiments. On the other hand, you might have decided that **oil pastels** were able to represent texture and colour. Here the work of an artist such as EDGAR DEGAS (1834 – 1917), in his pictures of dancers backstage in a theatre, might have helped you to understand this. In contrast, you may have come to the conclusion that **pen and ink** or **pencil** best portrayed the outlines of shapes and their textural appearance. Discovering an etching such as those by JOHN CROME (1768 – 1821) might have helped you arrive at this conclusion. If you can make connections such as these, it shows that you are aware of contextual pieces of information.

All of this suggests that if you take with you to the allotment sets of these various materials with their different qualities, you could enhance the range of possibilities for the work you carry out there. First, you could assess which material best suited what it was you wanted to draw at any particular time, taking into account why you wanted to draw it. This last point is essential. It means that if you decided to draw some cabbages because, say, of the linear pattern produced by their overlapping leaves and veins, then you could choose a material which best allowed you to do this. If, on the other hand, you were attracted to the textural qualities of the side of a shed, perhaps a rusting metal watertank and a bale of straw, then you could choose a material which would best suit what it was you saw in the objects and made you want to draw them. As a point of interest, which materials would you choose in order to do these two contrasting drawings? Remember, you can mix the materials in your work if you wish.

Alternatively, you could pick a scene and then portray it by using each of the materials you have with you in turn. In our opinion, it is essential that you do this in at least some of your drawings. The likelihood is that, as you do this, you will begin to see various qualities in the scene which did not strike you at first. You are likely to find that the nature of the particular material used each time will force you to see and draw things which it is best suited to, and which might otherwise have been overlooked.

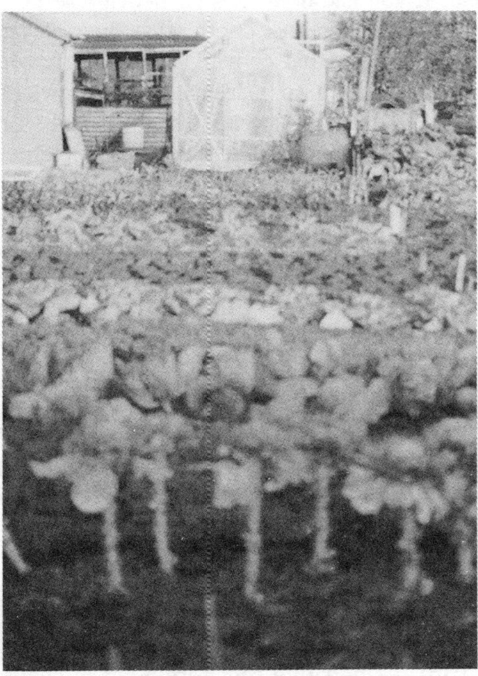

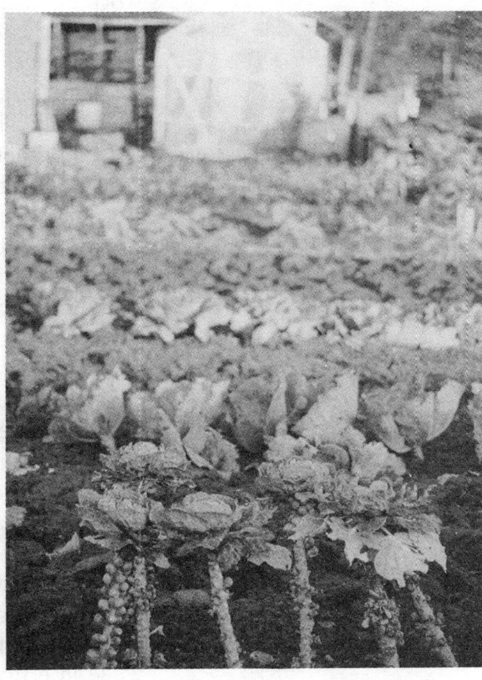

Figs. 2.3 a) and b) The allotment using the medium of film.

In figure 2.3a) and b), by focusing in one picture on the greenhouse and in the other on the brussels sprouts, two differing images of the same scene have emerged from the work. Using the photograph which focuses on the brussels sprouts, you could produce an original and creative work which ranged in contrast from 'detail' to 'impression', and which dealt with the problem of spatial recession.

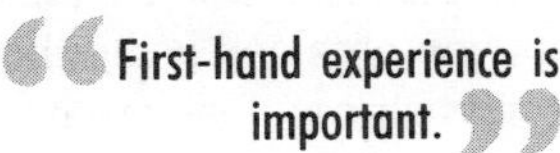

First-hand experience is important.

If you go to an allotment and use the basic approaches we have described, you will no doubt come away with a set of work which is varied, rich in quality and highly original.

You will also have seen things which you may not have predicted when you set out for the allotment.

In Table 2.1, in relation to doing personal practical work which reflects a sound working habit, we mention the terms 'analytical copying' and 'creatively original'. No matter how much theoretical and practical studying you do with regard to materials, technology and techniques, it will all be sterile if you do not translate your knowledge into something creative of your own. Doing creative practical work of your own is vital. Never think that we are suggesting to you that theoretical study is the be all and end all of modern art and design.

In art and design education and examinations there seems to be a strong aversion towards copying of any kind. People talk of 'the colour supplement syndrome', which refers to the way many students in schools merely take a photograph from a newspaper's magazine as an image to copy. This is indeed likely to be of little value, but more constructive copying can be an important aspect of learning in art and design. In this sense, while we would be very critical of your getting a photograph of an allotment from a newspaper and redoing it in, say, oil paint, such a photograph could help your studies if you *used* the information in it to tell you something about allotments.

By **analytical copying** we mean trying to copy not so much what it is an artist or designer has done, but *how* they have done it. Analytical copying of this kind can help you learn a lot about materials and techniques, and it was a traditional feature of art education in the past, when it was quite common to see students in a gallery working with an easel set up before a particular 'masterpiece'. The notion of 'learning how to do' by this means has its counterpart in other activities, most notably sport. By seeing a top sportsperson perform an activity, perhaps time and time again by the means of video, it is possible to imagine and copy the same mental and muscular cohesion and movement to the extent that you begin to feel that what you are doing is correct.

Trying to match how artists such as Cézanne, VINCENT VAN GOGH (1853 – 90) or GEORGES SEURAT (1859 – 91) mixed colours and applied them in juxtaposition on canvas can teach you a variety of things. These might include the qualities of the paint medium *they* used and the paint medium *you* may be using, as well as the theory of colour, the techniques of mark making and modelling they each used. All this can provide you with the beginnings of some understanding of the theory (or set of principles) behind the approach to their work in each case. If you had done this particular exercise, involving these three artists, you could later research in greater depth what their particular theories actually were. So you can see why we believe that copying of a constructive kind, which involves practical work of your own, can help to increase your knowledge and understanding. It may eventually allow you to do highly creative and original work of your own.

“Photographs and analytical studies.”

Photographs from any source, even colour supplements, can be used in analytical studies of this kind. Remember, a photograph is *not* an exact likeness of what it portrays Because of the materials used in its production it **translates** reality into something else. In the case of a photograph, reality is in the first place translated into a series of light impulses upon the emulsion of the negative film. This is then further translated by the printing process (as light is passed through the negative and a chemical procedure is followed) into marks, shapes, tones and even the colours this negative can produce upon photographic printing paper.

In the case of the 'photographs' in a colour supplement, they are not even photographs at that stage; they are prints in coloured inks taken from photographs. If you have a photo-litho or a photo-stencil printing facility in your school, it might help you to understand this and to be aware of the actual differences between negative film, photographic prints and prints made in coloured inks.

Let us return to the question of the allotments. If you first took a photograph of an allotment and then printed a photograph from the negative, you would have two versions of the same set of images – versions which are vastly different to each other. In turn as you well know, the negative in **black and white film** reverses the light and dark areas, while in **colour film** the negative registers a set of shapes and tones which come about because of the colours of the real objects it portrays. In both cases, the photographic prints which can then be made from the negatives look different again not only to the negatives but to each other.

Saving both the negative and the photograph, you could then transfer your work to a printing system, such as photo-litho or photo-stencil, and then print it using coloured inks. If you then collected together all the different images and results you obtained using these different materials, you would be able to see how the material in each case has created a particular effect upon what is identical subject matter. You could explore this still further, perhaps by using photographic printing methods such as polarisation, to produce some pictures, or by changing the colour scheme in your litho or stencil print.

An exercise such as this would greatly benefit your understanding of how materials both cause and affect what we do in art and design, as well as, in this case, contributing to your work upon the allotments problem.

By the term **creatively original** we mean work in which *you* originate the forms and images you produce, be they visual or written. Do not worry if you later discover that they might have been done by someone else at a different time. In 'creatively original' work there is no intention of copying someone else's work, even if it possesses certain similarities. It does not matter if some of the work you produce can subsequently be related to what other, maybe famous, artists and designers might have done. You cannot be expected to search out absolutely unique work to do, or a unique way in which to do it. If you were to be constrained in this way, you would never be able to do a landscape, or even an allotment, if it was known that you had seen a representation of one, say, in a painting by JOHN CONSTABLE (1776–1837). The same applies, of course, to any subject matter you might choose.

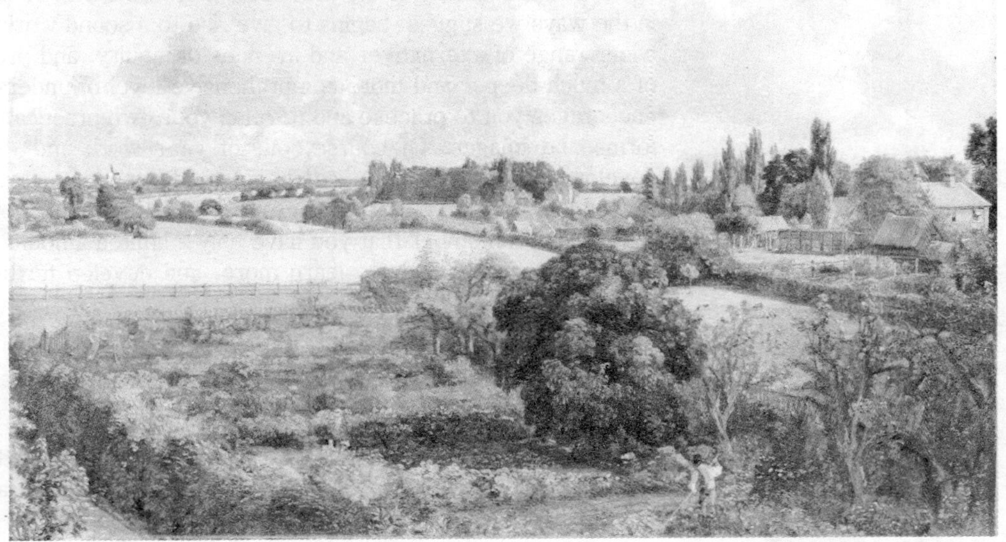

Fig. 2.4 'Golding Constable's Kitchen Garden', John Constable (reproduced by permission of the Trustees of the Ipswich Museum).

Fig. 2.4 shows the painting of an 'allotment' or kitchen garden from an unusual viewpoint, taking in the surrounding countryside. The principles behind it are not unlike those we used in taking the photograph in Fig. 2.2. Does this mean, then, that we should not have taken that photograph, since the apparent similarities between the photograph and the Constable painting could mean that we were 'copying'? Yet we can assure you that we found the work by Constable *after* we had taken the photograph and included it in this book! Clearly, it would be absurd to expect total originality in the work that you, or anyone else, does.

Historical traditions and contemporary practices and innovations

Here we look at the terms **historical traditions** and **contemporary practices and innovations** used in the first section of Table 2.1. We have separated the two in order to convey to you that the study of the past in your chosen field is an essential part of your work if it is to have any reasonable level of credibility. At the same time, however, the present moves on and new things occur which are instrumental in the furtherance and development of your field of study. In our modern technological world such developments occur at a rapid pace and some provide alternatives to what has gone before. The introduction of acrylic paints is an example of an alternative; other developments, such as the use of the computer and graphics, represent genuine innovations.

"Study the historical and the contemporary."

It is our experience that you should study both the historical and the contemporary side by side in this way. You cannot sensibly hope to understand the modern situation if you are not aware of the past. For instance, only by studying the past would you be aware of the short history of acrylic paints and the ways in which their uses differ from other paint media. Such historical studies might also help you become aware, for instance, of the effect upon painting of the invention and development of oil paints as a medium.

In turn, if you have been brought up in the midst of computer-graphic images, an understanding of their uniqueness and their effect upon the way they encourage us to see the world is most likely to come about by studying the types of images which existed *before* their invention. There can be little doubt that the 'image makers' of any time, and in any media, have influenced the way in which we see the world. Just consider the effect of television advertising upon our image of ourselves. Take pop-videos. While they reflect to a degree the world they portray, that portrayal also gives form to a much wider world, which in turn sets out to 'look like' the image the video conveys in the first place. While the paintings of the past may not have had the same intensity of impact, they too have helped to propagate an image of society. The paintings of the High Renaissance appear to reflect an image of a society based upon dignity, classicism and economy of detail and means, despite the fact that such a society hardly existed, except perhaps on a small scale within the whole.

We hope that you can see from this that if you have access to computer-aided printing processes, the next question you might ask yourself is, 'How do I use a computer in my studies of the allotments?'

Some conclusions

From this unravelling of the first section of Table 2.1 we trust you can see that working in the ways we suggest begins to give rise to a sound working habit. It offers you a much wider range of alternatives and avenues of inquiry, and provides you with the possibility of a much deeper and more comprehensive level of understanding. At the same time, it encourages you to practise and develop your own practical skills in making art and design forms and images. Of course, out of your work and the interests you seem to be developing, your teachers *will* begin to direct you in what you do, but they will be responding to what *you* are doing rather than to what *they* think you should be doing.

I pays to remember that you have only a limited amount of time for your studies. This being so, you are likely to learn more, and develop further, by adopting such a sound working habit.

ACQUIRING KNOWLEDGE AND INFORMATION

As Table 2.1 and the previous passages suggest, part of the knowledge and information you need for your studies can come from acquiring and practising your productive skills, provided you adopt the sound working habit we advocate.

“'Active' knowledge relates to the task in hand.”

If you work in the way described, you will also begin to encounter historical and contemporary knowledge and information relevant to the images in art and design, and the social and economic situations which surround them. What is more, your knowledge and the accompanying information you gather will together be what is known as **active knowledge**. That is to say, you will have acquired such knowledge in relation to things you were actually, and actively, doing and were interested in. You will therefore be encountering those parts of history which are relevant to your work and interests, rather than learning in some preselected order what someone else has decided for you.

There is nothing wrong with the fact that your historical knowledge will not be chronologically based. A chronological system is one in which things are ordered according to when they occurred. Chronology is a way of handling the problem of documenting and presenting history. As a system it is invaluable in understanding how one thing gave rise to another. It is also a most suitable system for learning, if you have plenty of time to study. But in the circumstances of your studies in art and design, chronology is likely to be of little relevance as far as you are personally concerned.

Of course one of *your* responsibilities in adopting 'a sound working habit', as described here, is to delve further when you uncover historical facts which are relevant to your immediate needs. You should then look backwards, sideways and forwards in history, in order to understand further the context of your discovered knowledge at any time. By this means you will begin to fill in the 'spaces in between' as regards your historical knowledge.

“Contextual knowledge is most important.”

Part of the system of teaching and learning described so far in this second section of Table 2.1 is concerned with **contextual knowledge**. Do not fall into the trap of thinking that you will be wasting time if you are *not* working on facts and figures which are exclusively part of art and design. In the *Food Programme* on BBC Radio 4 a confectionery cook said that apart from learning about the tools and materials necessary to ice cakes, he had learned about and acquired skills in metalwork, joinery and artistic expression while carrying out his trade. If it is appropriate for a person to do this when engaged in paid occupation, it is surely sensible for you to do so in your student/learning circumstances.

As Table 2.1 shows, historical knowledge is part of any contextual knowledge you might suitably acquire, but so also is cultural knowledge and social knowledge. These last two terms might need explaining.

Cultural knowledge

The distinction between cultural and social is not very easy to grasp because the two often overlap in common usage. We do not mean good taste or refinement by the term **culture**. Rather, we mean all that contributes to, and forms part of the intellectual, artistic and social state of development of a group. It will probably be best if you think of culture as meaning a group of people who can be identified by observing:

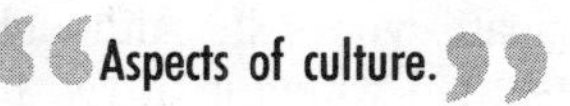

- the way in which they live and behave;
- the beliefs they hold;
- the objects and images they produce;
- the methods of communication they employ.

This means that *you* belong to a culture. That culture is part of the general society in which you live. For instance, if you live in the United Kingdom, you are part of the general 'British' culture. How you live, what you believe in, the things that you own, they way you communicate – are all governed to some extent by the institutions and people around you, whether you like it or not. In other words, you are influenced to a greater or lesser extent by British culture.

At the same time, you may be part of a **subculture** within that general culture, such as a minority group living in the United Kingdom. For instance, the fact that you are in your mid-teens will inevitably mean that you will be part of one or more of the various teenage subcultures which exist. Your own interests or hobbies may bring you into contact with many other subcultures in Britain: Christian youth, bikers, naturalists, vegetarians, etc.

In the way that you can see the differences between the teenage subculture and the general culture in which you live, so you can identify differences between that general culture and the general cultures of other nations.

In art and design terms, you are likely to be aware of the various (cultural) patterns and colours used on their blankets by individual North American Indian tribes. You will probably recognise that both the patterns and the colours differ from those used traditionally in the United Kingdom.

Social knowledge

Social, on the other hand, is more to do with the **structures** within a group which give rise to the society they represent. In this sense it is more about organisational beliefs, such as distinctions between 'classes' within a society, or the notion of mutual interdependence, which forms part of the basis of belief behind a social organisation such as the Welfare State.

The types of knowledge and the range of information which might come from cultural and social sources is wideranging. There can be no doubt that it is instrumental in understanding why things look like they do, why some things exist and others do not, why some things mean one thing in one place and another somewhere else, and why some things are accepted in one place and yet are taboo elsewhere. By finding out more about this type of information you are increasingly able to 'read' the codes which exist around you and which give shape to the culture and society in which you live. Part of such understanding can best come about by studying alternative cultures and societies on a *comparative* basis. We emphasise this last comment because we believe that the best way to grasp what underpins different cultures and social structures and beliefs is not by studying each, as if it were a separate and precious hot-house flower, but by attempting to identify the similarities in principles and beliefs which exist as well as any apparent differences.

We end up with (the rather lame) 'etc'. in Table 2.1 because although we believe that knowledge and meaning are tied up inevitably with the cultural or social reasons for their existence, you may well find it easier to regard knowledge under a range of conventional subject areas. By this we mean that you may find it easier to think of scientific knowledge, mathematical knowledge, geographical knowledge and so on – that is, similar groupings to the historical knowledge already mentioned as an important aspect of your studies in art and design. Do remember, however, that although areas of knowledge such as these appear to have 'absolute' values, in each case the meaning behind the apparent facts can often be linked to a culture, or to a society. Thus the same apparent thing could mean something quite different in another culture or society. For instance, it is fairly well known that the Western social and cultural concept of art is not something we can impose upon the forms and images present in an Asian culture. In the same way, colours have different purposes and meanings in different cultures and societies.

The next methods of study in Table 2.1 refer to primary and secondary sources of information.

Primary sources of information

A **primary** source of information is one which you originate yourself. Although a photograph is not the original subject matter which is represented within it, if *you* took the photograph yourself it would be regarded as a primary source of information for decisions within your work. This means that you could work from such a photograph in almost any way you wish, without criticism. There has been after all, a tradition for this in art and design ever since the invention of photography. Degas, in particular, springs to mind as an artist who used photographs in composing his work. It is known, for instance, that he used photographs in the preparation of his paintings of landscapes. At the same time, he was also recognised as an accomplished photographer.

Secondary sources of information

It is clear that your own drawings, written notes, poems, etc. documenting and recording the views of things you have, either real or imagined, must be regarded as primary sources of information when you use them in the preparation of other pieces of work. Yet if you make your written notes, or make your drawings, from the work of others, either from books or other media, you are using **secondary** sources of information in your work.

> "Acknowledge secondary sources."

When you do this, you must *acknowledge* your sources of information. There are many ways of doing this. Where a publicly accepted way exists, we suggest that you use it. This is particularly the case when you use books in your studies. There is a common way to refer to any book you use. Where we have got our information from a book as a secondary source, or we use a book to justify what we say, we put first, the name of the author, then the title of the book, followed by the publisher's name and where the book was published, and finally the date of publication. You can follow this accepted format in your own work.

It might be that you use information from an artist's work, or a designer's products. If so, acknowledge the fact, referring to any title the work or item might have and stating the name of the artist or designer; or use any other means of description you can discover or even invent. The thing to remember is that rather than being penalised for using secondary sources of information in your work, if you acknowledge them you will be rewarded for your skills and ability in discovering relevant information and knowledge, as well as for using it in a personal and profitable way.

So, remember, rather than attempting to conceal your sources of information, make them clear and acknowledge them, in order to get the fullest reward for what you do and the way that you do it.

Principles and criteria

Table 2.1 raises the question of getting, justifying and using a **personal set of principles** as the basis for the decisions you make in your work. This could be called the **criteria** you work to.

> "Develop your own, personal criteria."

It is a safe bet that whenever you do anything in art and design you *do* work to some principle or criterion. Perhaps the most common principle in the earlier stages of artistic development is the desire to produce work which might be said to have a 'photographic likeness' to that which we are trying to portray. Whether such a thing is possible or even desirable, is not the issue here. The point is that we, or you, have worked with a criterion or principle in mind – namely, to achieve a likeness. The trouble is that all too often we have not *voiced* this (or any other) principle in any way. We have often wrestled internally with the problem, before becoming frustrated with the outcomes of our work.

The criteria we seek to work to should, of course, be based upon the principles associated with art and design, such as those of composition and design, colour theory and so on. The definition of these terms and of the 'Formal elements' in the Glossary will help you to understand this.

"Make your criteria clear."

We would suggest that it is essential that you *make clear* and *specify* the principles to which you are working at any time. Above all else, this will provide others with the means to critically evaluate your work. For instance, if *we* tend to concentrate upon the use of colour in our work in art and design, it would be quite wrong for us to assess *your* work predominantly on the basis of this quality if you had been concentrating upon, say, 'getting a likeness'. Of course, it is difficult to give hard-and-fast examples of exactly what we mean, because in doing work in art and design we all call upon a mixture of qualities and desired effects, using a spectrum of principles and means to achieve them. The point is, however, that it is better to have your work evaluated and assessed upon the principles you used in producing it than to be assessed on the basis of the beliefs and principles we, or others, might hold about the nature and purposes of art and design. Therefore, you *must* make your principles or criteria clear at all times.

There are, of course, other factors which are not strictly to do with art and design but which might be considered by you in forming your principles. For instance, nowadays it is popular for people to express a 'Green' sympathy. If *you* do, how will this affect the decisions you take in your work and the appearance of your work? It might be present in the messages your work intends to convey. This need not be too obvious; you do not have to make each piece of work a poster for conservancy but you may choose to do pictures of peaceful landscapes. If you are politically minded, you may make your point by merely juxtaposing a belching chimney or a fuel-burning aircraft with an idyllic stretch of a canal scene, and so on.

In the same way your own moral and ethical beliefs, and the codes which come from them, are likely to influence the decisions you take involving your work. For instance, if you believe that war or exploitation is wrong, you might avoid choosing to do work which could further either of these aspects. Or you might have religious beliefs which discourage you from portraying certain images in your work.

Whatever your personal circumstances or views, the important thing is that you should begin quickly to identify the set of principles which will guide your work. These are likely to be based upon the personal religious, moral and ethical beliefs you hold. They will also come from the social and cultural standards to which you adhere. Many are likely to be based on the criteria which have been established theoretically and traditionally for producing work in art and design. You might, for instance, hold principles which affect your decisions about the composition in your work, the colour arrangements you use, the designs you choose to make, the materials you wish to select, and so on. When you are conscious of these principles emerging in the outcome of your work and in the way that you work, try to *articulate* them. Write them down in your notebook. When you can understand them, try to explain why you hold them. Then, set out to *justify* why it is that you do hold them. Finally, try to make it clear to your teachers, and then to your examiners, what the principles are that you are working to, as well as why you hold them.

Some conclusions

We hope you can see from the foregoing that adopting a very broad level of acceptance with regard to what might be useful to you in your studies is likely to benefit not only your work but also your examination result. There can be no substitute for knowing as much as you can about your subject and about the contextual circumstances surrounding it. The breadth of knowledge suggested here is very likely to lead to much more original and creative work on your part.

ACQUIRING AND DEVELOPING FUNDAMENTAL SKILLS AND CONCEPTS

We have already dealt indirectly with the first three methods of study listed in this section of Table 2.1. 'Working in depth' is covered in part by considering 'alternatives'. Both depth and the question of alternatives are helped by your willingness and ability to set up 'experiments'. The knowledge you gain from experimenting will lead to your being 'inventive'. In our discussion of Table 2.1 so far, we have been suggesting ways of working which will encourage and facilitate each of these three methods of study.

In the same way, particularly in our previous discussion about 'primary' and 'secondary' sources of information, we have already begun to explain what we mean by 'researching' and 'recording and documenting'. However, as researching, recording and documenting are highly important aspects of working soundly in art and design, we will define them more closely.

Researching

Researching is really about 'finding out', which art and design is most often done by going somewhere and looking. This was the essence of the approach we recommended you take to answer the allotment question. You might visit allotments in order to find out about them. In the process you might discover things you had not expected. If you do, you will find that you then have the means to be more inventive and original in your work.

Of course, there are other ways of researching, even in art and design. When you read books, look at slides of work, see films or videos on art and artists, and so on, you are conducting a form of research. You are finding out more than you might already know.

The term 'research' has scientific connotations. When scientists conduct experiments, invent new things, investigate diseases and so on, they are said to be 'researching'. The word is also used to describe the practice of bringing together useful information in order to clarify situations, such as the popularity of TV programmes, the success of advertising campaigns, the needs of a community, a profile of a group of people and so on. For example, when the Top Twenty records chart is compiled, it is as a result of research of this nature. A number of procedures might be used in these 'research' situations, including:

- conducting interviews;
- compiling and using questionnaires;
- testing materials.

In an art and design situation, the results you get from these procedures might be useful in guiding your decisions about what to do, and how to do it. Let us look a little more closely at the use of interviews and questionnaires.

Interviews

Let us imagine that you are going to investigate the topic of old age. To begin with you decide to make a **portrait** of an old person and chose your grandfather. At first you think it would be a good idea just to do a drawing of him, and then to make a painting from it later. This is very acceptable. After all, it is in the mainstream of the history of portrait painting. But imagine that when you go to ask him if you can do this, he is so excited by the interest you are taking in him that he begins to talk of when he was a youngster, the same age as you. At first you simply humour him, but then you find that he is very interesting to listen to. When you leave you find that you have not remembered to do your drawing!

Thinking about it, you decide that it could be a good idea to make your portrait as full and contextual as possible. Perhaps you realise that what 'makes' your grandfather is what he knows, what he has done, and what has happened to him, as much as what he looks like now. It might be that the next time you go to see him you take a tape recorder and a camera. You ask him to tell you about his childhood, his time as a young man, being a father and then a grandfather. As you conduct this **interview** and he talks into the tape recorder you move around him, photographing him in his armchair against his favourite things. You might arrange a **still-life** of his treasured possessions and photograph these. Perhaps, as he continues to talk, you sit down and make some drawings of him as well.

Later there will be many possibilities open to you. You can arrange an exhibition of your photographs and drawing, with your tape playing in the middle of it. You can add a large painted portrait of your grandfather to this. You may have taken your original photographs, or gone back to do so, on colour-slide film. If so, you could arrange a 'tape-slide' presentation of the event; perhaps as your tape plays it will trigger a slide to accompany what is being said. You might add other slides to illustrate what your grandfather is saying at any time. These could have been bought from museums or taken from pictures in books. They may have been, for instance, about harvesting in the 1930s, or pictures of the last world war, or illustrations of the various fashions in clothing that your grandfather has lived through so far. You could add to the tape of his voice, perhaps, by recording popular songs from the different times he spoke of. You might even decide to make a **video portrait** of your grandfather, going back to film him again with a **story board** worked out from your first tapes and photographs.

By being open-minded and receptive to unexpected ideas which might crop up, the possibilities in your work are endless, and each one will be refreshingly original and adventurous.

Questionnaires

On the other hand, within the topic old age you might decide to try to find out what it is people at a local old people's home most need to make their life more pleasant. If you ask ten people this without any boundaries for their answers, you will probably get ten different replies – not all of them serious! If, however, you construct a **questionnaire** which curtails the types of replies you receive according to the type of information you feel you need, then you will have some real exploratory evidence to work from.

Let us imagine that you visit such a home and talk to some of the people there. You look around and think the place looks bare. So you decide that you will find out if the people would like a piece of art and design work to hang or keep in their environment. To find this out, and what it might be, you construct a questionnaire. It might be something like this:

Q.1 Would you like something which livens the place up?

Q.2 Would you prefer a picture, a piece of pottery, a print, etc.?

Q.3 Is there anything you would like the object to be of?

Q.4 What colours should it be?

Q.5 What size do you think it should be?

Q.6 Where do you think the object should go?

The answers you get are hardly likely to tell you *exactly* what is needed and what it is you should do, but if you 'score' the answers in a table or chart, then you will get a quick visual impression of what is the *most important* conclusion to draw from your evidence.

To make the chart you might tabulate your headings vertically, and list those who answered horizontally, putting a tick at each intersection where a positive reply occurred. It may look something like Table 2.2.

INTERVIEWEE		1	2	3	4	5	6	7	8	9	10
Q.2	Picture	✓	✓			✓		✓			
	Pot				✓					✓	✓
	Print			✓			✓		✓		
Q.4	Reddish		✓				✓		✓	✓	
	Blueish	✓		✓							
	Yellowish					✓					
	Greenish				✓			✓			✓
Q.5	Big	✓			✓		✓	✓			
	Medium		✓	✓		✓			✓	✓	✓
	Small										
Q.6	Lounge		✓			✓		✓		✓	✓
	Dining room	✓									
	Entrance hall			✓	✓		✓		✓		

Table 2.2 Scoring information.

Of course, it cannot be claimed that any research system is absolute in the sense that an unquestionable conclusion can be drawn from the evidence. Nevertheless, certain things can be 'read' from the chart shown above.

It seems that, while the choice is by no means overwhelming, a picture might be the most appropriate thing to do. But at the same time, the 'scoring' could suggest that a piece of pottery or a print is equally appropriate. This means that you could choose to do whichever of these appeals to you most. A reddish-greenish piece of work appears also to be wanted, of a medium size. You would need to decide what you consider to be a 'medium' size, unless you do some more research work and ask the people concerned. The fact that the people you asked want the work to be in the lounge might govern what it is you choose to do and what might be regarded as a medium size. People sit around for long periods of time in a lounge, therefore it might help to produce something which can be studied closely and be interesting as well as something which is striking and visible from a reasonable distance.

Recording and documenting

These two activities are very closely related. You **record** things when you draw them, paint them, photograph them, write about them, talk about them and so on. These records are often a haphazard collection of things of differing forms and sizes. To make more sense of them in your studies, it is preferable that you **document** them. With regard to your work, in all its forms and variations, this means that you learn to:

- collect;
- sort;
- select;
- order;
- collate.

By doing this you will be in a better position to know what you have got, evaluate its relevance, and find it again whenever you want to use it in your work.

For recording and documenting artists most often use a **sketchbook**. However, in your work particularly with the range of modern techniques and materials available, you might well find that a sketchbook alone is insufficient for your needs. For instance, you cannot put a video or a tape recording on the pages of a sketchbook. Whatever means you use, though, documenting is a vital process in your education in art and design and can make a valuable contribution towards the final result you obtain in your assessment.

> "Use a variety of recording devices."

When you record and document what is going on in your studies, you are 'communicating visually and verbally', as we mentioned in Table 2.1. Try to discern when images and forms are the most appropriate means for you and when words, written or spoken, would be better. Do not fall into the trap of believing that all your work in art and design should be practical and visual. Remember, the well-rounded approach can lead to much more knowledge and improved work in the time available.

Critical skills

At all times in your work try to adopt a critical approach. Learn how to question all that you see and receive. Get into the habit of asking others to justify their views and decisions but, above all, learn how to do the same yourself with your own views and decisions. Once you have started justifying things, you will be surprised how much easier it is to make decisions. We have already pointed out the need to have a well-defined set of personal principles to aid you in these decisions. So the essence of the critical approach is having a point of view of your own and being able to account for it.

> "Be ready to justify your opinions."

You do not have to write something to express your judgements. You do so as soon as you choose to do one thing in preference to another, such as a pot rather than a print, or a picture of a landscape rather than a picture of trees alone. In the same way you express your judgements when you choose to work in one material rather than another. It is also true that the forms and images you produce can offer visual criticism of the things you see around you. The 'Disasters of War' etchings by FRANCISCO GOYA (1746 – 1828) clearly illustrate this point.

What is important is that you make it clear that you have made particular judgements and you give reasons for why you did so.

PREPARING FOR PRACTICAL EXAMINATIONS IN ART AND DESIGN

COURSEWORK

You should bear in mind at all times during your course of study that your coursework is preparation for an examination. In fact, in some syllabuses it is part of your assessment. Whatever the case, you can never ignore the significance of what it is you do – and how you do it – so far as your development and final grade are concerned.

Of course, this does not mean that you should 'play safe' and fail to experiment and explore deeply the things which interest you. If you do this, your work is likely to be sterile, unadventurous and limited in its level of final achievement. Art and design is a risk-taking affair. You dream, imagine or postulate in the initial stages, and all these approaches have within them the possibility of failure. Nevertheless, if you never risk working seriously and sincerely on something which might turn out to be inappropriate, you will be unlikely to arrive at very original and exciting conclusions in your work. If you never tackle work which you know in part to be beyond your ability at the outset of the project, you are unlikely to develop the level of your skills and ability.

Furthermore, if you do not take risks, you are unlikely to use, and thereby develop, your **critical** faculties to any extent. When you are working in unknown realms, then is the time when you need to have your 'sixth sense' working overtime. For artists and designers, their sixth sense is the ability to critically analyse what is going on in their work *as it is going on*! From this you will gather that being critical is a continuous state of mind you need to have throughout your practical work if that work is to have any significance and credibility. In painting a portrait, for instance, you may be considering whether a flesh colour needs to be warmer or colder, or whether the colour under the jaw-line needs to be of a darker tone, or whether the tonal and colour contrasts between two adjoining shapes define each shape, or whether some means of including a line to define the two shapes needs to be devised. The list is endless, and it does not stop with fine art. The designer may be considering whether the weight of the object is too heavy for its intended use, or whether one colour is likely to appeal more successfully to the intended market than another, or whether certain materials should be used in terms of strength, durability, 'green-ness' and so on. Again, the list is endless.

Coursework is therefore an essential part of preparation for your examination, because it instils in you a worthwhile way of working, whether or not it contributes directly to your final grade.

PREPARATORY STUDIES

Many examining boards allow you to have your question paper a number of days in advance of the actual examination. This is so you can carry out 'preparatory studies', making you better prepared to answer the question you have chosen.

We think it better if you regard this time, and the work you do in it, as a series of investigations which explore *all* the possibilities which may be present in the question you have chosen to do. The danger is that you might otherwise see the answer in your mind's eye and devote all your time to gathering together information to allow you carry out your preconceived solution. Of course, the very notion of preparatory studies means that you will come up with some idea of an outcome which will answer the question set. What we mean here is that you should not let your ideas become too fixed; otherwise your solution is unlikely to contain the unexpected, the exciting or the original. Cast your mind back to the discussion on the allotment question earlier in this chapter and you will see what we mean.

"Make good use of your preparatory studies."

If, on the other hand, you decide to use the time available for your preparatory studies to let your mind run free, it is likely that you will be able to find things out about your chosen question which did not come easily to mind in the first place. So, use your preparatory studies not to plan what it is you *will* do in your final examination work but to find out what it is that you *could* do.

Let us illustrate this by supposing that you have been set the task of doing some work based upon the **human form in action** in your final examination. You could start your preparatory studies by finding out how *others* have treated this subject in the history of art and design. You might also write down some places, such as the gymnasium, the swimming pool, staircases and gardens, where it is probable that you will be able to *see* figures in action. If you do this, what you have is not just preparatory; it is also exploratory, and it will be supportive at a later date so far as your work is concerned.

Your next step in this task might be to make some drawings and to take some photographs of people jumping, swimming, going up and down stairs and digging. At the same time, you could begin a **scrapbook** of cuttings showing people doing a much wider range of activities, in case your ideas change direction later.

Again, this work is as much exploratory as it is preparatory. So far you do not know exactly what it is you will end up doing, so it is not strictly preparatory work. At the same time it *is* supportive work, no matter whether you use any of the particular pieces of work or not. All that you are doing so far will support you in making your final decision about proceeding with the problem before you.

Imagine that you have got as far as deciding that you are going to produce a **statue in clay of a swimmer just leaving a diving board**.You might then find that, despite all your preparatory work, you do not have enough information about the way one thing follows on after another as a person dives off the board. So you have to return to the swimming pool, armed with a camera and the intention of taking a number of photographs of people as they dive from the diving board.

If you take the trouble to do this, what you are undertaking cannot be described accurately as preparatory studies. In the strictest sense, if you have already *started* to carry out your idea for the sculpture, your preparatory studies have finished.

To sum up so far, the word preparatory suggests:

- something done at the beginning;
- something done before you start work on your idea in its final form;
- your planning.

Whereas in practice, at all stages of their work, professional artists and designers:

- continue gathering information;
- redirect their ideas;
- change their mind altogether.

Therefore it would pay you to regard your preparatory studies as being:

- preparatory;
- exploratory;
- supportive.

THE FINAL EXAMINATION

If you have used your preparatory studies in the ways suggested it is likely that you will arrive at your final examination with what you are going to do, and the way that you are going to *start* doing it, firmly in your mind. At the same time, and this is most important, you will not have done anything which is a facsimile of what you intend to do in your final examination. In some cases, what you have done so far may not necessarily be even remotely like your intentions, as far as your final piece of work is concerned. That is to say, you may now have the information to support what it is you intend to do, but you will not yet have 'put it all together' in its final form. This is excellent. It means that your final work will be fresh and have about it an air of spontaneity.

"Work can continue to develop and change."

During your final examination you will be able to put into practice the sound working habit you have become familiar with during your coursework studies. As you do your work you will continue to develop and redirect your ideas and intentions in the light of how it is taking shape, taking into account any new directions suggested within it. If this is the way you work during your final examination, you will find yourself excited at the prospects opening up as you work, and your level of achievement can only benefit from this.

The alternative is, of course, to play safe. That is to say, before your final examination you have a 'dummy run' at the work you intend to do and then just repeat it during your examination. If you do this, you run the risk of being either bored with doing the same thing a second time, perhaps almost unthinkingly, or becoming so concerned with techniques and neatness that your work takes on an impersonal appearance. In both cases your examination result is likely to be limited by the restrictions that this approach imposes upon your work.

So, try to arrive at your final examination fired-up and excited at the prospect of exploring and presenting ideas which you have not so far covered in their entirety in your preparatory studies.

As regards getting yourself ready for any examination in art and design, be it practical or written, try to get a reasonable amount of sound sleep the night before. The best way of doing this, and of getting ready for the next morning, is not to break any of your habits. It is your regular habits which help to account for what, and who, you are. In your examination, especially in art and design, you are trying to convey this personal element in your work. Therefore, if you have a good breakfast normally, do not get yourself so excited that you cannot eat on the morning of your examination. If you are used to going to bed at about 10.30 p.m., do not go to bed so much earlier that you lie awake worrying, or so much later that you sleep heavily a wake up unrefreshed. Just behave normally. To do well at your work you need to be sharp and alert, yet relaxed. The best way of attaining this state is to behave as you always do. The examination will enhance and sharpen your mind and your reflexes without you having to do anything special about it.

WRITTEN EXAMINATIONS IN ART AND DESIGN

Some examining boards insist that you take a **written paper** as part of your end of course examinations in art and design. Others give you the option of taking such a paper during your end of course examinations. Both are listed in Table 2.3.

Some of these written papers are part of syllabuses based upon the study of a particular craft. Others deal more with either the history of art or the history of design. Again, these differences are shown in Table 2.3.

EXAMINING BOARD	SYLLABUS	PAPER/ SECTION	COMPULSORY/ OPTIONAL
AEB	ART – PAINTING/603	Paper 2 History and Technique	Compulsory
	Brief details **Mark Weighting:** 33.3 per cent of total marks for the examination. **Time Allowed:** 3 hours. **Other:** Answers may be illustrated wherever relevant.		
	ART AND CRAFTS/605	Paper 2/Option 25 History and Appreciation of Art	Optional
	Brief Details **Mark Weighting:** 33.3 per cent of total marks for the examination. **Time Allowed:** 3 hours. **Other:** Four essay subjects must be answered out of twelve set.		
	CRAFTS PRINTMAKING 662	Paper 2 History and Technique	Compulsory
	Brief details **Mark Weighting:** 33.3 per cent of total marks for the examination. **Time Allowed:** 3 hours. **Other**: One question must be answered from Section 1, and two further sections from sections i-v.		
	CRAFTS POTTERY/663	Paper 2 History and Technique	Compulsory
	Brief details **Mark Weighting**: 33.3 per cent of the total marks for the examination. **Time Allowed**: 3 hours. **Other**: Two sections set; three answers are required, drawn from both sections.		
CAMBRIDGE	ART AND DESIGN/9309	Component 3 Personal Study	Compulsory
	Brief details **Mark Weighting**: 30 per cent of the total marks for the examination. **Time Allowed**: Carried out during Coursework. **Other**: The work for this component may be written, a structured sequence of annotated images or a slide/tape/video presentation. It is essentially a research exercise with personal interpretation and critical analysis.		
JMB	ART AND DESIGN	Personal Study	Compulsory
	Brief details **Mark Weighting**: 30 per cent of the total marks for the examination. **Time Allowed**: Carried our during Coursework. **Other**: This work involves the techniques of research and investigation, but also demands that a personal interpretation and use of the information gathered should be present in it.		
	CRAFT (DESIGN AND PRACTICE)	Written Paper	Compulsory
	Brief details **Mark Weighting**: 20 per cent of the total marks for the examination. **Time Allowed:** 3 hours. **Other**: There are two sections in the examination. Two questions have to be answered from Section A, and two from different study areas in Section B.		
NISEC	SYLLABUS A	Paper V History of Art	Optional
	Brief details **Mark Weighting**: 33.3 per cent of the total marks for the examination. **Time Allowed**: 3 hours. **Other**: There are two parts to the paper. Five questions must be answered. These may be chosen from either part of the paper, or both. Answers may be illustrated where appropriate.		

<table>
<tr><th>EXAMINING BOARD</th><th>SYLLABUS</th><th>PAPER/ SECTION</th><th>COMPULSORY/ OPTIONAL</th></tr>
<tr><td></td><td>SYLLABUS B</td><td>Section 3
History and Appreciation of Art, Architecture and Design</td><td>Compulsory</td></tr>
<tr><td></td><td colspan="3">Brief details
Mark Weighting: Whilst this is a compulsory section of the examination, you may fail to satisfy the examiners in this section but still obtain your A-level certificate, provided you reach the necessary level in the other three sections of your overall examination.
Time Allowed: 3 hours, plus an extended essay.
Other: The examination comprises two parts. Two questions from Part 1, and one from Part 2 must be answered.</td></tr>
<tr><td>OXFORD</td><td>ART WITH
ART HISTORY/9894</td><td>Paper 1
History of Art</td><td>Compulsory</td></tr>
<tr><td></td><td colspan="3">Brief details
Mark Weighting: 20 per cent of the total marks for the examination.
Time Allowed: 3 hours.
Other: There are three sections in the paper. Four questions must be answered. These may be taken from one, two or all three sections.</td></tr>
<tr><td>OX/CAM</td><td>ART AND DESIGN
1991/9642</td><td>Component 3
Related Study</td><td>Compulsory</td></tr>
<tr><td></td><td colspan="3">Brief details
Mark Weighting: 20 per cent of the total marks for the examination.
Time Allowed: Carried out during coursework.
Other: The study may take the form of practical work supported by written work, a written paper or a video. The work should be directly related to your practical work in the overall examination, but should show the degree of your critical analysis, contextual knowledge and historical investigations.</td></tr>
<tr><td>SEB</td><td>ART AND DESIGN
(REVISED HIGHER GRADE)</td><td>Critical Evaluation and Historical Studies</td><td>Compulsory</td></tr>
<tr><td></td><td colspan="3">Brief details
Mark Weighting: 26.6 per cent of the total marks for the examination.
Time Allowed: 2 hours.
Other: The paper is in two parts. All three questions must be answered in Section A. Two questions must be answered from those available in Section B.</td></tr>
<tr><td>ULSEB</td><td>ART AND DESIGN
O20–027</td><td>Endorsed certificate
Critical and Historical Studies 027</td><td>Compulsory</td></tr>
<tr><td></td><td colspan="3">Brief details
Mark Weighting: The certificate carries the whole of the marks available in the examination in this particular certificate.
Time Allowed: The duration of your course, plus a 3 hour written paper.
Other: The work carried out during your course of study should result in either an A1-sized mounted sheet/sketch/notebook or a dissertation on a topic selected by you. The written paper on the History of Art and Design is in addition to this work.
Apart from this Endorsed Certificate, all the certificates, endorsed and unendorsed, insist that you include critical and historical studies in your work. This may be shown in any of the three ways specified in the previous paragraph, i.e., the A1 mounted sheet/sketch/notebook; or the dissertation; or the written paper.</td></tr>
<tr><td>WJEC</td><td>ART AND DESIGN</td><td>Critical Studies</td><td>Compulsory</td></tr>
<tr><td></td><td colspan="3">Brief Details
Mark Weighting: 25 per cent of the total marks for the examination.
Time Allowed: Either a 3 hour written examination, or an investigative study carried out over an extended period of time during your coursework.
Other: The written paper is in two parts. You must answer one question from Part One and three from Part Two. The investigative study is expected to show evidence of research as well as your own level of interpretation and evaluation of your gathered material.</td></tr>
</table>

Table 2.3 Written examination options in art and design.

There can be no doubt that when you take written papers of this kind you will be expected to know a number of facts and be able to recall them under examination conditions. This will necessitate a certain amount of revision on your part.

Even though the syllabuses make it clear that you are expected to respond, when answering a particular question, in a personal, interpretative and critical manner, you will need to know about, and remember, historical and technical facts. You cannot be critical or interpretative in a vacuum. That is to say, you cannot waffle on, talking about nothing. Here it is a matter of *using* the facts you know in order to convey your own view and opinions about things to the examiners. If you find this prospect daunting, then you should be taking an alternative examination syllabus (or an alternative combination of papers within the syllabus you are taking, provided the written paper is optional).

PERSONAL STUDIES

Some examination boards give you the option of taking a **special** or **personal** study of a historical and critical nature during your course of study. Before you jump with joy at the prospect of this, bear in mind that the requirements for this study will probably mean that you must have a considerable command of the skills associated with interpretation and criticism. These might well have to be learned and they will certainly have to be practised during your course of study. Fortunately you can practise them as much in your practical work as in your written work, so both areas of your work could benefit if you take such a written paper in your examination.

Some of those skills will, of course, be about seeking out, using and acknowledging authoritative sources of information. This means that you must be able to conduct **literature searches**, be capable of visiting and using museums and galleries in a competent manner, and show yourself capable of arranging interviews and conducting them sensitively. In other words, you will have to conduct your own research in a proficient and purposeful way. But remember, you will be doing this anyway, while carrying out your practical work in art and design. Because this option further develops these vital research skills to the benefit of all your work in art and design, we would encourage you to select this personal study option wherever it is available.

> “Take every opportunity of developing your research skills.”

We say this so emphatically because, if you work at your practical studies in the way that we propose, you will be equipping yourself with both the skills and the information necessary to deal well with a written paper of this kind. The greater the relationship you build up between your practical work and the content of any written paper, the more likely it is that you will be able to 'kill two birds with one stone'. Suppose your practical studies were centred around the production of studio pottery, then you might choose as the subject of your personal study the work of a potter such as BERNARD LEACH (1887–1979). What you then do in one area of your study will benefit and develop what you do in the other, and the reciprocation will be ongoing. For instance, in our example it is likely that your own pottery will be increasingly influenced by your study of the work of Leach. In turn, your understanding and appreciation of his work will be increased because of the experience and knowledge gained from doing your own practical work.

REVISING FOR WRITTEN EXAMINATIONS IN ART AND DESIGN

It is to be expected that your teachers will encourage you to study the history of your subject in an interpretative and critical way, in contrast to just asking you to learn and remember facts. If so, at the time of your written examination you will already be used to working in a sound way. All that you have to do is to make certain that you have some system for bringing to mind the facts and figures which are stored in your head as a result of your studies throughout the course.

The number of facts you need to know, or can know, will be controlled by two things:

- the amount of time allowed by your timetable for studying your subject;
- the narrowed-down selection from the history of art and design which each examining board imposes within its written examination syllabuses.

The syllabuses for each written paper divide the subject they cover into various historical periods. You will then elect to study one of these different periods in the history of art and design during your course of study. In turn, the questions in the written papers do not usually ask that you recite a long list of facts and figures. Instead, they are mostly worded to provide you with the means of writing about, and around, a particular person, time, event, situation, theme and so on.

But of course, in order to do so you will need to know and be able to recall (if you sit a written end of course examination) a large number of the basic facts about the period you are studying.

Even if you take the personal study option, you will still have to learn a large number of facts before you can begin to write your study, although in this case such facts are likely to be relevant to your particular needs, rather than be in the form of a general selection from the period you are studying. In the more formal type of question and answer written paper, you will need to know a lot of facts because your study must prepare you for any eventuality.

As far as revising for the more formal type of question and answer examinations, try to get used to *planning* your revision carefully, and then sticking to your schedule. You will find that you study best for a certain amount of time without a rest. Experiment early in your course to find out what this length of time is for you, perhaps by revising one evening for a specified period of time and then trying to write down all that you can remember the next evening. If there is a large gap between what you can remember and what you revised, with much of what you have forgotten being what you revised towards the end of the session the evening before, then you were revising for too long. Learn to set yourself revision tasks on particular topics, artists, themes, etc which just fill up the time you can profitably use for revision. Plan for these self-appointed tasks to take place on a regular basis during your revision, and stick to them come what may. It is essential that you create a discipline in your revision, as well as finding ways of testing yourself on the information you revised some time previously.

You can, of course, expect some 'fall out' as far as your memory is concerned. Nevertheless, it is important that you devise, and practise, some 'recall' methods. One of the most effective ways, in our opinion, is brainstorming.

Brainstorming

It usually helps to organise your revision on the basis of establishing **key facts** in your head in such a way that you can recall them later under examination conditions.

> "Brainstorming can help give a broad view."

In view of the type of questions that are often set, it will be best if each of these key facts can be related to, and connected with, a whole variety of **contextual surroundings**. In other words, when you recall a key fact, you should also be able to **brainstorm** a collection of **contextual information** which surrounds it.

You can do this at the time of your actual written examination. As you read through the paper in order to make your selection of questions to answer, note down on your answer paper all that comes to mind for each question, *even if you do not eventually answer that particular question*. By noting down all you know in relation to each question as you read it, you might find it best to answer a question you would not normally have tackled. This may be because you find you know quite a lot more about it than you thought at first sight. Even if you *don't* answer that question, you might find that you can use some of the information you note down in answering another.

What does all this mean in practice? As we have already encountered PAUL CÉZANNE earlier in this book, let us consider him in illustrating this technique. If we take him as a **key fact**, together with what we know about him, his name will spark other key facts if you have been studying properly. One of these might be IMPRESSIONISM. Depending on our original study and revision, we might also include another key fact – namely, CUBISM. So you will already have two, or even three, key facts in response to a question which mentioned either Cézanne, or Impressionism or Cubism!

Let us show you how you might write these key facts down. Put them on a clean sheet of paper, side by side but a distance apart, roughly in the middle of the height of the paper, perhaps with the name Paul Cézanne in the centre (see Fig. 2.5)

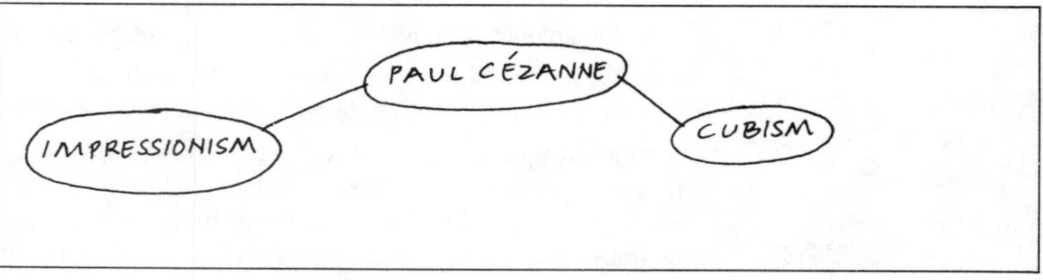

Fig. 2.5 The start of a brainstorming diagram.

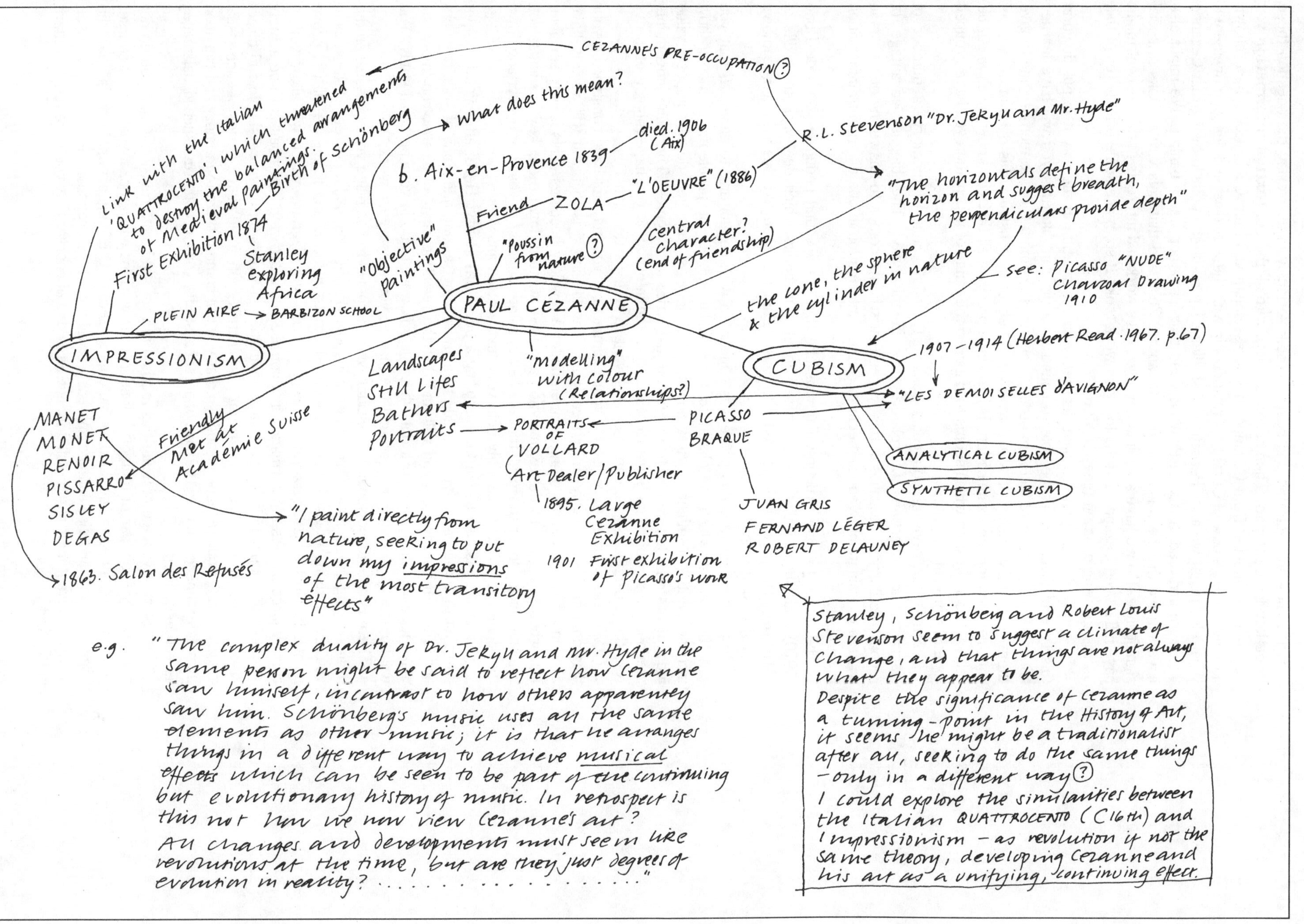

Fig. 2.6 The growing brainstorming diagram.

Let us now imagine that you begin to think seriously of answering the question these three key facts refer to. Then surround them with all the **contextual information** you can muster, moving from Cézanne to Impressionism and then Cubism. We have shown already that we know of Cézanne's relationship with these two art and design movements. What else might we add? Perhaps our studies have resulted in our knowing that Cezanne was born and died in Aix-en-Provence and that his father was a banker. We might also have learned that he was a friend of the author Zola, and that Zola wrote books of social significance. Do we have an opinion of how Zola's work and interests in this respect might have influenced Cézanne and the form his work took? If so, make some brief notes of this on the growing diagram (see Fig. 2.6)

It is unlikely that you will have learned your information in the way it is put down in this type of diagram. To be able to construct a diagram like this you will have learned about a large number of facts. In order to be able to commit them to memory and to give them some relationship, it would have been helpful to construct this diagram as part of your revision for the examination. It is really a précis of all that you know which *might* be relevant to a question which seems to call upon the range of information you have grouped together in your diagram.

During your revision you could construct, and commit to memory, a number of diagrammatic collections of related facts in this way. The biggest advantage of reconstructing your learning in this way is that when it comes to answering questions in written examinations, you can begin to connect information in one diagram to information in another.

The method of constructing diagrams like this has a sound pedigree. Both de Bono (1970) and Buzan (1974) have written about it in books which deal with the skills of **thinking**. The process associated with constructing a diagram like this has become known as **brainstorming**.

Properly conducted, this process is concerned with committing to paper *all* that you can think about which is related to a particular subject or problem, no matter how inconsequential it might at first appear. The idea is that you do not impose value judgements on what comes to mind; you just write as it comes. The value judgements creep in later, when you begin to select from the information you have thought of in this way those elements which are most relevant to your particular needs.

Of course, in order to revise for your examination, you may not have constructed your diagrams in this originally **uncritical** way. The likelihood is that you will already have condensed various items of information under a few key headings. This is only sensible. But when you get into the examination and have written down these key headings, you can still quickly 'brainstorm' all that the key headings suggest to you. Put everything down that comes to mind. It can only help your final written answers.

This system is also useful for compiling a **personal study**. Here, after you have put down all that you know, you can add to it by reading, asking questions of your teachers and so on. If you do this, you will find that the resulting 'map' of all that you know will make it easier for you to work out what it is you want to do in your personal study. You will be able to plot your way around the map as you shape your work.

There is one further point to consider when it comes to compiling your personal study, or answering questions in a written examination. Because the major content of the subject you are studying is visual that is to say, it exists in forms and images – it will prove helpful to work out illustrations, drawings, plans and diagrams which will allow you to convey large parcels of information in a concise and clear way. The point is to be acutely aware of the opportunity to turn large quantities of words into a more simple and direct visual image. In the case of a written examination, you could plan a series of such visual images during your revision period, so that you can commit them to memory and call upon them later if necessary. In the case of personal study, you can construct such visual images as you need them.

The great advantage of using this method in your study and revision is that you do not have to rely upon 'parrot memory' alone in your work or written examination. Of course, you will still need some kind of automatic recall. Our suggestion here is that the 'brainstorming' and visual image approaches will help the storehouse in your mind to open so that relevant information will flow out, provided of course, that you have put it in there in the first place!

Some final conclusions

This may seem to be a wide-ranging chapter, but this is really only because of the variety of examples we have called upon to illustrate our points. The important points in this chapter are, in fact, very few, and are concerned with outlining some useful approaches on how to study. Despite the variations in what it is you might be called upon to study in your syllabus, we have been stressing an approach to study which is consistent with, and therefore applicable to, all those variations. It does not matter if you are making a picture of an allotment or a scrapyard, or if you are painting pictures or making pots, or if you are doing practical work or answering written examinations. We are suggesting an approach to study which will stand you in good stead for whatever you are doing, and for any of the other aspects which exist in art and design but which are outside your current activity.

If you are in any doubt about what we mean by a 'sound working habit', we suggest that you go back over this chapter before proceeding any further with the book.

EXERCISES

At the end of some chapters in this book you will find a list of exercises for you to do. In each case they arise from the examples and suggestions already introduced in the text of the particular chapter. None of the exercises has a specific subject content, so they can all accompany any theme or subject which forms the basis of the project you may be doing. We offer the exercises because we believe they will help you to broaden and develop your work in a variety of dimensions and directions.

1 Select about four different media, such as water colour, pen and ink, pastel and collage. Choose four separate subjects, one for each of them, on the basis that the subject will match the qualities and possibilities of the medium each time. Make your four studies and display them side by side. Accompany them with a critical evaluation of the results, measuring the 'success' of your predictions about matching the qualities of the medium with the subject chosen.

2 Use four different media to do four studies of the *same subject*. Each time try to identify some aspect of the subject which will enable you to use the best qualities and possibilities of the particular medium you are using. Display your studies together and accompany them with a critical evaluation of the results, suggesting alternatives you would consider if you repeated the exercise. Perhaps undertake the alternative set of works and begin the critical evaluation all over again.

3 Identify four artists who, in your opinion, employ different methods in the use of paint. Using a similar paint medium as the original each time, copy at least a portion of the picture. Try to understand *why* the artists would have chosen to work in the way they did, and undertake an analysis of their work. Concentrating on *one* of the methods, choose a subject which you think fits the method and brings out the best qualities of both the method and the subject. Critically evaluate your results against the analysis you carried out at the end of the copying.

4 Make a set of photographs of a particular subject. In printing the negatives, experiment with the techniques of printing available to you. If you have access to a printmaking system which allows you to use your photographs to make up the plates or the screens, make a colour print of your subject from one of the photographs. Display the negatives, the photographic prints and your printmaking side by side. Compare and critically evaluate your results. If you have access to a computer which will allow you to produce images from your photographs, use this work in your final display.

5 Make a study of a subject which juxtaposes two contrasting elements. Try to make the images or forms you produce convey your feelings about the situation you are depicting. Do not use anything more than a visual means to carry out this exercise. You might ask your friends to write down their reactions to the work you produce in order to test if you have managed to convey to others your original feelings.

6 By means of written explanations, diagrams and pictures, show what you feel to be the differences between the contemporary work of PABLO PICASSO (1881–1973) and GEORGES BRAQUE (1882 – 1963) in their respective approaches to CUBISM. In this account do not be afraid of bringing into play your own feelings, rather than relying on other people's academic observations alone. It might help if you find out about their places of birth and personal circumstances, as contributory factors to the way that each of them worked.

CHAPTER 3

THE ESTABLISHED SYLLABUSES

AEB

JMB

NISEC

OXFORD

SOME OVERALL CONCLUSIONS

EXERCISES

GETTING STARTED

In this chapter we shall concentrate on what we call the **established** syllabuses. These tend to divide what you can do during your studies and for your examination into different art and design **practices**. In this established group of examinations you are often able to choose between practices. Different examination papers are set for the practice, or practices, you elect to do. This is explained later in the chapter.

Some syllabuses take a rather different approach, having recently been revised to take into account changes at GCSE level or in the Scottish Standard examination. We shall call these the **new** syllabuses and deal with them fully in Chapter 10.

To help you identify your particular syllabus, study Table 3.1. Whatever the nature of your syllabus, whether established or new, you will find much of relevance in Chapters 4 to 9, which deal with the various practices in art and design individually.

EXAMINING BOARD	SYLLABUSES ESTABLISHED	NEW
AEB	Art – Painting/603 Art and Crafts/605 Crafts – Printmaking/662 Crafts – Pottery/663	
CAMBRIDGE		Art and Design/9309
JMB	Craft (Design and Practice Advanced)	Art and Design
NISEC	Art – Syllabus A Art – Syllabus B	
OXFORD	Art with Art History/9894	
OX/CAM		Art and Design 1991/9642
SEB		Art and Design
ULSEB		Art and Design/020 Art and Fine art/021 Art and 3D Design/022 Art and Fashion/Textiles/023 Art and Graphic Design/024 Art and Photography/025 Art and Film and Video/026 Art and Critical and Historical Studies/027
WJEC		Art and Design

Table 3.1 List of established and new syllabuses.

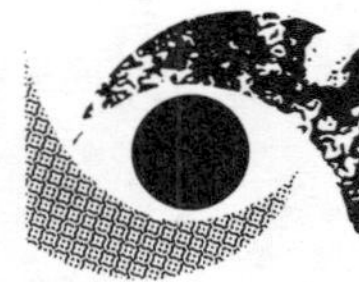

ESSENTIAL PRINCIPLES

To analyse each of the **established** syllabuses, we look at each examining board providing such a syllabus in turn. To save time, you can of course go directly to your own board and syllabus. If yours is a **new** syllabus, turn to Chapter 10 for details, before returning to the material in Chapters 4 to 9

In this chapter we consider the established syllabuses offered by the boards under four common headings:

- work requirements – i.e., the papers you must take, etc.;
- stipulations – i.e. regulations about size and presentation of work, etc.;
- values – i.e. the statements made about the nature and quality of the work you might do;
- mark schemes – i.e. what it is you get marks for in the examination.

AEB

The first thing to realise about the AEB is that it offers more than one established A-level examination syllabus. Do make sure that you have the correct one in mind at all times if you are sitting your examination with AEB.

ART – PAINTING/603	EXPLANATORY COMMENTS
Paper 1: Practical Test **Paper 2**: History and Technique **Paper 3**: Coursework	Candidates for Art – Painting are required to take both Paper 1 and 2 and are required to submit coursework. Details of objects required and poses are printed in the ART and CRAFTS M FORM
ART and CRAFTS/605	
Art and Crafts Paper 1 – Design and Practice of a Craft (for details of Craft options, see page 141 of the AEB syllabuses. **Art and Crafts Paper 2 – Option 20** – Drawing or Painting **Art and Crafts Paper 2 – Option 24** – Pictorial Composition **Art and Crafts Paper 2 – Option 25** – History and Appreciation of Art **Art and Crafts Paper 3 – Coursework**	Candidates are required to take Paper 1 and any two options from Paper 2 and are required to submit coursework Details and requirements are printed in ART AND CRAFTS M FORM
CRAFTS – PRINTMAKING/662	
Paper 1: Design and Practice **Paper 2**: History and Technique **Paper 3**: Coursework	Candidates are required to take both papers and to submit coursework. See ART and CRAFTS M FORM for further details
CRAFTS – POTTERY/663	
Paper 1: Design and Practice **Paper 2**: History and Technique **Paper 3**: Coursework	Candidates are required to take both papers and to submit coursework. See ART and CRAFTS M FORM for further details.

Table 3.2 'Summary of subjects' table, 1990 (reproduced by permission of the AEB).

The syllabuses available with the AEB for 1990 are listed in Table 3.2. The references to the Art and Crafts M Form in the table above do not need to concern you. The M Form is a document which gives your teachers details of the materials they should supply for your examination. It also outlines how the examination should be conducted and the work set off for marking when it is completed. Your teachers will ensure that the requirements listed in this form are met.

You can see from Table 3.2 which, and how many, separate papers you *must* take for any of the particular syllabuses the board offers. Those papers often have optional choices within them. Details of the various papers and the optional choices are shown in Tables 3.3 to 3.6.

WORK REQUIREMENTS

ART – PAINTING 603

Paper 1: Practical Test (Time allowed: 9 hours)

i) Pictorial Composition
ii) Painting from Still Life
iii) Painting from Life

(You may choose only one of these to do)

Paper 2: History and Technique (Time allowed: 3 hours)
(Coursework has to be submitted in addition to all this)

Table 3.3 Brief details of papers in Syllabus 603.

Pictorial composition, painting from still life and painting from life each represent a practice. When making your choice for Paper 1, you should obviously select a practice early enough in your course of studies for you to study it thoroughly, in time for your examination. Nevertheless, you may well follow a general course of study for a while before this is done.

ART AND CRAFTS 605

Paper 1: Design and Practice of a Craft (Time allowed: 15 hours)

Option 03: Embroidery
Option 04: Fabric Printing
Option 06: Lettering and Calligraphy
Option 08: Pottery
Option 10: Printmaking – Wood- and line-block cutting
Wood-engraving
Lithography
Etching
Screen printing
Option 12: Sculpture

You may choose only one of these to do, with the exception of Printmaking, where you may combine more than one method in a print)

Paper 2: Option 20 – Drawing or Painting (Time allowed: 3 hours)

Part (A) Still Life
Part (B) From Natural and Other Objects
a) potted plants, dried or freshly cut seed heads;
b) shells, stones, sea flotsam or urban junk;
c) bones, skeleton sections, animal or bird skulls.
Part (C) From Life
part i) two action poses (10 minutes each)
part ii) half- or full-length study (2 hours, 40 minutes)

You many choose only one of these options to work from)

Paper 2: Option 24 – Pictorial Composition (Time allowed: 6 hours)

Paper 2: Option 25 – History and Appreciation of Art (Time allowed: 3 hours)
You must take Paper 1, and then a combination of any two of the three Paper 2 options, as well as submitting coursework

Table 3.4 Brief details of papers in Syllabus 605.

(You may choose only one of these to do, with the exception of Printmaking, where you may combine more than one method in a print)

In paper 1 each of these options represents a practice, although for the purposes of this book we shall combine some of them into one chapter later on. In Paper 2 working from natural and other objects represents another practice as far as this book is concerned.

CRAFTS – PRINTMAKING 662

Paper 1: Design and Practice (Time allowed: Up to 15 hours)
Wood- and lino-block cutting
Wood-engraving
Lithography
Etching
Silk-screen printing

You may choose one method, or combine more than one in a print

Paper 2: History and Technique (Time allowed: 3 hours)
One general section
Five specialist sections

You must answer one question from the general section and two other questions from any of the specialist sections. Coursework has to be submitted in addition to all this.

Table 3.5 Brief details of papers in Syllabus 662.

CRAFTS–POTTERY 663

Paper 1: Design and Practice (Time allowed: Up to 15 hours)

Paper 2: History and Technique (Time allowed: 3 hours)

Historical section
Technical section

You must answer three questions in all, but at least one question must come from each section. Coursework has to be submitted in addition to all this

Table 3.6 Brief details of papers in Syllabus 663.

STIPULATIONS

A number of stipulations arise from the work requirements of Tables 3.3 to 3.6. First, there is a general level of control over the size of paper you can use in the syllabuses. It seems to be best to regard A3 as the smallest size to use. There is a very definite *upper* limit running through all the syllabuses, which is A1. You may choose to use any type and quality of paper you wish.

Your teachers will ensure that you do not exceed any weight or size limits for three-dimensional work or oil painting. You should get this information from them early on in your course. It would, for instance, be unhelpful if you got used to producing three-dimensional work during your course which later proved to be of a size which was not allowed in your *examination*. Nevertheless, there could still be advantages in working to various sizes and scales during your *coursework*.

It is stipulated that your coursework should be *substantially carried out in school*. The word substantially does not mean exclusively. The essential thing is that your teachers should be able to guarantee that the work you undertake in addition to that which you do in the classroom is your own unaided work. This means that field studies and homework remain an important part of your A-level work.

For your coursework studies, you may submit only two A1-size sheets to be assessed by examiners. These may include up to four photographs of any large-scale work you have done, but slides are not acceptable. If you do submit photographs, you must indicate the **scale** of the work in the photograph. This is usually done by including something well known in the photograph, such as a matchbox or a coin, to show the actual size of your work by comparison.

Being able to submit only two sheets of coursework means that you must carefully select what to include on the basis of worthwhile principles. Your teacher can help you in this, but we suggest that you try to show *how* you have worked at least as much as what it is you have *done*.

In all of the AEB syllabuses and examinations it is recommended that you should have a period of time between receiving your examination paper and starting the actual examination, in order to do some preparatory work. This means that you should choose the question carefully, bearing in mind that you will need access to appropriate information to enable you do such preparatory work.

The selection of syllabuses offered by the AEB means that you can choose to take more than one of them in the same year of examination. There are, however, certain stipulations about how you can mix them:

- if you take Syllabus 662 with Syllabus 605, you cannot take a 'Printmaking' craft in the latter;
- if you take Syllabus 663 with Syllabus 605, you cannot take 'Pottery' in the latter.

In your actual examination, while you may use tracing paper, you are forbidden to take tracings into the examination with you. This is, no doubt, in case you rehearse your final work and take a tracing of it into your examination. Nevertheless, you should not lose sight of the fact that tracing paper is a useful material for developing initial ideas in art and design. For instance, new ideas can be worked over the original on the tracing paper, allowing you to see through to the previous image each time.

VALUES

What we call the 'values' in a syllabus are highly important. Where they are contained within a syllabus they indicate to you how the examiners are thinking, and how they regard art and design.

In the traditional type of syllabus values are not laid out in any formal way, but occur dotted about throughout the syllabus. In the case of the AEB, we shall now deal with each syllabus in turn, picking the values out for you and giving our explanation of what they are likely to mean.

Syllabus 603 (Art – Painting)

In the AEB syllabuses there are a number of references which help indicate what the examiners probably have in mind. For instance, in this syllabus they explain that Paper 1, the Practical Test, is designed to test your **creative ability, skill and craftsmanship**.

This suggests that there is some difference in the minds of the examiners between skill and craftsmanship. We would suggest that you begin to untangle this difference. Skill might mean something like **the knowledge of art and design necessary to understand it, and the ability to practise it expertly**.

Craftsmanship might mean: **the ability to produce work in art and design expertly and in a traditional manner, where applicable.**

You can see from this that we regard the two terms as overlapping, rather than entirely distinctive. What is more important is that you evolve your *own* definition of these and other terms. Always remember, however, that a definition is never finished. As you become more knowledgeable and gain new experiences, you should be prepared to review your previous definitions.

It might even be argued that the term creative means much the same thing as skill, or at least something very similar. See if you can compose your own definition of creative. Write it down below in this book. Do not just copy out a dictionary definition, but try to explain it in your own words.

Creativity means
____
____
____

In Paper 2, History and Technique, the questions set are designed to test your **historical knowledge and technical knowledge.**

This, you might think, is straightforward enough. You learn about techniques both theoretically and by using them practically. In history, all you need to do is learn and remember some facts!

This explanation might be true of techniques, although even here it would help to be able to link certain techniques with particular artists, in order to explain and illustrate your knowledge of those techniques. For instance, you might first learn, through a practical exercise in painting, the difference between **glazing** and **scumbling**, before looking at how different artists have used these techniques.

In painting, glazing, as you might know, is the technique of applying a transparent film of paint over a previous coat of paint. This causes the effect of the first colour to be modified in a certain way, according to what the original colour was and what the colour of the glaze is. Thus an original surface coloured yellow is likely to glow in an orange hue if it is overpainted with a glaze of red. If you have done any pottery in the past you will already be aware of this. Even a clear pottery glaze will change the original colour of the clay used to make a pottery form.

Scumbling, on the other hand, is the technique of dragging a thick, opaque and almost dry colour over a first coat of paint, so that the new colour is applied in a series of broken and uneven brush lines. By this means, the original coloured surface is not completely covered and shows through the broken surface of the second coat.

Both techniques are most suited to oil paints – or gouache or poster paints if you add something like gum arabic to form the glaze – rather than water. Acrylic paints now offer similar opportunities.

However, if you knew all this, and maybe more, you would still be able to explain and illustrate your knowledge much more satisfactorily if you could refer to an artist, or artists, whose work exemplifies these techniques. Thus you might introduce an artist such as FRANS HALS (1581 *c* – 1666) or REMBRANDT (1606 – 69), or the Tachiste School of Artists, as typical exponents of these techniques.

Adopting this attitude in your learning and your answers is borne out as beneficial by the note in the syllabus which says that you should learn the **historical background as well as the traditions of painting**. It is also stated that you should **give your own personal reactions** in your answers. This means that just learning facts and figures parrot-fashion will not be enough.

What is also significant, and you should make sure you take full advantage of the suggestion, is that the examiners are willing to accept **drawings** as part of your written answers. As you can see from the example above, it would pay you to include drawings to demonstrate what you mean as far as glazing and scumbling are concerned.

Syllabus 605 (Art and Crafts)

In this syllabus, apart from the same reference to creative ability, skills and craftsmanship as in Syllabus 603, there is a reference to **the proper use of materials**. This is difficult to understand, and consequently to explain. After all, it might seem that the 'proper use of materials' is any which succeeds in communicating what it is you want to communicate, and is crafted sufficiently well for the materials to remain in the form you gave them in the first place.

What might be intended here is the notion that there are traditional ways of working materials, and you should know of, and obey, these ways or practices. If so, this is well within the generally accepted meaning of craft, in relation to art and design. The definition of a craft usually includes some reference to complying with the traditional designs, skills and uses of materials which are handed down, generation to generation.

In the case of the options available to you in Paper 2: Option 20 – Drawing or Painting, various values are implied in each case.

The Still-life option states that the objects you use should be of **varied shape and material**. This should alert you to infer that the individual shape of objects should be efficiently drawn in your work, and that you should be able to convey through drawing or painting the visual effect of different materials which the objects might be made of.

For the Natural and Other Objects option the examiners actually specify what it is they will be looking for in your work. They expect you to conduct **an analytical study of an object, or a group of objects, either in,**

a) direct sense or **b) leading towards a craft design** or
c) leading towards pictorial work.

In 'a direct sense' is likely to mean that you choose to work from direct observation, producing a work which exists in its own right as a solution to the problem before you. Choices b) and c) indicate that the work you do from the object, or the group of objects, would be a stage towards some other piece of work in art and design. A 'craft design' or 'pictorial work' reflects the other two sections of this particular examination, and it may be that a question in those other sections will allow you to pick up and use your ideas from this section. Even if this is not so, at least the process involved in this section of the examination should help your work in the other sections.

The Life option suggests a difference between two **short 'action' poses** and a much **longer pose**. This means that your drawing techniques should probably be developed in ways that allow you to work well within these two differing requirements. Your drawing techniques are likely to be varied as a consequence. We shall return to this point more fully in Chapter 4.

Paper 2: Option 24 – Pictorial Composition refers again to a test of your 'creative ability'. Here the question of what is meant by creative crops up again and you have to try and match your definition with what you think is intended by the use of the term in the AEB syllabuses.

- creative; the personal production of some original and inventive piece of work in art and design.

How does this compare with *your own* definition? You might even look up our definition in the Glossary (p.11), and compare all three definitions. When you have done so, before going any further, try to rewrite your own definition, using the space below.

creative means

____

____

____

The History and Appreciation of Art paper, 605/2/25, contains many implied values. These can be summarised along the following lines:

- you should study the presence of art and design in everyday life, as well as in the works of the great masters;
- you should visit galleries and museums not only to study their contents but also to study the buildings themselves, particularly in your own locality;
- you should develop not only a broad appreciation of art and design but also an appreciation of the interests present in your own practical work;
- you should use the information which reading gives you, but also introduce your own personal thoughts and reactions into your work.

This list puts into practice some of the observations we have already made on how to study in Chapters 1 and 2.

Syllabus 662 (Crafts – Printmaking)

In addition to the requirement that you should show your ability to **create skilfully, according to good standards of craftsmanship**, this syllabus also expects you to have **an understanding of the media used in your work**, and for you to **develop your ability to communicate**.

Your 'understanding of the media' concerned will be displayed largely in your practical work. Successful practical work reveals how much you understand the qualities of the material you are using, as well as your ability to design. Nevertheless, a comprehensive notebook with notes you have made about materials, their qualities and their possibilities might assist your final grade in this respect.

The question of 'communicating' is much more problematical. Some people believe that you communicate when you produce *anything* in art and design. Others think that you communicate via the better-executed pieces of art and design. But it could well be that your apparent 'artistic failures' reveal greater depths of communication than any other work you might have done. What we intend to convey is that where 'communicating' is considered to be an important value in the syllabus, then you should select work which most clearly 'communicates' your ideas and intentions for presentation, even if these items are not the best pieces of work in art and design that you have done. This means that you should *always* save all your work in any project you might do.

It would pay you to keep notebooks to explain and justify your work and the decisions you made in it, as well as to evaluate your results.

The syllabus includes a statement which says that the **examination seeks to be a creative test, in which the mere reproduction of a drawing or a photograph in print is not considered a sufficient answer at this level**.

This makes it clear that considerable value is attached to your ability to do more than produce just a technically sound and proficient print. You are expected to interpose some level of interpretation and development upon what it is you have seen and are using as the subject for your print. This is something we shall pick up again in a later chapter.

In the History and Technique Paper (662/2) again you are encouraged to use your personal and practical experience in your work and to offer personal reactions.

The value associated with studying prints and printmaking in a variety of contexts is stressed in this paper:

- social;
- historical;
- artistic;
- cultural;
- industrial;

This list should provide you with a suitable structure to work to in both your studies and the answers you give at the time of the examination.

Syllabus 663 (Crafts – Pottery)

One of the values in this paper emphasises that **practical work should be practised alongside theoretical study**. This is something we stressed in the previous chapter.

The expected nature of your practical work and its composition and structure is indicated in an aesthetic implication in the syllabus. Here it says that you should be concerned with **the interaction of**:

- mass and space;
- texture and pattern;
- balance;
- scale and proportion.

Each of these terms is part of the aesthetic vocabulary associated with art and design. Some of them are in the Glossary (page 11); where they are not, add them and write your own definitions as they stand at this stage.

We think the thing to bear in mind here is that you should consider not only the interaction within each set in the list above – for example, texture and pattern – but also the interaction among all four sets. This overall interaction is the thing which good art and design stems from.

That pottery products fulfil a variety of functions is implied in the syllabus, as is the fact that there are various ways of arriving at designs for your work. For instance, it is stated that in the questions set, opportunities will be included to make work which is:

functional	(pottery which performs a practical purpose, e.g., teapots, mugs, bowls, cruets, etc.)
organic	(ceramic forms which are often structured by growth-like repetition of related shapes)
imaginative	(work which comes from within yourself so far as its shape and intentions are concerned, even though these ideas are likely to be based, perhaps unconsciously, upon things seen or known to you already)
realistic	(work which sets out to reproduce things seen, or known, as visually accurate as possible)
expressive	(work which gives shape and meaning to things which you feel and ideas which you have)
abstract	(work which seems to have no clear basis of reality or representation within it; it stands as a form in its own right, being internally credible and justifiable)

The syllabus also differentiates between the notion of **designing as a result of problem solving** and **from source material**. In problem solving it is generally accepted that the criteria associated with an ideal, theory or identified need will be satisfied in the solution arrived at. When working from source material, it is usual that an interpretative process will result in a credible design which does not necessarily fulfil any other external controls and requirements (see the note above in the Natural and Other Objects option of Syllabus 605, Art and Crafts).

Finally, again there is an emphasis upon actually seeing, studying and analysing real examples of the work of others.

MARK SCHEMES

The AEB publishes mark-allocation tables in each of its syllabuses. There is a big difference between a mark scheme and a mark-allocation table. A **mark-allocation table** (such as Table 3.7) tells you how many of the total marks available for the examination are given to each section, or paper, within it. A **mark scheme** shows you how many marks you can get for making sure that, in your work, you attend to certain principles or criteria which are stated in the syllabus alongside the marks they command. Thus if you can see that there are ten marks available, for instance, for showing that you have the ability to create a harmony in your compositions or designs, then you know how to gain access to at least some of those marks. We say 'at least some', because even if you do achieve a harmony in your work, it is not likely to be recognised as totally successful. You must also bear in mind that the examiner will also have a scale of achievements in his or her mind, against which your work will be measured. Mark schemes which show the 'qualities' in your work which will be rewarded have considerable significance upon what it is you do and how you do it.

SYLLABUS 603 (ART–PAINTING)		
Paper 1: Practical Test		140 marks
Paper 2: History and Techniques		100 marks
Paper 3: Coursework		60 marks
	Total	300 marks
SYLLABUS 605 (ART AND CRAFTS)		
Paper 1: Design and Practice of a Craft		80 marks
Paper 2: Art Papers (80 marks for each option; see earlier note under 'Work Requirements')		160 marks
Paper 3: Coursework		60 marks
	Total	300 marks
SYLLABUS 662 (CRAFTS – PRINTMAKING) and SYLLABUS 663 (CRAFTS – POTTERY)		
Paper 1: Design and Practice		140 marks
Paper 2: History and Technique		100 marks
Paper 3: Coursework		60 marks
	Total	300 marks

Table 3.7 AEB mark-allocation tables (reproduced by permission of the AEB).

JMB

The syllabus discussed here is entitled Craft (Design and Practice) (Advanced).

WORK REQUIREMENTS

Three papers must be taken, as follows.

Coursework

In your coursework you must study in at least two of the following subject groups:

- Textiles/Fashion;
- Graphics;
- Three-dimensional Studies.

The content of these are explained in the next section. During your coursework you must also prepare and present for assessment a **Craft Study** on an approved topic.

Controlled test

A test involving up to fifteen hours of unaided work, following on from ten working days of preparatory studies relative to your chosen question.

Written paper

A three-hour test. The question paper is divided into two sections:

- general principles of craft;
- specialised knowledge of twentieth-century craft.

STIPULATIONS

First, work done for examination in this syllabus cannot be used for assessment in any other JMB A-level examination.

Coursework

The three areas of study for your coursework are divided further, as shown in Table 3.8.

SUBJECT GROUP A: TEXTILES/FASHION	
Study Areas	i) Printed Textiles: any method of application of colour to fabric.
	ii) Constructed Textiles: any form of fabric making technique.
	iii) Embroidery: any form of fabric embellishment, manipulation or assemblage.
	iv) Fashion: dress design, garment construction and illustration.
SUBJECT GROUP B: GRAPHICS	
Study Areas	i) Printmaking: any form of printmaking; relief; planographic; intaglio.
	ii) Packaging and Display: construction and decoration; typography; calligraphy.
	iii) Photography: any form of monochrome, colour, still, moving, animated.
SUBJECT GROUP C: THREE-DIMENSIONAL STUDIES	
Study Areas	i) Ceramics: any form of making any type of functional or decorative pottery.
	ii) Sculpture: any form of construction, modelling, carving, casting, utilising any materials or processes.
	iii) Theatre Studies: realisation of specific theatrical texts or dramatic performances within specific theatrical venues.
	iv) Jewellery: the use of any materials and construction techniques.

Table 3.8 JMB study areas (reproduced by permission of the JMB).

Although you have to produce work in only two of the specified study areas, your coursework can range through as many study areas as you like. You can choose areas of study which have an apparent relationship, such as Printmaking and Photography or Ceramics and Jewellery, or you can choose very diverse areas of study, such as Printed Textiles and Sculpture or Embroidery and Ceramics.

As a result of your coursework you are expected to find one study area emerging as more important than the others. This, it is expected, will in turn begin to dictate the complementary craft and historical studies you have to do during your course. It will also determine your choice of controlled test.

From your course of study you have to produce a craft workbook. This will be assessed as a compulsory and integral part of your coursework in the examination.

Craft study

This needs to be on an approved topic taken from **the broad context of twentieth-century craft**. The topic should involve first-hand experience and not be just theoretical. You might be able to interview a local craftsperson, or you could visit a local museum to select work to include in your study. You would then use books and other sources of information to reinforce your knowledge and to give authoritative support to your comments and views. It would seem beneficial to choose a topic which is closely related to your own practical work.

Controlled test

Prior to the start of your controlled test you will have ten days in which to prepare for the question you have chosen to answer. You may use the work you do during this time to assist you in your controlled test. These preparatory studies must be given in with your final examination work, whether you use them or not during your controlled test.

In your controlled test you will be given an initial session of two hours to work in, to get you started, and then you will have up to thirteen hours in the following three weeks to complete your work. The work you produce in your controlled test must be your own unaided work, and will be supervised at all times by your teachers.

If you need to do more exploratory work during your controlled test you can do this unsupervised during the three weeks given over for you to complete the controlled test. Such exploratory studies must be clearly presented with your final work.

Written paper

The **specialised knowledge** referred to in the written paper is divided into the same three subject groups specified for organising your coursework. Each subject group will have four questions relating to it. You must answer two questions, each from a separate **study area**. This means that your answers could be from one subject group only.

For the paper testing the general principles of craft the six questions set will cover the following areas:

a) pre-industrial craft methodology;
b) the industrialisation of the craft practices;
c) contemporary craft practices.

You have to answer two questions only.

VALUES

Many of the values attached to this examination are implied in the organisation of knowledge and activities represented by such things as the study areas. The separation, in particular, of craft and design activities into these various clusters demonstrates that a rather traditional and divisive view of a series of crafts is being upheld. This is so even when the twentieth-century influences are taken into account. For instance, there seems no justifiable reason to separate 'printmaking' from 'packaging and display', except that in this case it has been decided to do so. That it has been decided to do so is all right, as it is consistent with the content throughout this syllabus. You should, however, take full advantage of the invitation in the syllabus to work aspects of different study areas in together, if that is what you want to do.

This, we believe, is equally true in something like the **craft study**. Using the same example, you might choose to investigate how printmaking techniques helped give rise to packaging design. Although 'printmaking' is not included as a thread under 'packaging and display', it is obvious that packaging design could not have taken off on the scale that it did without the possibilities offered by being able to repeat the same design innumerable times.

So, all in all it appears to be acceptable that you should begin to integrate different activities during your studies, but you should also be very aware of the discrete nature of each activity and the crafts they are associated with. This is borne out in particular when you consider how the controlled test is organised and constructed, as well as the second section of the written paper.

The first section of the written paper has an implied value in its organisation. The notion of pre-industrial, industrial and contemporary craft practices suggests that the examiners have a view of the structure of the subject which it would pay you and your teachers to fathom.

We think, that pre-industrial craft activities are seen as involving a large amount of manual dexterity. But this is not exclusively true. For instance, both wheelwrighting and most pottery have some 'mechanical' aspects to them which do not rely upon manual dexterity. Yet the mechanical is something associated with industrial products in the minds of most people. If, on the other hand, it is thought that industrial methods provide mass-production of articles and craft activities do not, just consider how many baskets were, and are, made by hand each year! To find out more about the integrating of manual and mechanical methods in the production of craft items, we recommend that you read Sturt (1923). This book, while building up the atmosphere of men working skilfully with their hands, also makes you aware of the more mechanical processes involved in the making of a sound and satisfactory wheel.

As for the industrial aspect of craft work, again it would be erroneous to believe that everything is done by machines or furnaces blasting out sparks and heat in this method of production. JOSIAH WEDGWOOD (1730 – 95) was deeply involved with the Industrial Revolution in Great Britain, but the pottery craft products bearing his name still involve much work by hand on the part of individual craftspersons up to the present day. Even so, the Industrial Revolution can be regarded by you as a boundary between the period of the individual practising his or her craft – albeit that it was part of a common product much in demand – and the introduction of machines into the reproduction of many articles identical in size and shape for mass public consumption.

Contemporary craft practices are a little more problematical. Many people nowadays work alone in garden sheds producing things like wooden toys, but they often use electrical woodworking tools. At the same time many produce, exclusively by hand, articles such as artificial flowers.

We can see that the boundaries specified in this syllabus are probably designed to divide and make the history of the subject easier for you to study, but they might also confuse and inhibit you. You should try to investigate how others before you have satisfactorily completed their craft studies. It is likely that your teachers will have some still in their possession in school.

The craft notebook is intended to **inform and record your practical knowledge** and reveal the level of your **understanding of good practice**. These are two value-laden extracts from the syllabus. 'Inform' means that your knowledge should grow, so ensure that your notebook shows by just how much and in which ways this is so. In your notebook you should show the work you produce and how you produced it. This would include references to the materials you used and their technological properties. It would also include details of how your ideas evolved, by referring in part to the sources of your inspiration and the range of investigations you entered into each time, as well as why you took certain decisions. To explain your decisions you would need to specify the criteria you were working to. All this need not be formal. In fact, it is expected that it will not necessarily be so. According to the syllabus you should show your **reflective thinking and personal interests**. This means that you should find ways of making these aspects public and credible as the foundations in your work.

This element of personal commentary is reinforced by a note in the syllabus that you could include a diary or log of your working practice and that you might evaluate the success of your results against your original ideas and decisions. We advise most strongly that you get into the habit of doing this from the beginning of your course. In compiling your log do not forget the value of including drawings, diagrams, plans, templates, photographs and so on, as well as words.

The 'Aims' of the syllabus are included in this case (see Table 3.9). Aims give you a clear indication of the values the examiners hold about the subject at A-level, as far as the JMB is concerned.

The aims of the syllabus are to allow each candidate to follow a broad and integrated course and

a) to have first-hand experience of working in the field of crafts,
b) to develop a knowledge of the relevant processes, tools and materials,
c) to develop an understanding of crafts in relation to historical and social contexts,
d) to develop the ability to use processes, tools and materials creatively.
e) to express ideas and feelings through the sympathetic response to materials and processes,
f) to develop a critical awareness of craftwork.

Table 3.9 The aims of the JMB Craft (Design and Practice) (Advanced) syllabus (reproduced by permission of the JMB).

Many of the aims tend to concentrate upon acquiring manual and technical skills regarding processes, tools and materials. Yet the intention of the examiners is not as bad as it might at first appear. The syllabus states that its aims are to **encourage candidates to engage creatively . . . to use materials and processes with imagination and sensitivity through the exploration of the problems of design and production, . . . to develop a depth of understanding of the creative activity of craftwork**.

In this statement the value-laden terms are:

- engage creatively;
- imagination;
- sensitivity;
- exploration;
- depth of understanding;
- creative activity.

If you make craft objects only on a technically proficient basis, no matter what their quality, you will not be fulfilling the aims of this syllabus. You will be penalised in your examination result for failing to do so.

There are also other important factors in the published aims which require a broadening of your learning. We have stressed the reference to 'historical and social contexts' already and will continue to do so for the remainder of the book. In the same way, we believe most strongly in the value to be obtained from conducting your work within a critical framework and our views are upheld in this syllabus.

MARK SCHEMES

This syllabus publishes a mark-allocation table (Table 3.10), a set of aims and objectives (Table 3.11) and a table showing the weighting of marks against objectives (Table 3.12). In this respect you have a fairly comprehensive set of guidelines upon which to structure and produce your work throughout the course and in your examination.

Coursework (including Workbook):	45	per cent of the total marks
Craft Study:	15	per cent of the total marks
	(60)	
Controlled Test:	20	per cent of the total marks
Written Paper:	20	per cent of the total marks
	(40)	

Table 3.10 JMB Craft (Design and Practice) (Advanced) mark allocations.

We have divided Table 3.10 as shown and put in the two totals in brackets. These show you that 60 per cent of the total marks for the examinations are given to work which is not part of a formal, end of course examination. This signifies how important it is that you tackle your coursework with enthusiasm, setting yourself high standards from the very beginning. In the type of examination this syllabus represents there is no room for slacking along the way in the expectation that you will redeem everything in the final examination. This is reinforced by the fact that you cannot obtain even an E Grade for your work **unless you satisfy the examiners in all four parts of the examination.**

Table 3.11 shows how the objectives published in the syllabus provide identification of what it is necessary for you to do in order to satisfy the aims of the examination.

1 The examination will be designed to text the candidate's:

a) knowledge of relevant processes, materials and tools;
b) knowledge of the development of craft processes in the areas and periods specified;
c) knowledge of the social and economic influences on the practice of crafts;
d) knowledge of the practice of crafts against the background of appropriate industrial or professional methods;
e) ability to conceive, develop and execute a design or designs;
f) ability to select, and use appropriate materials and techniques;
g) ability to appraise work and processes;
h) ability to show evidence of a personal response;
i) ability to organise and present material in a clear form by means of the written word, diagrams, drawings, etc.

Table 3.11 Objectives of the JMB Craft (Design and Practice) (Advanced) syllabus (reproduced by permission of the JMB).

Good, thorough work, attending to all the ramifications of the values implicit in the syllabus, will mean that for the most part you will demonstrate that you have looked to the majority of these objectives. This means that you do not have to 'spell them out' Nevertheless, it would benefit you to make sure that your notebook did draw particular attention to things under the classifications offered by the list of objectives. By doing this you will draw your teachers' and examiners' attention to them during their evaluation and assessment of your work. This notebook, used correctly, could be the passport to a higher grade. It is up to you. No one can give you a recipe for compiling it. It must come out of the way that you work personally.

Table 3.12 shows how marks are distributed among these objectives. A few examples should enable you to use this table, but first let us explain that the asterisks identify where evidence is expected of you. The table tells you, for instance that the most important single objective in the examination concerns the level of your **ability to conceive, develop and execute a design or designs**. It is expected in turn that your ability to do this will be evident in your coursework and the controlled test, and not in the other sections of the examination. This means that the level of your ability in this practical work is highly important, which is not surprising.

2 Weighting and location of the objectives
The weighting of the objectives in the examination will be approximately as follows:

OBJECTIVES	TOTAL WEIGHTING	COURSEWORK	CRAFT STUDY	WRITTEN PAPER	CONTROLLED TEST
a	10	✓	✓	✓	✓
b	10	✓	✓	✓	
c	10	✓	✓	✓	
d	10	✓	✓	✓	
e	25	✓			✓
f	15	✓			✓
g	5	✓	✓	✓	
h	10	✓	✓		✓
i	5	✓	✓	✓	
Total	100 %	45 %	15 %	20 %	20 %

Table 3.12 The weighting and placing of objectives in the JMB Craft (Design and Practice) (Advanced) examination (reproduced by permission of the JMB).

What might be surprising is that your **ability to organise and present material in a clear form by means of the written word, diagrams, drawings, etc.** is not expected to be present in your controlled test. This is confirmed by a further note in the syllabus which says that, although you must present all your preparatory studies and any further exploratory studies you might do, along with your controlled test, these sets of studies will not be allocated any marks. Whether this is fair is another matter. After all, those studies might be the best demonstration of your ability to organise your material through diagrams, drawings, etc., and there is also no reason why you should not also include the written word in such studies.

A final word before we leave this syllabus. While 10 per cent of the marks are given for 'this' and another 10 per cent are given for 'that', you will not necessarily receive all those marks for presenting evidence of 'this' and 'that' in the appropriate areas of your work. The level of ability you show each time will determine what proportion of the total marks available you receive. By repeatedly paying attention in your work to the qualities represented by these objectives, you will begin to build up a pattern which shows the developing level of your ability in the particular objective, and this can only stand you in good stead in your examination.

NISEC

Two A-level examination syllabuses are offered by NISEC. They are Art Advanced-Level, Syllabus A, and Art Advanced-Level, Syllabus B (Art and Design).

Very broadly, they differ in that Syllabus A asks you to choose three out of the five papers available, and coursework does not form a part of your examined work except in Paper IV, while in Syllabus B you have to do each of the four papers contained in the syllabus, and one of these is coursework.

Let us explore the real differences more fully.

WORK REQUIREMENTS

Syllabus A

Five papers are set (Table 3.13). Your choice of three must be made *at the time of entry for your examination*.

PAPER I DRAWING OR PAINTING FROM LIFE (24 hours)
1) a 15 minute drawing of a standing figure
2) a 2 hour drawing of a figure sitting or reclining

PAPER II DRAWING OR PAINTING FROM NATURAL OR FASHIONED FORMS (3 hours)
either,
working from a plant or any other natural form
or,
from a group of common objects

PAPER III PICTORIAL COMPOSITION (3 hours)
a picture in answer to a question based upon history, literature or contemporary life
(question papers will be issued 14 days in advance of the examination)

PAPER IV DESIGN FOR A CRAFT (3 hours)
a 'design' only in answer to questions set for a very wide range of crafts
(question papers will be issued 14 days in advance of the examination)

PAPER V HISTORY OF ART (3 hours)
The paper is in two parts,
History of Architecture and Sculpture
History of painting
Questions may be answered from either part, or from both.

Table 3.13 NISEC Syllabus A examination papers (reproduced by permission of the NISEC).

Syllabus B

There are four compulsory sections in this syllabus (Table 3.14). You *must* satisfy the examiners in Section 1 and Section 4 and either Section 2 or Section 3. The questions for all the papers in Section 1 will be issued at least five school weeks prior to the beginning of the assessment period.

SECTION 1 – MAIN STUDY (15 hours)
You may choose just one of the following and then produce either an interpretation of a theme, or a proposal for a solution to a problem.

1 PAINTING
2 VISUAL COMMUNICATIONS
  a) Graphic processes
  b) Printing processes
  c) Photographic processes
3 THREE-DIMENSIONAL STUDIES
  a) Ceramics
  b) Jewellery
  c) Silversmithing and beaten metalwork
  d) Constructions
  e) Sculptures
  f) Plastics
  g) Furniture
  h) Interior Design
  i) Stage decor and costume
4 TEXTILES AND FASHION
  a) Dyeing and printing (Batik, tie-dye, block and screen printing)
  b) Weaving
  c) Dress design
  d) Creative Embroidery (Hand and/or machine)

SECTION 2 – ANALYTICAL AND WRITTEN STUDY (3 hours)
You may choose to work from just one of the following, using visual and written means.
a) Natural Forms
b) Manufactured Forms
c) Human Forms/Activities

SECTION 3 – HISTORY AND APPRECIATION OF ART, ARCHITECTURE AND DESIGN
(Time allowed: 3 hours for written paper, plus the presentation of an extended essay).

Written Paper
Part 1 History of painting and History of Architecture and Sculpture
Part 2 Appreciation of Design for Living
(You must answer two questions from Part 1 and one question from Part 2 in your answers to this paper.)

Extended Essay
You must submit an extended essay of between 2,000 and 3,000 words based on an aspect of study done during your course of study.

SECTION 4 – ASSESSMENT OF COURSEWORK
You are expected to set up a display of your coursework at the end of your course.

Table 3.14 NISEC Syllabus B examination papers (reproduced by permission of the NISEC).

STIPULATIONS

Syllabus A

The general stipulations for this syllabus state that you should not exceed A2-size paper in your work. You may use any medium you choose, but should bear in mind that your work will have to withstand travelling and handling. All the measurements specified in the questions set will be given in metric units only.

In Paper IV: Design for a Craft, apart from the list of crafts given in the syllabus and repeated below, you may apply, through your teachers, for the inclusion in the examination of another craft if it is not contained in the list. Questions in the examination each year will be set relating to:

- lettering and calligraphy;
- pottery;
- wood-engraving;
- fabric printing;
- embroidery;
- graphic design (posters, book jackets, record sleeves, and package designs);
- metalwork;
- stage decor and costume.

In Paper IV you produce a design only in answer to the question you choose. You do not execute the design as a finished article. You must include, however, a description of the processes you would use to carry out the design as a finished article. To show how well you can produce an article relevant to your chosen craft you have to submit a finished example of your work in that craft by 1 May in the year of your examination. This example of work would come, of course, from your coursework.

In Paper V: History of Art eight questions will be set in each part. You must answer five in all but, as is shown above, you can restrict your selection of questions to just one part of the paper or choose a combination from both. Where it is appropriate you are expected to include drawings in your answers.

The actual content you should study for the two parts of Paper V is specified in the syllabus and is shown in Table 3.15.

Table 3.15 Details of Paper V, NISEC Syllabus A (reproduced by permission of the NISEC).

HISTORY OF ARCHITECTURE AND SCULPTURE
Candidates will be expected to have a detailed knowledge of Greek and Roman Architecture and Sculpture, and Italian Renaissance 1400–1600.
HISTORY OF PAINTING
Candidates will be expected to have a detailed knowledge of Italian Renaissance Painting, and European Painting between 1850–1400.

Syllabus B

For some of the sections of this syllabus there are no stipulations other than those specified in Work Requirements above.

However, in Section 1, Part 4, Textiles and Fashion it is stipulated that during the five school weeks allowed for your response to a question from this paper, you should use the first two weeks to carry out your preparatory studies. In this time you should collect together information relevant to the question and your emerging answer. The investigation can include written as well as visual work. This preparatory work must be available at the time of assessment. You begin and complete your final piece of work during the last three weeks of this examination period. For this final piece of work you may use up to fifteen hours. Your work during this time must be supervised by your teachers, so it must be carried out in your school or college at all times. When you are doing this final work you must keep a log, showing all the periods of time you use and add them together to complete your work. In our opinion this log would also include, if possible, a description of what you did each time, as well as, perhaps, your feelings about the way things are going and what you might do next time. For this to be possible, you might need to design your own log rather than use one published by the examination board.

It is pointed out that Section 2 is not a design paper. The work carried out in answer to this section should be **strictly concerned with visual exploration and accurate, in-depth description**. This is obviously a paper expecting work from direct observation, in which you analyse what it is you are studying, paying attention to structure, texture, form, colour and appearance.

In Section 3, the written paper, twelve questions are set in Part 1 and six in Part 2. You choose from them as specified above. The actual content of the two parts of this section is shown in Table 3.16.

In both parts of this section you are expected to accompany your written answers with drawings where appropriate.

Section 4, Assessment of Coursework, stipulates that in your display of coursework you must include some evidence of the supporting preparatory studies material you used and also a **visual inquiry notebook** which you used and compiled during your course of study. In this section of the examination quality, rather than quantity, will be assessed.

PART 1	History of Painting and History of Architecture and Sculpture History of Painting Candidates will be expected to have a good knowledge of Italian Renaissance Painting *or* 20th-century International Painting *or* French and British Painting of the 19th Century. History of Architecture and Sculpture Candidates will be expected to have a good knowledge of Greek and Roman *or* 20th-century International *or* 19th century European (including Art Nouveau) Architecture and Sculpture.
PART 2	Appreciation of Design for Living In this paper you will be expected to know of the standards of design and production relevant to everyday objects and to be able to construct your answers as a critical appraisal based upon this criteria.

Table 3.16 Details of Section 3, NISEC Syllabus B.

VALUES

A number of values arise from the syllabuses, many of which have now been discussed.

Syllabus A

First of all, in Paper 1, Drawing or Painting from Life, the very title indicates that the examiners see 'painting' as something different from 'drawing'. We would suggest that while you could distinguish between the two on the basis of the media you might use, it would be better if you tried to define 'pure painting'. If you did, and then tried to work according to the criteria you came up with, then you would emphasise the difference between painting and drawing much more strongly. Pure painting is a matter of doing work which is 'painterly'. This is a term much used in art and design. It is usually intended to mean that images and their forms are shown by means which do not depend upon their outline. Instead they are shown by such means as patches of coloured light and shade. In work of this kind the edges of shapes and forms seem to merge softly into each other. All this is in direct contrast to showing form and shape by linear means, in which outlines are rather sharply delineated. Thus you could use paint and colour in a work which would, nevertheless, be regarded as a drawing rather than a painting. If you study the work of artists you will no doubt begin to see clearly what we mean by this argument. Murray (1987) gives TITIAN(*c*1487 – 1576) and REMBRANDT as examples of artists who adopt a 'painterly' technique, and BOTTICELLI (*c*1445 – 1510) and MICHELANGELO (1475 – 1564) as examples of artists who, despite their use of paint and colour, work in a linear – or drawing – way. The added advantage you can gain by studying these particular artists is that they nearly all fall within the period specified for Paper V, History of Art, in the examination.

Apart from this, as far as your working from life is concerned, the differences between a standing or a sitting or reclining pose, suggested in the syllabus, are really more about the needs of the model in your examination. It is obviously easier and more comfortable to sit for a long period of time than to stand. You should concentrate upon the time you have for each of the two poses you have to draw. As in other examinations from other examining boards, this aspect is concerned with your ability to use the time available to the best advantage. This will probably necessitate a different approach to each pose, but we shall deal more fully with this in a later chapter.

In Paper IV, Design for a Craft, the work you should do is specified in such a way as to make clear that you should distinguish between the appearance and function of your design and the processes necessary to produce it as a finished article. Of course, in designing it is usual for anyone to call upon their knowledge of materials and processes as well as attending to the needs inherent in the problem at stake, but this is usually all combined into one single activity. Here, perhaps because the paper is about 'crafts', you must show your intentions clearly by referring to the processes you had in mind in arriving at your design.

Syllabus B

The way this syllabus is laid out means that 'making and doing' are regarded as the major concern of the examination. You have to reach a pass standard in the Main Study and your Coursework (Sections 1 and 4). In both of these the majority of your activities will be of a practical nature.

This does not mean that you can afford to disregard the historical element in art and design, or critical evaluation and responses in your work. First of all you have to pass either Section 2 or Section 3. Both these involve critical analysis on your part. In addition, however, as we have been at pains to point out, studying the history of the subject in a critical manner can only benefit your own practical and creative work. What is more, if you choose your historical period and references carefully, you will mostly be 'killing two birds with one stone' in your studies. By this we mean you can choose the history of art and design covering what you like doing in you own practical work and, provided it is drawn from the historical period listed in the examination, what you study in this way will be appropriate for your historical, analytical and critical studies.

It will pay you to realise and remember that the syllabus calls for a really well-balanced course in art and design and you must respond to this, no matter what your preferences might be.

In Section 1, the Main Study, the terms 'to interpret' and 'to propose a solution' are used. This is in accordance with the generally accepted boundaries and standards which help to define 'art' in relationship to 'design'. Interpretation suggests that what you do is more personal and expressive. As a result you can make firm decisions of your own and the success of your work stands to a large extent upon how it measures up to the criteria you introduced and used in its conception and production. Of course, part of these criteria will include the historical traditions of 'art', which is why, despite the apparent emphasis on the practical work you do, it is so important that your studies should pay sufficient attention to the history of the subject you are studying.

On the other hand, you 'propose solutions' to design problems, because many of the criteria you use are bound up in the problem itself and must be answered in wider terms than the personal alone. It is your task to be aware of this criterion and to define it in terms of the way your solution is developing, but whatever happens, the success of your work is not on such a personal level as in 'art'. It is judged on much more public levels and in this sense your solution can never be more than a proposal for others to judge its effectiveness.

When, as in Section 1, Part 4, Textiles and Fashion, you get your question paper in advance of the time you begin your final test or examination, there are always certain values present in the notion of preparatory studies. The statement in the syllabus that they may be both visual and written indicates the thinking of the examiners. It suggests that you could study the works of other designers, as well as books on those designers, but also that you might conduct some research methods in defining the criteria you are going to work to. Again, we shall pick this point up more fully in a later chapter.

In Section 2, the Analytical and Written Study, you are asked to carry out a **carefully observed analysis and appreciation of the nature, character and qualities of the selected item in terms of structure, texture, form and colour in a descriptive visual and written manner.**

This statement is heavily laden with value qualities. To unravel it you need to begin to define some of the terms. This time, we shall attempt the first definitions, and then leave you space to write your own definitions in when you feel you understand enough to do so.

Observed analysis and appreciation. This means the translation of what you can actually see and understand into a series of marks which together make up an appropriate visual image to explain your understanding, and a series of words and terms which interpret what is seen into a publicly understandable language system.

Your definition

____

____

____

Nature, character and qualities. This means the content and aspects of an item which distinguish it from other items and which go to make up, explain and classify its being in terms which can be seen and understood, or heard or read and understood.

Your definition

____

____

____

Remember, at any time it is important to construct your definitions according to any specific clues which you get from a particular situation. As in most things, there are few absolute truths. In this case the task is to define something within the parameters which seem to apply in the particular examination and circumstances. This is why, as you work towards the examination, you should be increasingly in a position to revise your definitions in such a way that they reflect your growing understanding of what is required of you. What you might bear in mind as you try to do this is that this section of the NISEC examination demands that your work should be a **visual exploration and accurate, in-depth description**. We have tried to reflect this requirement in our definitions above.

The other terms in the quotation above – structure, texture, form and colour – have been dealt with elsewhere. Again, your understanding of the fuller significance of what these terms mean in art and design should be growing as your experience and knowledge grows. You might try to define even these traditional terms from time to time.

Most of Section 3, the History and Appreciation of Art, Architecture and Design, has been reproduced earlier in this chapter. The value-laden terms are those like **good knowledge**. This could mean that the quantity of knowledge you have should be large or that the quality of your understanding of it should be deep. It is probably best to regard the term 'good' as meaning both. It follows that you might not learn as much as you would if you set out to pick up knowledge 'by the pound', but what you do know will be clearly understood and reusable by you at a later date. If so, this will serve you much better than knowing the size of everything but the value of nothing.

The term **critical appraisal** is used in the Design for Living section of the examination. You should be familiar enough with its implications by now to attempt your own definition of it. It is accompanied with a reference to **the standards of design and production in relation to everyday objects**. These qualities have to be first learned and then applied as a criticism of everyday objects. The relevant information is beyond the scope of this book but can be quite readily picked up by you. You will find it in studies giving information on such things as ergonomics and British Standards, but it also comes from reading the leaflets which accompany everyday products, explaining their use and installation, as well as just keeping your eyes and ears open. Your mother and father will be able to tell you what they think of the products which exist in your home. What they, and others, have to say will contribute towards your understanding of what makes a good, successful design and what makes a design difficult to use and maintain – in fact, substandard. We suggest you get into the habit of including any material of this kind in a notebook you compile and keep over your course, but remember, any design must be judged according to its level of acceptability as well as its apparent effectiveness and the degree to which it measures up to production standards. Part of this 'acceptability' should include whether the product was necessary in the first place, and whether it is ethically and morally justifiable.

The Extended Essay does not have any value-laden statements to accompany it. It should be based upon your work in either Section 3 or one of the areas for study in Section 1. We believe it would be beneficial if, as the basis for this essay, you used:

- description;
- evaluation;
- criticism;
- future implications.

These terms, and the type of work which accompanies them, will allow you to use the values which are present in the other sections of your examination, as well as to display your ability at them in alternative dimensions. We intend the terms to mean that you will describe what it is you do and how you do it. Describing how you do it will necessarily involve aspects of evaluation, in which you begin to sort out why you do one thing in preference to another. Deciding this is a form of criticism, but you could add to it by criticising your working procedure and your results, building up a view of things for and against your decisions. This, in turn, will cause you to consider how you might have done some things differently and to better advantage, as well as how you might use your successes in different circumstances in the future.

In Section 4, Coursework, apart from specifying that you set up a display of your work, including the support work you do as part of your exploration and experimentation, the notes to this section of the examination include a sudden reference to a **visual inquiry notebook**.

We have dealt already with the types of work this should include. It sounds as if it should be a sketchbook, in which you draw, paint, make collages and so on – your responses to visual phenomena and your ideas – but also a scrapbook in which you collect and include things you find written and printed about the field of art and design studies.

You should be prepared to extend this field to include anything contextual which takes your eye or fires your imagination. There seems to be no reason why you should not include your own written responses and notes about things. In fact, in the light of Section 2 of the examination, it would pay you to practise this skill. The essential thing is that this notebook should be about your visual and mental awareness of all things to do with the study of art and design, and not be restricted to the projects or themes you actually work on during your course. This advice reflects the view we hold that studying successfully in art and design is more a matter of the *way* in which you work than the *subject* of your work and the technical skills you show in carrying it out alone.

MARK SCHEMES

The *NISEC* syllabus does not carry any mark schemes. There are no references to marks in Syllabus A. In Syllabus B the references state that:

- all sections of the examination carry equal marks;
- in Section 3 the written paper carries 75% of the marks for the section, whilst the extended essay carries 25% of the marks for the section.

OXFORD

The one syllabus and examination this board has is dealt with here, but it will soon be undergoing a major revision, for 1991 or 1992. The examination is entitled Art with Art History.

WORK REQUIREMENTS

The examination has six papers, as shown in Table 3.17. Of these, you must take three papers. One of these must be Paper 1. The others can only be taken in the following combinations:

- Paper 2 with Paper 3;
- Paper 2 with Paper 5;
- Paper 3 with Paper 5;
- Paper 3 with Paper 4.

Table 3.17 Alternative papers for the Oxford Art with Art History Examination (reproduced by permission of OXFORD).

9894/1	Written paper on History of Art (3 hours, maximum mark 50)
9894/2	Written from observation (96 hours, maximum mark 100)
9894/3	Imaginative work in two-dimensional media (extended period, maximum mark 100)
9894/4	A second exercise on the syllabus for Paper 3
9894/5	Imaginative work in three-dimensional media (extended period, maximum mark 100)
9894/6	A relief paper which may be offered instead of Paper 2

If you take the last combination, Paper 3 with Paper 4, you must work in two totally different media in responding to the problems set in each paper. The decision to take the relief paper, Paper 6, rests with your teachers, who may choose to use it because of timetabling or space problems. When it is used, it can replace only Paper 2 in the above combinations.

STIPULATIONS

Paper 1 History of Art

The paper is divided into three sections (as can be seen from Table 3.18) and you must choose to answer four questions. You can choose your questions from one, two or all three sections.

PAPER 1 HISTORY OF ART (A booklist is available on request from OXFORD)

The paper is divided into three sections; candidates must answer four questions which may be chosen from one, two or all three sections.

Section I. History of Architecture

i) Questions on the development of, and important influences on, English medieval architecture from 1066 to the middle of the sixteenth century, of which one gives opportunity for candidates to show local knowledge.

ii) Questions on the development of, and important influences on, architecture in England from the middle of the sixteenth century to the present day, of which one gives opportunity for candidates to show local knowledge.

Section II. History of Painting

i) A question calling for comment on a work of a great master of which a reproduction is supplied.
ii) Questions on Italian Painting of the fifteenth and sixteenth centuries, including the School of Venice.
iii) Questions on European Painting of the seventeenth century
iv) Questions on English Painting from 1700 to 1850
v) Questions on the general development of European Painting of the eighteenth and nineteenth centuries.
vi) Questions on painting of the twentieth century.

Candidates may limit their answers to *one* of the subsections (ii) – (vi).

Section III. Visual History

Candidates are required to study in relation to the British Isles, one short period, in its widest visual context (architecture, interiors, furnishings, costume, painting, sculpture and artefacts). Some general knowledge is expected of the periods immediately preceding and following the chosen period.

The periods are:
i) 1650–1700
ii) 1730–1780
iii) 1850–1900

PAPERS 2 AND 6 WORK FROM OBSERVATION

Instructions are sent to teachers giving a pose for a model and a range of objects, plants, natural forms, etc. Complete freedom in approach and in choice of medium is allowed to the candidates and, where possible, in the choice of objects, etc. If paint is used it must be of a quick-drying nature.

PAPERS 3 AND 4 IMAGINATIVE WORK IN TWO-DIMENSIONAL MEDIA

Topics are set which candidates may interpret in any two-dimensional media they wish. They may offer two pieces of work as Papers 3 and 4, provided that the works are in two totally different media, not in two different versions of the same medium or of similar media. Candidates are allowed three weeks in which to produce their work.

PAPER 5 IMAGINATIVE WORK IN THREE-DIMENSIONAL MEDIA

Topics are set for interpretation in three-dimensional media. Candidates are allowed three weeks to execute their piece of work.

Table 3.18 The content of papers for the OXFORD Art with History of Art examination (reproduced by permission of OXFORD).

Section I deals with Architecture in England *either* from 1066 to 1550 *or* from 1550 to the present day. In each case, one question allows you to include a building you know from your own locality.

Section II deals with Painting. You *must* answer a question on the work of a great master. A reproduction of the work concerned is provided in the examination. Otherwise you have to answer questions from the following subsections, although you could limit your answers to just one subsection.

- Italian Painting of the fifteenth and sixteenth centuries, including the School of Venice;
- European Painting of the seventeenth century;
- English Painting from 1700 to 1850;
- The general development of European Painting of the eighteenth and nineteenth centuries;
- Painting in the twentieth century.

Section III deals with 'Visual History'. This covers architecture, interiors, furnishings, costume, painting, sculpture and artefacts. You are expected to relate your study and answers to the British Isles. The questions are divided into three periods of time and you are expected to study in one of them. These periods are:

- 1650 – 1700; ■ 1730 – 80; ■ 1850 – 1900.

The syllabus states that you should possess some **general knowledge** of the years surrounding the periods you choose to study. This is what we call **contextual knowledge** and, in our opinion also, it should form part of your study of the actual years of your chosen periods.

Papers 2 and 6 Work from Observation

Here you are allowed *complete* freedom in approach and in your choice of medium, as well as in your choice of subject matter where possible. This means that it is essential for your coursework to prepare you for the level of independent choice this encourages.

Papers 3 and 4 Imaginative Work in Two-dimensional Media

Again, you have freedom of choice over your media, although you have to work to set topics. If you choose to do both these papers you *must* work in two totally different media. This means that you might be ill-advised to work in, say, water colour in one paper and acrylics in the other. Your teachers will know from experience how different the media you use should be.

Paper 5 Imaginative Work in Three-dimensional Media

In this paper you are allowed to choose and mix the media you use as you like. The ability to do this will come from the experiences you have gained during your course of study. The examining board will set the topics, or themes, you have to work to.

VALUES

Paper 1 History of Art

The term **local knowledge** in the History of Architecture section is important. It reveals that your learning not only need not but should not be restricted to theoretical and secondary sources of information. Instead, it should involve your going out, seeing for yourself and making your own appraisals and critical reactions.

This notion is borne out in Section II, History of Painting, where it includes the term **calling for comment**. Comment infers that you should introduce your own reactions in your work and not merely repeat what you have learned from others.

In Section III, Visual History, you are called upon to include a wide **visual context** in your study and to gather together some **general knowledge** in support of your work. This further reinforces the notion that the examination is concerned with more than second-hand, academic learning. Make sure that you take full opportunity of all this. It will help to distinguish your work from that of other candidates by making it personal to the study approaches and content you have adopted, arising from your own interests and your local opportunities.

Papers 2 and 6 Work from Observation

The fact you are allowed your own choice of medium and *complete* freedom of approach in responding to this paper means that you should carefully consider and plan for this choice during your coursework studies. Your coursework should not only enable you to practise the use of the media which most attracts you but also equip you with the knowledge to decide which media most suits a particular problem you are tackling. In this way you will be able to see both the media to use in your choice in the examination and also the qualities in the subject you are working from.

Papers 3 and 4 Imaginative Work in Two-dimensional Media

Here the term **interpretation** encourages you to adopt a personal approach in your work. By understanding what is possible and how to carry it out, you are able to be adventurous, original and creative in the work you do in response to the examination.

Paper 5 Work in Three-dimensional Media

Once more **interpretation** is the value-laden keyword in this paper, with all its accompanying opportunity to do work of a personal nature.

MARK SCHEMES

Apart from the maximum marks available for each paper, which are included above under Work Requirements, the syllabus does not include any other reference to marks. The term 'maximum' means that you can get all or a proportion of each mark, depending on the standard you reach in your examination work.

SOME OVERALL CONCLUSIONS

This is a long chapter, containing a lot of information. It is highly important that you read it carefully and understand it, because the contents are fundamental to the remainder of the book. You need to read about syllabuses you are not taking just as much as you need to read about your own syllabus. The information given under the section headings, 'Values', when put together, will provide you with a suitable set of principles and criteria to work to, no matter which syllabus you are taking. Getting as much knowledge of as many of the values as possible in art and design can only enhance your chances of achieving a high grade in your examination.

When you have read and understood this chapter, carry the information you have learned on to the next chapters, which deal with the various art and design practices. By this means you will be able to gain a wide, overall knowledge of your examination and at the same time, prepare yourself for working in depth in your studies.

You will find that you grow to know what is expected of you. This is much more important in your examination than knowing which pictures to paint, pots to make or objects to design.

EXERCISES

1 For any set of work in your coursework studies, try to write down how many aspects of the syllabus you are using for your examination that work has covered. You should find these aspects from the values, aims and objectives in particular, as drawn to your attention in this chapter.

2 Choosing one thing only from the period of history you may be studying for your examination, such as an artist or a designer, a painting, a sculpture or a designed object, try to list down all the information and knowledge you have upon it under the following headings:

- books read;
- dates known;
- specific historical fact;
- contextual historical facts;
- views of others;
- own views.

List your books properly, with name of author, title and so on, including the page numbers which apply to your studies. Remember, specific historical facts are about the person or object; contextual historical facts explain the times and conditions which surrounded the person or the production of the object. In writing your own views, try to use the views of others as a model for how you express your personal feelings and responses.

3 Choose one designed object of recent years which, in your opinion, was an unnecessary product. Describe the object by means of visual recordings and written accounts, and explain why it is an unnecessary product in your view. Try to justify the views you have.

4 Choose one object which has stood the test of time. Explain why you think this is so. Your object could be a designed object, a piece of architecture or a work of art.

5 Select a piece of architecture which you either like or dislike. Discuss your likes or dislikes, using visual as well as verbal means. Criticise the relationship of the piece of architecture to its surroundings. You might think the surroundings show it off well, that more recent developments spoil the piece of architecture or that the piece of architecture spoils the environment it stands in.

6 Discuss the effect of any reprographic system you chose upon the appearance of packaging and presentation of mass-produced articles. For instance, when it was invented, the reprographic process necessary to print coloured images on tinplate had a considerable effect on the toy industry. If you add to this the affective nature of fashion, trends or the popularity of some things at different times, you become aware of a technological, industrial, economic, social and cultural relationship in everyday things. The example of seaside metal buckets bearing the image of Mickey Mouse and his friends illustrates this.

CHAPTER 4

STILL LIFE

GETTING STARTED

Many of the examining boards include Still Life by name in their examinations. Whether or not you take this section of the examination is a matter for you to decide, because it is always optional. All the other examination syllabuses involving fine art would accept that you might include still life in your studies, even if they do not mention it by name. This is because it is such a traditionally accepted mode of work in art and design.

We have chosen to begin these chapters (4 – 9) involving the various practices with still life because we regard it as fundamental to most of what goes on in A-level and related courses of study, and in the actual examinations. We mean by this that studying still life, no matter what form of art and design practice you may consider to be your main interest and activity, provides you with a number of basic skills which are integral to anything else you might do in art and design. Those skills include the ability to develop your powers of:

- observation;
- drawing;
- spatial analysis and interpretation;
- colour analysis;
- colour mixing;
- colour usage;
- textural analysis and interpretation;
- pattern organisation;
- composition and design.

These are all basic skills in art and design, no matter what it is you may be doing. They are fundamental to two- and three-dimensional work, to expressive work or design-based work, to fine art or to craft, and so on. The major reason why still life is so convenient for studying and developing these skills is that the subject matter stands still and is unchanging, more or less for as long as you like.

Therefore, no matter what syllabus or practices you may be intending to follow, it is essential that you read this chapter thoroughly now.

This chapter sets out the format to be used in the following chapters (5 – 9), dealing with the other practices of art and design. We will not always repeat certain things within each of those chapters, so a full reading of this chapter will amplify some of the points raised later on.

Remember, studying the chapters on the practices is vital even if you are taking one of the newly written syllabuses which are covered in Chapter 10 of this book.

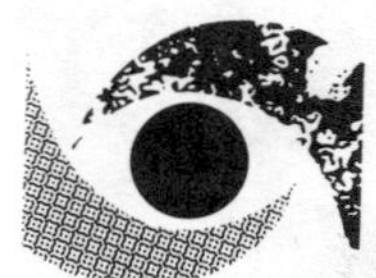

ESSENTIAL PRINCIPLES

CRITERIA IN STILL LIFE

In our opinion, whenever you work in art and design it is vital that you should not only make expressive and creative responses to what you see, or imagine, or are thinking, but also establish suitable criteria to describe what it is you are trying to do. This will help to focus your mind on the whole variety and range of qualities which should be present in your work. This applies just as much to *any* practice in art and design, as it does to still life.

The following are some of the criteria you might consider as forming part of your work, and on which it might subsequently be evaluated:

Criteria for your work in art and design.

- a definition of the practice (or genre) in art and design you are using or studying: DEFINITION OF THE TERM;
- an understanding and employment of the aesthetic standards essential in art and design work: AESTHETIC CONSIDERATIONS;
- a realisation of the qualities of materials and the appropriate use of tools and equipment: MATERIALS, TOOLS AND EQUIPMENT CONSIDERATIONS;
- a consideration of appropriate standards of craftsmanship: CRAFTSMANSHIP;
- a knowledge of the genre, derived from a study of the history of the subject: HISTORICAL FACTORS;
- the nuances and levels of understanding which an investigation of the contexts which surround us generally (as well as art and design specifically) might help to bring about: CONTEXTUAL CONSIDERATIONS;
- practical work within the practice concerned: WORKING METHODS.

In Chapters 4 to 9 it is our intention to analyse each practice or genre on the basis of these headings.

DEFINITION OF THE TERM

Defining the term will help you to understand what it is you ought to be doing. The sources of your information for doing this might come from dictionaries (both general and those specific to art and design), books on the history of art and design, leaflets published by museums and galleries, the collected writings and letters of artists and designers and so on, as well as from your own knowledge and experience.

According to the dictionary, 'still life' is 'a painting representing only inanimate things'. If you were to look up 'inanimate' in a dictionary you would find it described as 'dead, or lifeless'. Even a brief study of the still-life drawings and paintings which exist in books, art galleries and museums will convince you that sometimes cut flowers or fruit are included. Whether these should be regarded as 'dead, or lifeless' is, of course, a matter of debate. Most still-life works certainly do include objects such as vases, bowls, jugs and so on. The suggestion that even these objects should be regarded as dead or lifeless also seems somehow inappropriate. To be 'dead, or lifeless' suggests that at one time life existed. So, perhaps referring to a dictionary does not provide us with an entirely suitable criteria for working in still life. The last thing you want to achieve is a 'dead, or lifeless' piece of work!

“Defining 'still life'.”

The French term for the type of work usually included in still life is *nature morte*, which translated literally is 'dead nature'. Perhaps it might be more profitable to think of still life as, at least partly, still nature. Again, however, even the term 'nature' does not necessarily cover all that might be regarded as the subject matter of still life.

Moving towards a definition in this way is a first step in our quest to devise suitable criteria to work to. What is really at the heart of a clear definition of the genre in art and design is the recognition that *anything* can be included in a still-life arrangement.

- **The essence of still life is that the things included should remain static and largely unchanging over an extended period of time**.

This is necessary for you to investigate the relationships between these 'still' objects and produce work which shows the result of your analysis, as well as your creative responses to what you see.

AESTHETIC CONSIDERATIONS

In **selecting** objects to include in a still-life arrangement, most artists pay attention to such considerations as:

"Aesthetic qualities involved in selection."

- the shapes and sizes of the objects;
- the colours of the objects;
- the textures of the objects;
- the patterns on the objects;
- the harmony and contrasts between the shapes, colours, textures and patterning of the objects concerned.

When a specific question demanding a still-life picture is included in an examination paper it often includes qualitative terms about shape, texture, colour, contrast, and so on.

In **arranging** the selected objects into a group from which to work, most artists would then consider:

"Aesthetic qualities involved in arrangement."

- the juxtaposition of one object with another;
- the distribution and placing of colour throughout the group;
- the contrasts and arrangements of texture and pattern within the group;
- the views of the group which different viewpoints and different eye levels would provide.

All of this means that the general and detailed content and arrangement of the group would need to be well designed, according to some of the basic aesthetic values particular to art and design.

These aesthetic values are sometimes referred to as the **formal elements**. You may be more familiar with this term than with the phrase **aesthetic values**. To remind you, the formal elements are usually described as:

"The formal elements."

- line;
- shape;
- form;
- colour;
- pattern;
- texture.

We have included each of these terms in the Glossary (see page 9).

You can see that in the various lists already considered we have more or less covered the formal elements in art and design when speaking of aesthetic values.

MATERIALS, TOOLS AND EQUIPMENT CONSIDERATIONS

All media have certain characteristics which make a particular one most suitable for certain effects, as well as for communicating certain types of information. For example, imagine you had arranged a still-life group which depended for its composition and effect upon the colours of the objects you had chosen. While you would be able to convey certain information about the group by using a soft, black graphite pencil, a pencil would not necessarily be a very appropriate choice of medium to respond to and convey, the colour qualities concerned. If colour was an important factor in your choice and arrangement of objects, you would be much better advised to use a colour medium, such as pastels, crayons, coloured pencils, paint or collage for your work from the group.

Of course, in any still-life work you are seeking to find some useful knowledge about the group and the reasons for its appearance. Therefore, even if it was colour which attracted you in the first place you would still be well advised to explore the content and potential of the group further, using alternative media in a series of visual responses. At the same time, it would pay you to write down your descriptions of the group and an account of your responses to each situation and media used.

If you are in any doubt about the value of doing this you should look at a book of the edited letters of VAN GOGH (1958). This is a collection of Vincent van Gogh's letters to his brother, Theo. In these letters he uses a language to describe things he can see which is as rich, textured and colourful as any visual account of the same thing. It is our contention that by *writing* down such descriptions you will then be better able to portray the qualities you have described in your *visual* accounts of things.

We have just mentioned that you might work from a still-life group with a **soft**, black graphite pencil. It is worth noting that what you might render with such a soft pencil is likely to be at least slightly different to what you would do if you were using a pencil with thin, hard graphite in it.

Returning to colour, it sometimes seems to be very difficult to grasp just how affected we are by colour, especially as colour is such a constant part of our everyday life. In order to help you realise and understand the effect of colour, a good experiment is to take two photographs of a group of objects from exactly the same viewpoint and eye level, one with colour and the other with black-and-white film. When you see the two prints produced in this way, you might be very surprised at the things you can see and realise in each photograph which were not apparent to you from the group itself.

For example, you might recognise the wide range and distribution of tones in the group from your black-and-white photograph. Each colour is not just the result of the **hue** concerned but is also, in part, the result of the **chroma** and the **tone** of each colour. Whether it is in shadow or not, each colour has its own tonal quality – that is to say, one colour is darker or lighter than another. This is not always easy to see and understand when your mind is concentrating upon colour and your eye is desperately searching out the actual hue and chroma of each colour you can see. Yet it is the portrayal of the tonal quality of a colour which, when put together across a number of objects and a range of different colours, helps to create the composition of the group and the work you do from it. The black-and-white photograph should make this quality clear to you.

If you do carry out this exercise, see if you can construct a 'league table' showing the colours from their darkest to their lightest. The sort of questions you should then ask yourself are whether red is darker or lighter than blue; or where green and yellow are placed in the scale of the relationships you are building up. Of course, your answers can indicate only that *this* red is darker (or lighter) than *this* blue in *this* situation, and so on. In other circumstances the scale might be changed. If you play this game, start by trying to judge which colour is darker, and so on, using only your eye and *before* you take any photographs. You should write down the decisions you make and then use this estimated scale for reference when you have your photographs to work with.

As we have touched upon photographs, it is worth noting that the film medium you are using *changes* the visual effect of the objects within the group. The images of the objects on the photographs will look different from the images of the objects you might have painted. It is easy, of course, to see that a stick medium, such as pencil or crayon, is likely to result in an image which *looks different* to an image produced in something like liquid paint or collage. In all these instances, as we have said already, the difference is due to the qualities and effect each medium possesses. This means that rather than choosing your medium in order to portray the type of information from the group which you have decided is important beforehand, it sometimes pays to pick any medium and to work from the group, *searching out* the type of information the particular medium is most suited to portray. If you take this 'experimental' approach, then together with the accompanying analysis you will be carrying out, you are likely to develop a growing awareness and understanding of the widest possible range of qualities and characteristics which the group possesses. This can only benefit you when you make future decisions about how to carry out a major piece, or pieces, of work from the group. If you refer back to 'Exercises' at the end of Chapter 2, you will see that you have already had an opportunity to explore this phenomenon through some carefully conducted experiments which should result in positive and useful knowledge for you to work with.

CRAFTSMANSHIP

The term 'craftsmanship' is often used in discussion about art and design. Therefore it is worth trying to sort out what it means. Of course, words are often really a rather imprecise way of constructing definitions, particularly when they are used to describe things which cannot be tested empirically or measured. This is often the case in art and design, where even most of the 'tests' we might conduct with materials and the like lack scientific rigour. This does not matter, however. If you try to test something and then describe your findings, whether or not the conditions were entirely scientific your understanding will still be likely to grow. Anyway, there is no need for everything to be **quantitative**, in the sense that it *can be* weighed, measured, tested, etc. according to scientific standards. The **qualitative** is just as important, not least because in our appreciation of things, one complements and enhances the other.

There has been a long argument about what the differences are between 'craft' and 'art', a 'craftsperson' and an 'artist'. This kind of argument seems to us rather sterile. A more important question is what is 'craftsmanship' and to what extent does it influence the criteria we establish for our work, be it art, design or craft?

Again according to the dictionary, craftsmanship is 'high skill shown in making some object'. There can be no denial that you would wish to display high skill in producing your work; but what does 'skill' mean? Without some suitable knowledge and criteria to describe skill, it seems that anything might be considered acceptable as skilful. You could even be excused for producing your work 'craftily'! Look up that word in the dictionary and then work out how well your work would be received!

"Defining 'craftsmanship'."

There is a word which does not appear in many dictionaries, although it is used quite commonly in the field of art and design. That word is 'crafting'. We take this to mean producing a good idea or intention well. The term 'well' means skilfully, but it does not refer to the productive skills alone. It involves also the quality of your initial idea or intention; the aesthetic decisions which help give form to your work; the ways in which you select and use tools, equipment and materials; how you absorb and use historical knowledge; and how aware you are of the social and cultural influences which impinge upon your beliefs and upon the decisions you take.

So, it is clear that as far as we are concerned, craftsmanship is about the way you integrate all the knowledge, information and skills you have to reach decisions about the nature, form and appearance of your work and the reasons for producing it.

This interpretation of the term 'craftsmanship' can help explain why we, and many others, regard as sterile the debate on the alleged differences between craftspersons, artists and designers. We see no need to create boundaries between them at all. Those who engage in such debates often suggest that craftspersons work according to standards and methods which are traditional and conditional upon what it is they produce. That is to say, they produce work which obeys a variety of external rules and regulations which have grown up around the production of such work. This view, taken to extremes, sometimes seeks to deny that craftspersons include any personal decisions in their work. This is obviously nonsense. The very notion of 'hand made' suggests the inclusion of some level of personal creativity. Indeed, it is this *lack* of the personal that is one of the things often bemoaned in the type and quality of furniture available from some modern factory production lines. From time to time a cry goes up about a return to the values of 'craftsmanship' rather than those of faceless mass production.

At the same time, however, it would be foolish to think that artists and designers can afford to ignore historical standards and traditions in their work. The whole issue is an interwoven one and distinctions are more a matter of balance than stark contrast.

Even if your work is not essentially concerned with still-life, it may still be worth your while studying the works and writings of WILLIAM MORRIS (1834 – 96) in order to gain a deeper understanding of this problem.

HISTORICAL FACTORS

From much of what has gone before, it is obvious that we consider the history of art and design to be an essential component of your work. This does not, however, mean that you should learn the history of art and design parrot-fashion and in chronological order from the beginning of time to the present day. If you set out to do this you will need much more time than your course will provide you with! Knowing the dates of things *is* an important aspect of your ultimate understanding, but there is no necessity for you to be able to recite those dates in chronological order. If you find out the relevant dates concerned with the work on which you are currently engaged, after a while you will find that you can recall them **because they are part of your working knowledge**. What you have to ask yourself is whether there is some advantage *to you* in chronologically sorting and ordering your knowledge in this respect.

If you do look at the writings of William Morris, you will find that the knowledge of when he lived and worked is an important factor in understanding his points of view. Here we use him as an example of a situation where knowing the history of the subject helps to increase your understanding of what it is you might be doing yourself in the practice of still life. On the other hand, if you had to study the history in a chronological order only, the likelihood of your coming across William Morris would be fairly remote.

"Gaining historical knowledge and awareness."

We strongly advocate using this **point of access** approach in your practical studies. By this we mean homing-in on some specific information which is relevant to your needs at a particular time. If you do this, and get into the habit of extending your inquiry a little bit backwards and forwards in time when you do, you will also find that the various inter-relations between different periods of time will also become apparent to you. This does not always happen in a chronological study, which separates history into packages in order to sustain the process of teaching and learning. Of course, you cannot always be expected to know what to research in history as you work, but you will usually find that your teachers will 'clue you in' to something from the history of the subject which will help you in your own practical studies. The trouble is, they may give so many clues of this historical type that it is all too easy for you to think of them as being casual and unimportant. Nothing could be further from the truth as far as your ultimate levels of achievement are concerned. Therefore, it is vital that you get into the habit of asking your teachers for guidance about the sources of information when they suggest things to you, and that you then follow these up, using them to further your understanding and work on the project at hand.

To return to the question of dates from the history of art and design, it is undoubtedly important that you should know certain key dates, such as the historically recognised fact that **oil painting** was invented, or discovered, about the beginning of the fifteenth century. It is equally important to know, for instance, that GIOTTO (*c.* 1266 – 1337), HIERONYMUS BOSCH (*c.* 1450 – 1516), PETER PAUL RUBENS (1577 – 1640) or GIORGIO MORANDI (1890 – 1964) lived and worked when they did. From such information you can make important deductions. For instance, it is then clear that, despite the argument that oil painting was known from a much earlier date than the early 1400s, it is unlikely that Giotto painted in oils. All the other artists *could* have done so, which is not to say that they did, or that they always did.

Again, it is possible that Bosch might have used the traditional medium of **tempera** for his paintings, although this is unlikely if you also know that he was a northern European artist. We say this because the discovery of oil paint as a medium is credited to the VAN EYCK family, who painted in northern Europe in the first half of the fifteenth century. So Bosch lived at the time of the introduction of oil paint as a major painting medium. However, had he been an Italian painter he might have turned to oil as a painting medium only after it had been very well tried and established, and then spread across Europe. As a northern European artist it is much more likely that he *did* paint in the new medium because he worked in the area where it was most used in its earliest days. In this way knowledge of dates and places can be an invaluable source of information and understanding in art and design. However, it is much more likely that you will be able to *use* such historical knowledge profitably when you seek it out in relation to the particular project or activity that is the basis of your current work.

CONTEXTUAL INVESTIGATIONS

> "Contextual matters affect real art and design."

We have already begun to touch upon a range of **contextual information** in this chapter, which goes to show how fundamental it is to the success of your studies. For instance, if you study a selection of still-life works from *various times* you will begin to see changes taking place over and above the changes brought about by the use of different media, or the application of the different theories which the artists might have adhered to. Artists cannot exist outside the society and culture in which they live and work. Therefore, that society and culture will influence the way in which they work and some of the values they might hold. As society and culture changes, so inevitably will the work of artists and designers.

In Fig. 4.1 we can see an illustration of the work of EMILY STANNARD (1803 – 85). 'Still Life – Dead Ducks and a Hare with Basket and a Sprig of Holly' can cause us to ask certain questions, such as why subject matter such as dead game should be regarded as suitable for a painting; why there is a sprig of holly and a dead robin among the dead game; what the local environment of the dead game might be; what the environment shown through the hole in the wall might be; and so on. Some of the answers we might begin to come up with could lead us to reflect that in 1853, when the painting was made, game was an important part of many people's diet, even of the poor, who often seemed to manage to poach without getting caught! The painting was undertaken in Queen Victoria's reign, when a particular image of Christmas was being created, at least in books by authors such as Charles Dickens. Part of that image was good eating. The sprig of holly and the dead robin might be no more than associated imagery to convey the feeling of Christmas. The hooks, posts and sign around the opening in the wall suggest that the local environment is a shop. The view in the opening has been identified as the church of St Peter Mancroft, Norwich, so it is partly a documentation of Norwich in the middle of the last century.

Our intention here is to try and illustrate how the values of a society and a culture affect and influence the way an artist works. In attempting to do so, we have entered into a whole set of contextual references, involving what we might otherwise label history, economics, architecture, religion, dietary considerations, social conditions, cultural circumstances and literary sources. We hope you can see from the passage how relevant contextual investigations are to art and design.

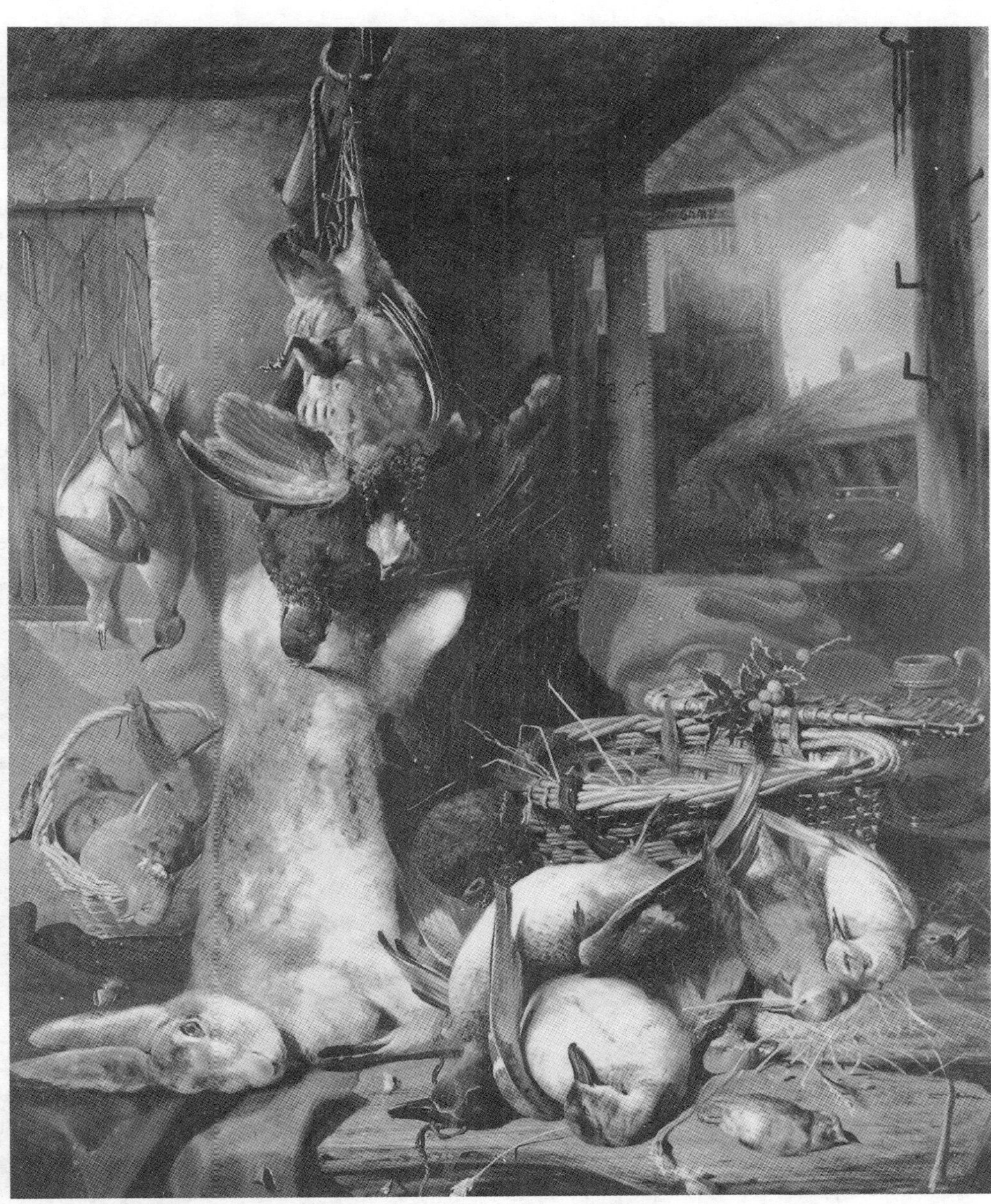

Fig. 4.1 'Still Life – Dead Ducks and a Hare with Basket and a Sprig of Holly', Emily Stannard (reproduced by permission of the Castle Museum, Norwich).

Think of how you might do a similar picture nowadays. Food in the shops at Christmas would look very different in content, form and presentation, would it not? The shop itself would be vastly different; today it might well be a supermarket. How does the church of St Peter Mancroft look now? Can it be seen from this viewpoint any longer? Does it still stand? What other buildings now surround it? Such changes around the church are likely to be quite dramatic in comparison with the changes that have occurred inside the church. Why is this so?

We think you can see clearly that both the values of the Victorian society and the culture they helped to create are markedly different from our own contemporary society and culture. Emily Stannard does not appear to be making any protest about the values of her society – or is she? The presence of the little dead robin might be a symbol of her protest against the carnage wrought so that one might eat. Or does this suggestion merely reflect a value which can have come only from a contemporary Green and conservation-minded society and culture?

We hope you can appreciate from all this how necessary it is to know and understand something of the society and culture in which the various artists worked in order to appreciate their work beyond the aesthetic alone. Such contextual knowledge is also vital if you are to be conscious of and understand the contemporary values *we* each bring to bear upon any work when we look at it. Our current social and cultural values are unlikely to have existed when the work was originally carried out. From this point of view, seeking out contextual knowledge is invaluable for a proper understanding of the work of others, as well as for understanding the changing world in which we all exist, what it is you do in your own work and why you decide to do it.

WORKING IN STILL LIFE

Still life before still life

Still life as a genre has a clearly identified history. Even before paintings and drawings were produced which could with some certainty be labelled still life (i.e. before the sixteenth century), a quick glance through books on the history of art would soon make it clear that artists have long included in their work little cameos which show, for instance, pots gathered on a table. There are many such examples, some done before the recognised beginnings of still life, some done after, but all of which have little to do with the genre itself. Fig. 4.2, 'The Supper at Emmaus', by CARAVAGGIO (1571 – 1610) is an example of this. The collection of objects on the table was not done according to the principles fundamental to the genre of still life, but they are nevertheless fine, perhaps unconscious, examples of the genre. The inclusion of an apparent still life within paintings such as this means that the objects in question are part of a work which sets out to obey the principles governing an alternative form of art and design. Such still-life cameos are included, for instance, in many religious paintings or in the mosaics at Pompeii. In both these instances, the notion of still life as we hold it today was *not* the governing factor behind the work concerned, any more than it was for Caravaggio. In many ways the drive behind his work was the pursuit of naturalism and an interest in story-telling.

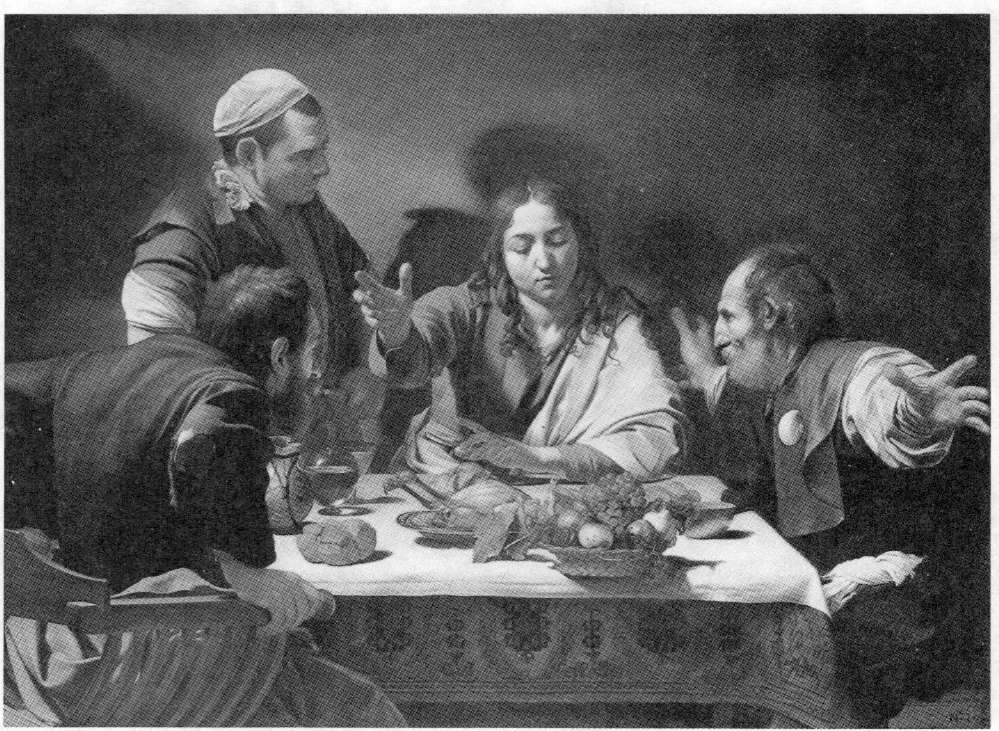

Fig. 4.2 'The Supper at Emmaus', Caravaggio (reproduced by permission of the Trustees of the National Gallery, London).

Still life as story-telling and documentation

In work which can be specifically labelled still life we can see more than one particular type of content. There are those still-life works which deal with whole interiors and include, for instance, kitchen furniture and equipment and food; or shot or trapped game, guns and dogs. Sometimes, although we may even label such works as still life, they are based upon additional principles as well. Thus some still-life works may be more concerned to show possessions, places or times, and so on. Artists who might be said to be associated with this particular aspect of still life and whose works are well represented in major UK and Irish cities include:

PIETER AERTSEN (*c*.1508 – 75)	Birmingham
JACOPO BASSANO (*c*.1510 – 92)	Cambridge, Edinburgh, London (National Gallery), Manchester
PIETER DE HOOCH (*c*.1629 – 1684)	Dublin, London (National Gallery, Wallace Collection), Manchester
JAN VERMEER (*c*.1632 – 75)	Edinburgh, London (Kenwood House, National Gallery)
EDOUARD VUILLARD (*c*.1868 – 1940)	Birmingham, Bristol, Glasgow, Liverpool, London (Courtauld Institute, National Gallery, Tate Gallery), Manchester

There are, of course, many other artists who could be said to have worked according to this particular genre. But throughout this book, when we present you with examples from the history of art and design, we try to select those artists and designers who have work on show in easily accessible galleries and museums. This is to enable you to either visit the gallery or museum concerned, or to write to them and purchase slides or postcards of the works.

Other artists may be found by referring to any book dealing with the history of art and design. However, in this case you will probably have to search out such artists for yourself, as you are unlikely to find that the book classifies artists under the headings suggested by this chapter, and by the others which follow.

As far as the list above is concerned, '*La Cheminée*' (Fig. 4.3) by Edouard Vuillard perpetuates a small aspect of an intimate domestic environment. It **documents** the scene for all time and also allows us to build up a story around the scene we observe. Can you write down aspects of the story which occur to you?

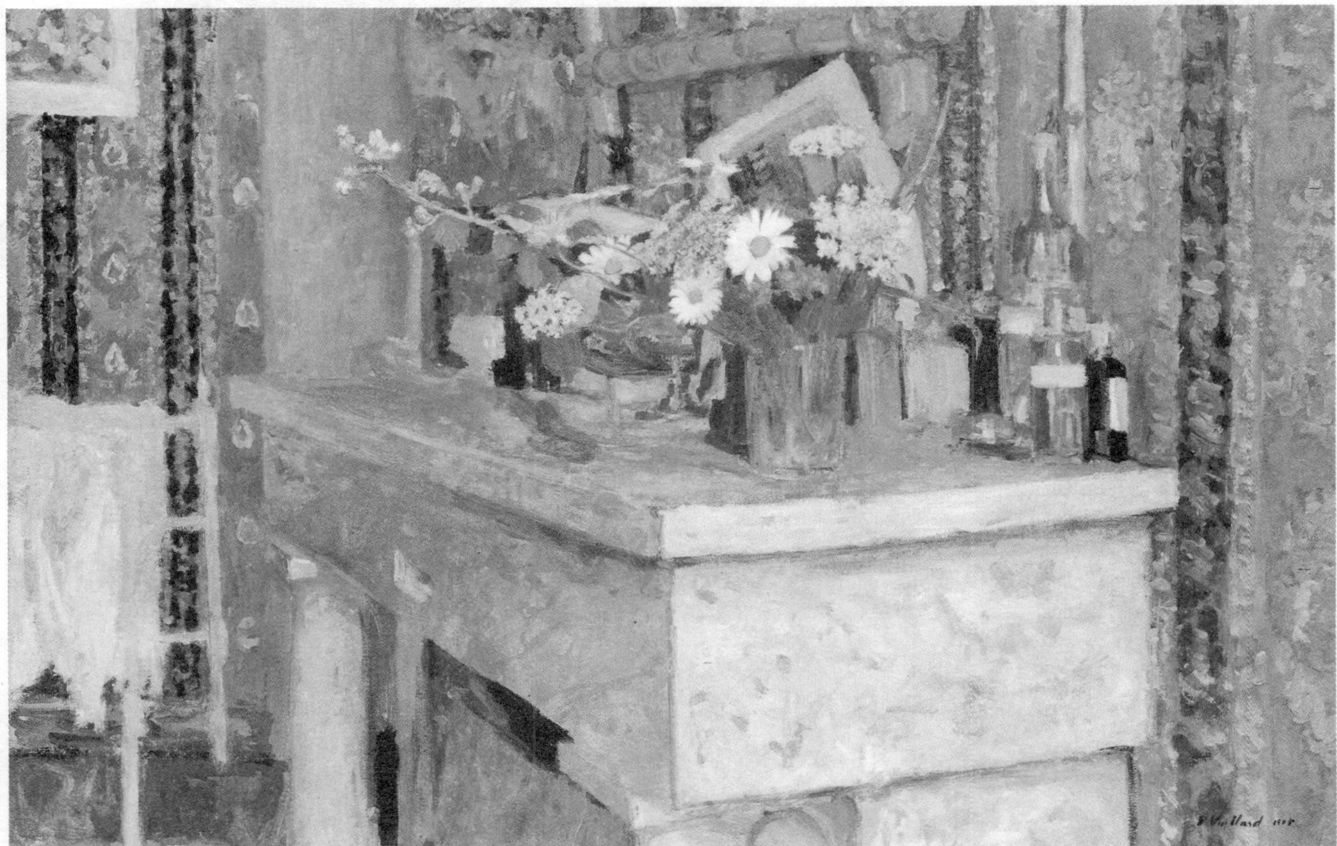

Fig. 4.3 'La Cheminée', Edouard Vuillard (reproduced by permission of the Trustees of the National Gallery, London).

Flowers and fruit in still life

Then there are flower or fruit pieces. These were done most notably by the Dutch painters in and around the seventeenth century, though many other artists can be identified who carry on the tradition right up to the present day. A selection of artists widely associated with flower paintings in still life is given below:

JAN DAVIDSZ. DE HEEM (*c*.1606 – 1683)	Birmingham, Cambridge, Cheltenham, Dublin, Edinburgh, Glasgow, London (National Gallery), Manchester, Oxford
JAN VAN HUYSUM (1682 – 1749)	London (National Gallery)
EMILY STANNARD (1803 – 1885)	Norwich

The Dutch term used to indicate work of this kind was **Silleven**. According to Murray (1987), it was this term which gave rise to the English 'still life'.

Flowers in a Terra Cotta Vase' by Jan van Huysum (Fig. 4.4) will suffice to show you the quality of the work of the Dutch Masters.

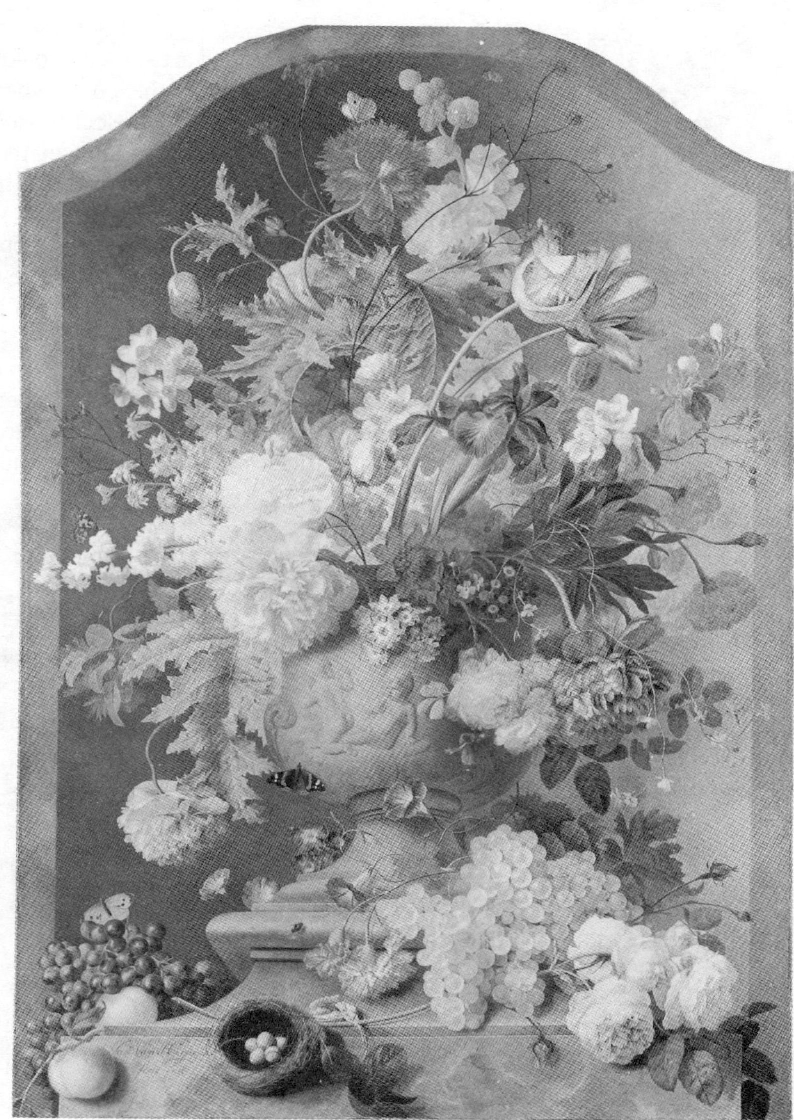

Fig. 4.4 Flowers in a Terra Cotta Vase', Jan van Huysum (reproduced by permission of the Trustees of the National Gallery, London).

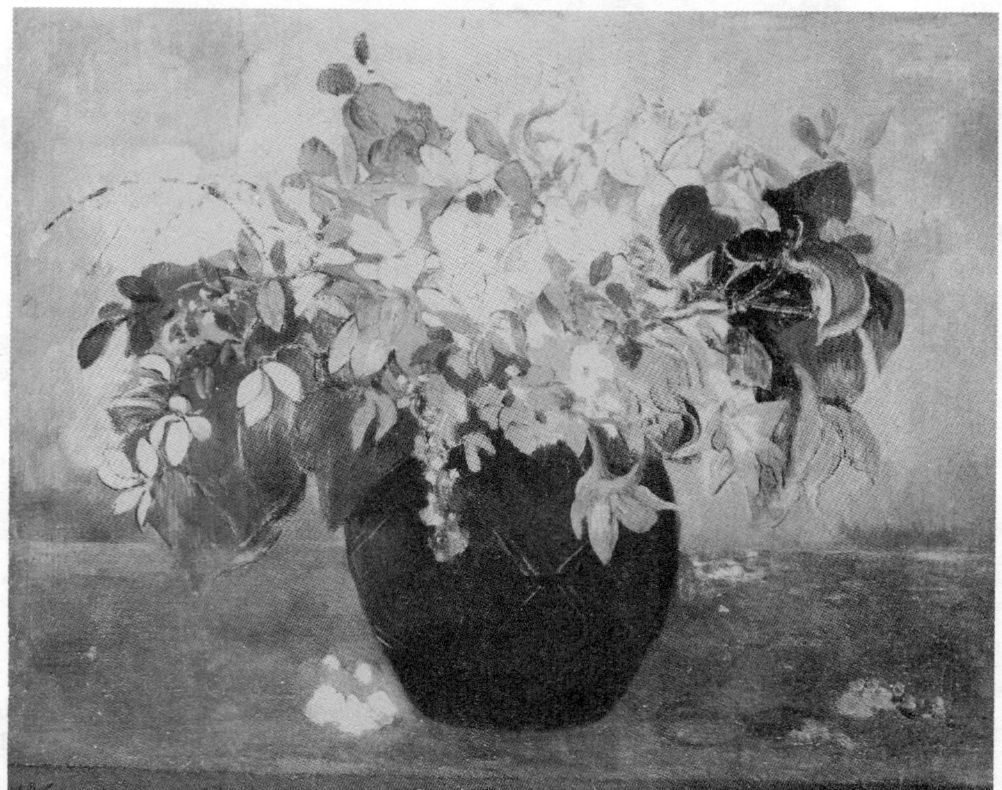

Fig. 4.5 'A Vase of Flowers', Paul Gauguin (reproduced by permission of the Trustees of the National Gallery, London).

In contrast, analyse how an artist such as PAUL GAUGUIN (1848 – 1903) painted a similar subject (Fig. 4.5). It soon becomes clear that there are no rules and regulations about how you portray what is before you. But one thing you *can* be certain of is that both Gauguin and van Huysum worked directly from their subject matter to achieve these results.

Still life for still life's sake

Since the beginning of the genre of still life, a few artists have arisen who have used the form as a pure form of personal exploration and expression. These artists have made still life their own, in the way that landscape painting is associated with JOHN CONSTABLE (1776 – 1837) and portrait painting with JOSHUA REYNOLDS (1723 – 92). These artists might be said to include:

GEORGES BRAQUE (1882 – 1963)	Edinburgh, Glasgow, London (Tate Gallery), Oxford
PAUL CÉZANNE (1839 – 1906)	Cambridge, Cardiff, Edinburgh, Glasgow, London (Courtauld Institute, National Gallery, Tate Gallery)
JEAN BAPTISTE SIMEON CHARDIN (1699 – 1779)	Dublin, Edinburgh, Glasgow, London
GIORGIO MORANDI (1890 – 1964)	Birmingham, Edinburgh, London (Tate Gallery)
PABLO PICASSO (1881 – 1973)	Various
WILLIAM SCOTT (1913 –)	Belfast, Edinburgh, London (Tate Gallery, Victoria and Albert Museum)

All these artists and their works are worthy of study, no matter what your particular still-life subject matter may be. Each artist represents distinctly different ways of working with the **medium** and each held a different **theory** as the basis of their work – except for Braque and Picasso, who both worked side by side through CUBISM. By studying them you will be able to discover the possibilities which are open to you in your own work.

The essential thing about these artists and their still-life works is that they largely used the genre to explore and develop their own theories and understanding about the practice of making art. Of course, in doing so they also produced excellent pictures. Explore the differences between the two still-life works reproduced in Figs. 4.6 and 4.7. If you try to read something about the artists concerned, you will find out more about the theories they held and the social and cultural influences impinging on their work, and therefore about the criteria underpinning their art. You will then be in a better position to identify and explain any differences (and indeed any similarities).

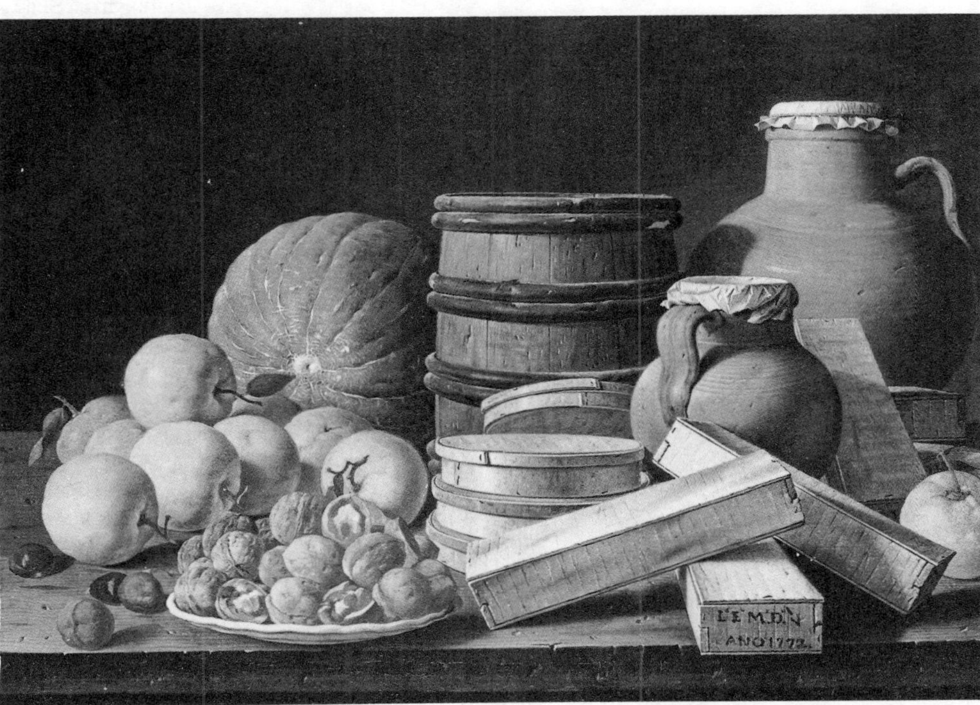

Fig. 4.6 'Still Life with Oranges and Walnuts', Melendez (reproduced by permission of the Trustees of the National Gallery, London).

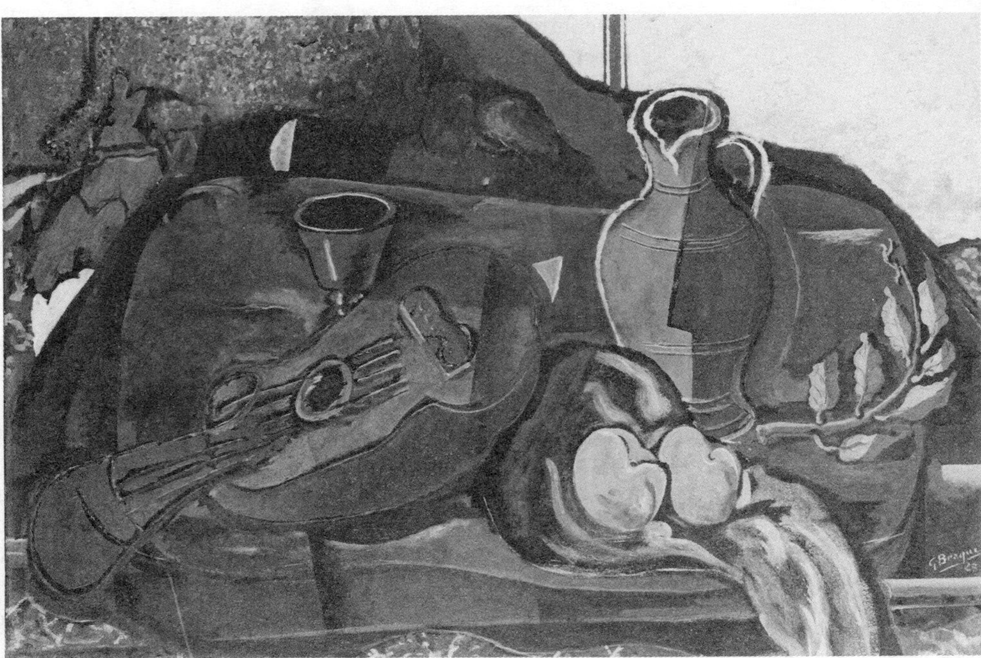

Fig. 4.7 'Guitar and Jug', Georges Braque (reproduced by permission of the Tate Gallery, London).

What the examination syllabuses say

Where an examination syllabus includes a direct reference to still life, what they say might influence what you do in response to this section of the examination. Table 4.1 indicates that not all the syllabuses carry a *direct* reference to still life. Where they do, we have already included the references and analysed them in Chapter 3 although they each had little to say which would guide you directly so far as still life is concerned. If *your* syllabus appears in Table 4.1, it would be useful at this stage to return to Chapter 3 and refresh your memory on what your own examination syllabus has to say about still life. It would benefit you more, however, if you looked through the *whole* of Chapter 3, gathering together all that is said about still life (or perhaps more helpfully about 'painting' and working from 'direct observation') from *all* the examination syllabuses.

EXAMINING BOARD	SYLLABUS/TITLES USED
AEB	ART – PAINTING/603 Paper 1 – Practical Test 603/1 (Time allowed: 9 hours) ii) Painting from Still Life Candidates will be provided with objects specified by the Board and will be expected to arrange their own groups. Paper 2 – History and Technique 603/2 (Time allowed: 3 hours) Paper 3 – Coursework 603/3 ART AND CRAFTS/605 Paper 2 – Option 20 – Drawing or Painting 605/2/20 (Time allowed: 3 hours) Part (A). Still Life Groups of objects of varied shape and material. Candidates will each be given a choice from the specified objects, and will be expected objects, and will be expected to arrange their own groups. Paper 2 – Option 25 – History and Appreciation of Art 605/2/25 (Time allowed: 3 hours) Paper 3 – Coursework
NISEC	SYLLABUS A Paper II: Drawing or Painting from Natural or Fashioned Objects (Time allowed: 3 hours) Paper V: History of Art (Time allowed: 3 hours) SYLLABUS B Section 1 – Main Study (Time allowed: 15 hours) 1. Painting Section 2 – Analytical and Written Study (Time allowed: 3 hours)

EXAMINING BOARD	SYLLABUS/TITLES USED
	Section 3 – History and Appreciation of Art, Architecture and Design (Time allowed: 3 hours, plus Extended Essay) Part 1 History of Painting Section 4 – Coursework
OXFORD	ART with ART HISTORY/9894 Paper 1 – History of Art (Time allowed: 3 hours) Section II. History of Painting Paper 2 – Work from Observation 9894/2 (Time allowed: 6 hours) Paper 6 – Work from Observation 9894/6 (Time allowed: 6 hours) *[See Table 3.18 about mixing Paper 2 and Paper 6]*

Table 4.1 Terms used to describe 'Still Life' in the various established examination syllabuses.

If you find that the syllabuses, even taken together, still say very little about what is required of you when doing a still-life work, this need not matter unduly. Your teachers will know what comprises good and successful still-life painting. As long as the values they come up with are in tune with the values the examiners hold, then all will be well. The likelihood of this being so is very high. The examiners, together with your teachers, are likely to have a deep, practical background in art and design which, combined with some shared knowledge of the history of the subject, will lead them to make very similar decisions.

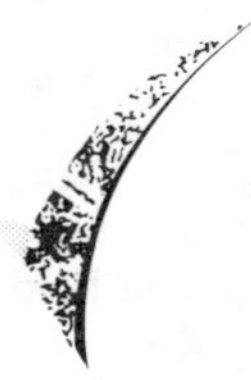

EXAMINATION QUESTIONS, STUDENT ANSWERS AND EXAMINER COMMENTS

In still life it is not usual for a 'question' to be set. You are usually given lists of objects to choose from so that you can arrange your own group. This has implications.

First, you will need to have some well-worked-out principles to apply in choosing your objects and arranging your group. These might come from your study of the history of the genre, as well as from your knowledge of aesthetics. Be prepared to explore alternative arrangements and viewpoints in your preparatory studies, so that you arrive at the best composition through experience rather than in a premeditated way.

Second, we believe you should *avoid* the trap of choosing to do those objects which appear to comprise a theme. By this we mean the collections of, say gardening tools or kitchen equipment which are sometimes set as possible choices. The problems of encompassing a tall, slender garden fork into a composition which includes some corms and a large, round garden sieve are almost insurmountable, at least in our opinion. Instead, choose those objects which can be grouped together according to some aesthetic principle or because their surfaces give you the opportunity of showing your ability to analyse and interpret them, or because their colours make possible an arrangement which you could explore further, and so on.

PRODUCING STILL-LIFE WORK

It may be helpful if we now set out to demonstrate to you just what types of opportunities and alternatives there are before you in your approach to still life. By introducing you to some of the identifiable alternatives, we will give you some relevant information which might either guide your choices and decisions in the future or reinforce the direction your work is already taking. To do this we shall depend largely upon examples of A-level work presented by previous candidates.

DIRECT OBSERVATION

If you have studied the examination syllabuses where still life is included, it should be apparent to you that the genre occurs in a section committed largely to working from 'direct observation'. This means that you work with your subject in front of you, observing and referring to it all the time.

As a result it is likely that your work will be concerned with:

- the visual appearance of things – what do they look like?
  – why do they look the way they do?
- the structure of things – what are they made from?
  – how are they made?
- comparison between things – what makes one thing different from another?
- the spatial position of things and the relationship between them – is one thing in front of another?
  – do they overlap?
  – are they on the same surface height?
- the environment things are in – is the background 'open'?
  – is the background 'closed'?

Even in work based on direct observation, remember that you are not necessarily setting out to obtain a photographic likeness between what you do and the original. This aspect is discussed more fully in Chapter 6 and you should refer to it, but for now let us point out that even from direct observation your work can be:

- illusory – in that it is made to 'look like' what you see;
- expressive – in that it gives significant meaning to what you see;
- interpretative – in that it explains the meaning of what you see.

There are, of course, other considerations which can enable you to carry out successful still-life works. They are:

- the characteristics of the various media;
- the effect of the media on the appearance of your work;
- the nature of the medium and its influence upon what you do;
- the style you work in, which results in part from the philosophy you hold about the nature and purpose of art and design.

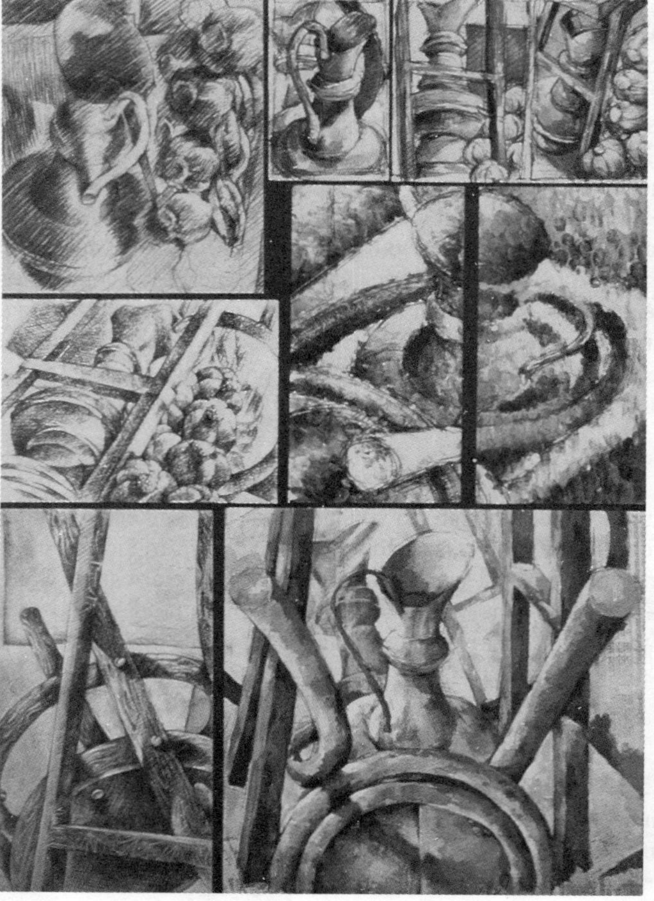

Fig. 4.8

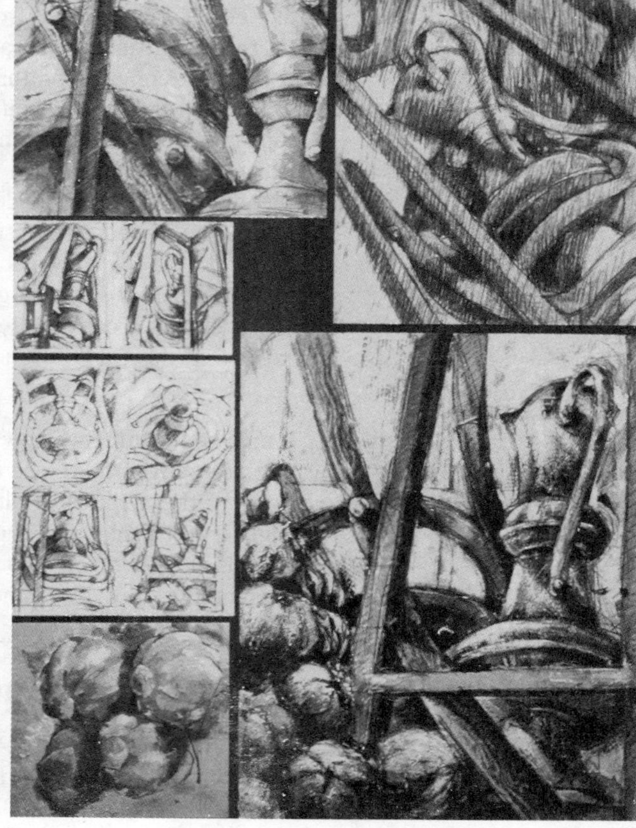

Fig. 4.9

In Fig. 4.8 we can see a candidate using media to good effect in exploring some of the visual aspects of the group. The drawings are vigorous, well executed and display good standards of observation and draughtsmanship. The works seem to combine an analytical and visual awareness of what is seen with an understanding of the qualities of materials.

In Fig. 4.9 the same candidate proceeds further in the work, showing a willingness to consider a large number of alternatives. In the final piece of work from these studies (bottom right in Fig. 4.9) the candidate clearly displays the ability to combine a good working knowledge of the qualities of materials with the nature of the still-life genre in the overall work.

Above all else, these studies show an adventurous spirit – in other words, a willingness to take unexpected and quite startling views of the subject matter being used. This has the advantage of making the compositions exciting, suggesting a marked element of risk in them. The views and the resulting compositions also get around the problem of dealing with objects of contrasting size and appearance. For instance, the candidate has avoided showing a tall, spindly stool standing up alongside other, smaller objects. The studies make the objects look as if they have arrived in their relative positions by chance and are likely to rearrange themselves if we turn away for a moment! There is a 'tension' present among them as a result.

In Fig. 4.10 we see a very sound painterly rendering of a still-life group. The composition, while is not startling, is more than adequate.

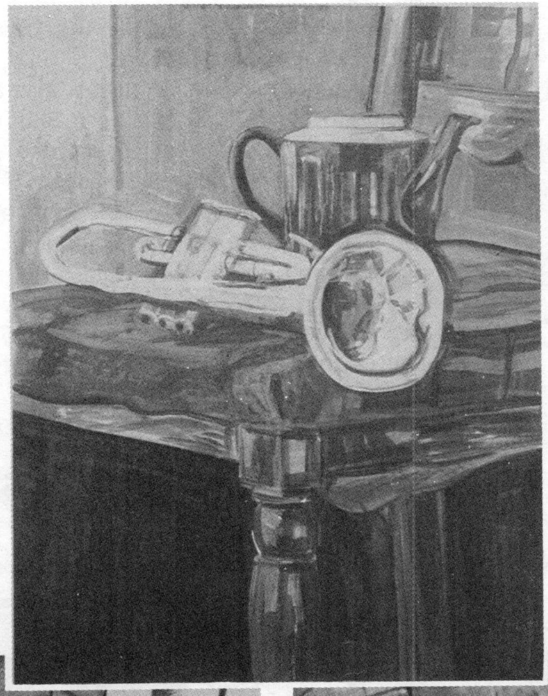

Fig. 4.10

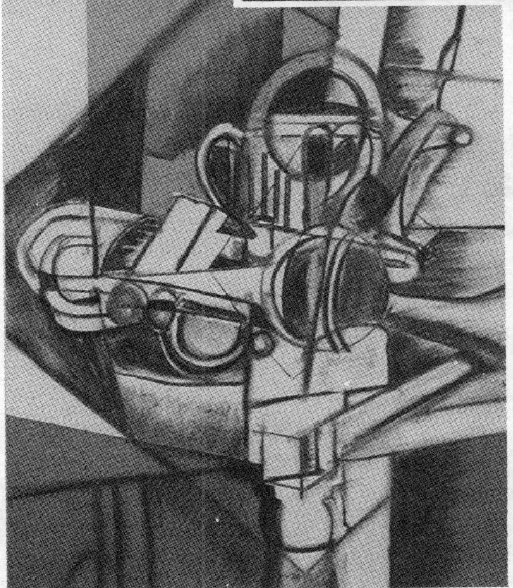

Fig. 4.11

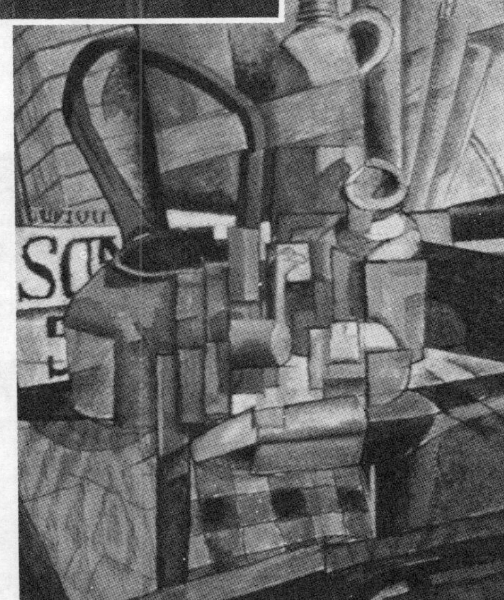

Fig. 4.12

For some reason, in Fig. 4.11 the candidate has done an alternative version of the group, from exactly the same viewpoint and with the same composition. In fact, it may have begun life as a tracing from the original work. In this second work the candidate explores a different form of alternative to that initially investigated. This is the alternative presented by a different theory of visual awareness and representation. In this case it seems that the candidate introduced a knowledge of the work of either BRAQUE or PICASSO into the approach. The knowledge involved and the 'success' of the work might be analysed by you, perhaps by comparing Fig. 4.11 with the work in Fig. 4.12, which was done by another candidate.

In the work of both the two previous candidates, it is difficult to know how they each arrived at the Cubist-like pictures. It might have been by no more than transcribing what they knew from their historical studies into what they saw, without any accompanying intermediary steps. On the other hand, in Figs. 4.13, 4.14 and 4.15 we are able to see how a candidate teases out many of the possibilities present in the still-life group in question, arriving *gradually* at a decision leading to the final work looking the way it does.

The danger in any abstract work is that your efforts seem merely to show an ability to copy how someone else does a similar picture. You must avoid this, and can do so by compiling a *written* critical analysis of abstract art, or of an abstract artist. You must show that you have understood how to 'take from', first, what you see, then what you have done, *ad infinitum*. If you wonder what this means, try to find some illustrations of how the artist PIET MONDRIAN (1872 – 1944) gradually transformed consecutive studies of a tree into what turned out to be the governing principle for his future – namely, totally non-representational art.

We do not make these suggestions to give your work an air of pseudo-academicism but rather to equip you with the means to work with understanding. It is all too easy for anyone to criticise your, or anyone else's, abstract work as a 'cop-out'. Just provide evidence to them that this is not so, if this is the way you want to work. After all, we are recommending here only what we in any case insist upon for anyone choosing to work in the field of traditional representation.

In the first preparatory studies (Fig. 4.13) the candidate shows an ability to draw what is observed well, using a strong, flowing line to do so. The studies reveal a willingness to experiment with changes of scale, which affect the content of each little study, no matter that they are all drawn from the same group. You can also see the candidate changing position and eye level in the work, to good advantage. All this helps to provide suitable criteria for making a decision about the final composition of the work.

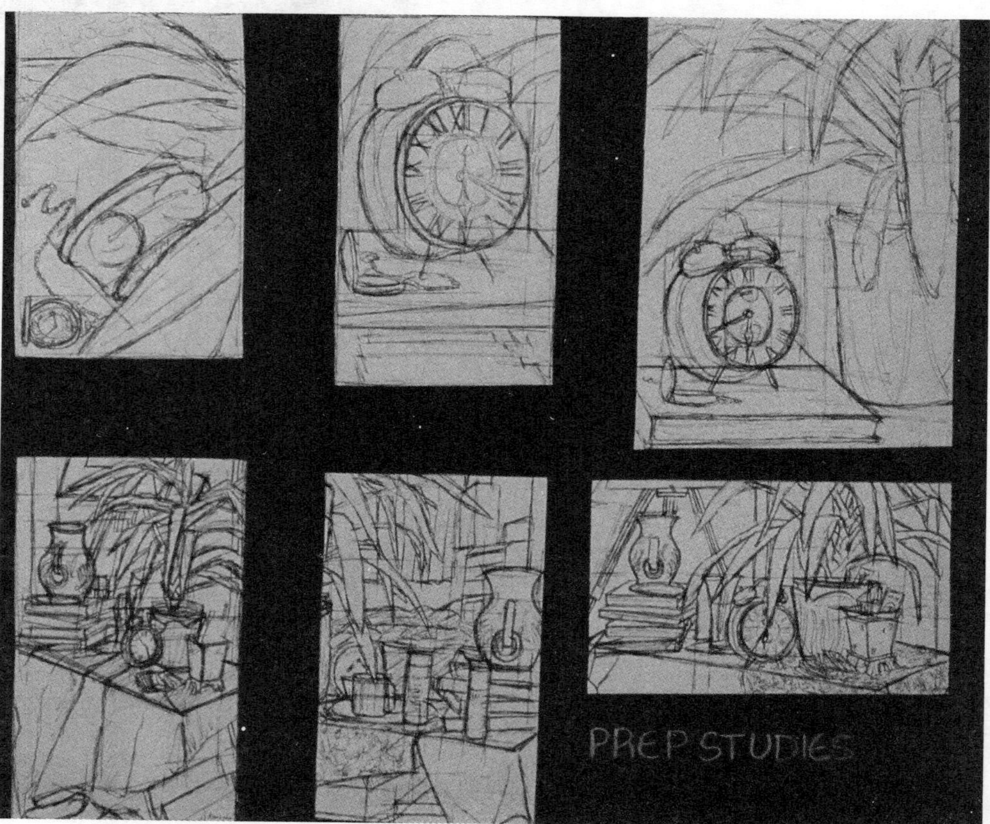

Fig. 4.13

It might have been this change in position and eye level that led the candidate towards the semi-Cubist appearance of the final work. After all, put over simply, one of the basic tenets of CUBISM was to see things from more than one place at the same time.

The second sheet of preparatory studies (Fig. 4.14) shows the candidate introducing a variation of medium into the work.

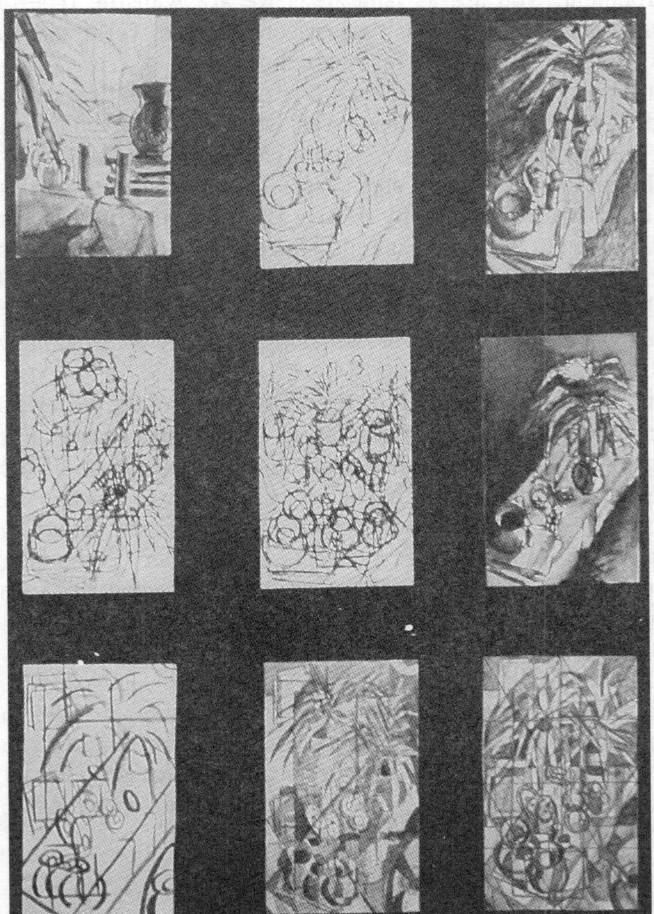

Fig. 4.14

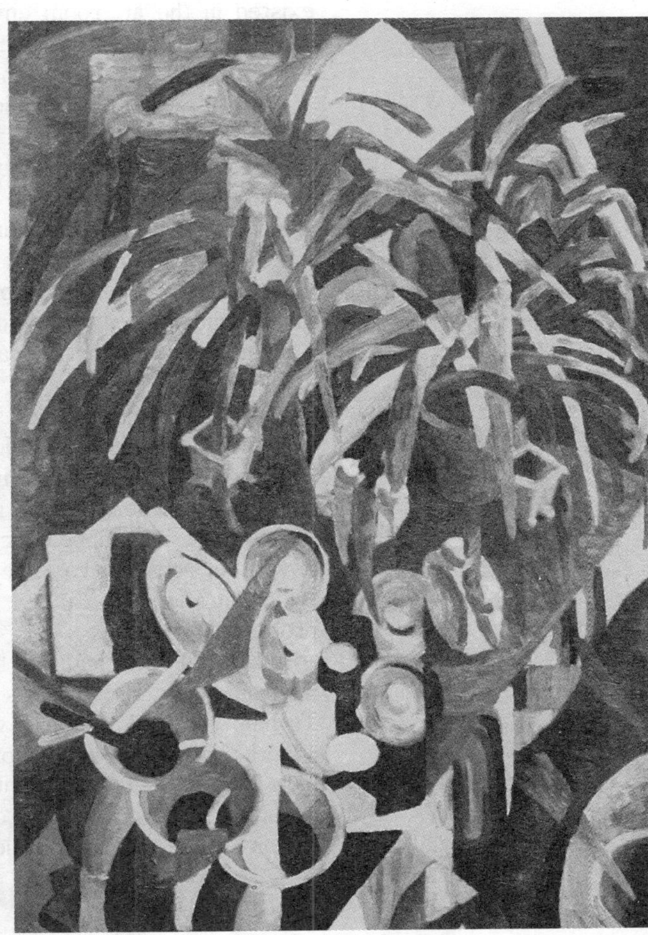

Fig. 4.15

The final work (Fig. 4.15) is an exciting result, well composed and expanding the interest right out to the boundaries of the picture. You might like to include this work in the analysis and comparison of the previous works we asked you to make earlier. It offers you a further variation on the Cubist theme.

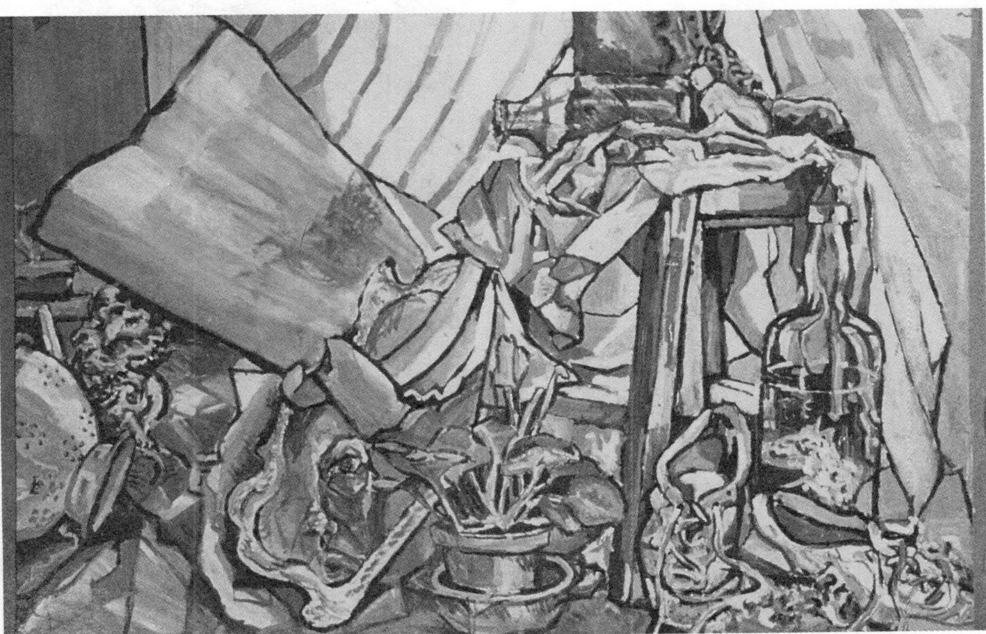

Fig. 4.16

In Fig. 4.16 we have an unsupported piece of work which is nevertheless a vigorous and successful still life. It points out, we feel, the problems of doing preparatory studies in which it is expected that you should explore the group visually. In this work, such preparatory studies were not carried out. Instead the candidate used the time to recognise a good, promising group, only the group was to be a more or less natural one which existed in the art room environment. You are as familiar as we are with the type of environment to be found in art rooms, and although this is obviously a well-arranged natural group, it captures the ambient conditions of many art rooms!

A further part of the candidate's preparatory studies was to further research the history of art. A modern British artist, JOHN BRATBY (1928–), was known to the candidate. During the preparatory studies period the candidate visited a gallery to see the artist's work at first-hand and read all that could be found about him. The influences of all this are present in the work, **but in no way is it a copy of any Bratby painting**, or just a mere pastiche of his style. A pastiche is when someone studies and learns an artist's style and just uses it to produce work, without necessarily having any fundamental understanding of *why* the work was as it was in the first place. In this case, the work is a natural response by the candidate to the stimulus of the subject matter, which is busy and chaotic.

One of the major problems in still-life work is to show the visual effect of the materials from which the different objects are made. Each has a different surface appearance. For instance, you might be trying to convey the **shininess** of chrome in contrast to the **furriness** of the skin of a peach. In addition, you might be called upon to convey the three-dimensional appearance of objects in works which are more usually flat. Studying how other artists have achieved this is important, as we emphasised earlier. In the next two illustrations we can see how two different candidates have come to terms with such problems.

In Fig. 4.17 the candidate has been confronting the problem of portraying glass, pottery, fruit and fabric. How well the problem has been solved overall we leave for you to decide. To help you to do this it is worth noting that if you have enough contrasting surfaces in a work, you are probably more able to build up a comparative scale of surfaces than if you have only one or two different surfaces among the objects in your group. What is significant in Fig. 4.17 is the way the candidate has used the surface pattern of lines on the fabric to convey the three-dimensional effect of the cloth in the picture.

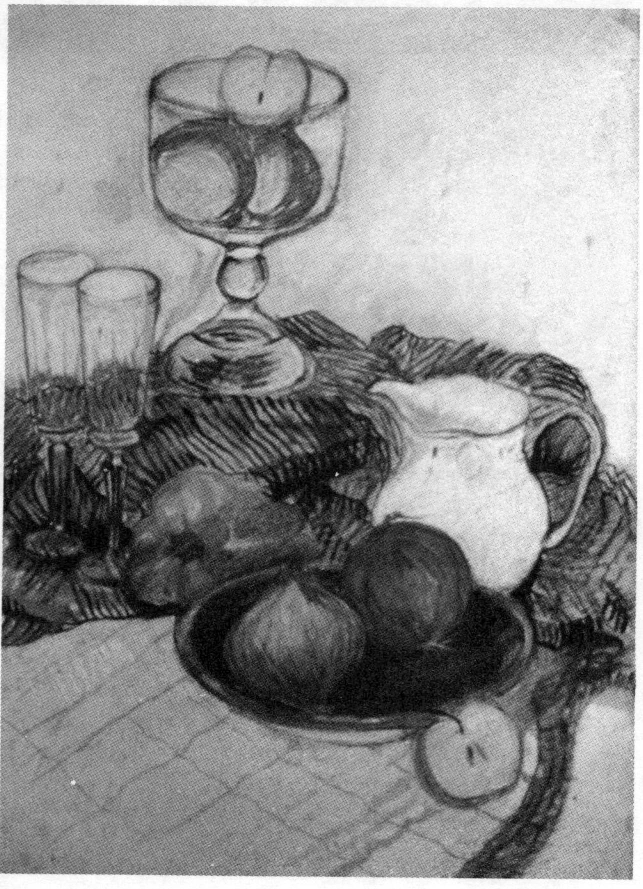

Fig. 4.17

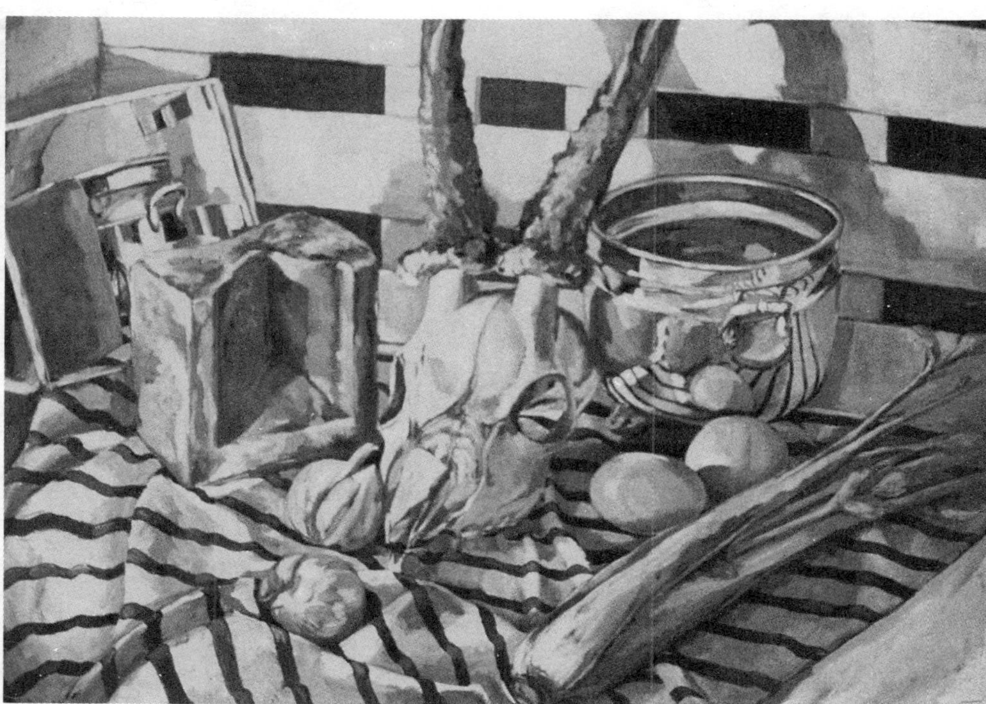

Fig. 4.18

In Fig. 4.18 different devices and paint-handling techniques have been used to show the differing surfaces of the objects within the group. The reflections in the large copper pot have been painted in a fluid manner. A linear technique for handling the paint in the celery has been very effective. For the half brick, the paint has been dabbed on in small patches of colour. Despite these variations, the result still has an integrated appearance.

Figs. 4.19 and 4.20 are examples of pure painting and are within the finest traditions of still life. Two of the studies in Fig. 4.19 show some tendency to experiment with viewpoints and eye levels. In Fig. 4.20 we see a simple but sound composition, where the size of the items within it is carefully related to the picture edges. We can also see a developed appreciation of the qualities of paint and painting techniques, a tonal distribution throughout the picture which adds to its sense of solidity, and a fine expressive feeling for the surfaces of the objects within the subject. All in all it allows a useful comparison with the work of someone like GUSTAVE COURBET (1819 – 77), whose work is illustrated in Fig. 4.21.

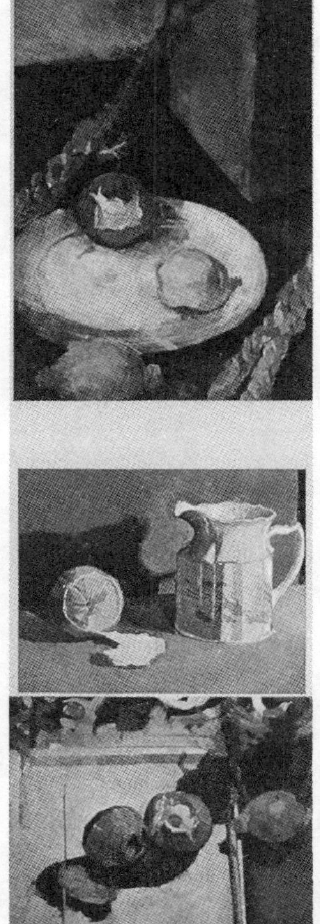

Fig. 4.19

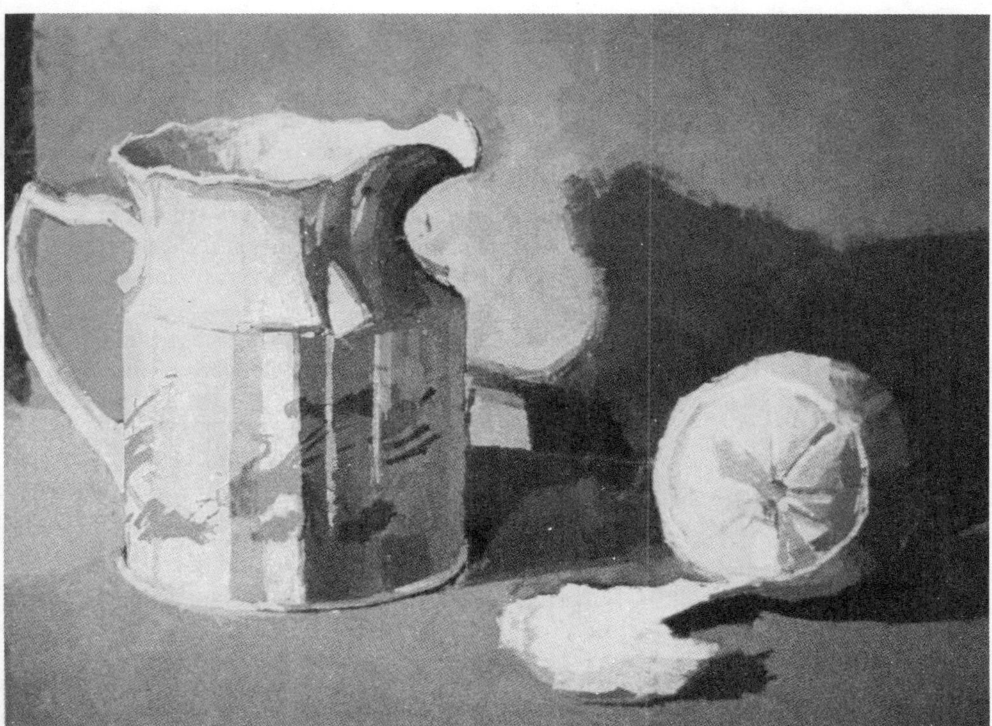

Fig. 4.20

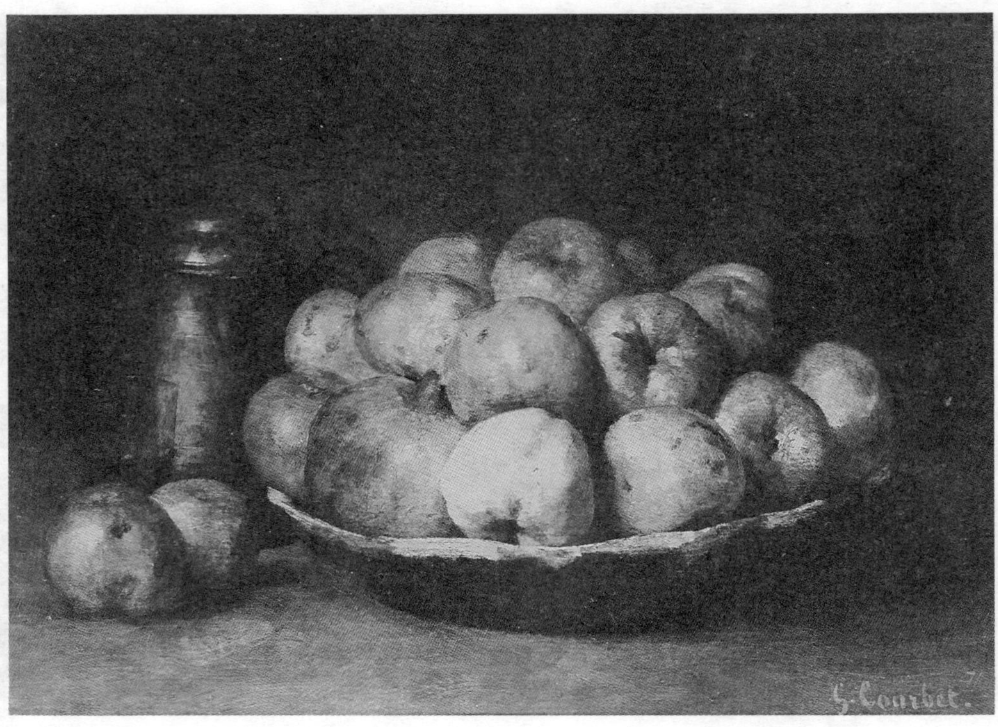

Fig. 4.21 'Still Life with Apples and a Pomegranate', Gustave Courbet (reproduced by permission of the Trustees of the National Gallery, London).

EXERCISES

1 Arrange a still-life group on the basis of the colours of the objects you choose to use. First, make a collage using coloured papers, doing no more than tearing your paper to represent the shapes of colour in your group. You should count the spaces in between objects as positive shapes. You may, if you wish, include colour changes on the surface of an object. Next, do a collage in black and white paper only, on grey. This time show the tonal changes within the group and the colours of the objects. You have only three degrees of tone (black, grey and white) to convey the changes you can identify. Now, disregarding the actual still-life group, make a painting in colour from your two collages. As you do so, alter the colour and tonal distribution shown in your collages, so that you *improve* the overall composition of your work without changing the size, shape or placing of the various objects in your picture.

When this is done, write down the changes you have made, why you made them and what you think of the result.

2 Study the work of the following artists:

IVON HITCHENS (1893 – 1979)
HENRI TOULOUSE-LAUTREC (1864 – 1901)
GEORGES SEURAT (1859 – 91)

Using only a coloured stick medium, such as a crayon, pastel or coloured pencils, arrange a single still life and try to portray it in the style of each artist, using the *same* stick medium each time. If it proves difficult or impossible to do this, first change the still-life group to fit the medium you are using. If it is still difficult or impossible to carry the work out in the style of *each* artist, change the medium you are using for any of the artists.

Collect and present *all* your works at the end, *including* the 'failures'. Try to write a critical appraisal of them and the work of the three artists concerned.

3 Arrange a still-life group which comprises fruit such as tomatoes and walnuts. Do a monochromatic and a coloured study of the group, portraying the fruit at least as big as footballs. That is to say, in your study the smallest fruit must be the actual, physical size of a real football. Show everything you can observe on the surface of each fruit in the group.

4 Arrange a group which has objects within it whose surfaces show the following qualities:

- the coldness of chrome;
- the soft warmth of wool;
- the wetness of fish scales;
- the smooth modulations of an apple;
- the transparency of water.

First, set up a series of experiments to test the effectiveness of different media to portray the surface of each object in the group in turn. Document your experiments each time. When you are satisfied that you understand the underlying qualities of each surface, then portray the whole group, integrating the appearance of your work into a satisfactory whole.

5 Collect reproductions of the still-life works of three artists where they have each tackled the same subject matter. We suggest you choose:

PAUL CÉZANNE (1839 – 1906)	'Still Life with Water Jug', the Tate Gallery, London
JAN DAVIDSZ DE HEEM (1606 – 1683)	'Still Life with Lobster', The Wallace Collection, London
MATTHEW SMITH (1879 – 1959)	'Apples', the Tate Gallery, London

Each of these three artists, in the pictures specified, painted apples. Investigate how they each worked and show your understanding of why their results look different, even though they were each painting the same subject matter.

6 Arrange a still life and do four studies from it. Each separate study should have as its essential nature one of the following principles, in turn:

- an illusory result;
- an expressive result;
- an interpretative result;
- an abstract result.

To do this exercise you will need to define most carefully what each principle means before you start work.

CHAPTER 5 PICTORIAL COMPOSITION

GETTING STARTED

Pictorial composition is sometimes called 'working from a Theme', or a 'Topic'. It is usual for you to be given a **title**, a passage of **prose**, a **poem**, or even a general **idea** to work from in your examination. For the purposes of this book we shall call all these things the **theme**.

In the question paper you will usually find that you have a number of such themes to choose from. This means that you must make a number of initial decisions, such as whether to include figures in your work; whether the environment represented in your work is to be an interior or an exterior; whether your subject matter is to be concerned with the urban landscape or the rural landscape; whether your subject matter is to involve the representation of land, sea, air or space, among other choices. Your choices will obviously be guided by what you have done during your coursework and by your interests. It is, of course, to be hoped that during your coursework, what you do will coincide more and more with your interests, although at the beginning it might be necessary to engage in activities that equip you more with the **means** to work than the opportunity to do what you want.

For your pictorial composition it will be normal for you to have your question paper a number of days in advance of the formal examination. During this time you prepare your ideas for what it is you will do during this test, by exploring the theme and by carrying out suitable experiments which will aid your final piece of work. We recommend most strongly that you do *not* use the time to do a 'dummy run' which you then repeat in the examination.

We regard it as essential that you read Chapter 4 *fully* and take its message in conjunction with this chapter. It is quite usual in A-level Pictorial Composition examinations to be told that your work must be done in colour. Still life is one of the most fundamental means by which artists develop an ability to control their media, which includes colour theory and knowledge, and to understand the traditional values and 'rules' associated with art and design. Therefore, most of what we have had to say in Chapter 4 will apply here. We would go even further and say that it would be in your interest to do some still-life painting, even if you consider that pictorial composition is the practice you will undertake for your examination.

In producing a pictorial composition many factors have to be considered. You need to concentrate on your ideas and intent; you have to grapple with the problem of working outside, or of combining outside studies with studio work; and you will often have to come to terms with the problem of a changing light. Because the contents of a still-life group stay still and can be studied in a fairly consistent light, you can learn a great deal about handling and controlling your medium in order to obtain certain effects. This will stand you in good stead when you are wrestling with the complex problems associated with pictorial composition. Again, doing a still life as a specific exercise to explore a certain problem can be both beneficial and time-saving in terms of pictorial composition.

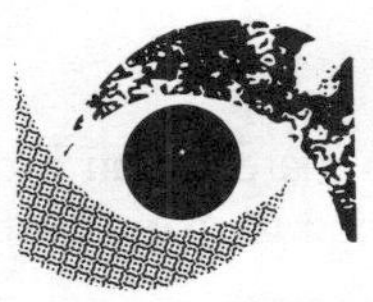

ESSENTIAL PRINCIPLES

DEFINITION OF THE TERM

Unlike the term still life, where the two words combine to form one concept, pictorial composition is a term which contains two distinct parts.

Composition

Composition is a traditional and familiar term in art and design. It is generally taken to mean **the arrangement of the component parts of a piece of work into a balanced and harmonious pattern or whole**.

This involves not only the objects or subject matter which make up the piece of work, but also the arrangements of colour and tone involved in the work, as well as the considerations of pattern and texture. It may also concern the problem of rendering on a flat, two-dimensional surface the interpretations of three-dimensional reality. We say 'may' because in some abstract work, and in all non-representational work, the two-dimensional surface of the work is the only reality. That is to say, because the work does not represent anything else, the only reality associated with it is its own material form and arrangement. The work is the 'real thing'. It does not set out to copy or stand in place of something else.

“Defining 'composition'.”

Composition in art and design means that the overall appearance of the work is more important than the quality of its component parts. Learning and then just obeying standards and rules will not necessarily result in work which is satisfactorily arranged for the 'eye to behold'.

Pictorial

The dictionary definition of pictorial is '**expressed by the means of pictures; illustrated**'. From this you can see that in pictorial composition you are setting out to illustrate your theme according to some set of values and standards which are already well established in art and design. That is to say, no matter what your subject might be or your personal approach to it is, you are **composing and presenting your ideas in a pictorial form which has certain recognisable qualities and traditions within it**.

“Defining 'pictorial'.”

AESTHETIC CONSIDERATIONS

In work using this practice or genre it is common to expect that you will show some degree of originality in your work. This comes from such things as:

“Sources of originality.”

- the media you choose to use;
- the way that you use such media;
- the viewpoint you adopt in responding to the set theme;
- the direction and degree of interpretation you introduce into your work;
- how you understand, use and adopt the work of artists from the past.

If you add these points *to* the principles inherent in carrying out a satisfactory pictorial composition – implied in the definitions we considered above – you have a checklist to apply to the aesthetic content of your work.

Once again, the 'formal elements' will feature strongly in your work. These are listed in Chapter 4. Refresh your memory before you go any further. Both the decision-making aspects of your work and the appearance of it will result from your consideration and use of the formal elements.

An important point about this practice is the need to understand the difference between what is known as **pure painting** and other forms of work carried out in colour. We have touched upon this before and if you remember, we distinguished between work that depends upon definite outlines to separate each form within it and work that determines the forms by means of colour changes alone. Later in this chapter we will consider the matter further.

MATERIALS, TOOLS AND EQUIPMENT CONSIDERATIONS

Your knowledge of materials will serve you well in this practice. When you are working from direct observation – a common approach for this genre – 'seeing' what a thing looks like depends as much upon your materials' knowledge as it does upon what you see. If something *looks* rough to the touch, this is because of the experiences which your sense of touch has given you as much as your sense of sight. If you then have sufficient materials' knowledge you will know that a thin wash of colour is hardly likely to convey this feel of roughness. It might well be that you will need to experiment with materials in order to get an effect you can 'see'. This might be because you have not tried to use a particular material to achieve such an effect before.

When you are working on a much more interpretative and **imaginative** level, as you often will be in pictorial composition, then again your materials' knowledge will be invaluable. Perhaps as an example of this Fig. 5.1, 'Snow-Storm: Steam-Boat off a Harbour's Mouth', by J. M. W. TURNER (1775 – 1851), will help to make the point. It is highly likely that Turner did experience an event such as the one he depicts here, but his painting depends just as much upon his knowledge of materials, his artistic intentions, his feelings and his imagination as it does upon 'sight'.

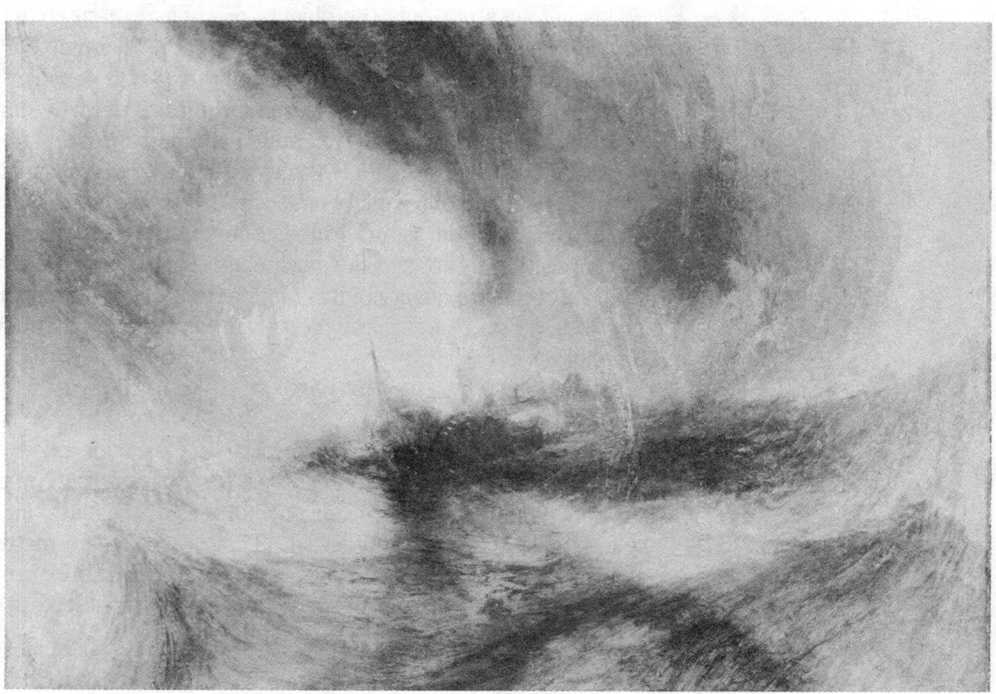

Fig. 5.1 'Snow Storm: Steam Boat off a Harbour's Mouth', J. M. W. Turner (reproduced by permission of the Tate Gallery, London).

“Use a varied approach.”

Because of this it is important that you should get into the habit of exploring your ideas and creating your responses to things you can see by using a wide variety of materials, tools and equipment. When you are beginning to investigate a theme, get into the habit of working in a way which adopts a variety of approaches, and uses a wide range of materials.

It is probably very easy to see that you could use photography to record the things before you; after all, as we have said before, this has been a fairly common approach since the invention of photography. The danger is that you will then use the resulting photographic image either to copy or to remind you of what it was you thought you saw in the first place. We advocate that you study your photographic prints much more closely and analytically than this. If you do, you will no doubt be surprised at just how much you had *not* seen in the first instance! The popular 1960s film *Blow Up* played upon this fact. In it a photographer who had been taking photographs in a park thought he could see a murder being committed behind a bush when he printed his film. As a result he kept on enlarging his negatives – hence the film's title – in order to see just what was actually happening. In *Blow Up* no murder was in fact captured on the photograph.

This film illustrates that as you enlarge a negative, the images become less a representation of reality and begin to take on a reality of their own. We mean by this that the grain of the paper gives an increasingly abstract image, in a series of increasingly disconnected 'dots'. As a result, instead of seeing more, you see something else. This is what we have been stressing about different media: each has an identity of its own which is distinctive and real; it does not exist merely to simulate something else. This is the kind of knowledge that is so important in your work.

In your investigative work try to be adventurous. Take risks. For instance, if you are trying to capture the effects of clouds scudding across the sky, why not model them in clay? It is difficult to see how to draw clouds so that they look solid, soft, wet, threatening and so on, but modelling them, perhaps only in relief, you can get your hands to 'feel' what they look like. The clay is soft and has an affinity with what it is you are seeing. If you then fire the clay and go on to rub oxides into it to show light and dark, you might then find that your work has a relationship with the cloud studies that someone like JOHN CONSTABLE achieved in paint and pencil. If this is so, your own practical experiences will have led you to a greater understanding of the way in which Constable worked, and then to a way of working in paint and pencil of your own. Get used to taking imaginative 'leaps in the dark' and then to connecting one thing you find out with another. This is a major contribution to the growth of artistic knowledge and a higher level of originality will result.

When you add the kind of materials' knowledge gained by personal experience to the knowledge gained by analysing how others have used similar media, then you have greater command and control over what you do than you would if you just learned a few 'techniques' in the medium concerned. The type of information and guidance you find in 'How To Do It' books, or receive from your teachers is invaluable, *provided* it is accompanied by a gain in your personal experience through experimentation and study of how others have worked, both in the past and in the present.

All of what we have said so far is tied up closely with the notion of **interpretation**. This goes on in all art and design works, even those which seem to be totally preoccupied with obtaining a 'photographic likeness'. When artists are working to get a photographic likeness, they still have to interpret and use the qualities of the media at hand. Of course, part of this interpretation is also tied up with their ability to discern what things in front of them *really* look like, which may be quite different from the initial impression given by the external facade.

A photographic likeness is sometimes referred to as 'reality'. The question is, what is reality? We suppose you might describe it as a form of the **truth**. Yet, the artist PAUL GAUGUIN said that art was a '***truth greater than naturalism***'. What do you think he meant by this?

CRAFTSMANSHIP

Again, you need to produce your work according to acceptable standards. What was said in Chapter 4 in this respect applies in full here, so we advise you to reread that section fully before going any further.

Study how an artist like JOHN WILLIAM WATERHOUSE (1849 – 1917) displayed such a high level of craftsmanship and command over his materials to create the effect of weeds, water and cloth when he painted 'The Lady of Shalott' (Fig. 5.2). In contrast, STANLEY SPENCER (1891 – 1959) in 'Swan Upping at Cookham' (Fig. 5.3) achieves another form of reality in portraying similar materials in his painting, but clearly displays the same high level of craftsmanship.

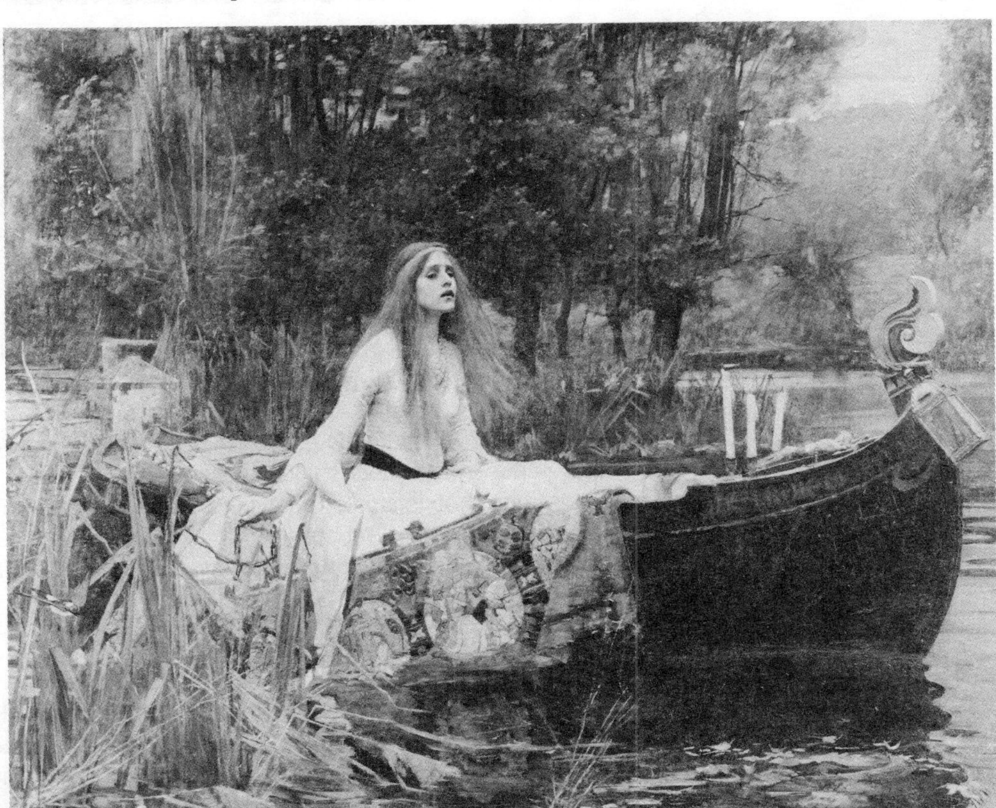

Fig. 5.2 'The Lady of Shalott', John William Waterhouse (reproduced by permission of the Tate Gallery, London).

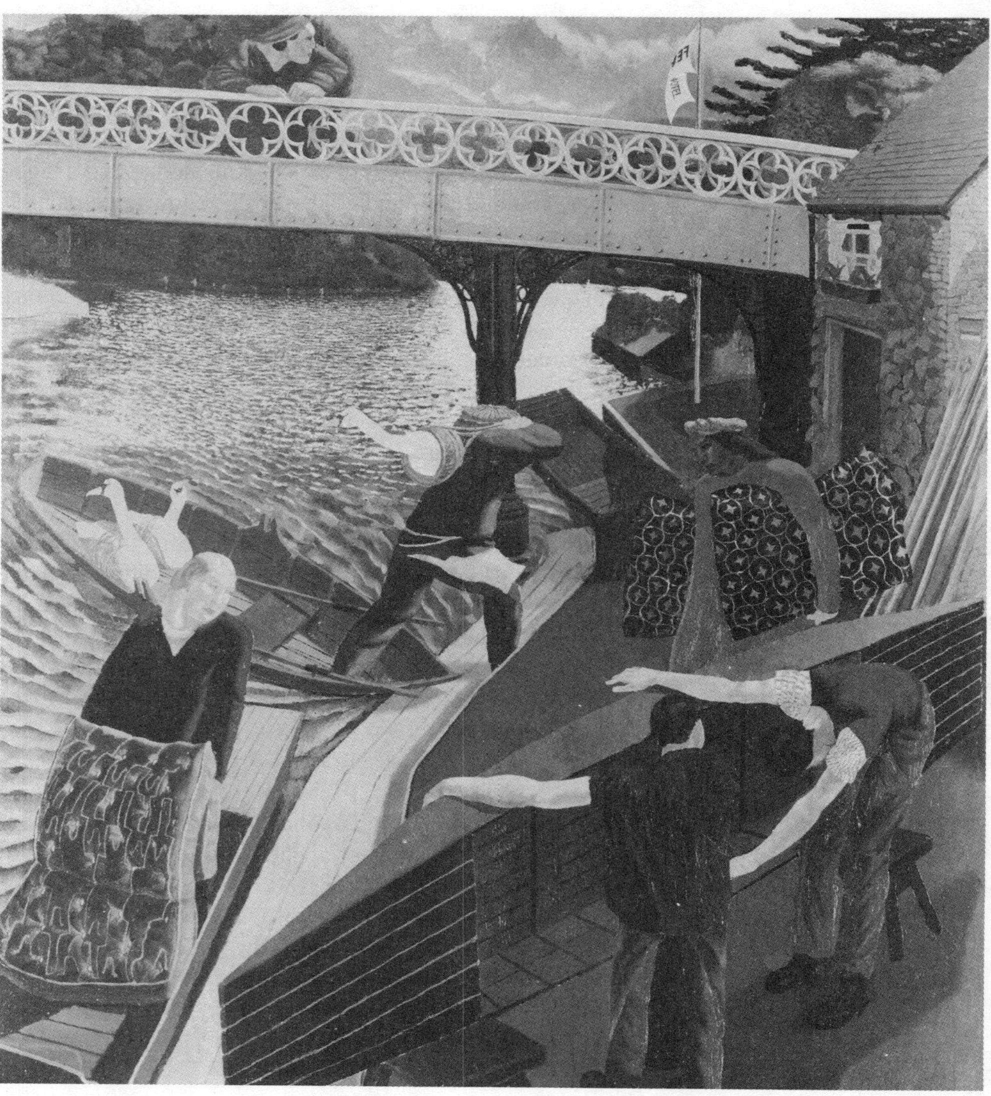

Fig. 5.3 'Swan Upping at Cookham', Stanley Spencer (reproduced by permission of the Tate Gallery, London).

Part of the craftsmanship in both cases is related to the clarity of interpretation each brings to bear in his work. It is not that Spencer is working on a *more* interpretative level but rather on a *different* interpretative level. Study these two reproductions closely and see if you can recognise and explain what each artist has done to achieve his results. We do not mean by this that you should merely give an account of how they have painted their pictures, although this would be part of your analysis; you should also try to explain what effect of 'reality' each artist decided to aim for.

There is, of course, another form of craftsmanship, to do with materials' technology. This involves using materials in a technically correct way, so that they will last, if not for ever, certainly for centuries. This is an important aspect of any artist's work. You may not agree, when your work has to last only two years – that is to say, until the time of your examination. Yet the possibilities which different materials provide are closely linked to their technical qualities. Therefore, it is important that you study the technology concerned. Apart from learning how to ensure that your work does not fade away or slip off the paper altogether, such knowledge can assist you in your decisions and interpretations. For example, knowing that grease and water do not mix can help direct your experiments using a mixture of wax crayon and water colour. Many other possibilities in your work can be opened up by an awareness of materials' technology.

HISTORICAL FACTORS

"Using figures in your composition."

Once more, all that we wrote in the previous chapter under this heading applies here. However, because this particular practice in art and design has a much longer identifiable history and a much wider set of boundaries than still life, there are many more examples for you to consider in your studies. Most of what has gone on in the history of art, and still goes on today, could be said to fall under the umbrella of pictorial composition.

If you find that a particular subject matter interests you, collect together as many examples as possible of how your subject matter has been covered throughout history.

For instance you might like to include **figures** in your compositions. The illustrations we have drawn upon so far in this chapter have presented you with work from only a limited period of history, roughly 1850 to 1950. Two of these contain figures. One is from this century and the other from the last century. You could collect an example of a figure composition from *each* century in the history of art and design. For example, you could get a picture, reproduced either from a cave painting or perhaps an Aboriginal tree bark painting. The Egyptian tomb paintings would give you something from about 1000 BC. Greek vase paintings could cover the period 500 to 200 BC. Roman mosaics would span the years from, say, 100 BC to AD 300. The Bayeux Tapestry is a good example of work from the eleventh century AD. After that you come into the period represented by some of the great painters of the world: GIOTTO (*c.*1276 – 1337), PIERO DELLA FRANCESCA (*c.*1410 – 92), EL GRECO (1541 – 1614), REMBRANDT (1606 – 69), GOYA FRANCISCO (1746 – 1828) and EDOUARD MANET (1832 – 83). Together these will give you some useful points of reference to guide you up to the present day.

If you do start a collection such as this, keep adding to it as you find further examples which come into your theme. You could add to your collection by purchasing postcards from galleries and museums and you could also photocopy some work from books. This is legal if it is a part of your study. If you do make collections such as this, you could *compare* the way that different periods approached what we are choosing to call a common theme, perhaps relating your findings and opinions to your knowledge about the history of materials in art and design. Of course, although here we are calling compositions with figures in them a single theme, over the history of art and design such compositions have been done for distinctly different purposes. You would become more familiar with this if you follow up your subject's contextual history. You might then be able to narrow down the focus of your attention to some particular context involving the use of figures.

CONTEXTUAL INVESTIGATIONS

For example, you might find out about religious painting, or the use of mythology and allegory in art, perhaps by following these aspects up in a book such as Gombrich (1975). This can lead you to some valuable contextual knowledge. Very broadly, when the Church provided patronage, artists often undertook religious paintings in response to that patronage. This is not to say that the artists did not hold deeply religious convictions of their own, but they worked at a time when patronage provided the traditional support and direction for art. On the other hand, when someone such as STANLEY SPENCER painted biblical stories this century, he did it for himself and entirely out of his own religious convictions. This is because the context surrounding the support of art and artists had long since changed. The Church no longer offered its patronage to the arts on the grand scale it had previously.

Even in the times of great patronages in the past, artists have not always obeyed the traditions and demands inherent in their particular brief. Of course, the culture represented by a particular society conditions most of what it is that artists and designers do and the way that they do it. Thus the values artists and designers hold are partly, at least, a product of the society and culture in which they exist. Nevertheless, it is still possible for any artist or designer to be at odds with the values represented by the society in which they live. When this is so, the result may well be work which appears to 'break the mould'. The various periods identified in the history of art and design are more or less indications of when the mould was broken. It is this inescapable fact that helps to account for some of the changes that have taken place in both the direction and the development of art and design, even though in retrospect those changes often seem evolutionary rather than revolutionary.

On some occasions an artist breaking the mould turns out to be a voice of conscience, helping to reshape and develop the society concerned. In our opinion FRANCISCO GOYA did this in 1810 when he began a series of etchings titled 'The Disasters of War'. He had previously enjoyed the royal patronage of the Spanish king Ferdinand VII, and might have expected to hold a similar position under Joseph Bonaparte, who was installed by Napoleon when he invaded Spain and drove out Ferdinand VII. Instead he produced his 'Disasters of War' etchings and two paintings, '2 May, 1808' and '3 May, 1808', both painted in 1814. These are works done in protest against the atrocities carried out by the French troops who upheld the rule of Joseph Bonaparte.

This behaviour was not untypical of Goya. He had earlier, while accepting commissions from the Church, published a set of etchings called '*Los Caprichos*', in which he made satirical attacks upon the various ways of the Church. In the case of the 'Disasters of War' etchings, the Spain of Joseph Bonaparte was the society and culture in which Goya lived. Perhaps because of the depth of his outrage at what he saw happening around him, his works make us even more aware of a society's influence upon an artist, even though Goya was in this case voicing a protest *against* the society and its ways. In his works he shows scenes of torture and killing in such a vivid way as to make us revile a society which could do such things. At the time they may even have helped the society in question to revile itself, and to search its own collective conscience.

In turn, PABLO PICASSO's painting 'Guernica', done in 1936, is another protest against violent happenings in Spain – this time the Spanish Civil War. In that war the Italians bombed the village of Guernica, creating havoc and disaster to men, women, children and animals. Although Picasso was living in France at the time, in a different society and culture, his work shows how the devaluing which goes on in one society can affect a much wider community. What happened in Guernica certainly affected Picasso adversely. As a result his painting stands as a personal objection to, as well as a monument against, a society's values which can condone acts as atrocious as those of Guernica.

In terms of your contextual studies, you should follow up our rather opinionated accounts above, trying to find out more about the society in each case. If you do so, you might find out *why* the society acted in the way it did. This could either help excuse its behaviour or reinforce your distaste for what happened, a distaste those two artists clearly held in common.

"The importance of contextual knowledge."

We hope you can see from all this that understanding what it is artists and designers do, and why they do it, is possible only when you have information and knowledge from a variety of contextual circumstances surrounding the works and their production. If you get into this habit, you will have much more than your own emotional level of response on which to base your critical opinion, and you will have access to a broader range of aesthetic standards and principles by which to judge the works.

It might help you to understand this more if you look at the photographs of DON MCCULLIN who has photographed recent wars. Because you know the society and culture he represents, and something of the wars he documented, you will be in a good position to conduct your own critical appraisal of his work. The key point in any appraisal is the notion that we can understand things really well only by being aware of their contexts.

WORKING IN PICTORIAL COMPOSITION

What the examination syllabuses say

The examination syllabuses offer you considerable insight into what it is the examiners are expecting in your responses. This might be because picture-making with a story to tell is widely recognised as being the essence of fine art. Table 5.1 outlines the established syllabuses which explicitly include Pictorial Composition as an element of their examinations. Of course, the practice is relevant to a much wider variety of syllabuses than those indicated.

EXAMINING BOARD	SYLLABUS/TITLES USED
AEB	ART – PAINTING/603 Paper 1 – Practical Test 603/1 (Time allowed: 9 hours) i) Pictorial Composition Paper 2 – History and Technique 603/2 (Time allowed: 3 hours) Paper 3 – Coursework 603/3 ART AND CRAFTS/605 Paper 2 – Option 24 – Pictorial Composition 605/2/20 (Time allowed: 3 hours) Paper 2 – Option 25 – History and Appreciation of Art 605/2/25 (Time allowed: 3 hours) Paper 3 – Coursework
NISEC	SYLLABUS A Paper III: Pictorial Composition (Time allowed: 3 hours) Paper V: History of Art (Time allowed: 3 hours) SYLLABUS B Section 1 – Main Study (Time allowed: 15 hours) 1. Painting Section 2 – Analytical and Written Study (Time allowed: 3 hours)

EXAMINING BOARD	SYLLABUS/TITLES USED
	Section 3 – History and Appreciation of Art, Architecture and Design (Time allowed: 3 hours, plus Extended Essay) Part 1 History of Painting Section 4 – Coursework
OXFORD	ART with ART HISTORY/9894 Paper 1 – History of Art (Time allowed: 3 hours) Section II. History of Painting Paper 3 – Imaginative Work in Two-dimensional Media 9894/3 (Time allowed: Extended Period) Paper 4 – Imaginative Work in Two-dimensional Media 9894/4 (Time allowed: Extended Period) *[See Table 3.18 about mixing Paper 3 and Paper 4]*

Table 5.1 Terms used to describe 'Pictorial Composition' in the various established examination syllabuses.

Pure painting

Part of any attitude about fine art involves this matter of what exactly constitutes pure painting. So far we have suggested that it is to do with defining shapes in a way that does not outline them. This is not the only way to work successfully using paint, but it is widely recognised as a measuring point in art and design. There are, of course a range of approaches, which might be said to run from pure painting on the one hand to filling-in between the thick black lines in a children's picture book on the other. There are a lot of stages in between the two extremes, as you will no doubt be aware.

The notion of pure painting is related to the development of **oil painting** in the history of art and design. This medium, in contrast to **tempera**, allows the images in a picture to be 'reworked' while still wet, and the edges of one form to be 'blended' into another because of this. In the case of tempera (which is powder colour bound with egg in order to make it workable), when the shapes are painted in, the colour dries almost immediately. This creates a defined, hard edge between the shapes. Of course, it is possible to use oil paints, or acrylics, in a similar manner if you so wish.

To explain the concept of pure painting a little further it is necessary to set out some of the terminology used in the theory of colour. This terminology is not jargon, but is part of the specialist language of the subject you are studying and as such should be learned by you. We advise you to obtain and study a good book on the theory of colour, such as that by Itten (1969).

Colour has various terms which define its qualities and content. The essential ones are:

"Terms describing the qualities and content of colour."

- HUE – that quality which distinguishes one colour from another, e.g. orange from red, red from blue, and so on;
- CHROMA – the measure of the pure colour content of a colour; the chroma of one colour is changed by adding a colour to the original which is opposite to it in the colour wheel;
- INTENSITY/SATURATION – terms used to convey much the same as chroma; a more intense version of a colour, or a more saturated version of a colour, is a purer value of that colour;
- TONE – the degree of light or dark that appears to be in a colour; the tone of a colour can be changed by adding either black or white to the original colour, although such additions can also change the hue;
- SHADE – the term given when black is added to a colour: thus maroon is a shade of red, navy blue a shade of blue;
- TINT – the term given when white is added to a colour: thus pink is a tint of red, sky blue a tint of blue;
- TEMPERATURE – the apparent visual warmth or coolness of a colour. The temperature of one colour is changed by adding to it the adjacent colour from the colour wheel: thus if you add violet to red you will make it cooler, whereas the addition of orange to red will make it warmer; from this you can see that blue is regarded as cold and red as hot in the colour wheel;
- WEIGHT – each colour appears to have a certain weight: thus in blues, ultramarine appears to be visually heavier than cobalt;

- COMPLEMENTARY – colours which are directly opposite each other in the colour wheel;
- JUXTAPOSITION – the placing of one colour against another. This involves consideration of a variety of qualities each colour could have and requires you to make critical decisions about the final, overall appearance of each colour concerned. It is these considerations which are so important in pure painting: you do not just paint each single object in turn;
- COLOUR WHEEL – a convenient way of laying out colours for reference in art and design; in this form, most of the terminology above, associated with colour, becomes self-evident (Fig. 5.4).

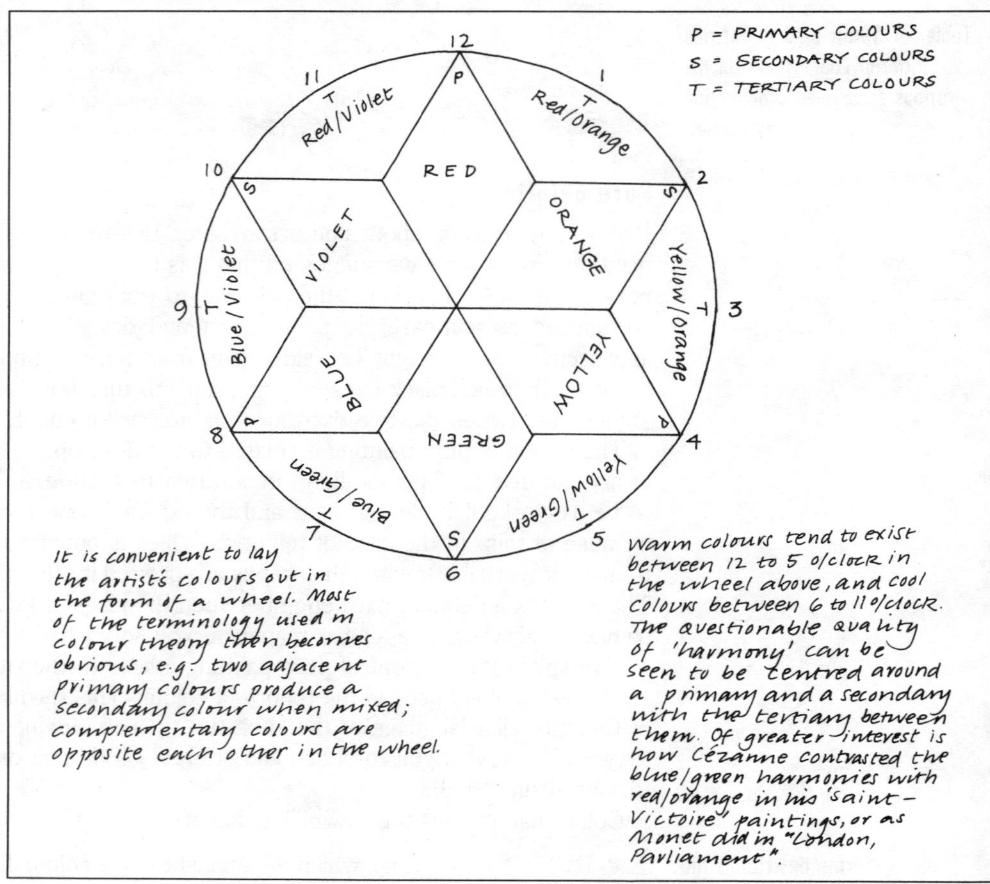

Fig. 5.4 The colour wheel.

To return now to the problems of pure painting, if you are *not* to define the edge of one shape with a line of some sort in order to distinguish it from the next shape, what are you to do?

It is obvious that if two shapes in juxtaposition are of two distinctively different hues, such as red and green, then each shape is easily and clearly defined by its contrasting colour alone. In the example here, the two colours are complementary – that is to say, exact opposites in most respects – which further exaggerates the contrasting situation.

However, you cannot always work your painting out so that you place contrasting colours in juxtaposition. What is more, you would be unwise to want to do this every time. When a red brick wall is seen against a red sunset, you need to consider qualities such as the tone, temperature, weight and saturation of a colour. It is likely that the wall will be in shadow. If so, this will alter the tonal quality of the red in the wall. It is also likely that the red in the wall will be cooler than the red in the sky. This will allow you to contrast the two items by means of the temperature quality each colour has. In turn, one red is likely to look heavier than the other. By playing up the quality of weight which is present, you can thereby define each item in your painting, without putting a line around, say, the wall.

In any situation there are many devices you can use in order to distinguish between shapes and forms in your work without resorting to the use of lines between them. Even so, two further things emerge.

The first consideration is whether it is necessary for you to distinguish distinctly between shapes! The eye does not do this in its immediate, overall view of a scene. It is when you look at each shape and form in turn that this separation begins to occur. Therefore, why not let one shape 'bleed' into another, with perhaps only the most subtle adjustment of the colours concerned. It is certainly sometimes helpful in your work to reconstruct two colours of contrasting hue so that they come closer and closer together. If you do not do this, there could be times when you might find it difficult to establish spatial relationships in your work, if that aspect is desired. For instance, you might have a bright-red car in your picture which is parked alongside a light-blue van. If you paint both 'as they are', it is likely that the car will appear to be closer to you than the van. The way to get over a problem such as this is to balance the intensity, temperature, tone and so on of the colours concerned.

The second consideration is whether it is possible to use lines in pure painting. We are not suggesting that you outline all around a form by this method, but you *can* put in lines which suggest shadows or optical effects. These usually depend upon the effect of complementary colours. Thus if you have fruit depicted in your work, you might introduce a blue line near the edge of the underside of an orange, to indicate a shadow. If you look at the colour wheel (Fig. 5.4), you will see that blue and orange are complementary colours, occurring opposite each other in the wheel. A close study of the still-life works of PAUL CÉZANNE will illustrate clearly what we mean by this device, which is central to the colour theory of the Impressionists.

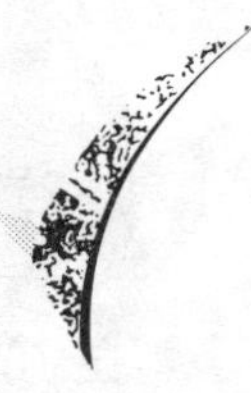

EXAMINATION QUESTIONS, STUDENT ANSWERS AND EXAMINER COMMENTS

As we said at the beginning of this chapter, in this section of your examination you are given a theme to work from. These themes are many and varied, covering a number of sources, such as poems or passages of prose, situations such as 'building sites' or 'market places', as well as concepts such as 'movement'.

To choose any one question to begin to answer will not only be inefficient but will also suggest that the content of the picture is more important than the way you approach the problem of pictorial composition. As we have stressed, we are emphatic that the *way* that you work is of paramount importance. Therefore, we shall 'answer questions' by analysing work by past candidates in response to a number and range of themes.

PRODUCING PICTORIAL COMPOSITIONS

Suggesting time and movement

We have already implied that nearly all that has been done in art, especially in two-dimensional work, is a form of pictorial composition. Much of it is a form of telling a story, recording an incident, conveying an idea, giving visual form to the imagination and so on, by the means of pictures. Of course, in art these pictures are static and largely stand in isolation from what we might call the reality of life. That is to say, pictures do not, or cannot, give a sense of the passage of time, even though they might reflect a time. At best they are most often seen as recording real life and at worst as recording mere frivolities as far as 'real life' is concerned.

Some work in art does try to get over this problem of art being rather static and isolated. In the first half of the eighteenth century the British artist WILLIAM HOGARTH (1697 – 1764) was 'telling stories' by means of a **series** of pictures. 'The Rake's Progress' and 'Marriage à la Mode' (Figs. 5.5 and 5.6), are examples of this. In the series 'Marriage à la Mode' there are six sequential pictures in the National Gallery, London. Postcard reproductions are available for purchase. Here we include the first two in the sequence so that you can see the ways in which Hogarth suggests the passage of time.

Hogarth's approach is similar to what we recognise now from comics, the only differences being, perhaps, that he did not include 'speech words' in his pictures, nor undertake so many pictures in order to tell his story. You may think that it was only right that he did not do so; after all, art is surely more serious than comics!

Well, ROY LICHTENSTEIN (1923), an American Pop artist, went so far as to include 'speech words' in his pictures and even copied some of his work from comic-book pictures. What do you think of this? Is it 'art'? It is often by trying to answer such questions that you develop your understanding of the subject you are studying. It might even be that if you

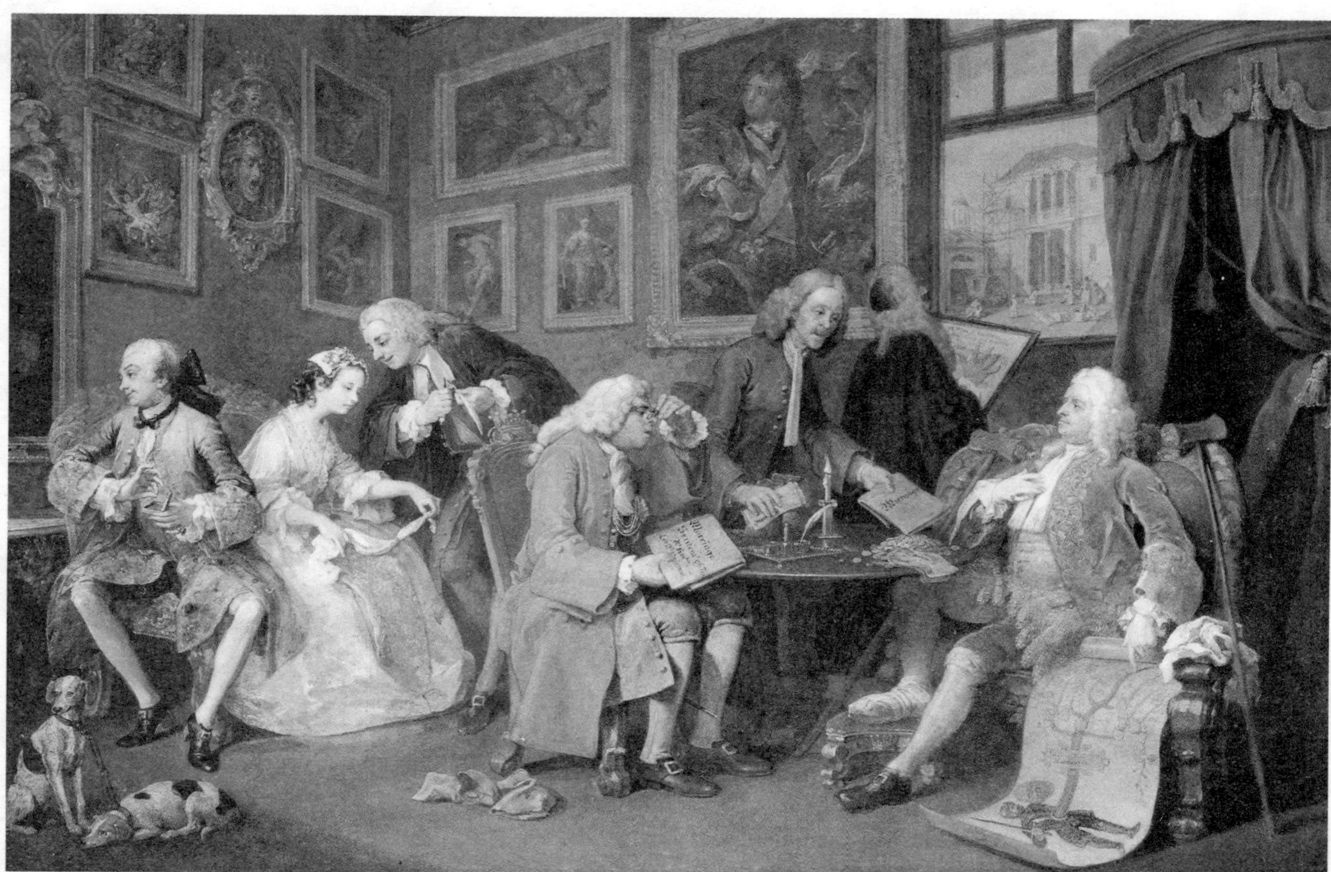

Fig. 5.5 'Marriage à la Mode: The Marriage Contract', William Hogarth (reproduced by permission of the Trustees of the National Gallery, London).

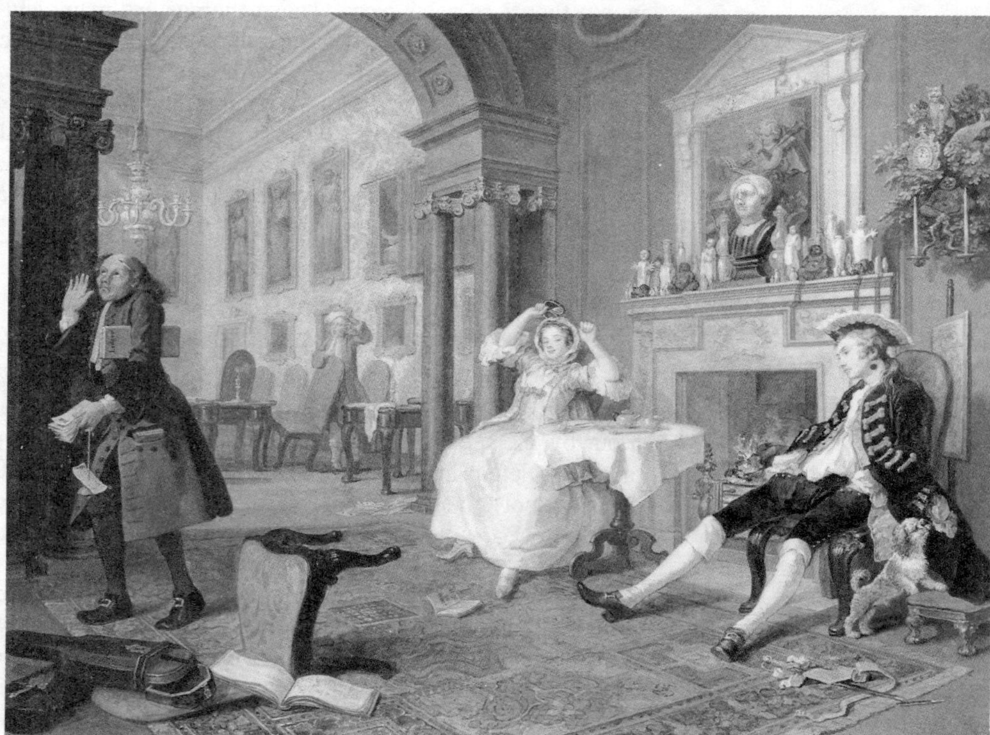

Fig. 5.6 'Marriage à la Mode: Shortly after the Marriage', William Hogarth (reproduced by permission of the Trustees of the National Gallery, London).

really wanted to work from such popular imagery as comic books, you will already have worked out your own justification for doing so!

Our view is that the work in comic books is an important sociological and cultural wing of art and is worthy of serious consideration as 'art' in its own right. Many comic-book artists produce work which not only obeys all the values and standards of art and aesthetics but also is executed much more proficiently than some recognised art. In any case, whatever the artistic value of the work in question, it is interesting to use such sources when studying the problem of portraying time, movement and changing location, and seeing how this has been overcome in comic-book work.

This aspect of time and motion has, of course, been taken up in films. Films are no more than a series of still pictures which simulate movement when projected at the correct speed. Are films anything to do with art? What about video? In this medium we no longer have even a series of single pictures as the basis of what is seen.

You may feel that there is no need for you to consider questions like this in your work, let alone begin to answer them. Our belief is that you *should* consider such things. It is the way your grasp of the subject grows.

Although repetition and practice is an important element in the improvement of your artistic ability, the level of your overall knowledge and understanding of the subject is also an important factor in such development and improvement. Above all else it encourages you to have a broader perspective, both in your thinking and in your work. You will then be more willing to take risks.

Words in art

We used the term 'speech words' earlier because it has long been the case that artists depict 'actual words' in their work. For instance, this is obviously true in the case of missals, manuscripts and the Bayeux Tapestry, as well as in many modern paintings by artists such as PABLO PICASSO. It is also true of Japanese art. If you study the woodcuts of, say, HOKUSIA (1760 – 1849), you will find that this is so. In Western art, GIOTTO (*c.*1276 – 1337) included a 'label' word in his wall painting in the Capella dell'Arena, Padua. This work is called 'Faith', and the word is painted as if engraved on a stone tablet in the picture. So we have examples of the use of words in pictures from more than one culture, from many societies and throughout the history of art and design. If this is the case in what we usually regard as fine art, why should we object to the inclusion of words in the circumstances in which an artist such as Lichtenstein uses them?

Some paintings are based almost entirely on words. We mentioned Picasso above. He painted pictures which are even known by a word which is visible within them. Another artist who used words as the subject of some of his pictures was KURT SCHWITTERS (1887 – 1948). He used the pattern of the letters, the visual shape and appearance of the words, the meanings of the word and the many emotional associations which various words have to compose his pictures and to give them meaning. He worked largely in collage, picking up pieces of paper, cards, tickets, packets and so on for inclusion as the basis of his pictures, but he also added paint to his works.

In Fig. 5.7 we see an A-level candidate using such an approach in pictorial composition. The subject seems to be a newspaper. Is it a headline we can read? The overlaying sheets of colour seem to create the feeling of a newspaper – namely, of revealing its story to us only bit by bit. In an actual newspaper we get the headline, then the subtitle. The story is gradually unfolding. Then we have to start to read the story, only to find it continues on another page. Folding and unfolding is one aspect of reading a newspaper. This candidate's work invokes that feeling. Shapes are carefully considered for size and position. All in all it seems to be a good piece of work. What do you think?

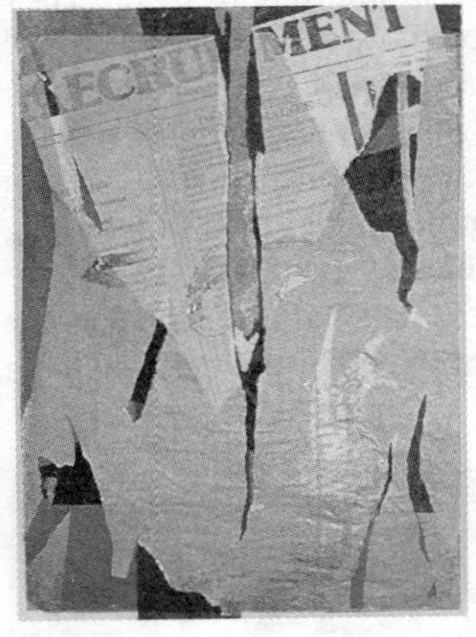

Fig. 5.7

Figure compositions

We have said already how important figure compositions are in the history of art. Most examinations include at least one question which will allow you to include figures in your work. It sometimes seems that the overwhelming majority of candidates choose to use figures in their examination work. We have already suggested that it would benefit you to study the use of figures in the compositions of others. Nevertheless, we feel most strongly that at your stage of development, if you *do* include figures in your work, you should use either *primary* sources for them – that is to say, models, friends and relatives who will be willing to pose for you – or *secondary* sources, such as photographs you have taken yourself or even photographs in papers, magazines and books.

The human figure is a complex structure and arrangement of parts. Its mobility and three-dimensional aspects are best analysed and understood by working directly from an actual person. If this is impossible, then good photographic references can help. 'Good' means that you have taken the photograph yourself, so that the figure is in the exact pose you planned, enabling you to take a series of photographs from all around the figure so that you can fully grasp its mass, weight and posture. Or a 'good' photographic reference could mean that you are using one of the collections of figures produced for the use of artists and designers. Or it could mean that you have found a photograph which gives you the real information you need, rather than leaving you having to guess most of it.

If you do end up working from photographs, beware of just copying their 'photographic' appearance. It is most likely that your final pictures will *not* look as if they have been copied from a photograph, and that being so, you do not want to introduce the incongruous element of a figure which looks more like a photograph than a painting or a drawing. This means that you need to do a lot of interpretation when working from a photograph.

Introducing the idea of secondary sources inevitably raises the question of whether you should copy the work of others in your own work. First of all, let us emphasise that you should *never* copy another artist's pictures. The examining boards insist that you avoid this and it is no use thinking that nobody will know the picture you are copying. Work where a picture is copied in its entirety has an appearance about it which seems to alert other artists, especially examiners! But the major reason for avoiding copying is that if you have made your course of study worthwhile, you will have no need to copy. Your own work will be interesting and exciting enough in itself and you will know enough about the standards and principles at stake in art and design to produce good, original work. It is only likely that you will feel a need to copy the ideas and work of others if, in your course of study, you have concentrated too much upon techniques and failed to equip yourself with the broadest knowledge and understanding of art and design in its fullest contexts.

Nevertheless, there *are* reasons for some copying from other artists during your course of study. Where this is done as an analysis of how another artist worked, it is a speedy way of gaining knowledge which can be easily absorbed into the framework of your own working approach.

In the past it has been reasonably certain that well-known artists have 'lifted' the compositions of others. The similarities between *'Déjeuner sur L'Herbe'* by EDOUARD MANET (1832 – 83) and the painting generally attributed to GIORGIONE (*c.*1476 – 1510), both in the Louvre, Paris, represent a classic example of this. In these works, whereas Manet's figures are clothed and enjoying a picnic in a park, Giorgione's are naked in a similar landscape, but grouped in essentially the same composition.

Rather than getting agitated, about the morality of copying, which is what Manet apparently did, it seems to us that the reasons for his clothing his figures are of more importance. These reasons are bound up with the contextual circumstances surrounding the two works and their production, and are worthy of exploration.

The thing to remember in a figure composition is to ensure that your figures are not just illustrating a story, or caught at an indefinite moment in an impromptu pose. They should form an essential part of the means by which you show how well you understand the principles of composition. Like the actors on a stage, they do not just happen to be there by accident. On the stage the director groups and arranges his or her actors visually from the point of view of the audience. That is to say, they are composed into a pattern or picture. You should do the same with your picture. Part of this might involve adopting a different viewpoint to the one you first thought of, or a different eye level. These are things which the director on the stage cannot do because the stage and the audience are mostly in a fixed physical relationship. So take full advantage of the opportunities you have as an artist in composing your pictures.

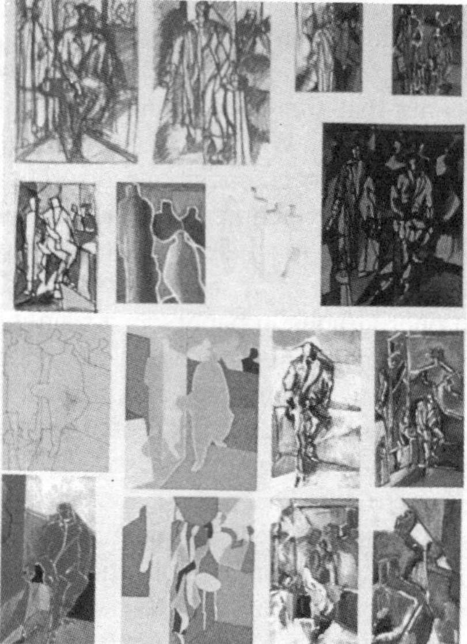

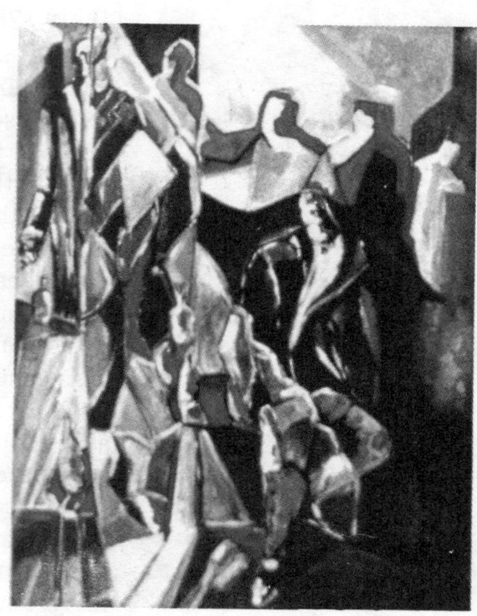

Fig. 5.8

Fig. 5.8 illustrates how a candidate has arranged, and then rearranged, the composition of the figures in the work. In addition, a wide range of media have been used during the preparatory studies. At the same time, the candidate seems to have explored different appearances in the work, which range through the representational to the almost abstract arrangement of shapes. The final composition and its appearance is very reminiscent of the work of EL GRECO. Try to find out why El Greco's work looks like it does, and then see if this candidate's preparatory studies lead logically to similar conclusions in the final composition and its appearance.

One of the major features about this set of work is the quality and complexity of the actual compositions in the various studies. They show an awareness and consideration of the rectangular frame the paper provides. This, after all, is the starting point of any composition. If the actual shape and size of the paper is *not* taken into account from the beginning, you are unlikely to arrive at a completely satisfying composition. All too often in art and design we see examples of work which is simply 'done in the middle of the paper'. The paper in art and design is a lot more important than it is in fish and chips!

Because of such awareness in these works, the shapes in between the figures and behind them are an important and integrated part of the whole jigsaw of the shapes which together make up the pictures. The successful arrangement of all the shapes, the negative as well as the positive ones, is a fundamental problem to be solved in any good composition. It is a matter of mixing large shapes and small shapes, square shapes and round shapes, spiky shapes and smooth shapes and so on in a satisfying and exciting arrangement. If you can think of your work in this way, rather than as a matter of including a man and a woman, a boat or a bus or whatever, you will find that your powers of compositional skill will develop beyond recognition.

Interiors and exteriors

Many examination questions allow you to set your own scene. Whether your picture is an interior or an exterior can be largely up to you. What, then, are the pros and cons of the alternatives?

The major distinguishing feature seems to us to be the question of light. In a daytime **exterior**, the light in your picture is mostly coming from all directions above your scene. This means that apart from using colours which convey a sense of the outdoors, you do not have too much of a problem in this respect. If you study some of the work of the Impressionists, you will see what we mean by being able to include in your work an overall sense of daylight. Actually 'painting' light was the essence of much of the work of the Impressionists, but that is another matter.

If you want to include strong sunlight, then you have the problem of painting defined shadows and keeping a level of consistency throughout your work. By this we mean that you will be unable to see the same shadows for any extended period of time because the sun will move. In these circumstances there seems every reason to take a black-and-white photograph of your scene, in addition to the other studies you will do in preparation for it. Once you are back in the studio, you will be able to see just what shapes the shadows actually made. One of the advantages of choosing to include a very strong source of light, such as the sun, is that you can make extra shapes with the shadows within the shapes of other things, or you can combine many shapes into one by means of a shadow. This is a good compositional aid, as well as being highly relevant to pure painting.

In an **interior** scene you will find that there is usually a single source of light which has a considerable effect upon what it is you see. While you still have all the incumbent problems of handling a strong, single source of light in your portrayal of a scene, because it is an interior you can observe the same situation for longer and as often as you like. You can even do some preparatory studies by setting up small 'environments' and lighting them in a controlled way.

These environments need not be full-sized. For instance, you could construct, or use, a doll's house and light particular scenes within it using torches. Or you could arrange spotlights in the studio to light in a consistent and controlled way the full-sized environment you may have built for your work. This, in fact, might have been how the work in Fig. 5.9 came about. Here there is a strong and directed source of light which is used in a compositional and dramatic way by the candidate concerned. The shadows are cleverly used to 'draw' the legs and other parts of the man sitting on the edge of the bed. The large shadow in the corner of the room and across the ceiling gives an atmosphere to the work. At the same time, the large shadow makes a new shape within the areas which make up the content of the room. Its presence creates a compositional effect which is

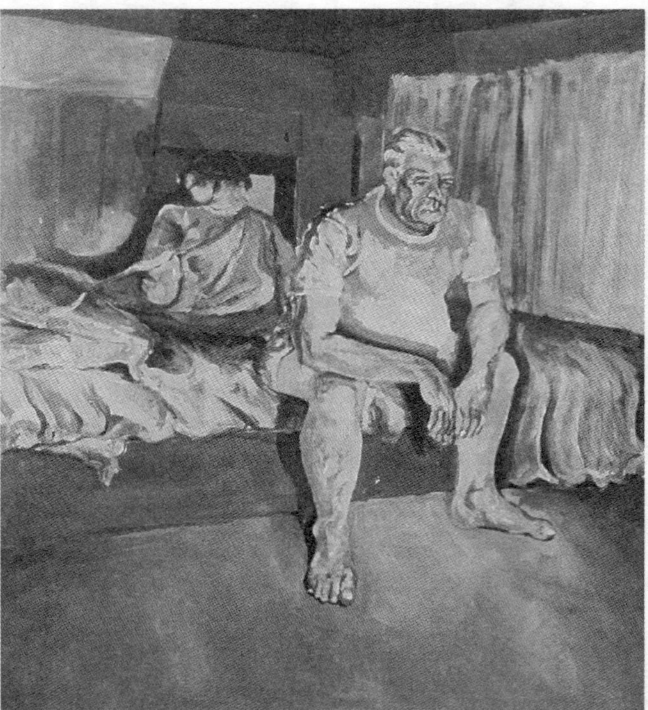

Fig. 5.9

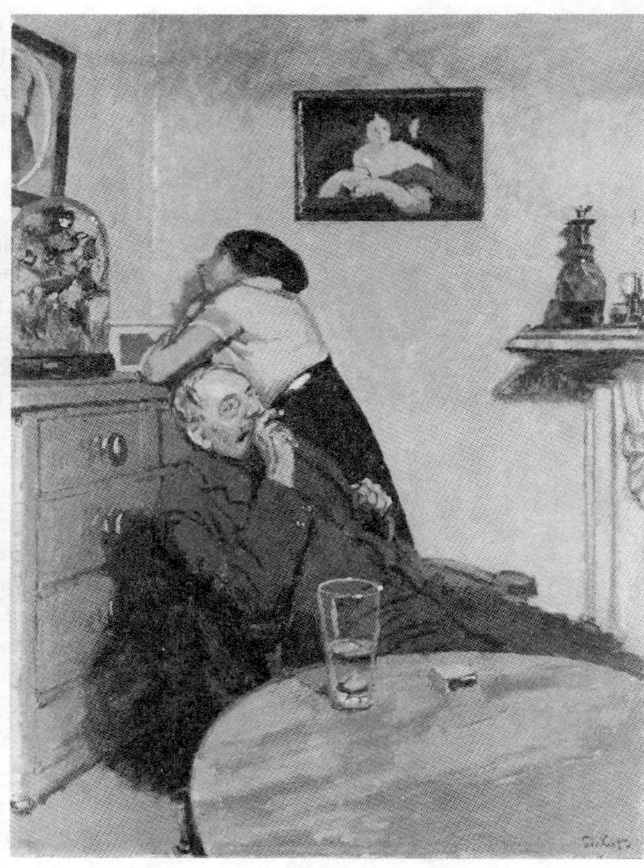

Fig. 5.10 'Ennui', Walter Sickert (reproduced by permission of the Tate Gallery, London).

different from one which would have been achieved by the clear intersection of the two walls and the ceiling.

The whole work has the air of a story which has been stopped in its tracks for a brief moment. It is due in part to this that we consider the work to have an atmosphere. This aspect has, of course, been well conveyed before, by the British artist WALTER SICKERT (1860 – 1942) among others. In his painting 'Ennui' (Fig. 5.10) we can feel the very boredom which hangs heavily on the air. We think that the candidate's work has the same effect, making us feel that we are part of the story being enacted. Thanks to the efforts of both the A-level candidate and Sickert, we are in the privileged position of being an observer of the scene and of the drama being enacted.

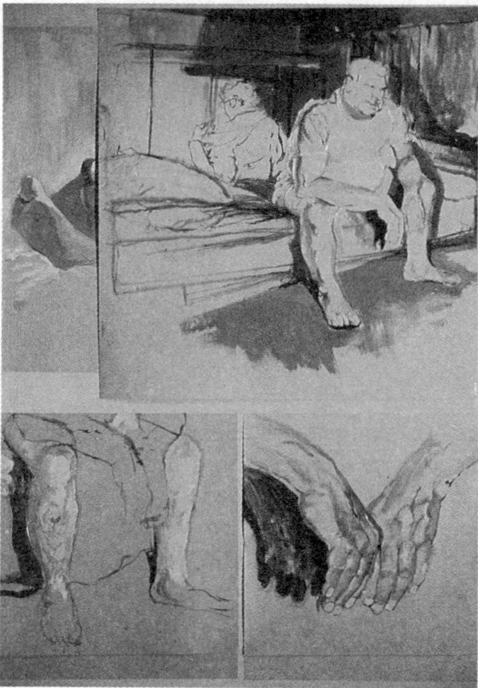

Fig. 5.11

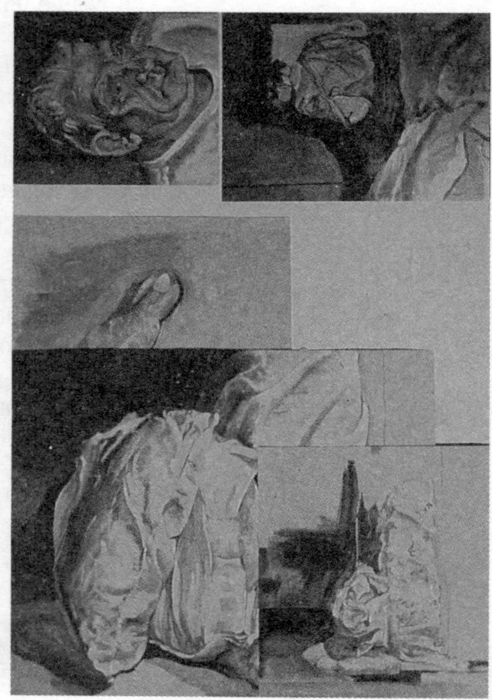

Fig. 5.12

The preparatory studies for Fig. 5.9 (Figs. 5.11 and 5.12) are excellent examples of work from direct observation. The figure painting experiments would be worthy of any A-level Life Drawing papers. The feel of the work is taken up and maintained in the final work, suggesting that it was done for the first time in the examination and not 'practised' beforehand during the preparatory studies, although the composition was obviously considered beforehand. This is an ideal example of what we mean by *not* using preparatory studies as a 'dummy run' in your examination.

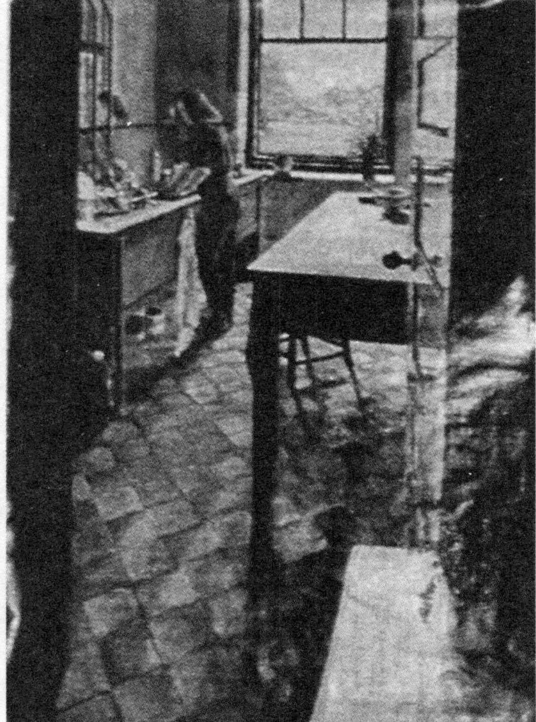

Fig. 5.13

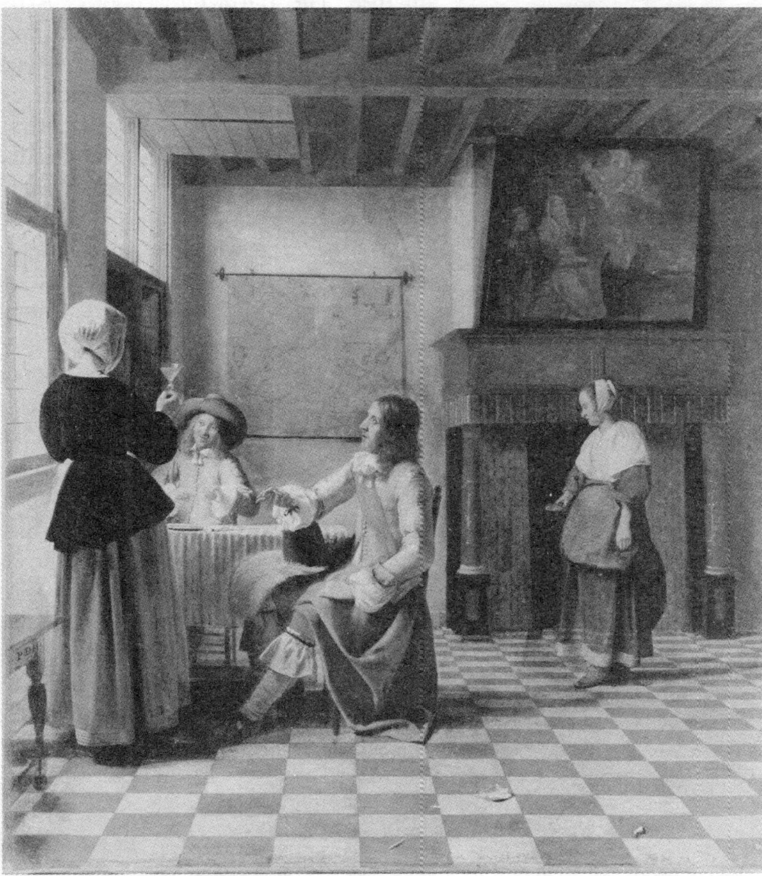

Fig. 5.14 (de Hooch/Vermeer)

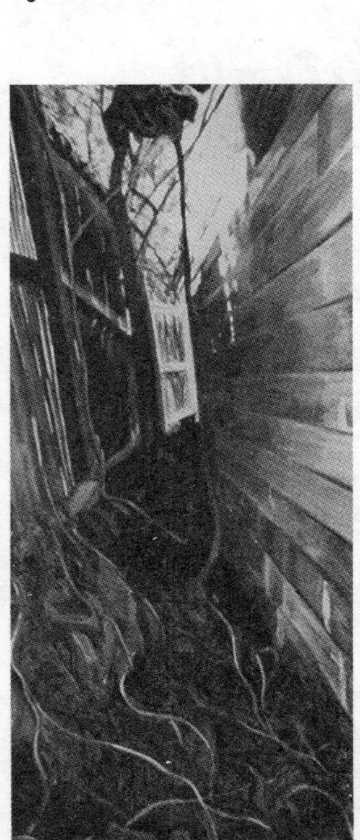

Fig. 5.15

In Fig. 5.13 we see an interior which is very reminiscent of the great Dutch interiors of artists such as PIETER DE HOOCH or JAN VERMEER (Fig. 5.14). The scene has a monumental air of cool calmness about it. This is built up largely by the refined perspective which goes to make up the composition. A work such as this could well be an unusual and original solution to a question which sets a theme such as 'work'. It would be refreshing to see such unusual viewpoints introduced into themes like this instead of some of the commonplace contents and compositions which so often creep into candidates' work. Compositions such as the one illustrated here tend inevitably to produce the type of work which results in the higher grades in the examination. With regard to the theme of work, the commonplace is successful if you manage to achieve what an artist such as WILLIAM HOLMAN HUNT (1827 – 1910) did in his painting 'Work'. This is reproduced in many books on art.

The intimacy of the two interiors in Figs. 5.13 and 5.14 can also be achieved in an outside work. By careful selection of viewpoint, the open air can be turned into an enclosed environment which matches either of the works above. Fig. 5.15 also uses perspective in a clever way to achieve its effect. It is interesting to note that none of these works seems to be a perspective exercise. It is just that the advantages of using perspective are understood and applied to good compositional effect in the works of all three artists here.

Urban landscape or rural landscape

The advantages of such landscapes, despite the problems regarding light we have already mentioned, are that they exist and you can work directly from them.

It is worth noting that the majority of artists work from preparatory studies back in their studio when painting scenes such as these. Even that genius of landscape painting JOHN CONSTABLE did this. It is known that for 'The Haywain' he both worked in his studio in London on the painting from drawings and also sent a friend in Suffolk a message, asking him to make a drawing of a Suffolk cart because he, Constable, was no longer certain of the detail.

On the other hand, there are artists who insist upon working in front of their subject matter. The Barbizon School of Artists was a nineteenth-century group of artists who worked 'on the spot'. In the same way, working in the open was an essential part of the principles present in much of the work of the Impressionists. The only trouble you will have if you want to do this in your examination is the problem it sets your teachers for supervising and overseeing what it is you do, as you do it. Nevertheless, if you want to work before your subject, after making a set of preparatory studies to allow you to do so efficiently, you should encourage your teachers and through them your examination board to allow you to do this.

Whether you work outside or inside a studio, you should be aware that artists make selections as part of the interpretation in their work. By this we mean that they are not merely cameras; so, even when depicting an actual scene, they miss things out, move things about, change the size of things and so on.

Examples of rural landscapes abound in art and are easy to find in books or on visits to any art gallery. For that reason, let us now consider some urban landscapes.

One of the advantages the urban landscape has over a rural one is that it provides you with an opportunity to keep your view and composition much more 'closed'. By restricting the boundaries and depth within your picture it is often easier to control what you are doing Fig. 5.16 shows this. Nevertheless, by using various means, such as the close-up of the fence in the foreground, the perspective in the buildings, the changing scale and the effect of light as the buildings recede into the distance, a good feeling of depth and spatial relationship is arrived at. This is the commonplace used very well. Rather than feeling, perhaps, that it would be better to look for something more 'beautiful', such as a cottage with roses round the door, the candidate has taken a familiar environment and interpreted it in such a way that it becomes a successful work.

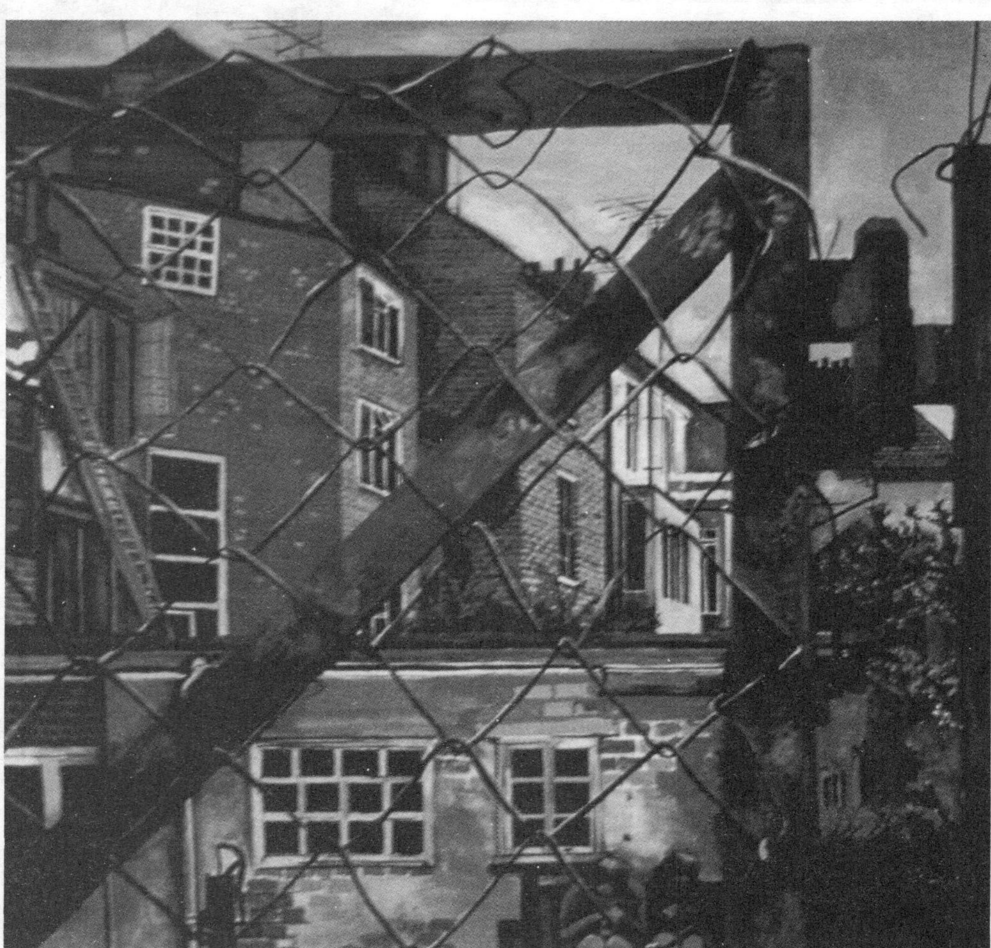

Fig. 5.16

Fig. 5.16 is a fairly straightforward representational work. It is, of course, not necessary to use this approach. Even in landscapes, both rural and urban, a greater degree of interpretation, even going as far as abstraction, is perfectly acceptable. The two works in Figs. 5.17 and 5.18 show this.

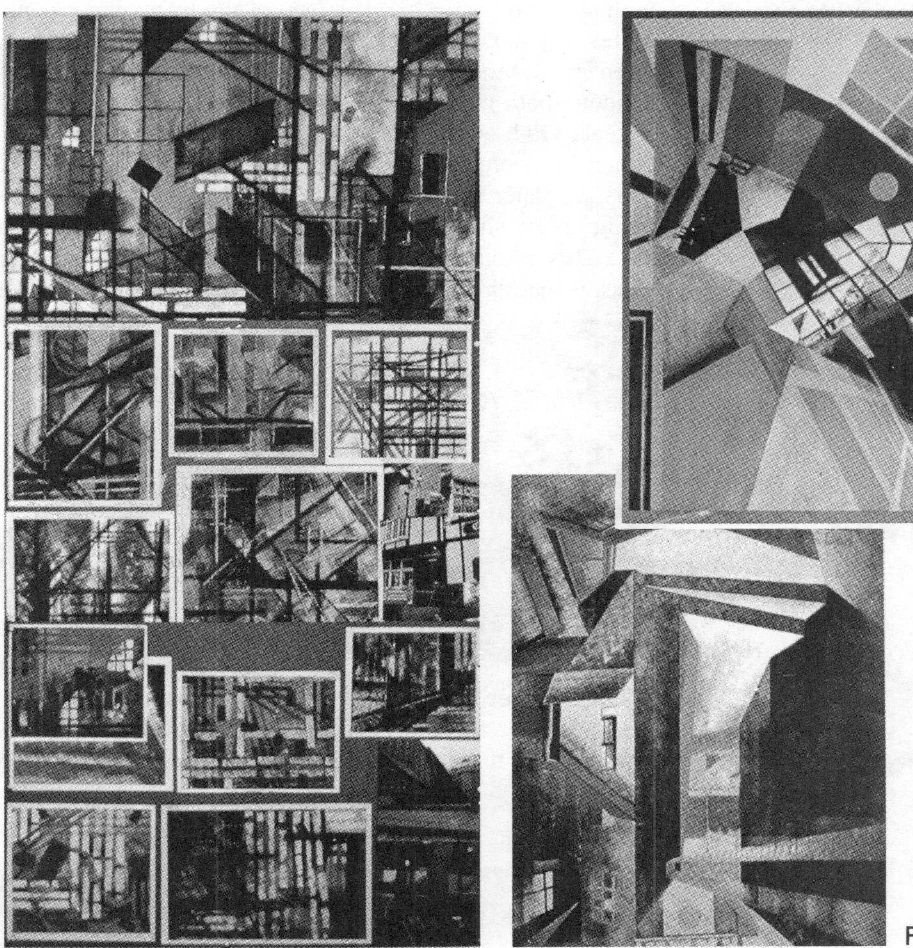

Fig. 5.17

Fig. 5.18

In Fig. 5.17 the candidate has moved what obviously began as observational work into a form of abstraction. The subject matter is a building site. It may have been the skeletal structures of scaffolding, ladders, steel building frames, door and window frames and so on which led the candidate to the approach adopted in the work. If so, it is not only a sound approach but one which would benefit by including some written notes about why the candidate chose to 'see' things the way they have been portrayed. We believe that an accompanying work journal is very likely to lead to a higher grade in the examination at all times, but particularly so here.

The candidate in Fig. 5.18 has chosen to paint a form of collage or, more accurately, montage. The scenes depicted could clearly not have existed as they are, but a number of what must have been very sound direct observational drawings have been juxtaposed to make up two successful compositions. The styles used are also very appropriate in both cases. The two works are not done in exactly the same style. In one the approach builds up an atmosphere which is akin to a number of human emotions, such as familiarity, foreboding, isolation and so on, according to your own 'reading' of the picture. In the other the style is crisp and unemotional, stating almost dispassionately a reaction to a number of architectural features and details.

In this section we have used a few terms which would probably benefit by being defined. They are:

- ABSTRACT – work where a natural source is fundamental, no matter how 'unreal' the work and the images might seem;
- NON-REPRESENTATIONAL – work which has no natural source, existing only in its own right as an arrangement of lines, paint, surfaces, forms and so on;
- MONTAGE – building up a single composition by juxtaposing a number of originally separate images.

Poems and prose

The work done in response to a question which is based upon a direct quotation from either a poem or a piece of prose is most often **illustrative** in nature. That is to say, a picture is composed to illustrate the quotation as if it were a picture in a book. There is nothing wrong with this. It is one of the many dimensions of art and design. Work done in this way mostly has what is described as an illustrative style. This means that there is often little attempt to portray spatial dimensions, or three-dimensional reality, in the work, although both might be present in some illustrations. It is usual, however, for this type of reality to be waived in favour of conveying the essence of the 'story' that is present in either the poem or the piece of prose. In fact, both are usually chosen for inclusion in the question paper in the first place because they are rich in descriptive, narrative language.

Fig. 5.19 shows a typical illustrative response to such a quotation. Despite the necessary imaginative content of the work, a number of preparatory studies exist which indicate that direct, observational drawings were carried out.

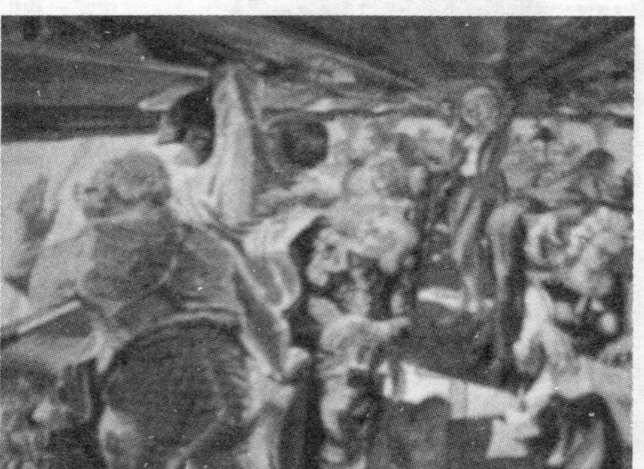
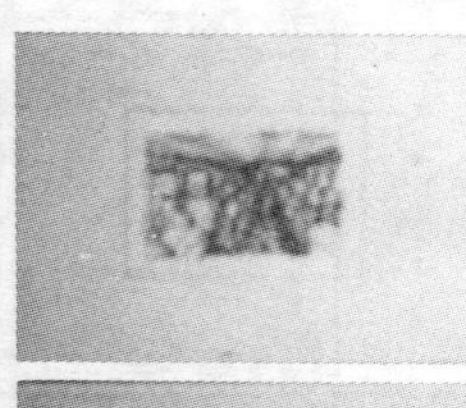
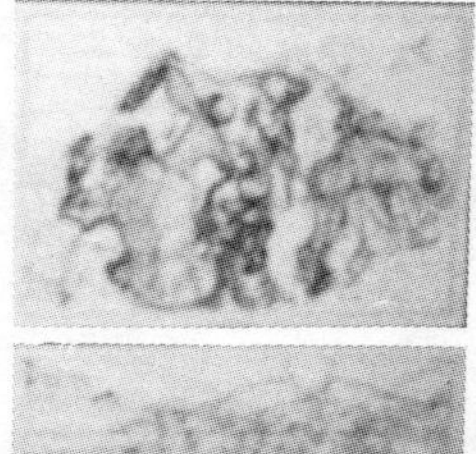
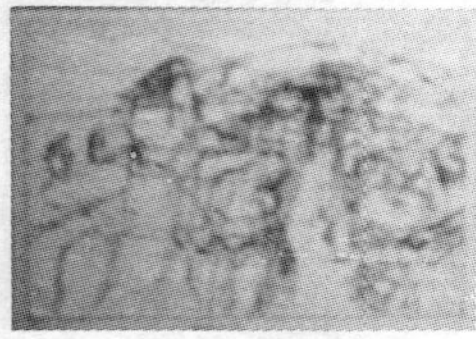

Fig. 5.19

On the other hand, Figs. 5.20 and 5.21 take a poem, in this case, and build up a personal response to it which seems to elaborate upon the emotional stimulus the poem gave the candidate. In this sense it is not necessarily an illustration of the poem but an imaginative, expressive and creative piece of work which is similar to the poem itself, but not a picture of it.

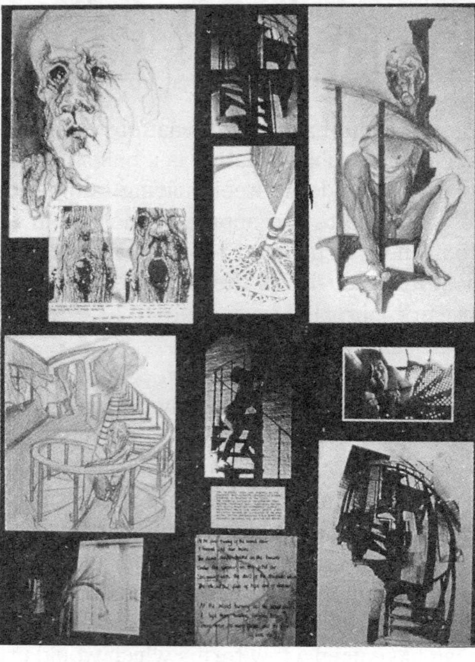

Fig. 5.20

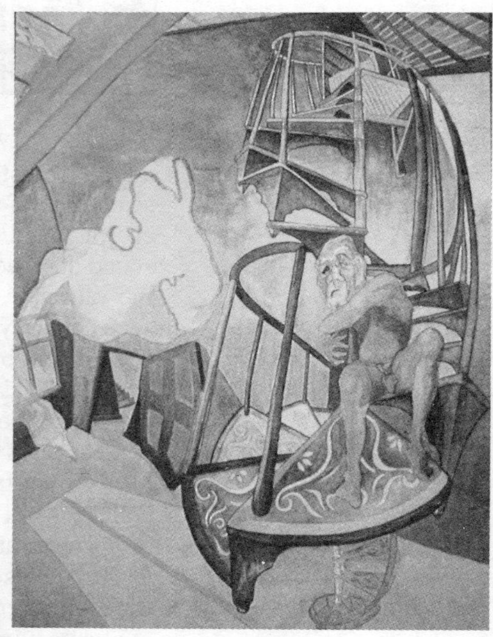

Fig. 5.21

Preparatory studies

As we have indicated above, if you intend to work in front of your subject during your 'test piece', your preparatory studies need to be geared towards allowing you to do this in an efficient and planned manner. This means that if your preparatory studies are made with the intention of working from them in a studio, they are likely to be substantially different from studies made when you intend to work directly from your subject in the open.

In your preparatory studies, you should bear in mind that you are doing a number of things. You are:

- thinking through your ideas;
- exploring the possibilities which exist;
- making investigations;
- gathering together information;
- formulating your intentions;
- preparing yourself to carry out your intentions.

While all this represents an integrated process, it comprises a number of separate and discrete activities, each with their own criteria. If you can identify and itemise the various criteria concerned, you will find that you can begin your preparatory studies in a much more meaningful and directed way.

None of the things you are doing are primarily concerned with producing works of art in themselves, although it is likely that you will produce a number of highly satisfactory works in your preparatory studies which are well able to stand up by themselves.

It is our experience that, in practice, the only criterion present in most preparatory studies is the intended outcome, which has often been finalised *before* the preparatory studies begin. By this we mean that a candidate gets a theme, for instance 'Allotments' (see Chapter 2), and then decides what to do before finding out anything about a real allotment, which is usually easy enough to investigate. As we said when discussing this theme, working out in your head what you will do as a final piece of work inevitably means that you fail to see all the possibilities which exist in the theme. Further, it will usually mean that the studies you make in preparation for your final work turn out to be inefficient, possibly inhibiting your ability to continue developing your work during the final composition. If this is so, and it often is, then when you are in the examination room you will be stranded!

Figs. 5.22, 5.23 and 5.24 show how preparatory studies can give rise to an almost unexpected final pictorial composition. In Fig. 5.22 the mother and child are explored, but almost as if they no longer mattered, with the candidate drawing pieces of other subject matter haphazardly over the remainder of the paper. One idea seems to be emerging in Fig. 5.23, but this is finally superseded in Fig. 5.24 by what has become the final work. In a way, even the final work is part of the preparatory studies. It is easy to imagine that this candidate will go on exploring alternative ideas which emerge, given enough time.

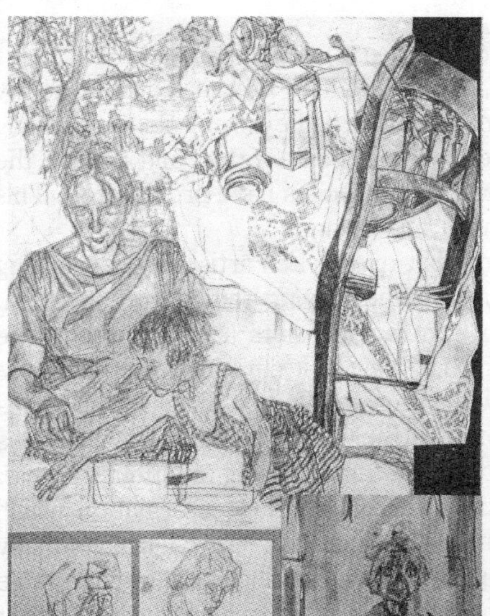
Fig. 5.22

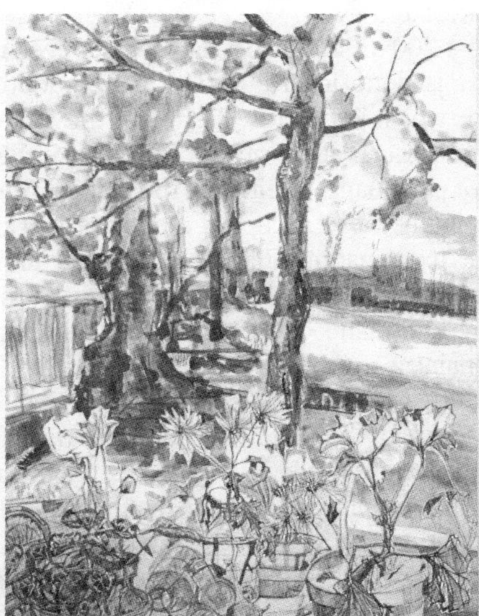
Fig. 5.23

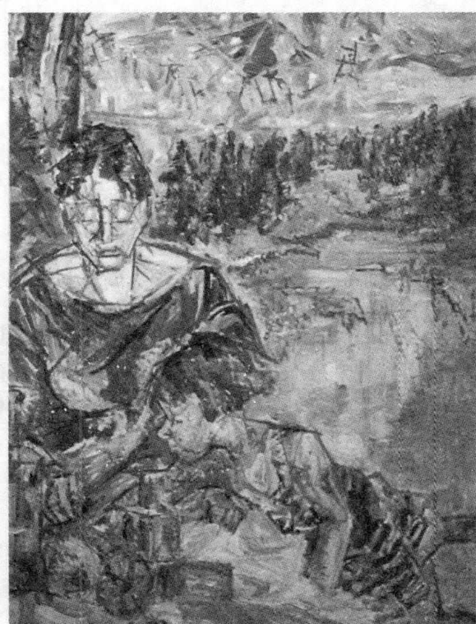
Fig. 5.24

Subject matter

The subject matter for your pictorial composition will be decided, at least in part, by your examiners. They will set questions and you will choose one of them to respond to. Even so, as we have said, there is still considerable choice for you to exercise as far as the actual form and content of your response are concerned. We have already touched upon this in dealing with some of the examples of candidates' work.

To equip yourself with the ability to so select your subject matter and content that it does not remain commonplace, it is probably preferable that you study the sources of inspiration for the many pictorial compositions which exist, past and present. A glance at paintings in a gallery or reproductions in a book will make you aware that, despite the number of works of art which exist, they all seem to be related to just a few sets of subject matter. It is the **using** of this subject matter in a fresh and original way that counts. This usually involves the content of your pictures and the way it is arranged within the picture. Being original does not necessarily mean that you will be unique, Unknown to you, it is very likely that someone else has been doing something similar. Indeed, to be fresh and original it is vital that you should study the work of others. It will enable you to recognise the many alternatives that exist in similar situations, as well to be aware of how different styles and approaches are governed by differing social and cultural criteria thereby giving rise to different results.

A prime source for so much art is obviously the Bible. There are hundreds of works which could sensibly be labelled religious paintings. This means that art has long been associated with story-telling. We have already used CARAVAGGIO's painting 'The Supper at Emmaus' (Fig. 4.2) to illustrate our point that many works contain what might be called still-life examples within them. Others have used it to explain foreshortening or the effects of light and so on. It is, nevertheless, a religious picture at heart. The amount of religious pictures which exists is hardly surprising. Art depends a lot on patronage, and for centuries the Church was the prime patron of the arts. Because patrons set out to get what they want, many religious works inevitably exist. It is interesting to note that at the time of the great patronage of the arts by the Church, the majority of the people were illiterate. As a consequence, the paintings were meant partly as books, in that they conveyed biblical stories visually. In this sense, one might even claim that they are the forerunners of comic-books. In religious paintings, if you know your Bible well, you can identify different saints and characters by the things they wear or are carrying.

Another source of subject matter is the ancient world. Here works tell in pictures mythological stories, stories about great love, heroic deeds and a world peopled by quarrelling gods.

Much painting, particularly from the seventeenth and the first part of the eighteenth centuries, was concerned with allegorical subject matter. In allegorical work it is usual for a general truth to be depicted in visual form by means of giving concepts a visual identity. Thus we could have pictures which portrayed the 'Blessings of Peace', by PETER PAUL RUBENS in which Peace is shown as a woman and, among other things, a panther is playing on its back, like a cat.

In the last 200 or so years it has become less necessary to tag such prestigious purposes on to what is done in art. Artists have adopted the freedom to do what artists nearly always did, which is portray the world they live in, even when they were also portraying religious, historical, allegorical or mythological events. As a result of this, and despite the demands of patronage, their own theoretical reasons and purposes have proliferated. This has led to many more accepted modes of work in art and design.

For your examination, it will help to bear in mind that even when artists were working in these strongly identifiable subject areas, they were portraying things around them, which they knew and could observe. Thus when Caravaggio paints a biblical figure, he may well paint a neighbour, friend or relative. STANLEY SPENCER certainly did this in the present century, when he used his family and events from his family life, as well as his fellow villagers at Cookham, to depict scenes from the Bible. In the same way, Rubens portrayed the countryside as well as the people in the allegorical painting mentioned above.

This should emphasise to you that you must try to use sources of information which you can observe directly in your own work, no matter how imaginative it might eventually be. If you want to include a person, draw a person; if you want to include a kitchen table laden with breakfast things, draw such a table. The degree of your imagination is evident in your idea and how you compose your picture, not how well or how badly you draw a person from memory and imagination. What we describe here has been the method of the artists of the past, as well as the present. It is one of the reasons why drawing skills are regarded so highly as a component of artistic ability.

We present the remaining illustrations in this chapter as examples of alternative and original solutions to problems similar to those illustrated above. Where we link them to the works of other, established, artists, it is not to suggest that they are derivative but to reinforce our point that little is new in art and design. Indeed, to understand the subject, and the possibilities which exist in your work, you should study the work of others.

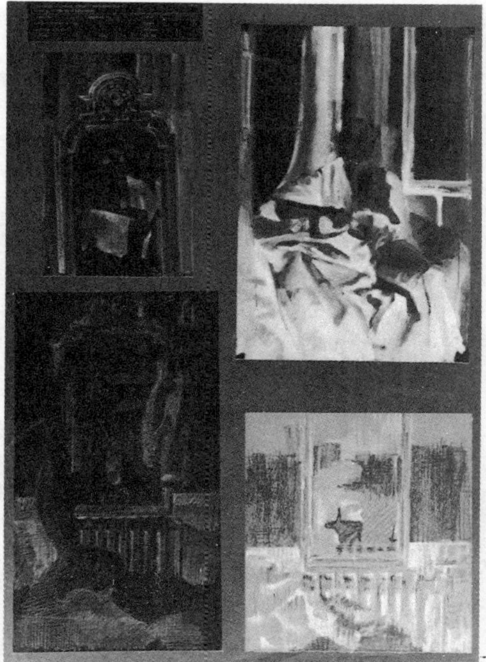
Fig. 5.25

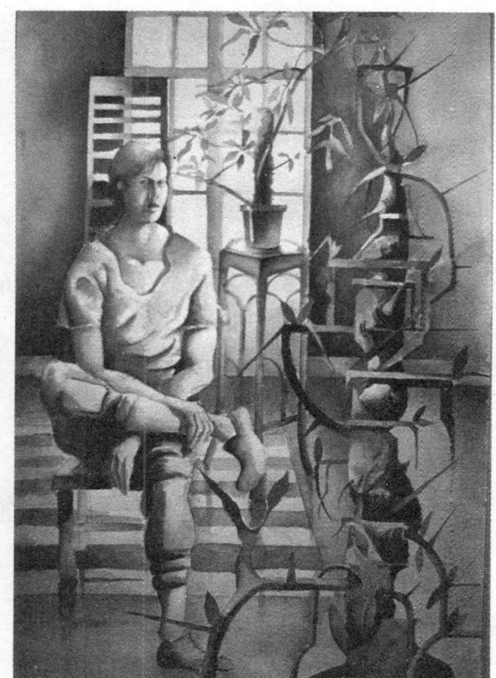
Fig. 5.26

Figs. 5.25 and 5.26 show alternative versions of figures in an interior. The first is Sickert-like, as was the work in Fig. 5.9. The second is rather different in style, as well as being much more of a **portrait** of the person in the picture. A portrait is built up not only from a likeness of the sitter but also from their belongings, all of which go to create an understanding of the character of the person being portrayed. In this sense, the picture is also another example of story-telling. Fig. 5.26 has an appearance which strikes a chord with the works of JOHN MINTON (1917 – 57) and artists such as GRAHAM SUTHERLAND (1903 – 80).

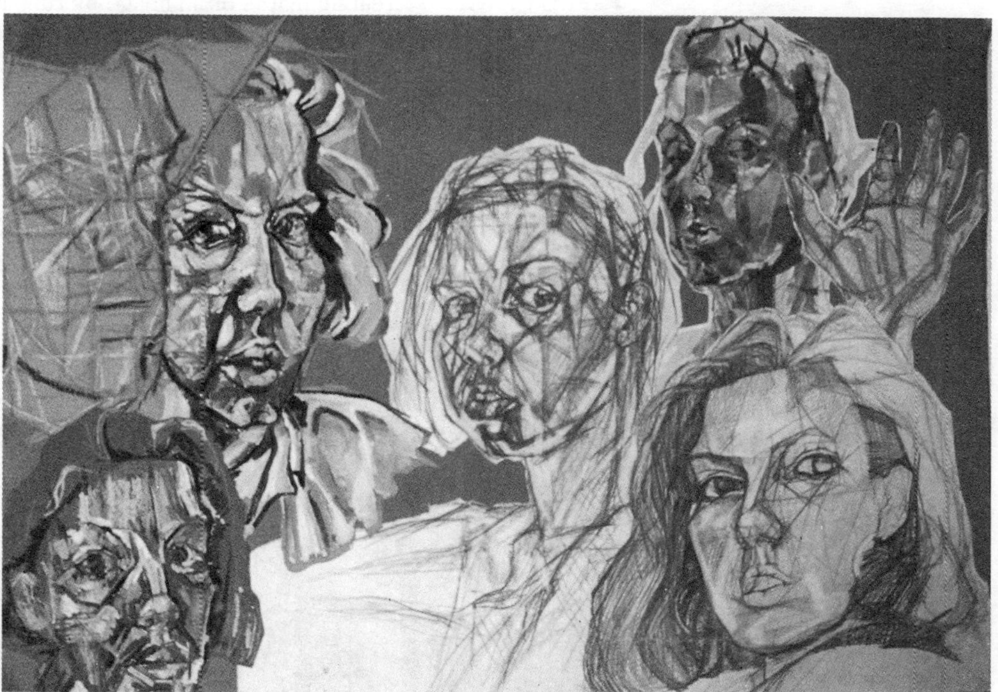
Fig. 5.27

Figs. 5.27, 5.28 and 5.29, the works of a single candidate, are the results of an obvious interest in something, in this case the face. For some reason the feeling of alarm, or threat, comes into the candidate's understanding of what is being done. This is developed through two further works. What do you think of the two more complete works? If the theme was fright, how well do you think each deals with this emotion, especially in terms of composition and aesthetic qualities?

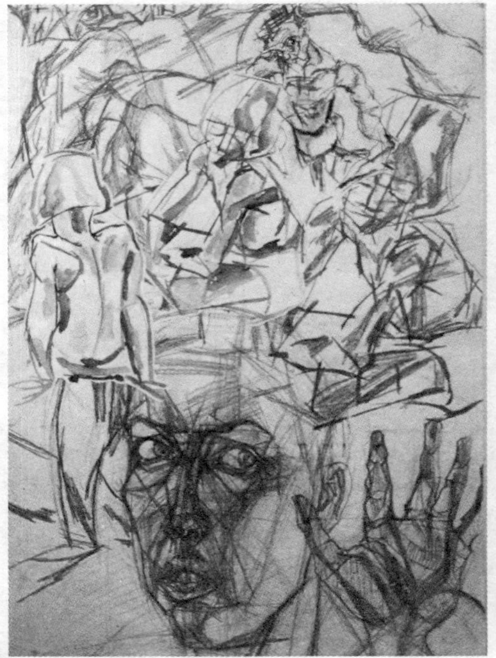

Fig. 5.28

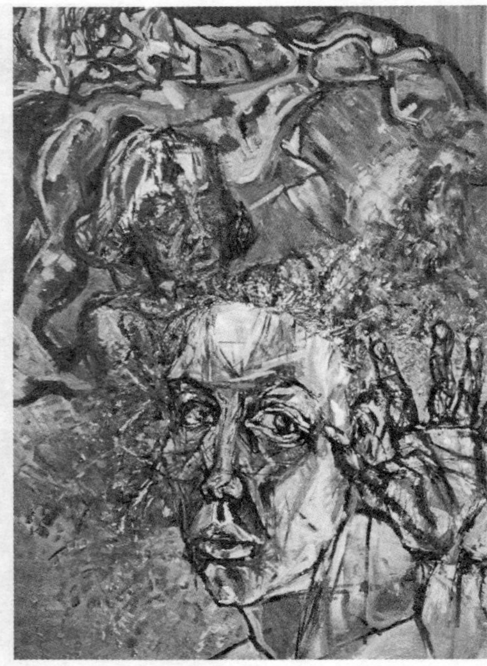

Fig. 5.29

We have obviously been at pains throughout this book to stress the importance of recognising and using the **qualities** of materials. Quality, in this case, is less to do with technical advances or techniques, and more to do with the 'natural' facility each medium possesses for portraying certain things. If we have made it sound as if you need to pick the *one* medium most suitable each time, this was not our intention. You might well need to mix your media in a single work, and this is well within the traditions of art and design. If you do this, in order to achieve the various effects you desire, your task then is to unite the media in a satisfactory way. Fig. 5.30 shows a candidate combining **paint**, **collage**, **montage**, and **frottage**.

- FROTTAGE – creating marks or an image by rubbing a texture or an image in one medium to another, paper usually: brassrubbings are an example. Artists such as ROBERT RAUSCHENBERG (1925) have used a technique to transfer printed images from magazines to canvas.

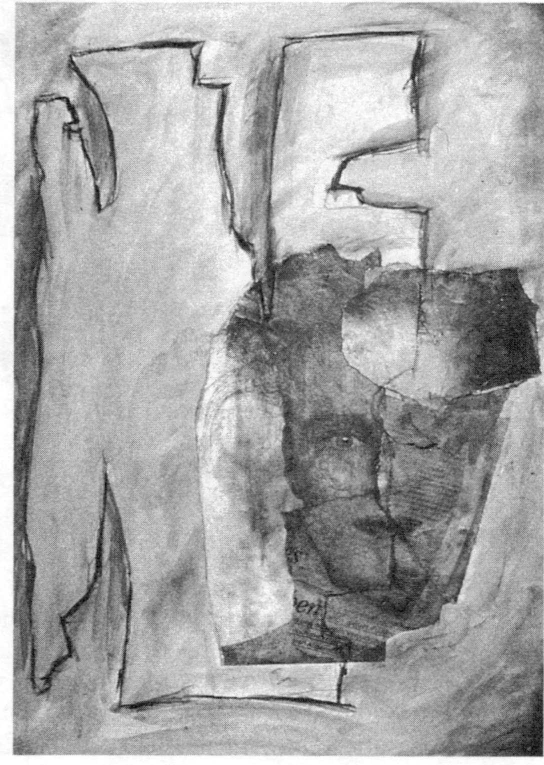

Fig. 5.30

The information in this section has been necessarily condensed in the overall interests of this book. Some might say it has resulted in a travesty of the truth! We would prefer to think that it offers you a further small insight into what you are studying. Follow up this discussion by referring to Gombrich (1972).

EXERCISES

1 Either go to a scene or select an interior to work from. Spend about one hour making studies of what is before you so that you could create a work from it when you can no longer see the environment you have chosen. Then go to a similar environment. This time spend about one hour making studies which give you the information necessary to work directly from the scene before you at a later time.

There is no need to do the two final works. Instead, see if you can identify any differences in the types of studies you did in each case and the type of information you sought each time.

2 Select a scene to paint, one which has a number of contrasting colours within it. In your painting use only one hue, such as red, to convey the scene. Do not put lines around things within the scene, but use the qualities of the colour to portray what it is you see before you.

3 Choose an environment to work from. It can be either exterior or interior. After you have made some investigative studies of it, produce a series of works which move from the photographic to the most 'abstract'.

It might help if you also studied the work of about four artists to do this. We suggest ANTONIO CANALETTO (1697 – 1768), PIERRE BONNARD (1867 – 1947), HENRI MATISSE (1869 – 1954) and PIET MONDRIAN (1872 – 1944).

4 Choose one of the following quotations. Try to produce a work which uses as its basic principles your interpretation of the chosen quotation. You may work from either imagination or direct observation.

'I want a red to be so sonorous, to sound like a bell; if it doesn't turn out that way, I get more reds and other colours until I get it.'

'Colour in nature is grey – built up on the palette by the use of colour.'

'Use only three primaries and their immediate derivatives.'

'Colours in vibration, pealing like silver bells and clanging like bronze bells, proclaiming happiness, passion and love, blood and death.'

'My choice of colours does not rest upon any scientific theory: it is based on observation, on feeling, on the very nature of each experience.'

5 Do a painting from direct observation which has a number of strong shadows in it. When it is finished, by means of tracing do it again, only colouring all the shadows black and everything else white. Study your result critically, analysing it as a composition of abstract black and white shapes. Do whatever you can to improve the composition of the shapes. Either work over the black and white picture you have already, or stick new pieces of paper over parts of your original work and then work again on to them, or do another piece of work altogether. When this is finished, paint another version of your first painting, from direct observation, but amending the distribution of shadowed areas to match your final abstract black and white work.

CHAPTER

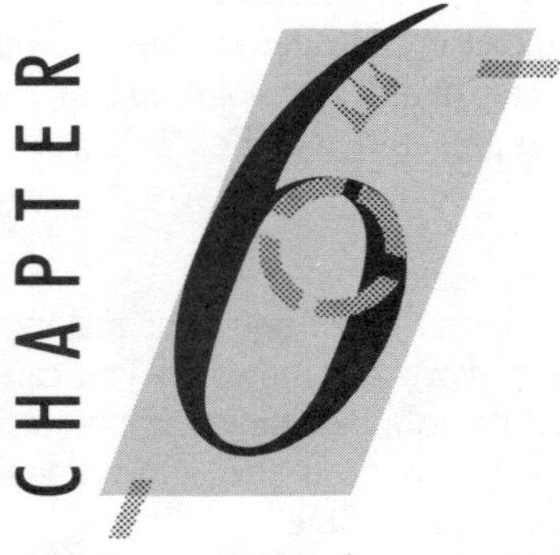

OBSERVATIONAL DRAWING

GETTING STARTED

The practices included in this chapter are

- drawing from life;
- plant drawing;
- drawing from natural or man-made objects.

These practices might be called something slightly different by each examining board, but the general meaning is clear enough for us to use these particular titles.

You should note that it is usual for still life to be included under the heading 'Drawing from Objects' in most examination syllabuses, even though we have treated it as a separate practice (Chapter 4) because it is fundamental to learning how to draw and paint, and also because the problems involved in still life are different to those encountered when drawing a single object.

The essential nature of work in the set of practices considered in this chapter is that **you must work from direct observation**.

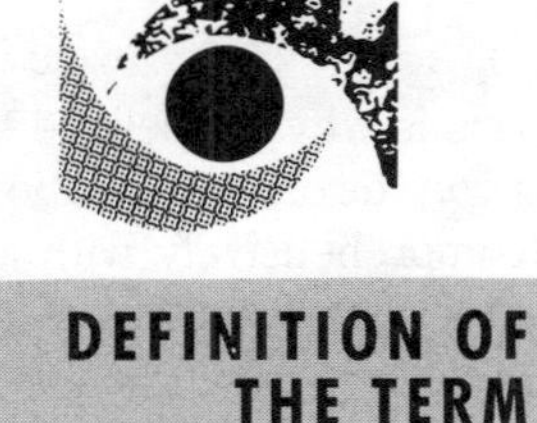

ESSENTIAL PRINCIPLES

DEFINITION OF THE TERM

The term we are setting out to define is '**direct observation**' and our definition will apply to all the practices listed above.

Direct

The easiest part of the term is 'direct', so let us get that out of the way at once. According to the dictionary it means 'without intermediary'. You can find many further additions to the definition quoted above, but this is the essential one for our purposes. Despite saying that it is the easiest part of the term to deal with, it is surprising how many students fail to grasp its significance to their work. Many candidates *do* work directly from the appropriate subject source during their preparatory studies, but then carry out their examination work away from their source material, using their first drawing as the sole basis for their information. When they do this, the first drawing is acting as an 'intermediary' of a particular kind. This is an accepted way of working in an area such as pictorial composition. Where artists work in studios using the direct observational work done in front of their subject, but it is totally against the requirement of the particular practices covered in this chapter. In drawing from life, plant and natural or man-made objects, it is expected that you will work directly from your primary source material *throughout* your examination.

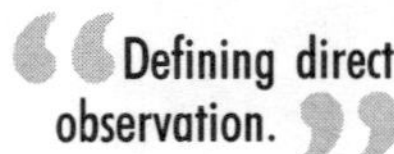

Of course, you may choose to do more than one study from your source subject, but each one should be taken directly from it, even though the knowledge and information gained from the first work will act as an intermediary of a kind as far as the next work is concerned, and so on. This is unavoidable, and we will discuss this aspect later in the chapter.

Observation

'Observation' is a much more complex term, and is one which is interlaced with hidden meanings in art and design. The dictionary says that it is the 'act of observing'. This bears out the need to work directly from your source subject each time in the examination. If you work away from your subject, you are not engaged in an act of observing. The dictionary definition continues: 'especially scientifically; remark, criticism'.

This begins to indicate that observational work is not just registering unthinkingly what is in front of you. More scientific processes are involved, such as:

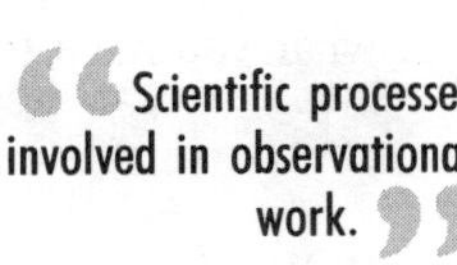

- analysis;
- discrimination;
- dissection;
- weighing;
- measuring;
- accurately describing;
- ascribing.

These offer us much more guidance as to what should be done in observational drawing.

This is what we meant earlier when we said that the term was interlaced with hidden meanings in art and design. Observational drawing is not just about reproducing something which stands for something else, which is how photographic likenesses might fairly be described. It is, among other things, about:

- finding out;
- taking apart;
- understanding;
- explaining;
- communicating;
- conveying.

In this sense it concerns making a 'remark' about what you observe. Tied up inextricably with the whole process are the level and extent of your own ability to conduct a critical appraisal.

This is borne out as the dictionary definition continues: 'facts collected and recorded'. If you are going to show only what your source subject 'looks like', you will barely have begun to explore the range and extent of the facts contained. This is why we believe the list above is an important checklist to work to when making *any* direct observational drawing. Working in such a way will equip you to deal more comprehensively with any preparatory studies you may do in any of your work, no matter which section of the examination is involved.

This last point is an important factor for you. So far in this book we have suggested that:

- your own practical work should be linked to any historical studies you may be following, and vice versa;
- still life is an important aspect in developing the skills necessary for you to execute a successful pictorial composition.

Now we link observational drawing and *all* your preparatory studies. What we are saying is that no matter what you do in art and design, it is all interrelated. The apparent separation of subjects is only a matter of convenience for teaching and examining the subject.

AESTHETIC CONSIDERATIONS

In this section of the examination, while the points mentioned in other chapters under this heading (like the 'formal elements' and so on) will still apply, the following are also most important:

"Additional aesthetic considerations."

- STRUCTURE – the way in which the many and often complex parts of your subject source are interrelated;
- CONSTRUCTION – the way in which the parts combine to make the whole;
- GROWTH – the way in which a form increases in size or multiplies in terms of developments of other kinds.

Each of these aspects applies equally to the different practices listed at the beginning of this chapter. They form the main reasons for your work in this section of the examination. You achieve them by employing the **processes** listed above, such as **analysis**, **discrimination** and so on. To render your findings visible and to demonstrate your understanding of structure, construction and growth, you can then employ the aesthetic factors we have already mentioned in earlier chapters.

One examining board asks for a 'written description' in this section of their examination. Even if you are *not* taking this board's examination, we suggest that you include written accounts in your work during your course of study. The words you use will probably inform you of just what it is you are observing and guide you in what you have to do in visual and aesthetic terms.

MATERIALS, TOOLS AND EQUIPMENT CONSIDERATIONS

In direct observational work it is common to use the term 'drawing'. We do so ourselves. The trouble is that in artistic circles it does not have the restricted meaning it usually does in other contexts.

It *can* mean rendering a likeness in pencil. The likeness could, however, be carried out equally well in any stick material, such as pen and ink, crayon, charcoal and so on. Creating a visual likeness is, however, not the only purpose in drawing.

"Defining 'drawing'."

In turn, the term 'drawing' is often used by artists when materials such as paint and collage are also used to make the image. So, when the term is used in art and design, the dictionary definition 'make lines or figures with pencil' does not necessarily apply. We suggest that a better definition is **to form a representation**.

This avoids linking the use of a pencil alone to what might be done as a drawing. The term 'representation' allows 'drawings' to serve more than one purpose. In the dictionary the term 'representation' is defined as: 'describing, drawing, depicting, making clear to the mind, symbolising standing for, an example of, signifying, meaning, making a statement of arguments'. In other words you must confront a broad range of media in your work and involve yourself in a variety of explanations about the widest nature of what it is you see.

The range of media you use cannot sensibly be restricted to two dimensional alone. For instance, trying to draw something in wire, or to model it in clay or cardboard, could well enable you to find out more about your source subject, as well as explain it more comprehensively, than perhaps drawing it in pencil alone.

This suggests that you might be well advised to do more than one study in your examination, and use a variety of media to do so. While most examinations seem to expect that you will show your ability to draw the **shape** of your source subject, they also accept that you may be able to express more by rendering just parts of that subject, using alternative media if need be. So as long as you ensure that you make one study which shows very clearly the shape of your source subject, you are likely to gain more credit if you then go on to explore that subject more fully and to make further studies which explain your comprehensive knowledge of both your particular subject and art and design generally. Whereas in the initial study, which showed the shape of the object, you might well have used a stick medium of some kind, in these further studies you would be wise to use the media most appropriate to your needs at any time.

CRAFTSMANSHIP

The degree of craftsmanship you display will depend to a large extent on the clarity of mind you display in your work. If you are unable to 'see' what there is in your source subject, you will be unlikely to produce well-crafted work. By see we mean here **realise**, or **understand**, as well as noticing the shape and form of a thing with your sense of sight alone. Your ability to learn to see in this way will be built up and developed over your course of study, if you work in the way we have been suggesting throughout this book. In this sense your later work will have the skills associated with craftsmanship built into it. That is to say, you will be working in a proven and even a traditional way, but this will in no way stop work being either original or personally creative.

HISTORICAL FACTORS

There can be no doubt that the 'masters' of the past have built up a series of techniques regarding the use of materials and mark-making which explains the nature and appearance of substances and surfaces in their original source material, as well as its shape and form. The so-called 'science of perspective' is just one of these techniques. If you study these techniques closely, you will find your own ways of doing likewise.

A pencil portrait drawing by PETER PAUL RUBENS or ALBRECHT DÜRER (1471–1528), for example, will show you how to portray the effect of flesh, its forms and the shadows which are part of it. On the other hand, a drawing of the human figure by MICHELANGELO (1475 – 1564) will show you how the effect of strongly developed muscles can be understood and portrayed. Anatomical studies by LEONARDO DA VINCI (1452 – 1519) not only explain to you how the human figure is composed but also show you how to draw what it is you can see, especially if, like him, you were able to attend medical classes where corpses were dissected. Of course, while this is unlikely, you would perhaps be able to sit in on a biology class when, say, a rabbit is being dissected. In turn, a drawing in water colour, 'The Hare' by Dürer will convey to you some of the ways in which fur and hair can be rendered in art and design.

To learn about drawing it is preferable that you do *not* stick to the examples provided by fine art, as we have done in the paragraph above. Studying how an architect draws a building so that it may be constructed by someone else, or how a DIY book draws something for you to make, or how an electrical or electronic circuit is drawn and so on will provide you with a much greater understanding of what the process of drawing is about. What is more, drawings such as these will develop your understanding of what it is you might see in your source subject material. As much as anything, such drawings convey the underlying structure of forms and objects, as well as the ways in which they work, and look.

As an example, let us consider how you might begin to draw an object which works. Imagine that you have as your source subject a 'Mincer'. These are kitchen machines of the past which are operated by hand. They are used to mince, or grind, a variety of foodstuffs. Because of the variety of foodstuffs concerned, the machines have distinctive appearances according to the purpose for which they were designed (Fig. 6.1). Therefore, to show what one or some look like is perfectly in order, if not essential.

So that you can make such a study – that is to say, one which has a visual likeness to the original machine – you might study the work of the Dutch Masters who painted interiors, such as JAN VERMEER or PIETER DE HOOCH. Or you might study the still-life work of painters such as WILLEM KALF (1619 – 93) or PIETER CLAESZ (*c*.1597 – 1660). In the paintings and drawings of these and other artists, although you may not find a mincer, you will be able to see how they portrayed other kitchen items, such as pots and pans. What you are looking for in your studies are examples showing you *how* other artists have successfully portrayed the surfaces of objects, as well as their shapes and forms.

As mincers are mostly made from metal, a study of the work of advertising artists and even comic artists might provide you with even more means to portray metal in your

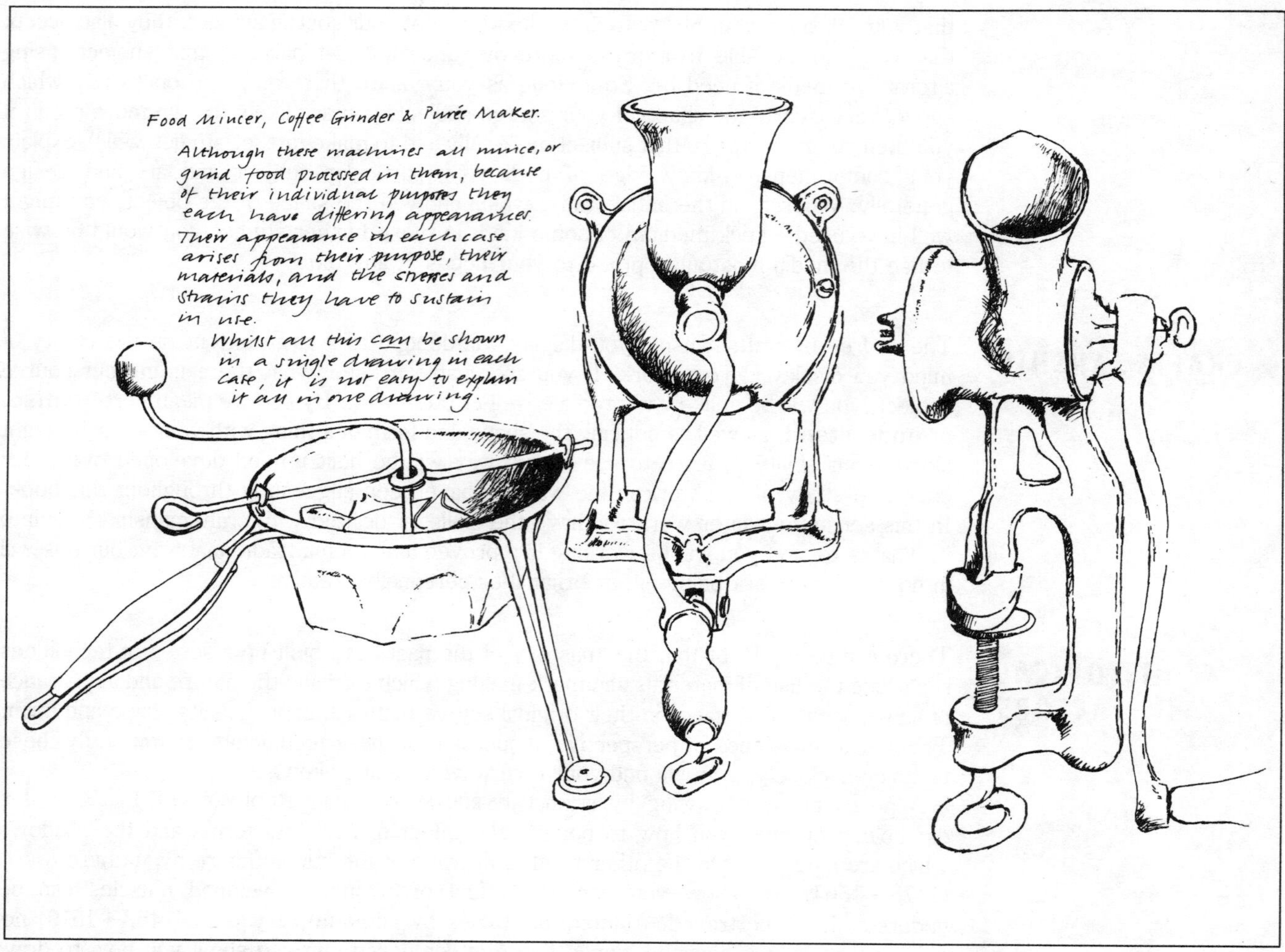

Fig. 6.1 Examples of mincing machines.

drawings. Metal is hard, usually reflective to a degree, and of an indeterminate grey colour, unless coated. *These* are the qualities you should be trying to show in your work.

Apart from the visual appearance of a mincer, the fact that the machine works and performs an operation is an essential aspect of the object. Fine artists, as well as graphic artists and designers, have show how machines operate for a long time past. If you study the drawings of LEONARDO DA VINCI which explore his ideas for flying machines and battering-rams, you will see how a fine artist tackles the task of showing how a thing works. On the other hand, the leaflets which accompany and explain, for instance, a food processor, which is no more than a modern mincer, include drawings done by graphic designers. These show the user how to operate the various parts of the machine. At the same time, they also contain drawings done by various types of technical artists. These usually explain things such as how the machine should be installed and maintained, or how it should be wired up and so on.

From a comprehensive set of studies such as those suggested above, showing how others have worked on similar subject matter, you will be equipping yourself not only with the means to carry out satisfactory drawings of your own from your primary source material, but also with an understanding of what to look for in your subject. Of course, in this example it will also probably be necessary for you to take the object apart in order to **see** how it works and also to be able to **explain** how it works. If you do, this calls for other forms of drawings, such as:

“**Forms of drawing.**”

- 'exploded' drawings – the various parts are shown in their relationship to each other, but separated slightly (Fig. 6.2);
- 'cut-away' drawings – solid parts of the object are drawn as if they have had parts of the solid area cut away, allowing us to see through and be aware of the detail which would otherwise be hidden (Fig. 6.3);
- annotated drawings – a combination of words and visual images are used to record and explain what can be seen (Fig. 6.4).

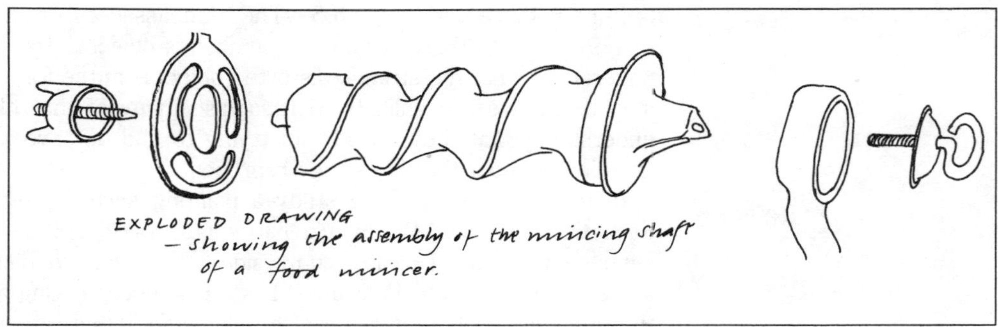

Fig. 6.2 'Exploded' drawing of a mincer.

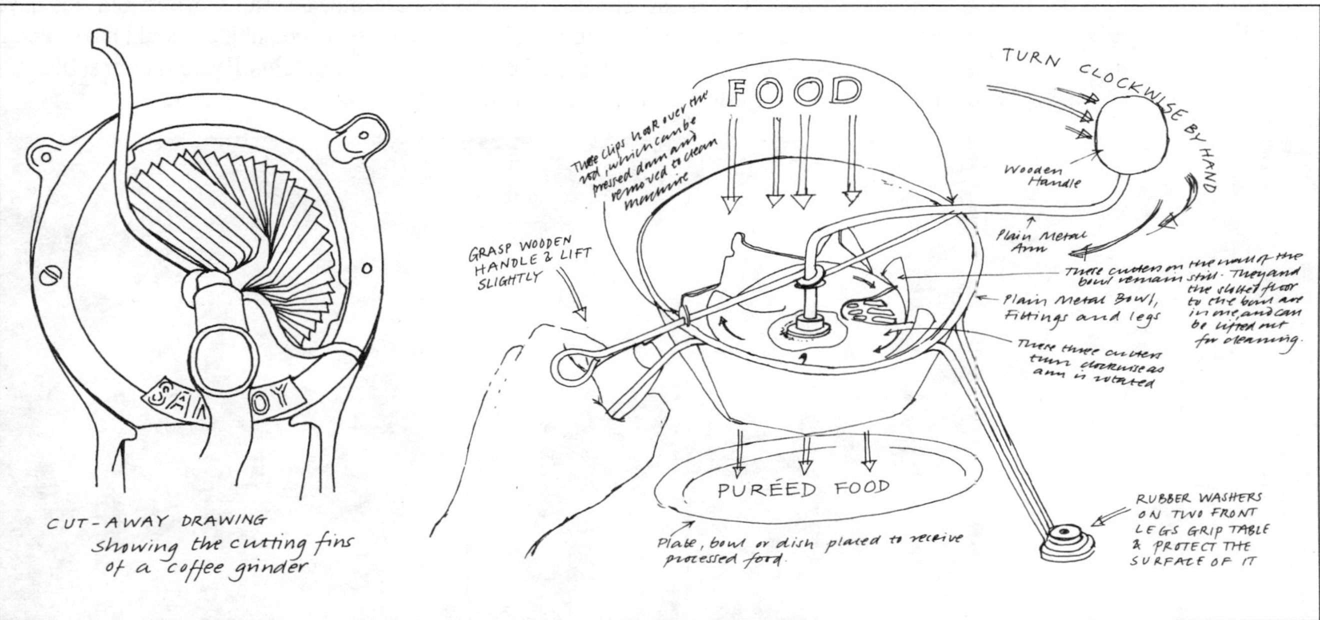

Fig. 6.3 'Cut-away' drawing of a mincer.

Fig. 6.4 Annotated drawing of a mincer.

CONTEXTUAL INVESTIGATIONS

Because direct observational drawings are taken from the real world at the time they were done, they are contextual documents in themselves. They document and record the time at which they were done. This might mean that they show us which individual things existed, as well as the ambience or environment in which they existed.

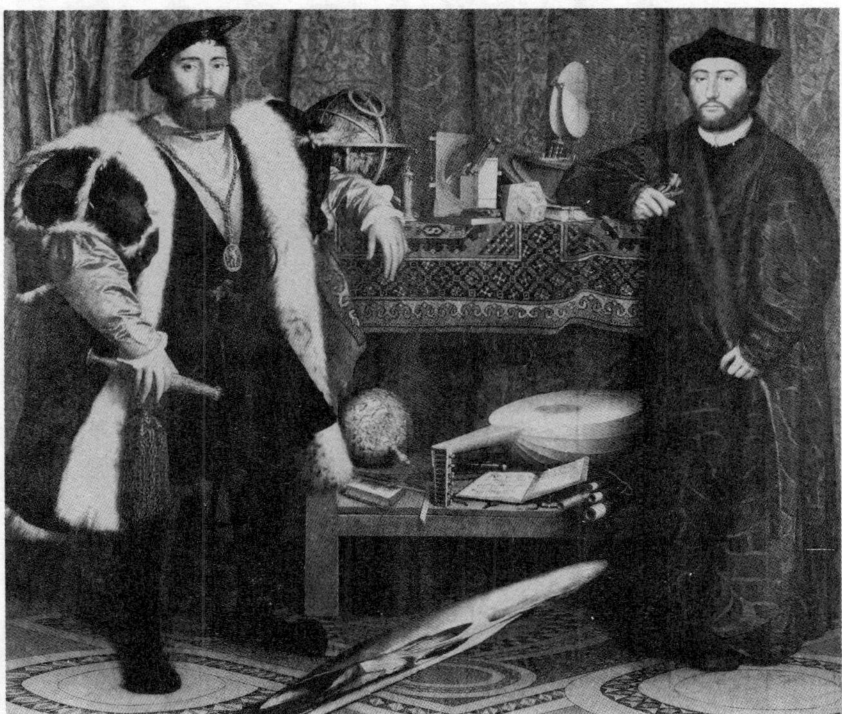

Fig. 6.5 'The Ambassadors', Hans Holbein the Younger (reproduced by permission of the Trustees of the National Gallery, London).

For instance, in Fig. 6.5 'The Ambassadors' by HANS HOLBEIN THE YOUNGER (*c.*1497 – 1543), there are a large number of objects. Apart from the problem of trying to understand what the strange distorted object is in the foreground of the picture, and why it is there, we are unlikely to recognise many of the other objects in the picture, or understand what they are for. In trying to find out, we shall discover much contextual knowledge about the times they represent.

In the same way, if we study a painting such as Fig. 6.6, 'The Martyrdom of St Sebastian', done in 1475 by ANTONIO POLLAIUOLO (*c.*1432 – 1498), it seems reasonable to suppose that the Tuscan countryside in the middle distance and the background is somewhere known to Pollaiuolo. If so, it is documenting and telling us something about the times in which he lived. It also tells us something about the development of art. In a similar subject done much earlier, such as a Byzantine mosaic, the work would not have included a pictorial background, since the religious nature of the subject would have meant that the background was unimportant, or even unacceptable. This Byzantine practice has been carried on in the icons of the Russians.

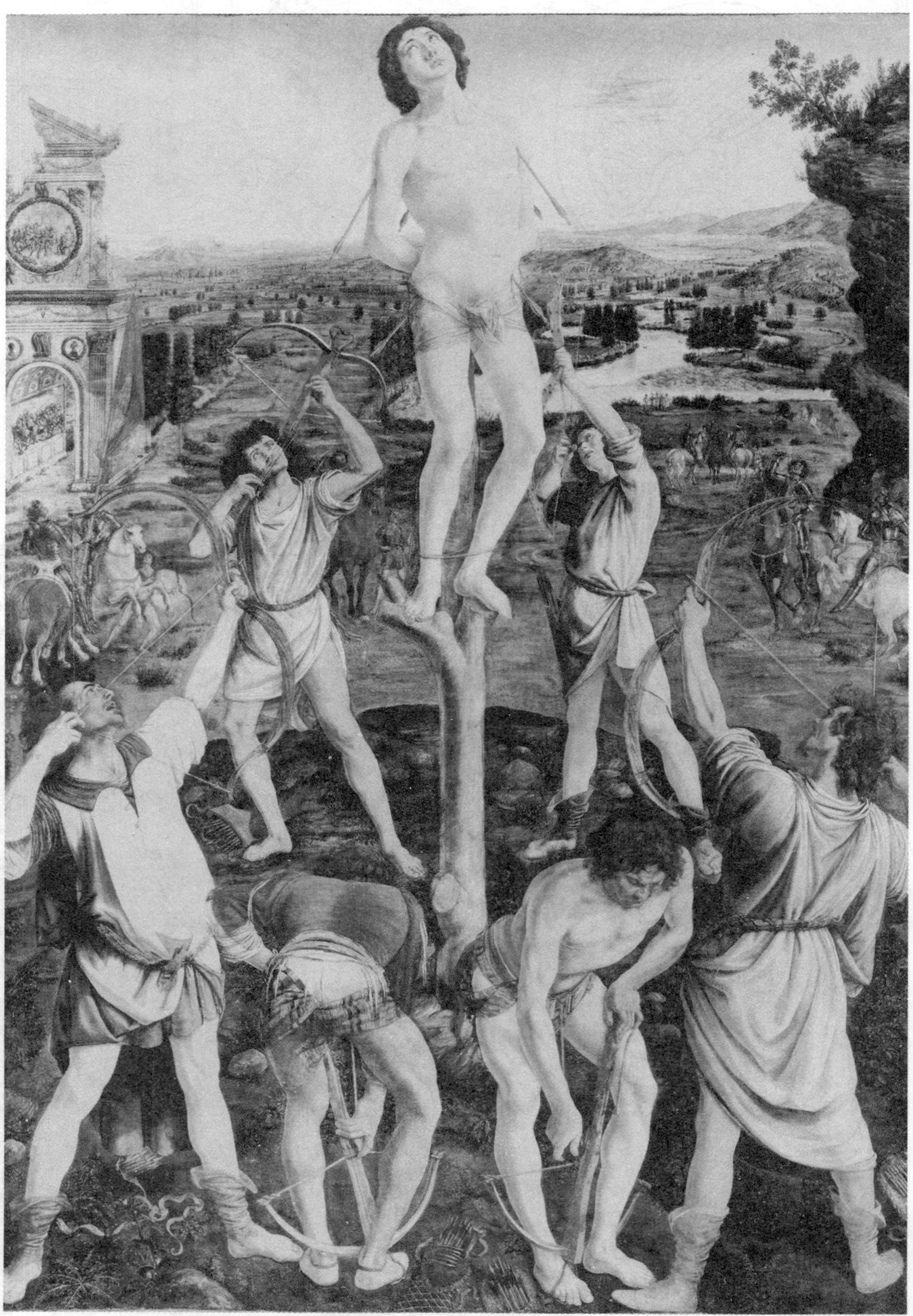

Fig. 6.6 'The Martyrdom of St Sebastian', Antonio Pollaiuolo (reproduced by permission of the Trustees of the National Gallery, London).

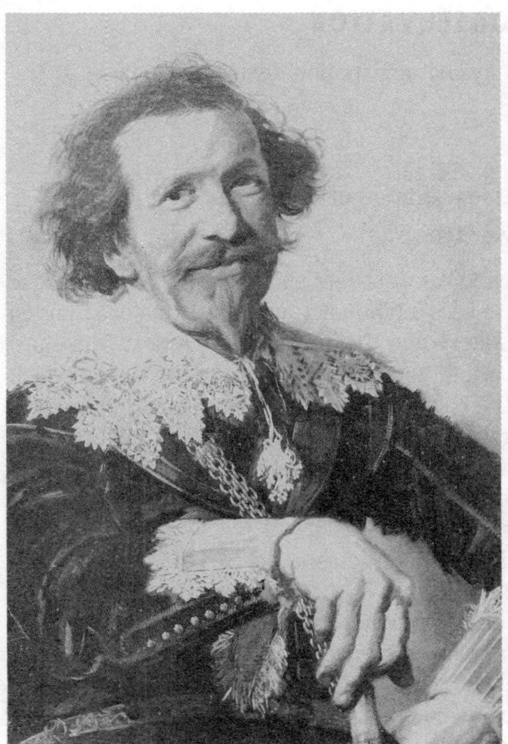

Fig. 6.7 'Pieter van den Broecke', Frans Hals (reproduced by permission of the Trustees of the Iveagh Bequest, Kenwood House, London).

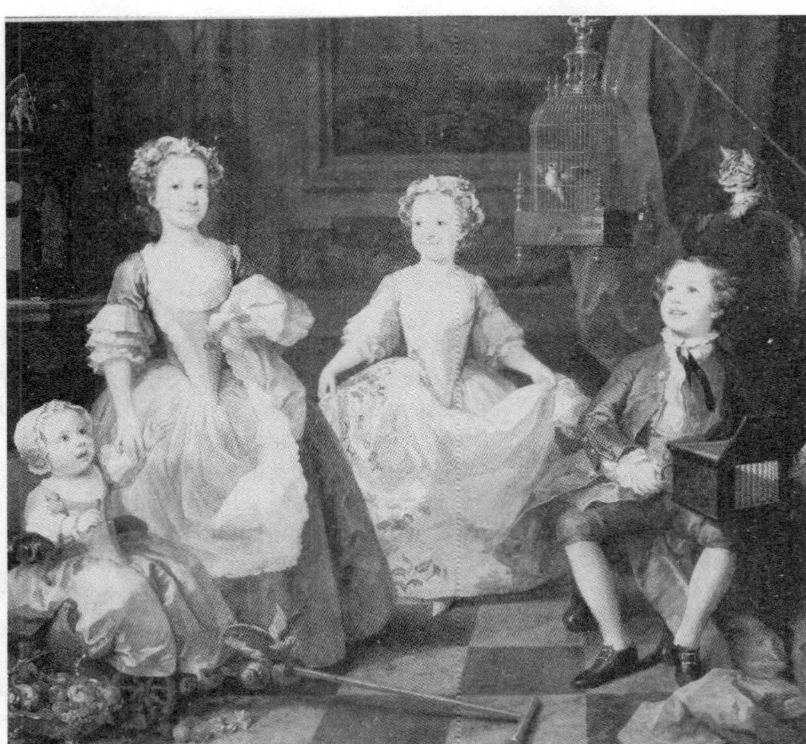

Fig. 6.8 'The Graham Children', William Hogarth (reproduced by permission of the Tate Gallery, London).

Portraits in particular tell us much about the costume worn at the time of their production. If backgrounds are included in the picture we can learn much more from them, but even if they are not, research into the historical background of the work can often inform us accordingly. Thus we are able to compare the variations of costume not only over different periods of time but also in different social and cultural circumstances. Take, for instance, Fig. 6.7, 'Pieter van den Broecke' who was a merchant-adventurer, according to Gombrich (1972), painted by FRANS HALS (*c.*1581 – 1666) and Fig. 6.8 'The Graham Children', by WILLIAM HOGARTH. The Hogarth work gives us plenty of visual clues to follow up, whereas in the case of the Hals portrait it is necessary for us to do some reading in order to find out something about the sitter and his times.

WORKING FROM DIRECT OBSERVATION

What the examination syllabuses say

The examination syllabuses bear out the approach we have recommended so far in this chapter, and indeed throughout this book. Terms and specifications in the syllabuses such as 'analysis', 'objects of varied shape and material', 'work from observation', 'analytical and written study', 'descriptive visual and written studies', 'appreciation of the nature, character and qualities of the selected item', 'structure', 'texture', 'form', 'colour' and so on are those we have already picked up in order to guide you in your studies in these sections of your examination. It is important that you bear such terms and specifications in mind at all times. If you do so, your drawings will take on a particular identity and appearance which comes from recognising and fulfilling the criteria contained in the examination syllabuses.

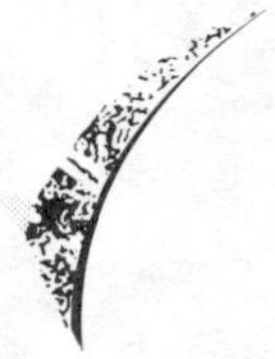

EXAMINATION QUESTIONS, STUDENT ANSWERS AND EXAMINER COMMENTS

Once more, there can be little advantage in considering just one examination question. In all the activities covered in this chapter, the examiners will usually direct your teachers to set up particular poses with the model for the life drawing you are to provide, or give you lists of things you may draw from.

PRODUCING WORK FROM DIRECT OBSERVATION

Direct observational drawing is part of the way that artists and designers:

- explore their world;
- understand their world;
- record information in his own right, or for use in other directions;
- produce work which stands up in its own right.

If you doubt any of this, try to see the sketchbooks of artists such as JOHN CONSTABLE or J.M.W.TURNER. Both these artists have their sketchbooks in three major London collections: the National Gallery, the Tate Gallery and the Victoria and Albert Museum. These sketchbooks show you how, and how often, each made studies of the things which attracted them. The sketchbooks also show the background each artist deemed necessary for some particular work he had in hand, or how he undertook a series of experiments which furthered his knowledge. By this means both explored their world, gained an understanding of it and collected information which might have been needed at once or which stood them in good stead at a later date.

Both Constable and Turner, as well as artists as diverse as RAPHAEL (1483 – 1520) and REMBRANDT, STANLEY SPENCER and DAVID HOCKNEY (1937), produced direct observational drawings which we can appreciate as works of art without worrying about the other uses and intentions which may have accounted for their existence in the first place.

On the other hand, artists such as Raphael and LEONARDO DA VINCI also produced direct observational drawings that are obviously studies made in preparation for something else. The fact that they were made specifically for another purpose is somehow self-evident in the drawings. If you look at Raphael's studies for 'The Virgin in the Meadow', you will see what we mean. There is a reproduction of this in Gombrich (1972).

Each of the practices covered in this chapter has its own distinctive character. They have all grown up in the history of art and design, with their own sense of tradition. It is important to accept this from the beginning. In your studies, no matter which particular practice you are doing, work in the ways we have suggested and maintained throughout this book. These ways are not revolutionary. They are designed to pick up and reinforce the strongest traditions of art and design.

Life drawing

Life drawing has a long history. From the very earliest days, studies were made in preparation for figures to be included in other works, as they still are today. This is especially so in the case of religious works.

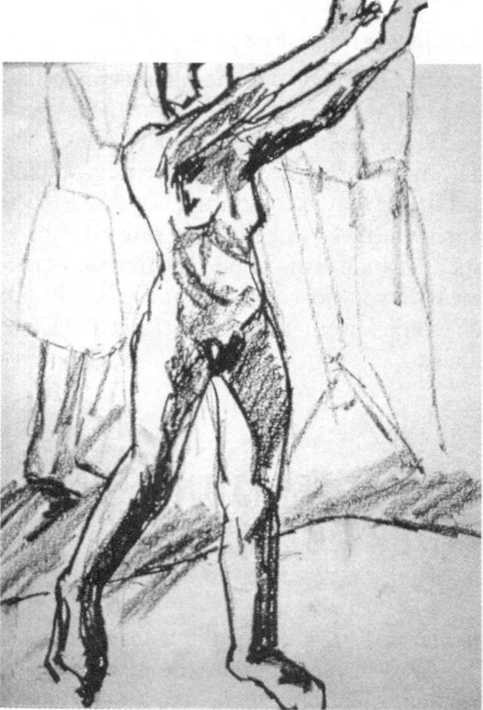

Fig. 6.9 Short poses.

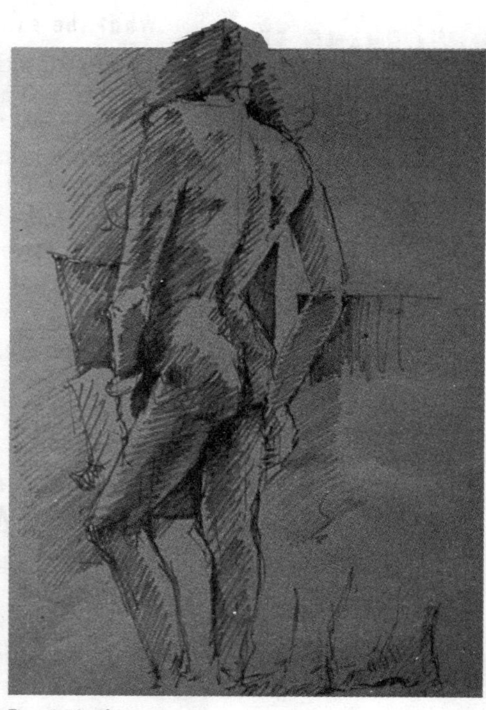

Fig. 6.10 Short poses.

Life drawing was formerly a central facet in the emergence of the portrait. Now, in art and design examinations, as well as in the training of artists and designers, it has been elevated to an art form in its own right. This means that a strongly identifiable level of expectation is present in the life drawing you do for your A-level or related examinations.

Part of this level of expectation is bound up in the requirement that you should do one or more short poses and one long pose in your examination. The different problems inherent in each and the stipulations for these two drawings impose a set of requirements which result in solutions which are likely to create distinctive and different visual results. Time will dictate what you can do in each.

Let us begin by showing you some examples of the work done in response to the short pose requirement in A-level examinations. We will then look at some examples of long poses.

The essential quality of Figs. 6.9, 6.10, 6.11 and 6.12 is the vigour, without loss of discipline, of the technique used in each case. The techniques are distinctive, but at the same time they can be seen as part of a continuum. That is to say, in slightly different ways they search out and portray very similar information.

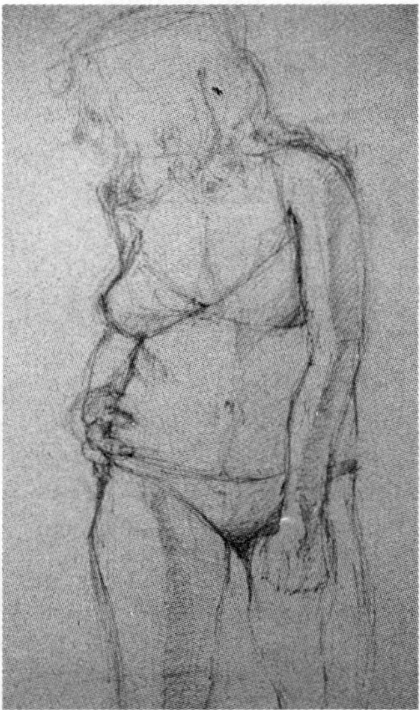

Fig. 6.11 Short poses.

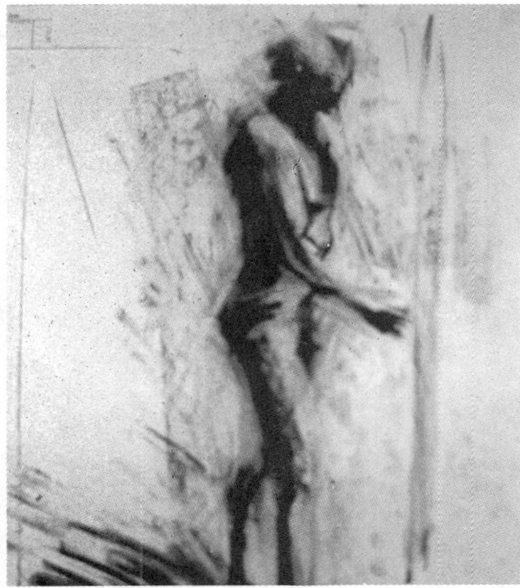

Fig. 6.12 Short poses.

The difficulty with short poses concerns the restraint of time. You have roughly fifteen minutes at the most to make this drawing. Therefore it is essential that you do all that is required of you in a way that allows you to work at speed, but accurately. To do this, before you bother about drawing techniques, decide on the criteria which will determine what it is you are trying to fulfil in doing your life drawing. The criteria might involve the following:

- showing the proportion of all of the parts;
- showing the relationship of one part to another;
- emphasising the pose;
- expressing changes in direction;
- showing weight;
- conveying differences in surfaces.

While these criteria have been composed with life drawing in mind, they are equally applicable to plant or object drawing. All you need to do is disregard the terms which have been used with the human figure in mind, and substitute terms which are more appropriate to either plants or objects.

Each of the short pose drawings included here makes good use of the time available. Because of the restriction of time, they are *broad* in execution and lack detail, each one:

- is well proportioned;
- is aware of the relationship of one part of the body with other parts;
- captures the pose well;
- illustrates and emphasises the changes in direction within the body;
- shows the distribution of weight in the pose.

What they probably fail to do is show the differences between the surfaces which go to make up the human body – for example, skin and hair. This is due partly to lack of time, but also to the fact that the techniques involved in each medium are not particularly suited to achieving this quality in the drawing. All in all, we would suggest that this is not a problem in the short pose.

Each drawing has within it a technique which amply records and imparts information about the nature of the body. In Fig. 6.9 there is a broad 'blocking in', using what looks like either a chalk medium or something more fluid such as ink. This technique begins to express the mass of the body. In Fig. 6.10 this blocking-in technique is used in a much more sophisticated manner, but is clearly related to the first example. Fig. 6.11 further refines the same basic technique for showing form and mass. It does not matter that one seems more refined than another. The technique comes from a well-documented and established method which can be identified throughout the history of art and design. In the work of the candidates the technique is used to good effect in each case; the 'refinement' of the technique seems to reflect the different media used, as is proper. As we have said repeatedly, each medium has its own characteristics. Fig. 6.12 exemplifies this. Here the drawing is almost a drawing of the medium being used, rather than of a figure in a standing pose. That is to say, the drawing can be appreciated for its own surface effect and imagery, without any necessity for it to be appraised as a drawing of the human figure. If you are able to look at examples of the black and white work of either FRANZ KLINE (1910–62) or PIERRE SOULAGES (1919), you can see what we mean by this unique identity of the medium and the marks it makes. Both these artists have work in the Tate Gallery, London.

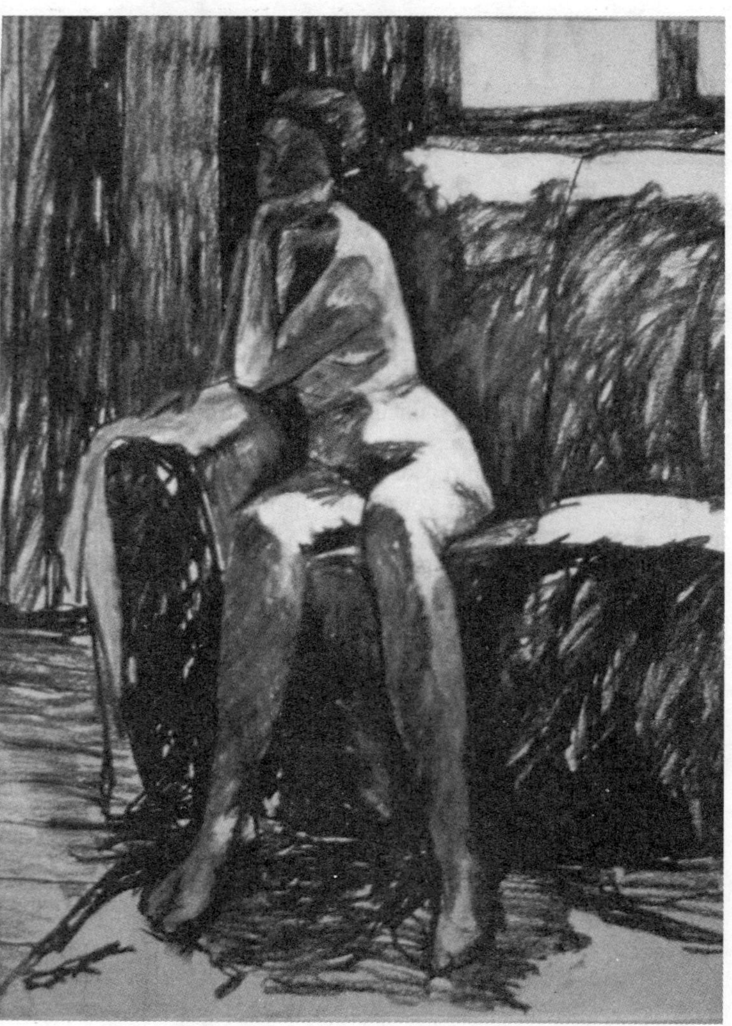

Fig. 6.13

The next set of illustrations were made in response to the **long pose** in the examination. We believe the differences between these and the work done for the short pose are visually self-evident. As we have said, this is inevitable. The purposes behind a drawing, the media used, the time available and so on all contribute to the appearance of the drawing – at least as much as the subject and the person who drew it.

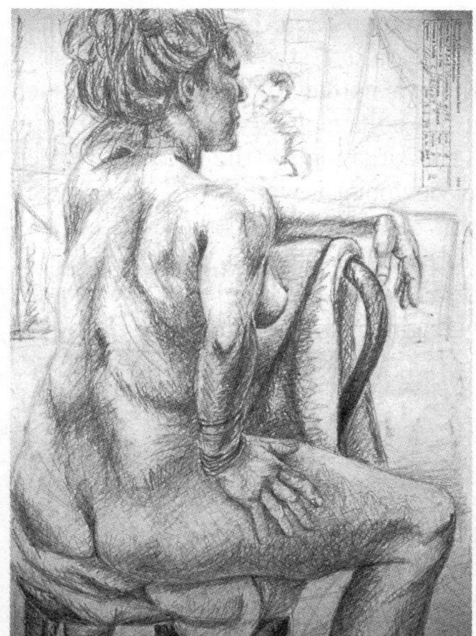

Fig. 6.14

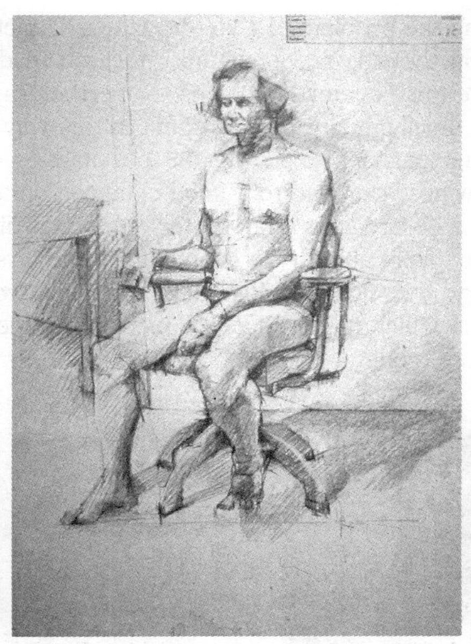

Fig. 6.15

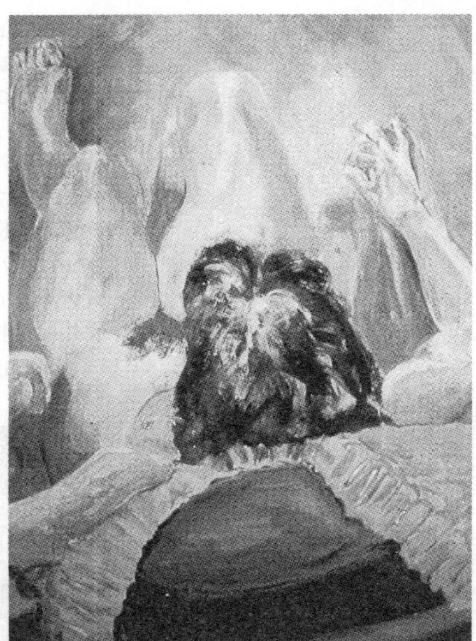

Fig. 6.16

In Fig. 6.13 we see a version of the technique used for the short poses, but here it is developed a lot further. Nevertheless, it still retains a free and impromptu approach to the problem. It is interesting to speculate on how the candidate would have treated the work if, say, a further two hours had been available. The drawing in Fig. 6.14 is perhaps an almost 'traditional' example of A-level life drawing. It is safe, well done and confronts all the problems without running away from any of them. For instance, the viewpoint introduces the problem of the dramatically foreshortened right arm, from the elbow to the wrist. You can see that the drawing adopts the same technique as that used in the drawings of the short poses, carrying it almost to its logical conclusion, because of the extra time available. We would question whether this is necessarily a good thing, but it cannot be denied that this approach succeeds in scoring highly in examinations. In contrast, Fig. 6.15 appears to use the extra time available for exploring a number of spatial relationships between the figure and his surroundings. As a result, even though it again uses the same basic technique as the previous illustrations, we feel that it has a lot more merit than Fig. 6.14. What do you think?

Fig. 6.16 is carried out in paint. This creates a different effect in the picture, as you would expect. The work shows a risk-taking approach in the selection of viewpoint. It could not have been easy to set up a situation permitting work from the eye level in this picture. Nor could it have been easy to draw and control the extreme foreshortening in the work in the way that has been achieved. The successful resolution of these self-imposed problems, however, is what leads to good results. Because of the opportunities this viewpoint provides, the overall composition of the picture is well worked out, and the work benefits from this.

We have largely used works involving the nude figure. To have a nude model is not always convenient in schools, and even when it is possible, there are problems as well as advantages. However, although it is very obvious where proportion throughout the figure goes wrong when drawings are done from the nude figure, it does allow you to show in a drawing how the figure is articulated and 'works'.

Many schools do not use the nude figure in their life drawing examination. Fig. 6.17 shows that this need not be a disadvantage. In this illustration we have two very powerfully worked-out designs, or compositions. The possibilities for contrasting black and white areas, because of the colour of the clothing, have been very well used, contributing to the impact of the pictures. You can show the articulation and form of the figure very well with clothing. If you remember the example we gave you in the chapter on still life, showing the use of a 'lined' pattern on a fabric to convey a three-dimensional effect, the same advantage can be used in life drawing. Lines, folds on the fabric of the clothing or even the shape of a cuff can be used to show, for instance, the roundness of an arm. At its boniest points, such as the elbows or knees, the body is very apparent, even through clothing. Look for these points and use them in your drawings to explain the form underneath the clothing.

In Figs. 6.18 and 6.19 we can see how a candidate has done preparatory studies, approaching the problem of a life drawing as a pictorial composition. In this section of the examination there is no opportunity for you to do preparatory studies over a period of time before the examination begins. Nevertheless, there is nothing to stop you doing such studies. A small amount of time spent in this way at the beginning of your examination in life drawing, perhaps exploring the possibilities of the situation by the means of quick pencil drawings, can lead to a good composition and viewpoint in your work. In this way you could well produce a far better work than if you had just tackled the subject from where you happened to be standing in the first place. We suggest that because of preparatory investigations Fig. 6.19, the final work, is a well-designed and worked-out composition which has produced a picture in its own right, rather than a study from the human figure alone.

Fig. 6.17

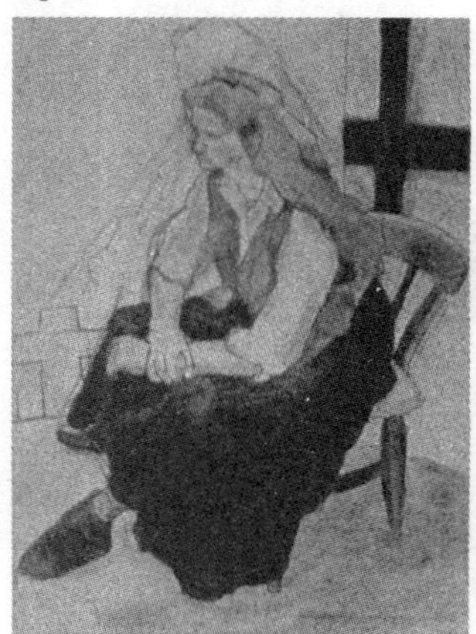

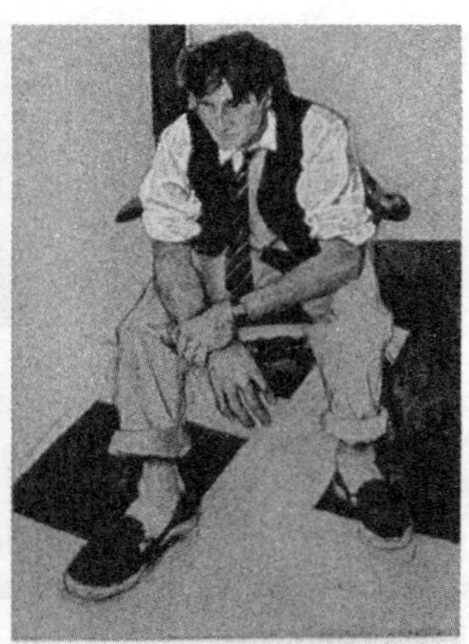

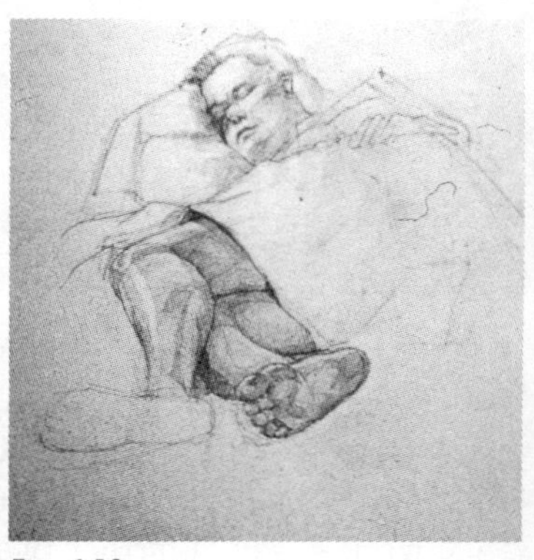

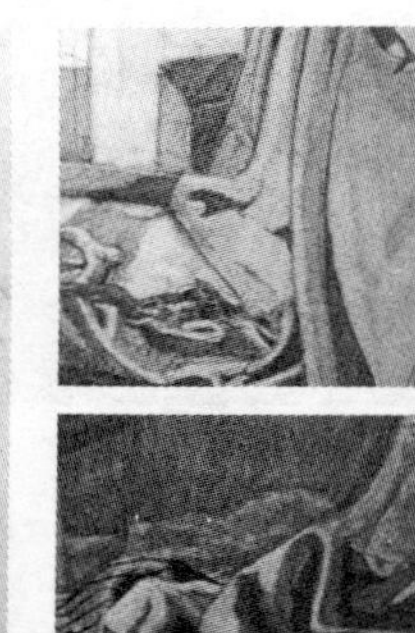

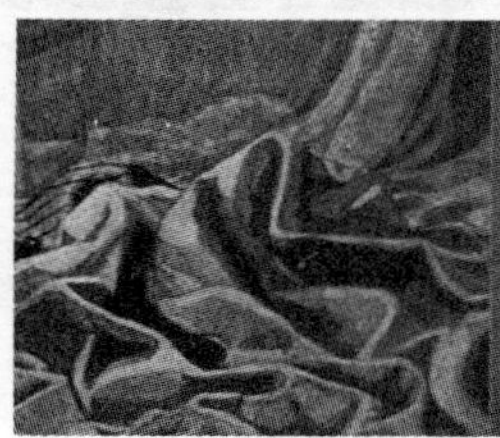

Fig. 6.18

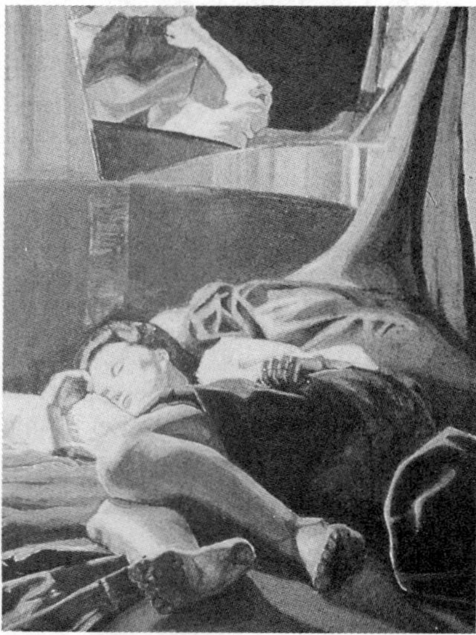

Fig. 6.19

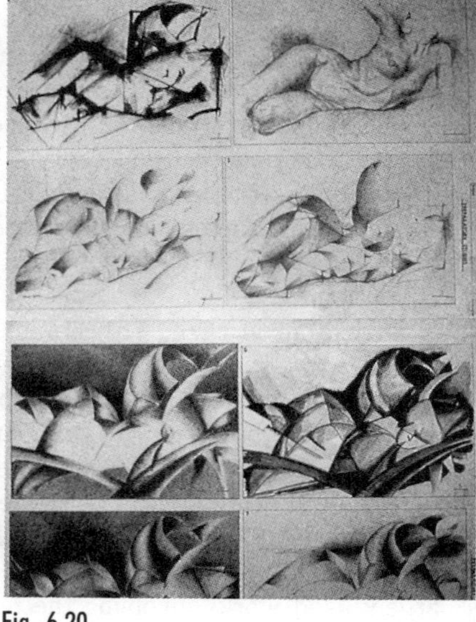

Fig. 6.20

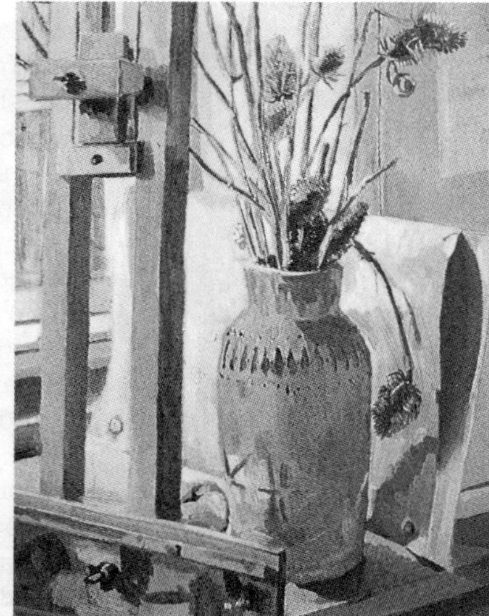

Fig. 6.21 (*opposite*)

In Fig. 6.20 this approach has been carried even further. Here we can see an approach which mirrors the most thorough work done for pictorial composition. Even though this examination was a test of drawing and observational skills, these skills are a product in part of your historical and contextual knowledge. This work indicates the breadth and depth of such knowledge. As a consequence, we believe that this is a set of work which should be allowed to participate in the life drawing section of the A-level examinations and rewarded very highly.

Plant drawing

Plant drawing has many traditions associated with it. Artists have always drawn and painted from plants, making expressive responses to what they see. Botanists use plant drawings to document and explain their scientific explorations and understanding of plants. Such drawings may show, for instance, the growth pattern of plants and the characteristics of their species. It has been the habit in the United Kingdom for artists to accompany scientists on their voyages to countries with different climatic conditions to our own, in order to draw and document the plant life discovered. Kew Gardens in London, in particular, has many fine examples of such drawings. Gardening publications use drawings of plants to show the aesthetic qualities of plants *and* their scientific characteristics. The above are all useful sources of reference and information to get you into the habit of studying plant drawing.

The fact that people have different reasons for making plant drawings is reflected in the way that the drawings take on significant and discrete appearances in each case. This is not to say, however, that botanical drawings do not have aesthetic qualities which are comparable to those in expressive drawings. They do, and what is more, such qualities are often all the better for the clarity of purpose behind the drawing.

We have not included many examples of plant drawing here, nor object drawing for that matter, as we believe that we have covered both well enough in Chapter 4. If you apply the criteria we specified at the beginning of this chapter, you will be able to produce good plant drawings. Whatever your speciality, remember to study *all* the drawings in this book, as well as particular historical and contextual sources we recommend for plant drawings above. Analyse what is good in them, and then apply what you discover to your own drawings. The main thing to remember about plant and object drawing in contrast to still life is that there is no need to relate either the plant or the object to its environment. You are drawing a single item. What you might do is design a good composition on your whole sheet of paper, perhaps by including more than one view of the subject, and including annotated drawings, rubbings, collages and so on.

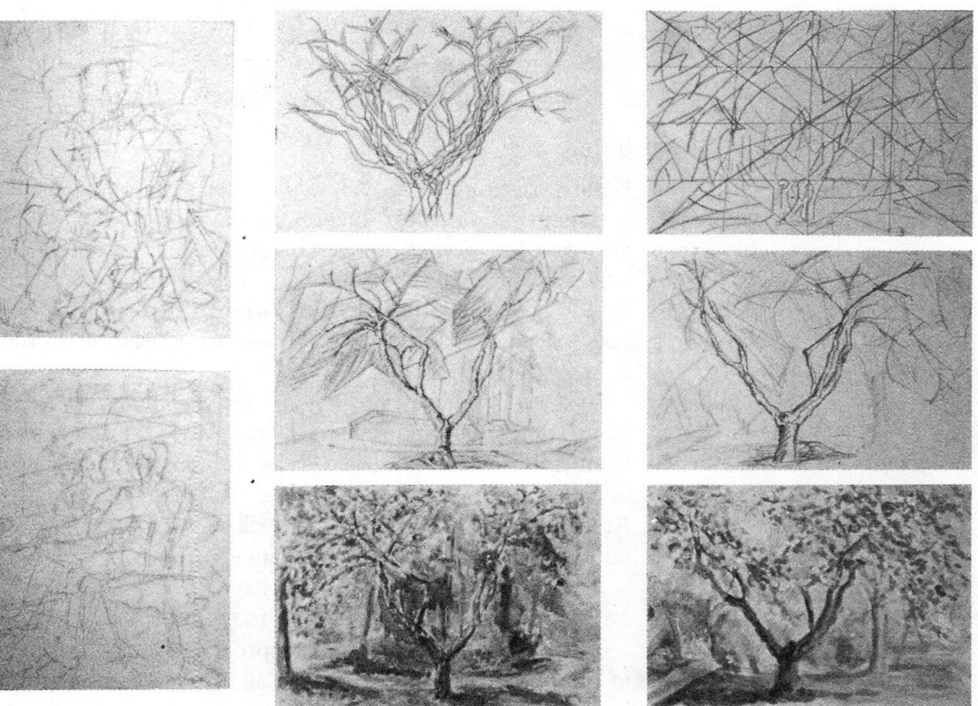

Fig. 6.22

In Fig. 6.21 it seems that the candidate was unclear about whether to do a still life or a plant drawing. As a result the work in not very satisfactory on either count. The plant is too insignificant in the work and was not observed closely enough to be drawn in an analytical and descriptive way. Even so, perhaps because the student was concentrating on the plant, the composition of the still life was also unsuccessful. Be clear in your mind at all times about what you are setting out to achieve.

The progressive series of studies in Fig. 6.22 and 6.23 shows an awareness not only of the growth pattern of a particular tree but also of various aspects of the history of art and design. Whether or not they would be accepted as suitable evidence of plant drawing by *your* examining board, we cannot be certain. You would have to rely upon the advice given by your teachers in this respect. However, we feel that the overall approach represented in these works could result in a very powerful response to the plant drawing section of most A-level examinations. For the approach to be more centrally placed within the ethos of plant drawing, we feel you would need to:

- work on site, directly from a tree;
- make close-up as well as overall studies of the tree, detailing and documenting its growth pattern;

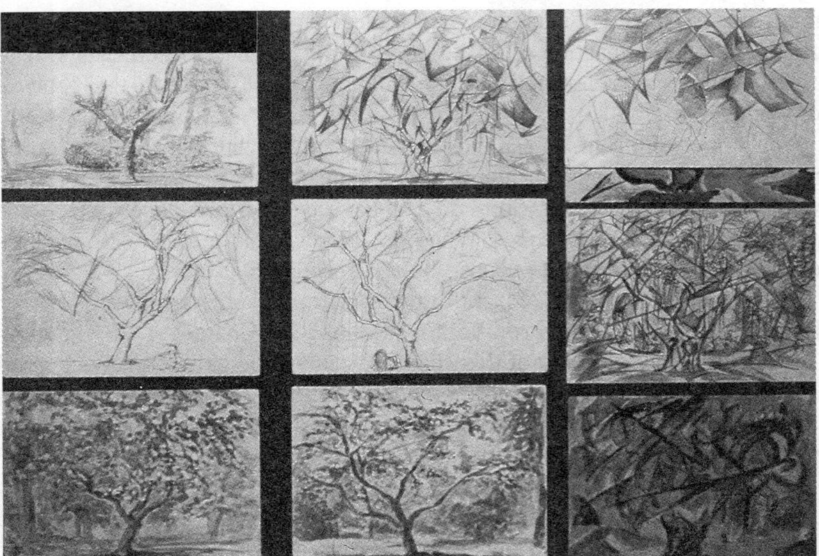
Fig. 6.23

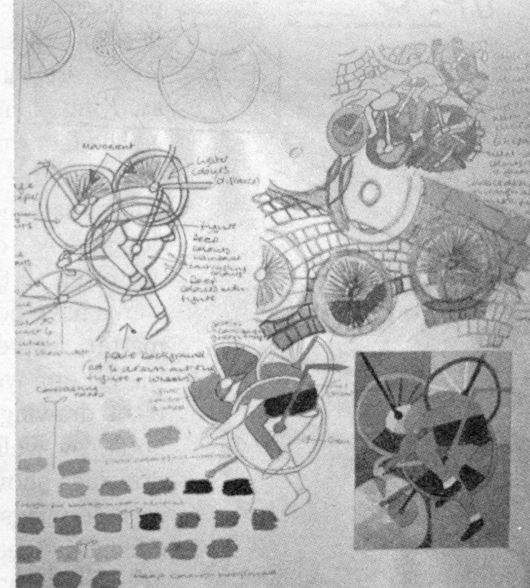
Fig. 6.24

- 'take from' one drawing to another, and so on, in your studies;
- clearly demonstrate your understanding of the tree in as many dimensions as possible, and not its visual appearance alone.

Object drawing

Before starting this section it is best to point out as clearly as possible why we distinguish between still life and object drawing. We take still life to mean the assembly and arrangement of a collection of objects which will remain static and more-or-less unchanging while you are working from them. In working from them, one of your major concerns will be to show **the spatial relationship of one object to another**. At the same time, you will be concerned to show the relationship of all the objects to the overall design of your picture.

As for object drawing you will be working with one object only. You will handle this object, turn it around, take it apart, place it at different eye levels and so on as you work from it. Your aim will be to show your understanding of it as an object in its own right, but also your understanding of the relationship of the parts within the object to the whole. At the same time, the object will show your ability to use a variety of media in an interpretative and illustrative manner (Fig. 6.24).

Again, the still-life works we have already included so far demonstrate a lot of these criteria, so we are not including too many illustrations of object drawing here.

Fig. 6.25 shows the worst approach to object drawing. Although there are a number of objects in the work, they are all observed as separate items, the eye focusing closely on each one in turn. Of course, given time, maybe the work could be pulled together, but the odds seem stacked against this. In turn, the explanation of what each object is, how it was made, how it grows, how it exists, what it does and so on suffers because of the approach.

In Fig. 6.26 we see a satisfactory, if commonplace, version of a still life work. We include it here because, although it is competently done and the parts (represented by the objects) are related to the whole, it nevertheless concentrates upon a single aspect of the objects concerned. This aspect is centred in the techniques associated with using a pencil in drawing. Despite the fact that the group includes a metal can and cut oranges and apples, only a limited account of *some* of their visual appearances is portrayed. The visual appearance portrayed deals with shape and the effect of light upon the surfaces of the various objects. As we have said, under these terms the work is competently carried out, but in terms of object drawing, is it enough? Our contention is that it is not. There are so many other qualities which are vital in conveying your knowledge of what the object actually is, why and how it exists and how it functions. This short list applies as much to natural objects as to manufactured objects.

In both Figs. 6.25 and 6.26 there are some very positive statements made, but they are largely **factual**. The possible **qualitative** values which exist in the objects concerned are to an overwhelming extent ignored.

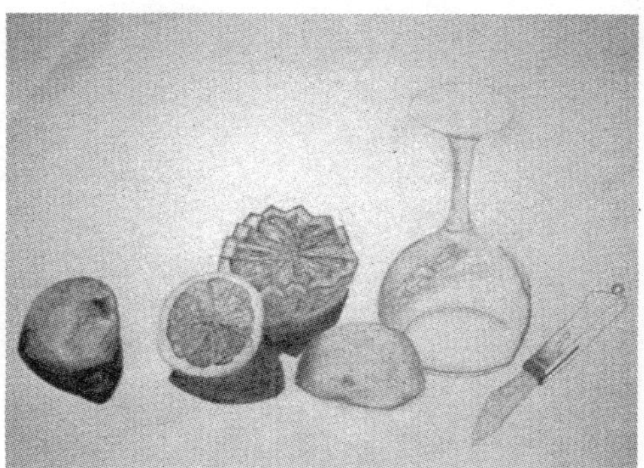
Fig. 6.25

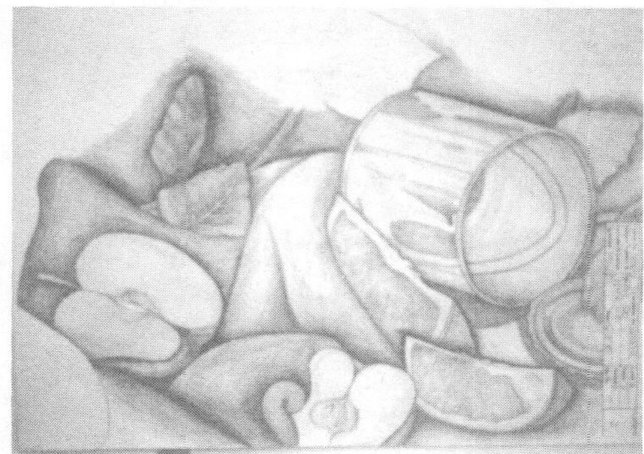
Fig. 6.26

Try writing a list of studies you would have made with regard to 'tin cans' 'apples' and 'oranges', in order to show as many of their qualities and functions as possible. When you have done so, carry out the studies, using any objects you choose, not necessarily tin cans, apples or oranges. The point is, the criteria in your list should be applicable to *any* objects, plants or human figures you wish to study.

In drawing from direct observation, no matter what the subject matter, your task is to do more than show what a thing looks like. Your work should explore the subject matter thoroughly, showing your knowledge and understanding of it and conveying this information to others. The information is bound up inextricably with the types of 'work evidence' you produce, which in turn depends upon your knowledge of, and experience in, the materials you choose to use, and why you chose to use them, as much as what it is you can see with your eyes. Cézanne once remarked that 'drawing is thinking with your eyes'.

EXERCISES

1 Get someone to pose for you in clothing which is:

- all striped;
- just black and white;
- all white;
- all black.

Make studies of *each* of the alternatives, trying to show the form of the person beneath the clothing. In each case, take from the effect of the clothing the best formula you can think of for showing form.

2 Choose a painting from the history of art and design which has a single, posed figure as its subject matter. This might be a portrait by someone such as FRANZ HALS, VAN DYCK, REMBRANDT, MANET, or CÉZANNE, each of whom did plenty of paintings suitable for this exercise. Pose a similar figure yourself, clothed in colours which are like the original and set in a small local environment which continues the colour theme of the original. Make a painting of your subject in the style you usually work in.

3 Select a natural object you can take apart, such as a fruit or a fir cone. Do a series of studies which help you to understand the various qualities the object might have. Reconstruct your drawings into a handbook which explains your object to potential users. Use as your model for this handbook a manual on a product such as a vacuum cleaner, a food processor or a video system.

4 Select about six different objects with contrasting materials in their structure. Using just a pencil, do a drawing of each, setting out to convey what the surface of each object feels like.

5 Do a series of studies which set out to convey the following qualities of objects in turn.

- shape;
- form;
- colour;
- weight;
- articulation and movement;
- feel;
- size and scale;
- beauty;
- ugliness;
- geometry;
- use and function.

You can use either the same subject matter for each study or choose different subjects which, in your opinion, suit the problem each time. In each study portray just *one* quality from the list above, until you have covered them all. Portray and describe the quality in each study both visually and verbally. You can use annotated drawings if you wish.

CHAPTER

GRAPHICS, GRAPHIC DESIGN AND PRINTMAKING

GETTING STARTED

The meaning of the term graphic has been extended as cultural changes and developments have come about, which is why it can apparently mean different things to different people.

In the first place the term was used in respect of fine art to describe the drawn output of an artist in monochrome – that is to say, using *one* colour and various shades of it. Often people mistakenly believe that monochromatic work is done only in black and shades of grey, but this is not necessarily so. For instance, many drawings were done in red chalk at the time of artists such as RAPHAEL.

The important thing to note is that under this definition of the term it was originally intended to refer to drawings, in contrast to work done in colour. We have already pointed out that a narrow definition of the term drawing is not really applicable today. As a consequence it is necessary to look for a wider definition of graphic.

Apart from its link with drawing, the term graphic is also applied to the work an artist does in the various printmaking processes, such as engraving, lithography, wood engraving and so on. This is a worthwhile broadening of the definition, but it does lead to some confusion. Many printmaking processes are used for more commercial and industrial purposes nowadays, and not by artists alone. The work involving printmaking in this case is produced by people we now call designers, but who, a short time ago, might have been known as commercial artists.

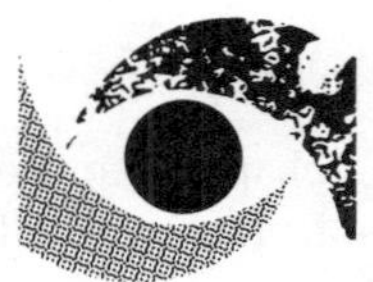

ESSENTIAL PRINCIPLES

DEFINITION OF THE TERM

A definition of graphic is best attempted if we separate artists from designers. Let us try to define the term first for artists.

Artists

“'Graphic' to the artist.”

Graphic work is two dimensional and is not constructed from paint or collage. It can be drawn or involve any of the printmaking processes. In the case of artists, it is usual for the work to be an expressive response to some observed phenomena or an idea they hold.

Designers and graphic design

For a designer the term would have a different but related definition. First of all, there would be no need to exclude certain media from the intended scope of the term. This was necessary for artists, when we excluded paint and collage and three-dimensional work. Second, the idea that the work is of an expressive nature is not applicable to designers. Of course, the work of many designers and many designed images do contain a very strong element of the expressive, but it is arguable whether this can ever be the prime element in the work of the designer.

“'Graphic' to the designer.”

Graphic design produces two-dimensional work finally, in any medium, for a purpose external to the needs of the designer alone. As such, while it might be partly personal and expressive, it obeys external criteria which give it purpose and help to shape its form and identity. The results are measured primarily against these criteria.

In this definition we have said that the work is finally two dimensional because it is often possible that graphic designers create their designs in three-dimensional form, using materials such as clay, card, wood and so on. They then photograph, film or video their results, thereby turning them into a two-dimensional image.

We have arrived at a definition of the term which proposes that for artists it refers to work which they do in media other than paint or collage. Under the terms of our definition you might find that you want to exclude further media in addition to paint and collage. On the other hand, we notice and accept that for designers the term has a slightly different meaning, although there must be certain similarities between the work of artists and designers.

Now let us consider a dictionary definition: ‘expressed by visual symbols; diagrammatic; vividly descriptive’.

The qualitative terms in this definition, ‘visual symbols’, ‘diagrammatic’ and ‘vividly descriptive’ are clearly applicable to the work which both artists and designers do. Although the terms do not offer any account of what it is you might do in your graphic work, they certainly do provide you with a valuable account of how you might do it!

The idea that in art and design visual symbols might be extended along a spectrum from expressive drawing to the diagrammatic is a useful reminder to you in your work, whether you are an artist or a designer. That your work should be vividly descriptive strongly suggests that you should be doing work which has vitality and originality – in short, work which is risk-taking.

Printmaking

This chapter also covers printmaking. Defining this is a rather more straightforward matter. **Printmaking is the variety of means and processes by which an image may be multiplied time and time again. Between the printed image and the original stimulus there is an intermediary, this comprises the materials and techniques which go to make up the particular printing process.**

This covers the essential aspects of a print. The first is that it can be repeated time and time again. The second is that there has grown up a variety of processes which allow us to produce prints. With regard to the latter, it seems to us that any method which will allow basically the same image to be repeated at least twice may be looked upon as a printmaking process. In this respect, blotting a wet painting at least once could be regarded as a form of print. Here there is no need for each print to be absolutely identical, as we would expect in printing processes which produce items such as commercially sold books, magazines and newspapers.

AESTHETIC CONSIDERATIONS

All that has been considered as regards aesthetics in the preceding chapters applies also to your graphic work, be it graphics, graphic design or printmaking. This work, like all things in art and design, must be well composed and executed.

Producing work which is well composed is a matter of sorting out what it is you want to do as an artist or designer. As always in art and design, remember that there is no right or wrong way to compose your work. What you do is either appropriate or inappropriate.

Knowing what is appropriate, or when a thing is inappropriate, is a matter of knowing 'the rules of the game' *at all times*. Of course, it is usual for artists to make up for themselves most of their own rules, whereas designers have to accept a lot of their rules from others. Of course, the rules of the game change each time you work on something new. In a new work, while you will call upon your previous experiences, you are working under an entirely new set of conditions once you have begun. This applies as much to artists as to designers. Further, because of their previous accumulated experience neither artists nor designers are ever in a position to start from the same point of knowledge and experience in each new work. So, no matter how similar a new task may be to work they have done before, they are involved in a new game with different rules.

For artists in particular, the rules of the game can change quite starkly as they are working on something. Artists learn how to react to the form their visual image is beginning to take rather than carrying on blindly with a preconceived intention. It is often said that once you have made *one* mark on a clean sheet of paper in art and design, the next mark has to be related not only to what it is you are looking at, or have in mind, but also to the next mark and its relationship with the sheet of paper. Of course, this process continues with the third mark, and so on. In this sense drawing, or indeed making any art, is a complex matter. Knowing how to make decisions about the problems which confront you repeatedly, taking into account all that has gone before, is a matter of having sufficient aesthetic knowledge to work with.

If what we say here is *not* a description of the way in which you currently work, it is likely that you carry on working in a largely uncritical way once you have begun what you planned. If this is so, it is likely that in your work you seldom take risks or arrive at invigorating and unexpected conclusions.

In the case of designers, they also find that their work changes as it goes on, but it is likely to be influenced by other, more controlling, matters which do not always allow them to take up the possibilities unfolding before them as they work. Nevertheless, as a designer you also should always be aware of this ever-changing situation, and respond to it, even if your explorations are later rejected in your work. Once undertaken, such explorations form part of a valuable set of evidence for the purposes of your examination, and should not be scrapped. Seeing what you have tried, even if it is rejected, leads your teachers and examiners towards a greater understanding of why you chose to do what you did in the end.

These other, more controlling, matters which designers work to might include things such as ethical considerations. For instance, as you work as a designer you might find that you appear to be condoning a sentimental attitude towards animals, or a romantic attitude about war. If you believed that such attitudes were wrong to hold, you could decide that you must change the nature and message of your work, provided it does not conflict with the requirements of your client. If it does, then you have to decide whether or not to continue with the work.

Designers might also be affected by economic considerations. These could be about time as well as money. If you were an advertising designer, you might find that your glorious idea to sell the product concerned on television would take about four minutes to achieve, and multiply the planned budget by about ten times! If so, you would have to react to the conditions surrounding your work, although you would not necessarily abandon the basis of your idea.

MATERIALS, TOOLS AND EQUIPMENT CONSIDERATIONS

Once more, the media you are likely to be able to use in your graphic work have their own respective qualities and possibilities. We have so far dealt extensively with the drawing and painting media. Here let us consider the other materials used in all forms of graphic work.

It cannot be denied that the printmaking materials and techniques call upon aspects which result in markedly differing results. Intaglio, planar and relief processes in printmaking will exercise firm controls over the appearance of your final work (see Glossary). Again, what you can achieve with a process which allows you to print large, flat shapes of colour in contrast to a process which does not is quite considerable. For instance, if you wanted to show how a field was ploughed into a linear pattern, it might be best to choose lino-cutting rather than silk-screen. On the other hand, silk-screen might be the better medium to use if you wanted to show how the green shape of a field contrasted with the blue shape of the sky, and perhaps the red shape of a wall.

In your graphic work, no matter whether you approach it as an artist or a designer, have the confidence to experiment with your media. Do not be afraid to mix them. For example, in the scenes above you might come up with something more vividly descriptive if you printed the brown shape of a field using a screen-printing process. Then you could experiment with overprinting it with a lino-cut which showed the textual pattern of the lines of the ploughing. Or you might choose to experiment by overprinting the green, blue and red silk-screened shapes with another medium, or even media, in order to enhance the image they present.

Find out what happens if you **draw** on top of a print such as a silk screened one. After all, there is nothing to lose in a printmaking situation. It is easy enough to have a number of identical prints at your disposal and to conduct a number of experiments on them without fear of failure. You are likely to learn from your first experiment and be able to investigate some aspects of your new knowledge in a second experiment using another copy of your original image, and so on.

We have not yet mentioned *photography* in this chapter. It is a strong and immediate graphic medium, as well as one which fulfils the criteria for a printmaking process. It can be used in a number of ways other than just recording what is before you. Used in this basic recording way, the selection of the subject matter each time is often decided on the basis of either narrative or aesthetic criteria. By this we mean that it is all too easy to take photographs which are selected because the scene reminds you of something you like and wish to preserve, or want to convey to others. Or it was selected because you thought the scene was beautiful. There is nothing wrong, of course, in doing any of these things, but we are keen that you should explore to the full the possibilities available each time in any medium you use. Photography can be used in a much more critical way, as we will consider more fully later in the chapter.

Before we leave the subject of materials and processes in printmaking, let us remind you that computer-produced graphic images are as much a part of the current educational scene as lino-printing is. The possibility of reproducing the same image a number of times, as well as of experimenting with the form of the image at speed, complies with any of the previous criteria used to describe and define printmaking. We shall pick up this newer aspect of art and design in Chapter 10.

CRAFTSMANSHIP

Some of the media you use in your work in the practices covered in this chapter will lend themselves easily to considerations of craftsmanship. The printmaking media, photography and some of the materials associated with graphic design have a strong technical content. It is this technical content which largely accounts for what is called craftsmanship in art and design, as well as in other activities. For instance, we call a joiner or a carpenter a good craftsperson if they use their materials in a professional and time-honoured way. Of course, we may ask them to make things which were previously unconsidered, but even then, if it is to be made of, say, wood, we can expect them to use the skills and traditions of their craft in producing it.

Where a medium does not appear to have this sense of tradition, it still has particular levels of expertise associated with it. It is up to you to ensure that you know of these, in part by a theoretical study and in part by personal, practical experience. What we are saying is that it is of little use using a pencil to produce something if you use it unthinkingly and without knowledge of its full potential. You *can* use it in such a way, but the likelihood is that you will not extend your range of skills in the medium, nor receive a very high reward for your use of it in your examination. This is not to deny that if you use any medium time and time again, you will be most likely to improve your skill. But the danger is that you will be using it only on a very limited front and that your range of skills will be restricted as a consequence.

The implication of all this is that although it is very satisfying and rewarding to produce, say, a finished etching, you should not lose sight of the need to do a certain amount of work which runs a high risk of your not having a finished item, or at least not a very satisfying one. This can only benefit your progress, and ultimate level of achievement, in art and design. Remember, if you experiment, you will add to your experiences, even if this results in a 'failure'. Such experiences will be of benefit in your next piece of work.

If you do take risks in your work, the most likely outcome is that you will be suddenly aware of a major breakthrough in what it is you do and how you do it. On the other hand, if you work in a 'safe' way all the time, while you will improve in the limited skills you are using, you will be unable to do anything different at the end of your course.

HISTORICAL FACTORS

In previous chapters we introduced you to the work of a number of artists. Some of the works we have mentioned have been what, in the fine art sense, we would call the graphic work of the artist in question. Therefore it is sensible for you to look again at these references in the earlier chapters, so that you can refresh your memory of some of the important historical references in your studies.

Apart from those examples, the development of the various genres represented here, and the media associated with them, is fairly easy to discover. This is because, as compared with art and design at large, some of the graphic practices have a relatively recent history.

Let us take printmaking first. **Engraving**, in its various forms, has a history of about 500 to 550 years. The first woodcuts date from the end of the fourteenth century, and etchings from around the early sixteenth century. A number of artists employed these processes, but you may look at the work of DÜRER so far as woodcuts are concerned and REMBRANDT for the study of etching. **Wood engraving** is a relative newcomer, dating back to only the mid-eighteenth century. The work of THOMAS BEWICK (1753 – 1828) is a fine example of this particular medium. **Lino-cutting** and **potato-cutting** are simpler forms of printmaking. Here you might study the work of a contemporary printmaker such as MICHAEL ROTHENSTEIN in order to see and understand the potential of even such apparently simple media. **Lithography** was not invented until the end of the eighteenth century. As examples of the use of this medium you would be well advised to study the work of artists such as HENRI TOULOUSE-LAUTREC and KATHE KOLLWITZ (1867 – 1945).

If you do study the lithographs of Toulouse-Lautrec, you will be able to see clearly what we mean when we say that each medium has its own language and form. A glance at his paintings and drawings will quickly convince you that he used the media concerned in a linear fashion for the most part. That is to say, he made up shapes of colour by juxtaposing lines and dashes of colour side by side. This was a technique which EDGAR DEGAS (1834 – 1917) used in his pastel works, and which influenced Toulouse-Lautrec. Whether it was pastels, chalks, conté crayon or paint which Toulouse-Lautrec used, they all lent themselves to the particular technique which he had developed. As such, we can say that a linear effect is part of the language of each of these media, although it is clearly not the only possibility each possesses.

Yet, when Toulouse-Lautrec came to use lithography for his posters for the Moulin Rouge, he used the medium in a series of large, mostly flat, shapes of colour. Of course, lithography lends itself to this form of language. At the same time, however, lithography can also be used in a stippled effect, or a textural manner, and so on.

The examples of work from artists we have discussed will allow you to see how they have used the media concerned in a personal and creative way, thereby expanding their own expressive output and creating new and original outcomes. Nevertheless, the media of printmaking have also been used from the start to reproduce pictures and other works of art which already existed in their own right. That is to say, to make and distribute reproductions of the original works of art.

This facility to reproduce a number of identical copies has led to the use of printmaking processes in distributing information, particularly with the arrival of the means to print the written word. This method of conveying information was also steadily developed and extended in other directions. The invention of lithography allowed artists such as Toulouse-Lautrec to design and print posters. Posters are a means of distributing information and as such should perhaps strictly be thought of as graphic design. In Toulouse-Lautrec's case, however, his posters are also regarded as works of art. It is unlikely that he consciously intended them to be that, particularly in the beginning. It was the overall technical and aesthetic qualities which he introduced into their design and production which seem to have given rise to this situation.

All in all, Toulouse-Lautrec's posters are a fine example of an artist working according to external criteria yet achieving a high level of personal and expressive content in his work. That is to say, although he had to inform the public as to what was on at the Moulin Rouge, and when it was on, he managed to do this in a highly developed aesthetic way.

In more recent times we have seen the mass production of items, particularly foodstuffs, which in turn has given birth to the mass production of labels. Such developments have created a need for artists who are able to design a whole variety of images in a wide range of media, so that things might be advertised and sold. At first, to distinguish between these artists and those producing more personal and expressive work of their own, the former were known as commercial artists. Nowadays they are generally known as designers.

Such has been the specialist development of the design world in recent years that we now have designers who specialise in certain areas of work only. Thus we have **industrial designers**, who design most of the products we use, ranging from can openers to cars, **textile designers**, who design the fabrics we use in our everyday lives; **interior designers**, who shape the appearance of the spaces we inhabit; **environmental designers**, who create the environments we move through; and **graphic designers**, who design things ranging from book jackets to television advertisements, and so on.

All this means you should study not only what is obviously the past history of your subject but also the present, because history is being made as you read these words. The great advantage of this is that you do not even have to go to a gallery or a museum. A history of the contemporary visual world and the times we live in is being brought into your home each day in the shape of television, newspapers, magazines, record sleeves and so on, as well as being displayed in places such as shops and garages.

CONTEXTUAL INVESTIGATIONS

Since the development of many of the practices covered in this chapter are so closely tied up with our everyday life, we have offered you considerable contextual knowledge as we have gone along. Even so, here are some additional contextual considerations. As the facility to reproduce images has improved and become so readily available, we have become conditioned to accepting reproductions of art in our homes. How else do we explain the mammoth industry which now allows many high-street businesses to exist purely by providing us with the means to decorate our walls with, for instance, VAN GOGH'S 'Sunflowers', or CONSTABLE'S 'The Haywain'?

The Victorians began the habit of collecting, and displaying on their walls, the reproductions and prints which were suddenly made available as the technology surrounding their production developed. At the same time, the whole business of accumulating possessions was accelerated by the Industrial Revolution. The availability of the means to mass produce items meant that things were suddenly within the price range of many families. The desire to possess seems to be part of humanity's character. If you doubt this, just look at a painting by THOMAS GAINSBOROUGH (1727 – 88) called 'Mr and Mrs Andrews', which is in the National Gallery, London. It is said to serve not only as a portrait of Mr and Mrs Andrews but also as a documentation of Mr Andrew's possessions – including apparently, his wife!.

The Industrial Revolution not only made many items economically available; it also led to a higher level of economic success, on both a national and a personal level. This is not to say that the conditions on which this new-found wealth were based were entirely acceptable! However, leaving that issue aside, one of the side effects of making money, it seems, is that after a while it is accompanied by the apparent need to 'make redemption'. Making redemption seems also to include making contact with the finer things in life, such as the arts. So we decorate our walls with reproductions.

On the more positive side, the various graphic practices have made it possible to convey information, which must be desirable. Certainly, one of the ethical considerations underlying our contemporary life is access to information and, of course, to the means of communication. An example of the desirable consequences of this can be seen in the recent history of America. Around the turn of the last century, there was mass immigration to America from Central Europe. People arrived by the boatload, unable for the most part to speak English. To deal with the problem of conveying information to this immigrant population (information which, for the most part, did little more than enable them to exist and settle in America) visual images were produced which told a story. It is often said that these little visual stories gave rise to the American comic-books, which now, of course, serve a different purpose. Or do they?

It is feasible to conjecture that a British comic-book called *The Eagle* helped to create a more informed situation in which the technological and scientific advances of the 1950s and 1960s could be accepted and absorbed by the inhabitants of the United Kingdom, if not most of the English-speaking world. If this is the case, it seems inescapable that the ease with which visual images can be reproduced, plus their strong emotional and intellectual power, can also lead to a situation where they can be readily used for propaganda purposes. Again, if you doubt this, study the imagery and its purposes on the sides of the 'Agit-Prop' trains in the early days of the Russian Revolution. Or reflect upon what we said earlier about one of the underlying purposes of much religious painting.

Remember, we are entering into these considerations of the contextual circumstances which surround the production of works in art and design because we believe it to be of the utmost importance that in your studies you should find out and understand what influences artists and designers in the production of their works. We are not setting out to tell you what to think, but to try to get you to think!

The more you study the subject of art and design and its implications in all of its contexts, the more you begin to understand that art and real life are inextricably interwoven, despite what is often said to the contrary. The result is that, even when artists seem to be working on a 'pure' level, they are still subject to the influences of their surroundings and their times. It would be beneficial for you to study something like CUBISM on the basis of the times in which it originated, as well as the philosophical reasons behind the works and their aesthetic qualities. In this way you could well see *why* those philosophical reasons existed when they did. This would lead you to a much greater understanding of Cubism than you would gain by just studying the works, or the statements, say, of PABLO PICASSO or GEORGES BRAQUE alone.

We said earlier that we would return to photography. Because of the nature of the medium, it is largely unselective. That is to say, after you have chosen what to point your camera at, the film records all that is within the scope and range of the lens of the camera. This is borne out by the number of times we are surprised at what is in a photograph when we see it printed. In selecting what to point the camera at, we most often choose subconsciously to ignore everything in our line of vision which we do not consider to be part of the *reason* for taking the photograph in the first place. As a result, photography is highly involved in contextual matters, revealing much that surrounds our often highly selective subject matter. This surrounding material is a visual illustration of what we mean by contextual.

This factor can be used most effectively in photography to draw contextual matters to the attention of others. For instance, by selecting your viewpoint carefully, you can highlight the juxtaposition of things which are at odds with each other. This might be the proximity of a power station to an idyllic meadow scene, or a motorway to a children's playground, and so on. Doing this puts things into context in a way that artists are so often at pains to avoid, whereby they select and include only that which enhances the attitude they already hold towards what attracted them in the first place. By means of a photo-montage, for example, you can show how changing the context of something can improve and enhance a situation.

WORKING IN GRAPHICS, GRAPHIC DESIGN AND PRINTMAKING

What the examination papers say

Table 7.1 outlines the established syllabuses which explicitly incorporate the practices of this chapter. Familiarity with what we have discussed will benefit your work even if your syllabus is not one of those shown here.

EXAMINING BOARD	SYLLABUS/TITLE OF AREA OF STUDY
AEB	ART AND CRAFTS/605 Paper 1 – Design and Practice of a Craft 605/1 (Time allowed: 15 hours) Option 06: Lettering and Calligraphy Option 10: Printmaking – Wood and lino-block cutting – Wood-engraving – Lithography – Etching – Screen printing as an autographic process Paper 3 – Part of Coursework 605/3 CRAFTS – PRINTMAKING/662 Paper 1 – Design and Practice 662/1 (Time allowed: up to 15 hours)

EXAMINING BOARD	SYLLABUS/TITLE OF AREA OF STUDY
	– Wood and lino-block cutting – Wood-engraving – Lithography – Etching – Screen printing as an autographic process Paper 2 – History and Technique 662/2 (Time allowed: 3 hours) Paper 3 – Coursework
JMB	CRAFT (DESIGN AND PRACTICE) (ADVANCED) Subject Group B: GRAPHICS Study Areas i) Printmaking: Any form of printmaking; relief; planographic; intaglio ii) Packing and Display: construction and decoration; typography; calligraphy iii) Photography: any form of monochrome, colour, still, moving, animated *[These areas cover your Coursework Studies and your Controlled Test]* Controlled Test (Time allowed: up to 15 hours) The Written Paper (Time allowed: 3 hours) Craft Study (Done during your Coursework, and assessed by your teachers)
NISEC	SYLLABUS A Paper IV: Design for a Craft (Time allowed: 3 hours) lettering and calligraphy; wood-engraving; graphic design (to include poster, book-jacket, record sleeve and package design) SYLLABUS B Section 1 – Main Study (Time allowed: 15 hours) 2. Visual Communications a) Graphic processes b) Printing processes c) Photographic processes Section 2 – Analytical and Written Study (Time allowed: 3 hours) Section 4 – Coursework

Table 7.1 The examining boards' titles for areas of study covered in this chapter.

The majority of examination papers develop the idea that work in these various practices is regarded in much the same way as work in still life, drawing and painting. That is to say, the examinations seem to accept that the majority of work practices will be part of the fine art approach. However, there are glimpses that much more might be intended, even if this is present more in what is *not* said than in what is. In any event, if you apply the standards and range of enquiry suggested in this chapter, and throughout this book, we are confident that your work will benefit and your grade improve.

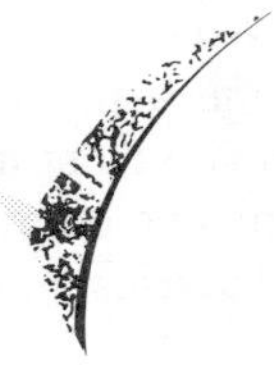

EXAMINATION QUESTIONS, STUDENT ANSWERS AND EXAMINER COMMENTS

Once again, the range of questions involving these practices makes it impractical to discuss a single question. It is far better to consider a variety of questions indirectly, by discussing work by previous A-level candidates. In these sections of the examination you tend to get a number of themes to choose from. Apart from the more obvious themes, which can easily be deduced from those described in previous chapters, particularly Chapter 5, this area of the examination also sets problems as questions. The notion behind a problem is that it contains a number of criteria which must be satisfied in your solution to it. In this sense, it is like having a design task to do for a client. No matter how creative and expressive your response to a problem is, bear in mind that at all times you should tease out the *specific* requirements of the problem, write them down and check from time to time to see that you are satisfying them.

As an example of what we mean, consider the following problem, which might be set as part of your examination in graphic design.

- A toy manufacturer has produced a plastic model of an electric locomotive, to 10 per cent life size, and wishes it to be packaged and sold as part of a Christmas toy campaign in shops and stores around the country. Design the package and propose a suitable decoration for it.

There are a number of things you need to find out and consider long before you begin to decide what your package will be made from and what it will look like. These include:

- What does an actual electric locomotive look like?
- What size is a real-life electric locomotive?
- What suitable materials can be used in the construction of the package?
- What is significant about Christmas as far as the campaign is concerned?
- Is the product part of a wider range of goods?
- To what extent should other products in the range be considered?

Once you have come up with answers to questions such as these (which you may ask yourself), there will be a certain number of **specific criteria** to which you must work. These might include the following:

- Will your package be a box, a bubble pack, an object which reflects its contents?
- What colours will you use on your package?
- What image(s) will you include on your package?
- What type of lettering will you use on your package?
- What will the lettering say?

This example gives an idea of the various decisions which surround work in the design spectrum of art and design.

Producing work in graphics, graphic design and printmaking

Because the evidence of this work is so widely available, we suggest that you compile your own documented accounts of the practices concerned. For instance, it is fairly easy to obtain examples of the graphic work of **graphic artists**. If you look through any magazine you will find illustrations reproduced. Cut them out and collect them as part of your study and as a basis for future reference material. At the same time, the work of **graphic designers** is everywhere around you. Identify this and begin to collect it. Printmaking need not be the prints which artists produce for sale, but can include examples which range from postcards and birthday cards to expensive reproductions of well-known paintings. Make the broadest collection of these that you can.

Once you have started your collections, we suggest that you then sort out, and classify, what it is you gather together. To do this you might try to write down some classifications which you derive from the terms used in this chapter. For instance, you could classify your collection under the different **processes** of printmaking as well as the different **forms** of advertising, such as posters, leaflets, magazines and so on. When you have done this, explore to the fullest extent the historical background of some aspects of your collection. You might choose these aspects on the basis of what you like most in what it is you have collected, or the items you think you will find most information on by reading and by going to sources of information such as galleries, museums, libraries and shops.

Graphic work

The type of work which might be reproduced using the graphic material of art and design, such as pencils, stick media, pen and ink and so on, has been well covered so far in this book. Therefore there can be little point in just repeating it with further examples. We suggest that you reread the other sections of this book which deal with the principles behind producing any successful work in graphic form, no matter which medium you may wish to use.

There is one further aspect of this section of the examination, however. Most of the examining boards include in their syllabuses a strong reference to **lettering and calligraphy**. This means that you must practice and develop your skills at producing lettering and calligraphy during your course of study. This will mean that you should be well able to produce hand lettering or fluent penmanship. Apart from the skills involved in shaping your letter forms in each case, you will also need the ability to design layouts and produce good compositions in your work. In this respect, both lettering and calligraphy are not unlike drawing and the rest of art and design.

In these sections of the examination, particularly where they move more towards the graphic design end of the spectrum of work, you are usually able to employ transfer lettering in your work as well as typography. There now seems to be no reason why your work should not include word processing and other computer-aided letter forms and images.

In calligraphy you will often include visual images, perhaps where you are lettering and depicting a poem. In any lettering work you could perhaps also include visual images. Therefore, rather than submit a set of works illustrating lettering and calligraphy alone, we suggest that you study the lettering in some of the responses to graphic design which are shown later in the chapter.

Graphic design

This section of your examination involves certain public criteria which you must set out to fulfil for each problem, in addition to producing a good piece of work in art and design. A good piece of work in art and design will involve attention to aesthetic content, demonstration of relevant materials' knowledge and expertise in handling materials. It will also depend upon the extent of your overall craftsmanship and the depth of historical and contextual awareness in your designs.

The examples we have gathered together all exemplify this overall awareness and ability to take into account the varied range of criteria, both public and personal.

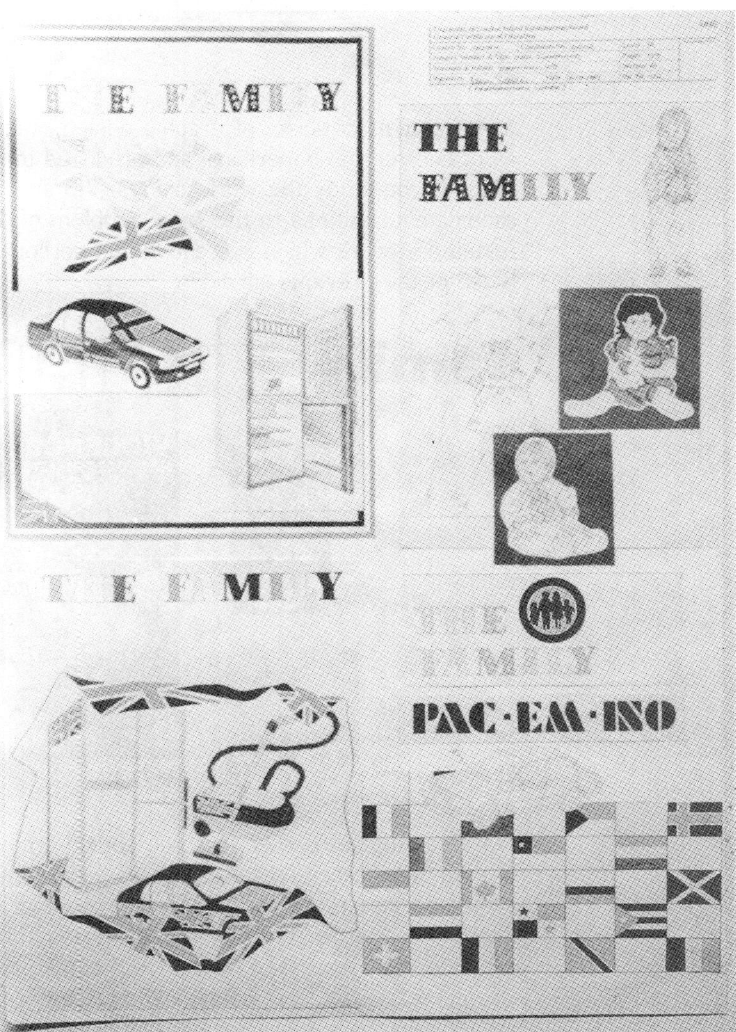

Fig. 7.1

In the first illustrations, we see a candidate working on the graphic design of a magazine cover. Fig. 7.1 shows the candidate considering a number of alternative ideas and propositions for the eventual designs. In these, a particular style has arisen. This might have resulted from a set of studies we cannot see here. If this is so, the examination result can only be improved by *including* those studies in the work presented for the examiners to see. In Fig. 7.2 the candidate has made certain decisions according to the public criteria inherent in the problem and the personal criteria involving the form and content of the solutions. The overall work is coherent, reflecting the fact that preparatory studies have been carried out, and can be evaluated, in part, using the values the candidate has personally set up as important in the problem and its solution.

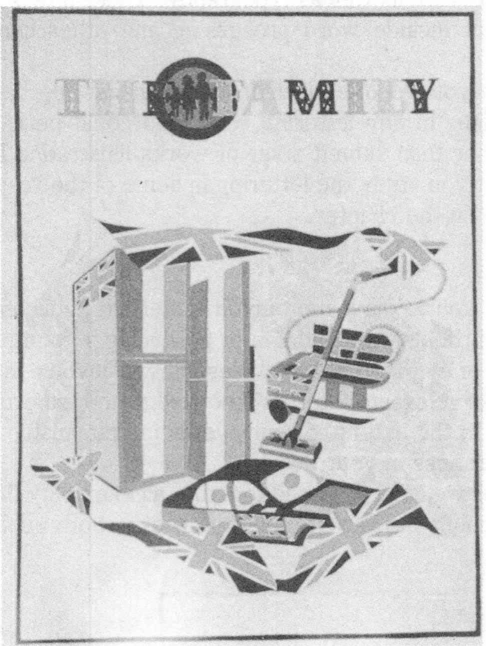

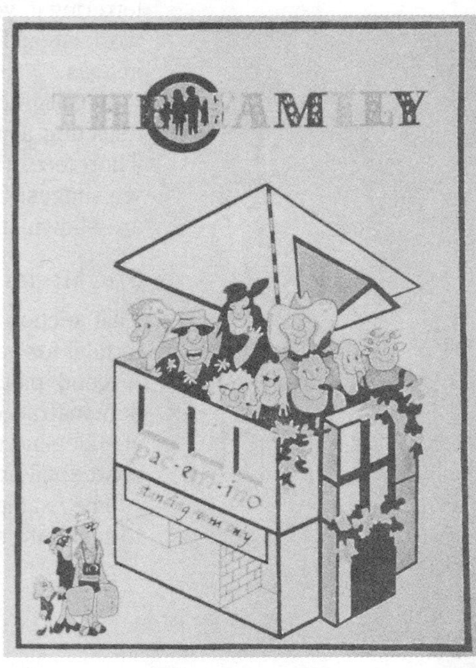

Fig. 7.2

A frequent criticism of graphic design, and indeed of all forms of design, is that the work is often too impersonal and produced to too restricted a formula, so that it all looks alike. If you study the work in Figs. 7.3 and 7.4, this is shown to be a fallacy. Another candidate's solutions to the same problem of designing covers for *Family* magazine have resulted in work which is creative and personal, as well as being dramatically different to those of the previous candidate.

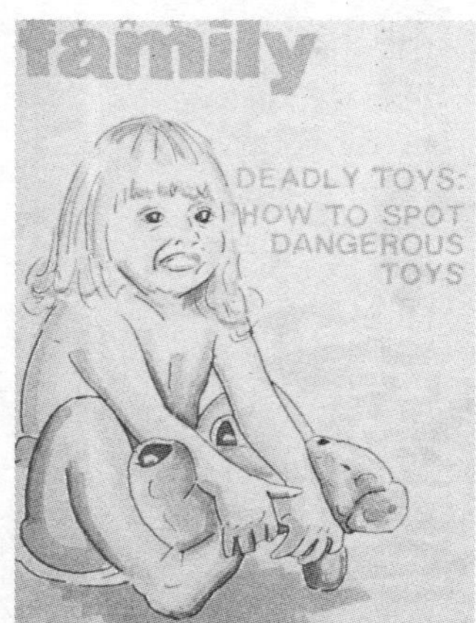

Fig. 7.3

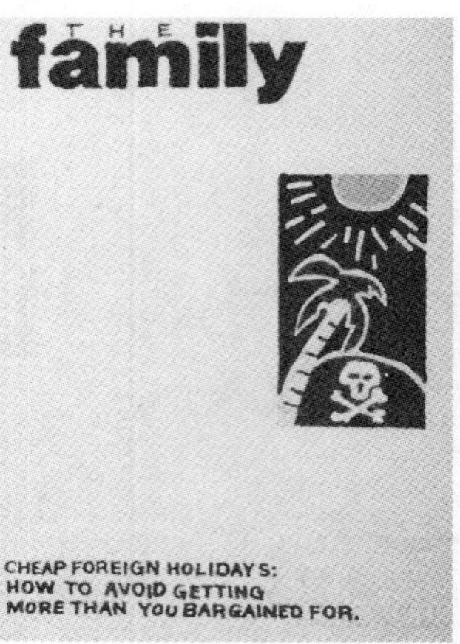

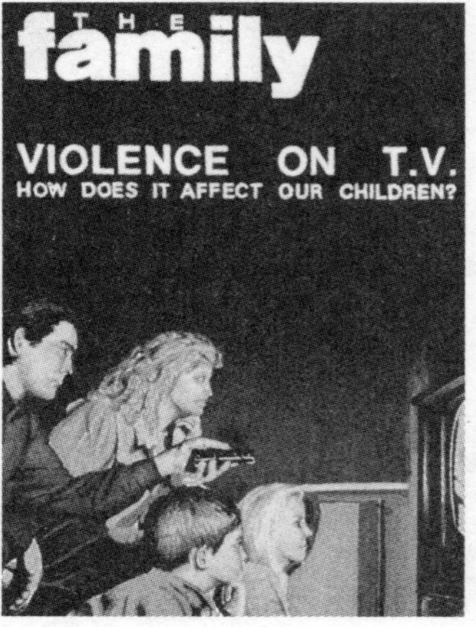

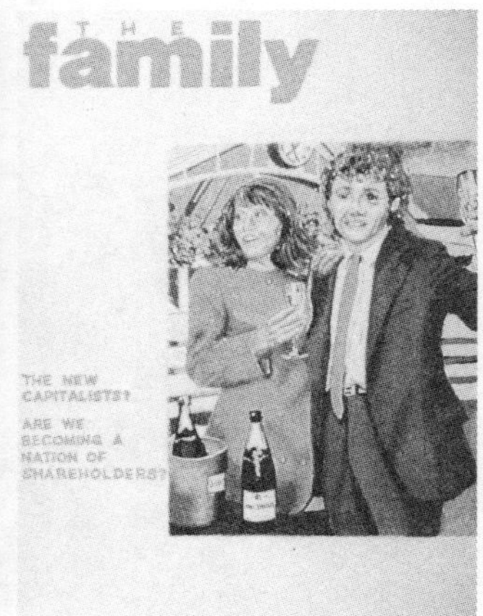

Fig. 7.4

We mentioned earlier that you should study the examples in this section with regard to their significance for lettering and calligraphy. The work of these two candidates offers a fine opportunity for this. The letter forms are different in both. What came first, do you think – the letter forms or the illustrations in the designs? This is, of course, an unfair question, because it is a chicken and egg situation. We simply do not know! The point is that in both cases, the nature and qualities of the illustrative matter on the covers match the lettering used in a very satisfying, aesthetic way.

In Figs. 7.1 and 7.2 the lettering is bright, colourful and light, whereas in Figs. 7.3 and 7.4 it is firm and sturdy. Why do you think the respective candidates chose to do what they did in this respect? Could it have had anything to do with their personal perspective of what a 'family' is, or should be? Try to write down a description of family life that the lettering and the illustrations used by each candidate suggests.

We believe that you are likely to have come up with accounts which suggest that the first candidate's view of a family appears to involve fun and pleasure. On the other hand, the second candidate appears to build up an image of family life which, while it contains pleasures within it, is primarily about stability, concern and responsibility. Do these brief accounts square up in any way with those which you wrote?

The whole point of this discussion is to emphasise that the overall content of your work can convey your feelings and meanings just as easily as it can portray anything else.

In the example of poster design shown in Figs. 7.5 and 7.6, we can recognise the considerable contextual awareness the candidate has shown in the design. The sprocket holes from the side of the film stock, although they have been used before in designs, are included and rendered here in a forthright and aesthetic way. The candidate has also shown a sensitivity to the whole genres of film, choosing as illustrative material one of the classic film productions of all time, *Casablanca*. The imagery captures the essential nature of the film, showing 'Rick' yet again disappearing into the background of the leading lady's life. In a single decision about which film to specify in the design, and by using two simple (but carefully related and rendered) images, the candidate has managed to convey the whole genre of the cinema in the poster design as well as the essence of the chosen film itself. The simplicity of the illustrative material and the forthrightness of the film sprockets pattern have been maintained and echoed in the bold, well-executed Gill Sans lettering.

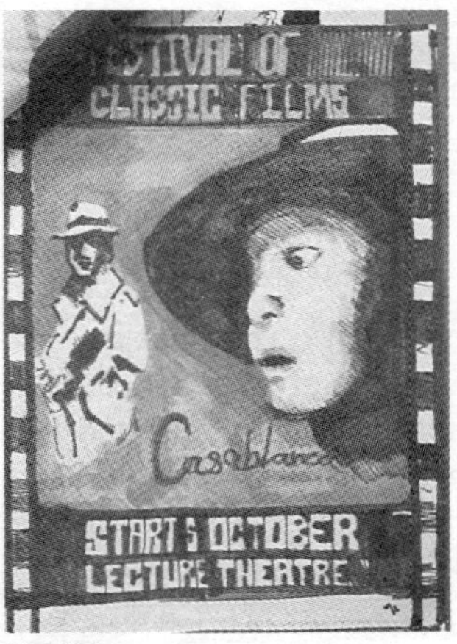

Fig. 7.5

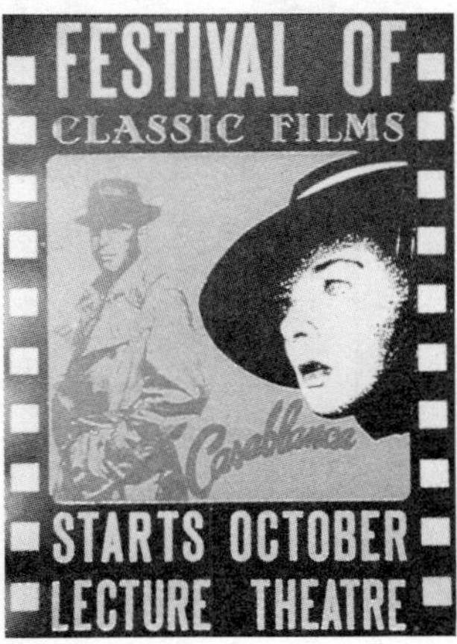

Fig. 7.6

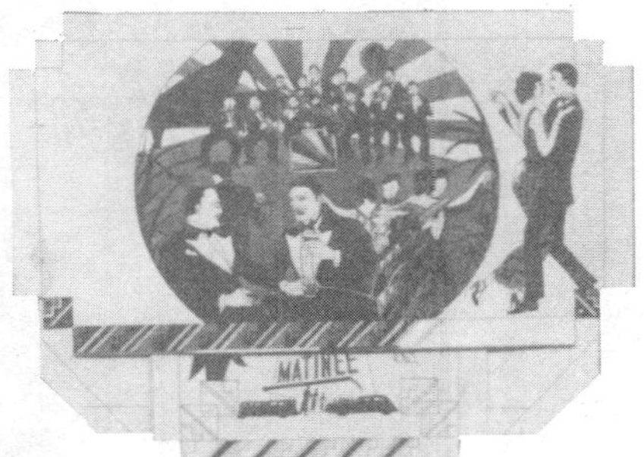

Fig. 7.7

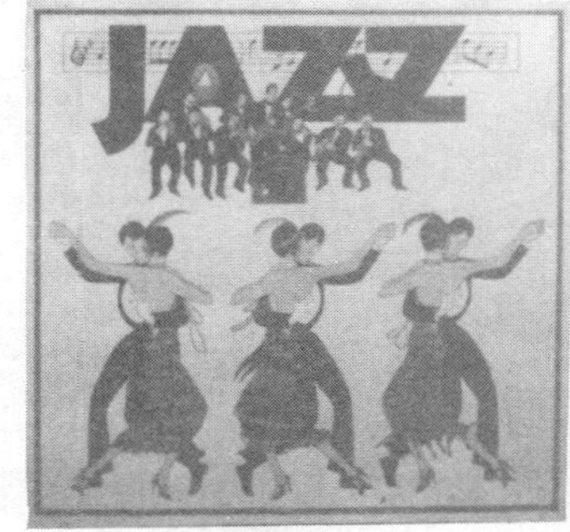

Figs. 7.7, 7.8 and 7.9 show a candidate's awareness of the fact that the fashions of an era can be resurrected and reconstructed into a contemporary design. This has been an aspect of professional design work for a fairly long period of time now. It depends, in part, upon the concept of 'nostalgia' for its success, but it does call for deeply researched information of both a qualitative and a contextual nature so that enough of the original wave of the 'fashion' can be discovered and understood to allow sincere and original designs to come about today. The danger of this approach is that the work might end up as no more than a pastiche of something from the past, which is neither explored nor understood sufficiently well.

One of the ways to judge success in this design approach is to see how well all the component parts of the design match and complement each other. It is easy enough to pick up something from 'here', something else from 'there' and to put them all together in a rather haphazard manner. This is certainly not the case with Fig. 7.7, which shows how discovered imagery and a rich contextual awareness can be designed into a fresh and original form. The work on 'Jazz' retains many of the original shapes and much of the style from the original era, but it reconstructs them into a personal and creative composition and message.

Part of the success of this set of work relies on the fact that it is produced in answer to a problem which has little to do with the era used for the imagery in the designs. The problem involves producing images which are to identify and publicise other activities, such as parties and restaurants. Because the principles inherent in the particular *purpose* of the designs have been kept to the forefront by the candidate, the results are original and fresh no matter whether we have seen the imagery before.

Like the film poster before it, the level of materials' knowledge and craftsmanship in this work is very high, as is the aesthetic standard. All this contributes to the overall success of both sets of work.

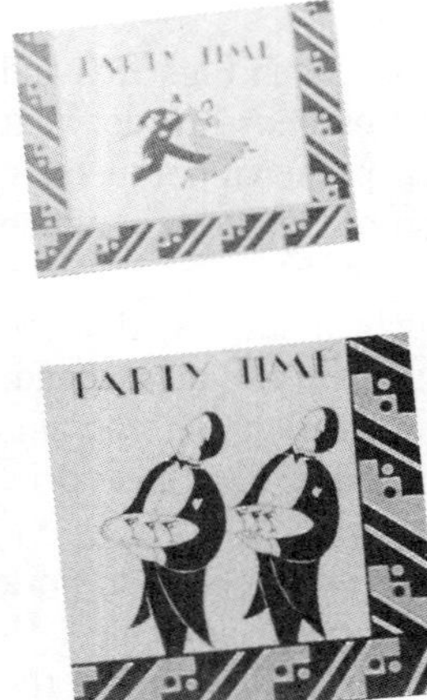

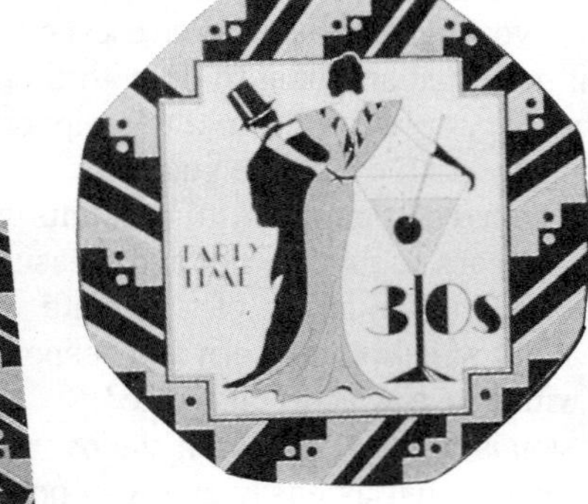

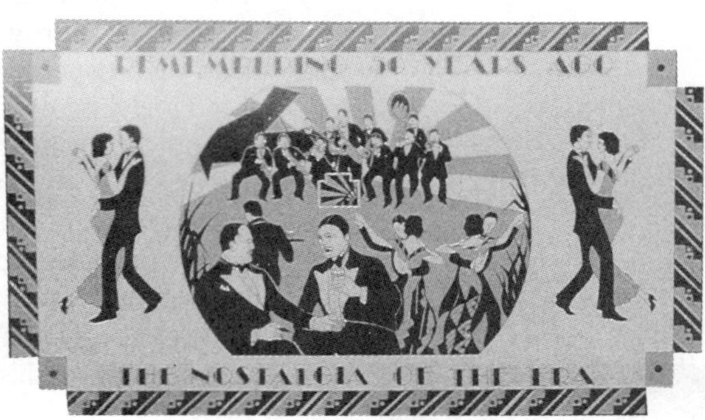

Fig. 7.8

Fig. 7.9

Printmaking

The print in Fig. 7.12 is silk-screened. It could, of course, have been carried out using a number of other processes. Had this been so, what would have been at issue is whether the particular process chosen corresponds as well to the imagery finally used, and the message it conveys, as is the case in this print. It is likely that the candidate would have needed to explore the subject further, in order to discover an alternative *aspect* of the subject which would fit in with the alternative *printing process*.

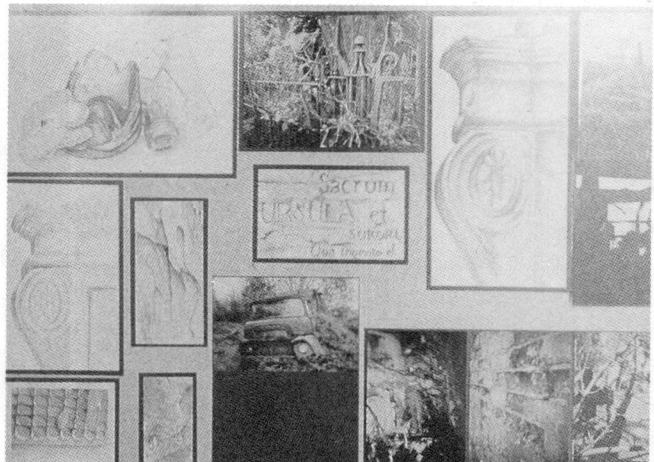

Fig. 7.10

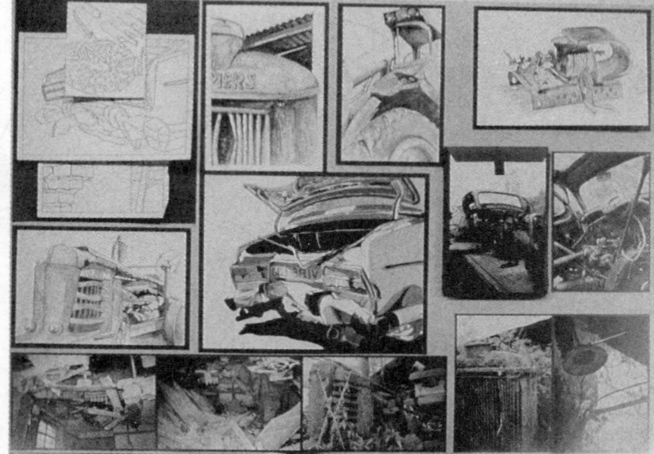

Fig. 7.11

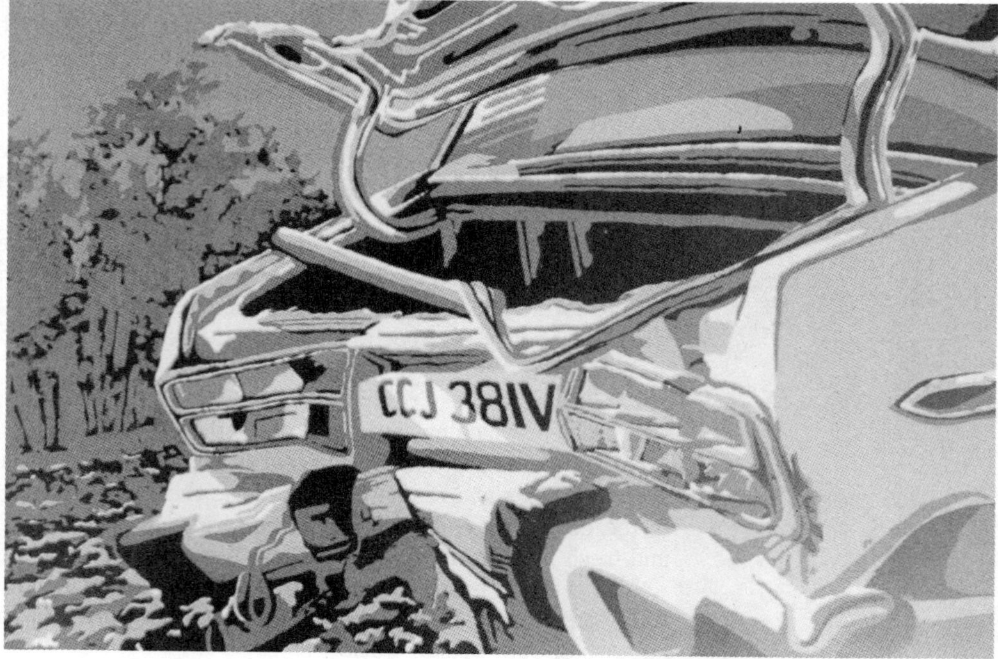

Fig. 7.12

In this work the original, investigative preparatory studies in Fig. 7.10 show an awareness and feeling for pattern and detail in what the candidate could see. This is extended further in the preparatory studies in Fig. 7.11, in which the final composition and print can be seen emerging, as if from a chrysalis, as the various studies proceed. The governing factors of **pattern** and **detail**, as well as sound **compositional aesthetics**, combine to produce a result which contains a high level of technical materials' knowledge and craftsmanship.

What this work indicates is that in printmaking there is no need to concentrate exclusively upon the techniques of the printing process concerned. Neither is there any need to set out to depict what is there exactly as it is there. This is a very figurative piece of work, yet it is also highly interpretative. This quality has caused us to praise the work of various candidates repeatedly throughout these recent chapters.

As is now becoming obvious, no matter what practice you may be studying, it is certainly not the ability to carry out work in a sound and proficient technical way alone that leads to the better results in your work. What you should be realising by now is that there are a few basic principles common to anything you may do in art and design. Learning about these, and attending to them first and foremost, is likely to lead to a good still-life painting, an exciting pictorial composition, as informative observational drawing, an effective piece of graphic design, or an original print in any medium.

EXERCISES

1 Using a postcard of GAINSBOROUGH'S 'Mr and Mrs Andrews' as the basis, choose two pieces of work which reflect the practices covered in this chapter and which, in your opinion, are pictures about people and possessions. Discuss the media used in each case and the contextual circumstances which surrounded each work at the time it was produced. Critically evaluate the purposes, values and achievements of each work.

2 Using the elements of solid shape, texture and colour, experiment with at least two different print media, exploring the facility the medium in each case has in relation to each element. Display your results so that they form a visual, comparative evaluation.

3 Design and produce some kind of image, images or sets of images which set out to convince someone to comply with something they might not necessarily agree with. For example, you might take as your theme 'A justification for rearing pheasants in order to shoot them as food', or 'Why the environment and its control is the concern of us all'. Use any media suggested in this chapter, or combinations of such media.

4 Choosing a single subject, produce images of it in at least four different media suggested in this chapter. Compare the effect the medium has had each time upon the images it produces and explain the differences you notice. You might do an expressive drawing in some graphic material first, directly from your subject. After that, you could work directly from the same subject again and again, or you could work from your first, intermediary, drawing each time, interpreting it in terms of the qualities you see each fresh medium possessing.

5 Take a series of photographs of a local environment which 'tells the truth'. The subject could be your home, your school or a much wider environment. You can adopt an attitude which is either supportive or destructive of what you see. You might even try to combine both attitudes in your work, pointing out the good and bad features of your subject matter.

TEXTILES, FASHION AND STAGE COSTUME DESIGN

GETTING STARTED

In this chapter we shall discuss the various individual practices which fall under the general heading of textiles, fashion and stage costume design. In some of the examinations you are called upon to create a design only. That is to say, you do not go right the way through the process and produce your design as a textile, fabric or actual costume. It is worth remembering this even if you are doing an examination which *does* call upon you to carry out your design as a practical piece of craftwork. The reason for this is that it brings home to you the importance of your **design** in these areas of the examinations. You are likely to find, where you do have to make your product, that it is all too easy to concentrate upon the craft techniques necessary to produce a length of fabric, for instance, and to end up carrying out something which is possibly not worth doing in the first place.

Learning the techniques and processes concerned is a fairly straightforward affair. It is better to concentrate upon learning how to produce good, worthwhile designs.

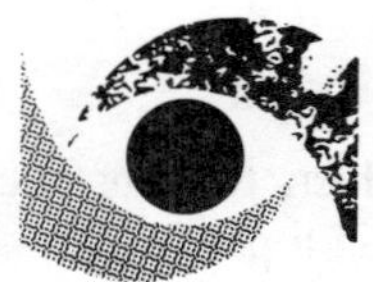

ESSENTIAL PRINCIPLES

DEFINITION OF THE TERM

Textiles

If we take the strict definition of the term it means 'a woven fabric'. This must be taken as part of the meaning so far as we are concerned here, but it is a very limiting definition for our purposes. 'Woven' is an adjective deriving from the verb 'to weave', which means 'to form threads into a fabric by intertwining; plait'. In turn, the noun 'weave' means 'a particular pattern of a fabric'. So far, then, we are certain that the term 'textile' means 'a fabric created by a weaving process which creates a particular pattern in its appearance'.

"Defining 'textile'."

This, however, although helpful, is still not sufficiently wide to describe the content of this chapter. Weaving is not the only way to produce textiles, and we intend to cover all the ways of producing textiles here. Some of the other ways in which textiles can be produced include printing, collaging and embroidering. Therefore a definition of the term which might be closer to our intentions that textile means **any cloth, fabric or material which is produced by any method or process. The pattern on the fabric, cloth or material can be formed by the production techniques of the actual fabric, cloth or material, or by adding visual symbols and/or tactile textures to it**. In practice this is borne out by the fact that in the A-level and related examinations it is common to refer to, among others:

"Types of production."

- woven textiles;
- constructed textiles;
- printed fabrics;
- embroidery;
- applique.

But even this is not the whole story. The examinations carry with them the notion of what textiles might be used for. Such uses could include:

"Types of use."

- carpeting;
- upholstery;
- curtains;
- dress.

This is straightforward enough, but tied up in all this there is still the notion of 'fashion'!

Fashion

Fashion is linked inextricably with aesthetics. This means that the term helps to emphasise the importance of the design aspect of work in this area. Fashion is also to do with contextual matters. That is to say, it is common to design textiles which correspond to a prevailing trend or style, usually of colour or decoration. Of course, someone, somewhere, has to begin the trend or establish the style, but even so, it is most likely that the trend or style comes about almost subconsciously from a variety of influences which exist in a society or culture and which are developing at that moment.

"Defining 'fashion'."

The dictionary definition of fashion is most helpful to our intentions here. Fashion is 'style, appearance; prevalent custom or taste, vogue, mode; latest or most admired style of clothes'. This definition encourages us to encompass dress design, which is a specific part of some examinations. It also concentrates our mind upon the appearance of a textile, which reinforces what we said about the importance of **design** in your intended textile.

Stage costume

Stage costume has a particular quality which is not necessarily present in the other practices covered by this chapter: its products, while needing to withstand the rigors of a long theatrical run, are nevertheless of an isolated and transient nature. That is to say, they are designed for a specific and confined purpose and once that purpose has been fulfilled, they are no longer of any relevance. Of course, in recent years it has become fashionable to buy articles of stage costume, particularly those used by pop stars. Exactly where these are then worn, though, is not very clear. It seems more likely that once bought they are treated as possessions rather than as articles to wear. In this sense the costumes remain isolated and confined to their original purpose.

"Defining 'stage costume'."

The dictionary provides us with a very sound basis upon which to construct our definition of the term: 'period or fantastic clothing worn by actors in a play'.

Even the most sedate costumes are often historically correct enough to be evocative of a fashion or era. That is to say, they have their particular 'period' quality and credibility, which is created as much as anything by a slight overemphasis, according to the judgements of the designer involved. On the other hand, the notion of the fantastic is often present in the costume designs for plays and other staged productions. This is a notion we believe you should bear in mind at all times. In most staged productions, it is necessary to be a little larger than life.

We might now proceed a little further with our definition of the term stage costume design. It is **the design and production of clothing to be worn by performers on the stage. The designs might be either historical or fantastic in origin; the costumes are of a fleeting and impermanent nature**.

By impermanent we do not mean we wish that the costumes should be badly or unsatisfactorily produced; rather we wish to emphasise that their life is restricted to the stage, and usually to one production only. We therefore do not require *all* the traditional techniques of dressmaking in their construction.

AESTHETIC CONSIDERATIONS

The aesthetic quality of your work in this section of the examination concerns two aspects. The first is straightforward enough. It is using and combining the elements, such as **line**, **tone**, **colour**, **texture** and so on, in your design for a textile, item of clothing or a stage costume. As we have pointed out, this aspect runs throughout everything you do in art and design.

To understand how the elements of art and design are combined into **patterns** for textile designs, we recommend that you look not only at other textiles but also at:

"Acquiring knowledge of patterns."

- nature;
- paintings;
- reproductions of mosaics;
- pottery decorations;
- illuminated manuscripts;
- armour;
- fairgrounds and canals;
- the history of fashion;
- the history of furniture.

The list could go on and is bounded only by your own level of imagination and receptiveness.

Do not look at these things in order to copy the designs you find, but rather to study how the elements of art and design have been arranged into patterns within them. Because of the mixture of two- and three-dimensional material among such sources, their study should gradually equip you to deal with the complex demands of textile design.

The second aspect of aesthetics calls upon a broader knowledge of contextual matters. For instance, you need to know how to distinguish between a design which is suitable for a furnishing fabric and one which is suitable for a dress. At the same time you need to consider how to design in such a way to take into aesthetic account the three-dimensional appearance of most textiles when they are in use. That is to say, you may create your design on flat paper and then print it on a flat length of cloth, but when it becomes part of an armchair, a set of curtains, a suit, a dress or a costume worn by a performer on the stage, it is then a *three-dimensional* object and is no longer seen to have the pristine, flat appearance it initially had as just a length of fabric. Also bear in mind that it will be seen in a new and different environment to the one it was designed in.

To understand all this you need to study textiles and their uses. You might go to your local high-street shops to do this, as well as places which house collections of examples from the past, such as museums and country houses. You could study the costumes worn by performers on television. If you are studying stage costume design, you should definitely go to productions in a range of theatres, such as local repertory, popular 'commercial' and major national theatres.

MATERIALS, TOOLS AND EQUIPMENT CONSIDERATIONS

Because this area of the examination involves an essentially craft-based set of approaches and techniques, the tools and equipment you use in producing an actual length of fabric are very strongly governed by traditional factors. The best way of learning these approaches and techniques is to practise and use them – by actually producing lengths of textiles, or whatever. No matter what you might read about screen-printing a design on to a length of cotton, or how often your teachers might explain the process to you, you will learn most by actually printing your design on to the cotton yourself. Make no mistake about it, your skills in this direction will be measured in your examination.

Therefore, once again, gain experience and develop skills by conducting a large number of quick experiments. The results will not matter very much and neither will the quality of your designs. In fact, you could include in your experiments a method of exploring 'design possibilities', perhaps by systems such as overprinting or by using a series of planned colour changes. In other words, learn the techniques of screen-printing, or any alternative process, by practising and developing your designing skills. Of course, some investigations and projects can be done quickly, others will take longer, and some could profitably be explored and developed in considerable depth over a very extended period of time.

You will be using the materials, tools and equipment associated with the various crafts-based approaches:

- batik;
- block printing;
- screen printing;
- weaving;
- machine embroidery.

You will also use the familiar media of art and design to work out and draw your designs. In these, again, experiment with the uses of commonplace media so that they might contribute positively towards the solution of your problem. For instance, if you are trying to create a design for a piece of machine embroidery, use ballpoint pens, or pen and ink, or technical pens to draw your design. On the other hand, if you look at the fascia of a line of buildings and decide that they have a linear visual effect, and consequently choose to draw them with pens, try your results out using machine embroidery. You need not carry out the whole of your design. At first you could do a portion of your drawing, just to see if it works in machine embroidery. If it does, put your experiment aside and plan your design anew in order to carry it out as a machine embroidery. If it does *not* work, save the experiment, but try another one in an alternative textile medium.

If you want to screen print a textile, why not design it using collage? The flat shapes of colour are rather like the effect of a screened pattern. They can also be cut out of folded sheets of paper, so that you can quickly see what the design will look like when it is repeated side by side. If you think of the strings of dancing figures cut from folded paper when you were a child, you will see what we mean by this.

Just get used to using the general materials of art and design in this way – that is, in ways which are appropriate to the craftwork you are doing at the time. If you do, you will find that you not only expand your materials knowledge but also improve your **design** skills; and remember, in this section of the examinations, these are as important as your **craft** skills.

As for making your textiles into articles of clothing, furnishing or stage costume, devise ways of experimenting on a small scale. This will enable you to try things out very quickly. For instance, you might take a doll as your model. When you work out a textile design, you could very quickly print it on to a sheet of paper by means of, say, photocopying the pattern a number of times in order to construct it into the repeat pattern you want. Many photocopiers will allow you to reduce your pattern in size, in order to fit the scale represented by your doll. If you use a material such as sugar paper, you will find that this is soft and strong enough to withstand cutting and joining. It will also provide a number of background colours to your design, as it is available in a variety of self-colours. When you join up your paper, use glue, double-sided adhesive tape, pins, needle and cotton, anything. You are concerned only to conduct an **experiment**. When you have the results of your experiment, store them safely for the purposes of your examination, but take a set of colour photographs of your work in case anything happens to the original experimental work.

This aspect of joining and constructing materials by means of glue, stapling and so on is very relevant to stage costume design. Because of the nature of these garments, they do not necessarily need expert and traditional needleworking skills and techniques in their construction.

CRAFTSMANSHIP

We have already given you plenty of examples as to how you might develop your levels of craftsmanship. Craftsmanship does not necessarily mean that you work in a slow and careful manner. It is more to do with the level of your understanding as to the technical possibilities of the materials you use at any time. This understanding is likely to come about faster if you learn how to plan and conduct suitable experiments. Get into the habit of asking yourself the question, 'I wonder what would happen if I . . . ', and then find out!

When you know some of the answers, you will be in a position to design in a more profound way for the task in hand. The ability to do this will be a strong measure of the level of craftsmanship in your work.

HISTORICAL FACTORS

Once again, studying historical examples will provide you with the means to develop your skills of both craftsmanship and design. The history of textiles is as long as the history of life itself. If you are a Darwinian, the history of textiles began with animal skins. If you have religious beliefs it began with fig leaves.

We believe it is best in this section of the examinations to study a variety of objects, artefacts and practices in art and design, rather than textiles alone. It soon becomes apparent that a good textile design is the product of a broad level of visual awareness and knowledge. Also, it can often be seen to derive from a series of contextual circumstances which have exercised some control over the way that the design has come about and been developed. Later in this chapter we will look at this point in more depth.

For now, let us press you to study things from the history of art and design such as:

"Useful historical studies."

- PAINTINGS – for the examples of textiles and costume they contain;
- ICONS – for the rich, decorative colouring they contain;
- ANCIENT POTTERY – for the examples of costume and decoration it contains;
- JEWELLERY – for the examples of design and pattern it contains;
- CARVINGS – for the pattern effects the carving processes contain;
- MULTI-CULTURAL OBJECTS – for their diversity and the broadening effect they can have upon our thinking.

Where it has been well documented, you would be advised to carry out a theoretical study of some historical activities where the production of textiles has been an important part of the particular activity. For example, you might well study the ARTS AND CRAFTS MOVEMENT in this country. Or you might research the activities and beliefs of the BAUHAUS in Germany earlier this century. In these movements the design of architecture, furniture, textiles, paintings and so on were all considered as a form of *integration*. The study of the life and work of architects such as FRANK LLOYD WRIGHT (1869 – 1959) or artists such as HENRI MATISSE (1869 – 1954), PIET MONDRIAN or THEO VAN DOESBURG (1883–1931) will provide you with a wealth of understanding upon which to base your own original ideas and designs.

In other words, do not copy the work of the examples we provide, but do try to sort out and grasp the principles held and worked to in producing the work in such examples. If you do this, you will be better equipped to produce genuinely fresh and original work of your own.

CONTEXTUAL INVESTIGATIONS

Textiles, fashions and even costumes are extremely relevant products so far as living is concerned. They are not just a decoration tagged on to our mode of life, but are an essential and fundamental part of it.

Why is there a need to decorate textiles with patterns and colours? After all, are not the functions of textiles in clothes to keep us warm and to add comfort to our existence? If so, there can surely be no need to embellish things. Yet humanity has an apparently insatiable desire for pattern and colour and to decorate almost anything in sight. A wide variety of research indicates this, ranging from studies of primitive communities to studies of the culture within our own society.

Because textiles and fashion are so relevant to our everyday life, in order to understand their **appearance** it is essential to study the reasons for their **presence**. This means that it is vital to tease out the values of the times and circumstances which surrounded their particular production.

In very simplistic terms, it soon becomes clear why textiles in ancient times used only particular colours as part of their decorative adornment. The technology of the time was restricted largely to earth colours. In turn, we can soon understand why cheap cottons were produced in the United Kingdom after the start of the Industrial Revolution, and why they had the appearance they did. It is equally possible to see why such products are no longer produced in the United Kingdom in the quantities they were about sixty or more years ago, and why they are now produced in such great quantities in Third World countries. If we *do* work all this out, we can then understand why, over time, the appearance of cottons has changed to such a large extent in Britain.

Again, once we investigate the ways in which men and women are regarded in a society such as ours, then the fundamental differences between men's and women's clothing in much of the contemporary Western world can be understood. This gives rise to an appreciation of why the decorative appearance of the textiles used to make clothing for each gender is so different. This deduction is then borne out if we study, say, men's contemporary clothing in a Far Eastern country, where more traditional cultural values persist, in contrast to our society, where the current traditions are social rather than cultural.

Understanding why the shape, size and style of contemporary clothing changes so frequently demands that we study the contextual relationship between **warmth, comfort, design** and **economics**. Grasping why the changes are what they are is another matter. For this we need to study a whole set of social and cultural factors, so that we can discover their subtle influences upon the design of textiles and the development of fashion. For instance, is it reasonable to expect that the shapes of clothing will become more austere and economical at times of financial difficulty and of concern over conservation, and so on? It is certainly maintained that the post-war 1950s fashion, the 'A-line', was a deliberate move against the then existing austerity.

As an exercise study Fig. 8.1, 'Music in the Tuileries Gardens' by EDOUARD MANET. Manet painted this in 1861. Consider how things have changed since then. The gathering of people in masses in public places to hear music played may have been unusual then, but is commonplace today. What are the cultural and social changes involved? What are the changes in fashion as regards dress, and why have they come about? It would help 'flesh out' the exercise if you also compared these two extremes with another similar event, such as listening to a band playing on a bandstand, either in a park or on a pier, in about the 1930s. Present your thoughts in written form, with illustrations to help make your points.

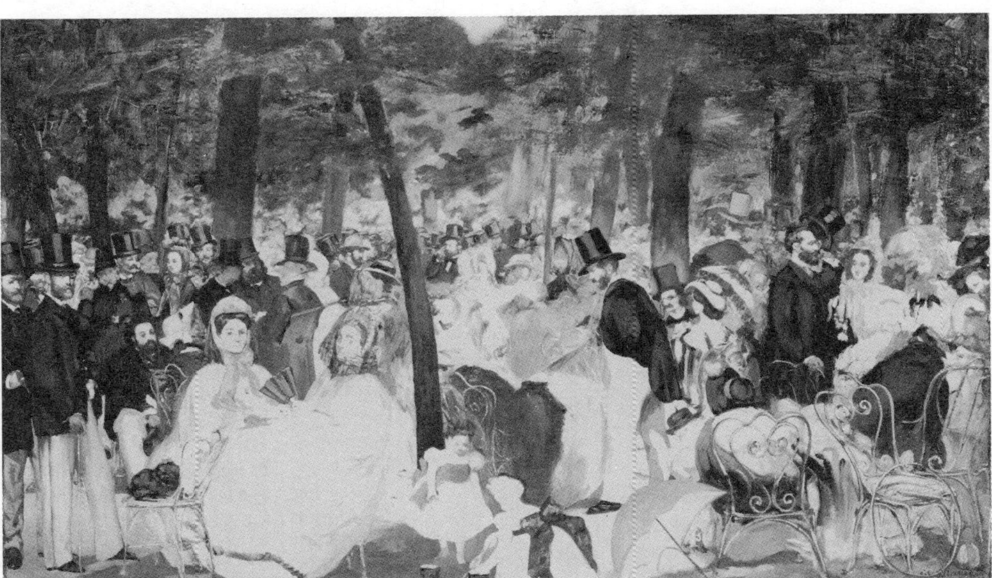

Fig. 8.1 'Music in the Tuileries Gardens', Edouard Manet (reproduced by permission of the Trustees of the National Gallery, London).

Becoming conscious of the social changes which gradually allowed more and more people to own, say, a blanket or a tablecloth, enables us to understand how such possessions grew and grew. The growth, of course, enabled a whole industry to arise and be sustained. The concern of this industry was to satisfy demand. This demand gradually made it more and more necessary for competing designs to be produced, as businesses fought for ever larger shares of the market. So, it might be argued, it was economics and not aesthetics which gave birth to the species we nowadays call designers! Or was it? The point is that here, as before, we want you to stretch your imagination in trying to find out more and more about your subject. This is the way you will best succeed.

WORKING IN TEXTILES, FASHION AND STAGE COSTUME DESIGN

What the examination syllabuses say

Table 8.1 outlines the established syllabuses which explicitly refer to the practices covered in this chapter, though their study will be beneficial even if your syllabus is not mentioned here.

EXAMINING BOARD	SYLLABUS/TITLE OF AREA OF STUDY
AEB	ART AND CRAFTS/605 Paper 1 – Design and Practice of a Craft 605/1 (Time allowed: 15 hours) Option 03: Embroidery Option 04: Fabric Printing Paper 3 – Part of Coursework 605/3
JMB	CRAFT (DESIGN AND PRACTICE) (ADVANCED) Subject Group A: TEXTILES/FASHION Study Areas i) Printed Textiles: any method of application of colour to fabric ii) Constructed Textiles: any form of fabric-making technique iii) Embroidery: any form of fabric embellishment, manipulation or assemblage iv) Fashion: dress design; garment construction and illustration *[These areas cover your Coursework Studies and your Controlled Test]* Controlled Test (Time allowed: up to 15 hours) The Written Paper (Time allowed: 3 hours) Craft Study (Done during your Coursework, and assessed by your teachers)
NISEC	SYLLABUS A Paper IV: Design for a Craft (Time allowed: 3 hours) fabric printing, embroidery, stage costume SYLLABUS B Section 1 – Main Study (Time allowed: 15 hours) 4. Textiles and Fashion a) Dyeing and printing (Batik, tie-dye, block and screen printing) b) Weaving c) Dress Design d) Creative Embroidery (Hand and/or machine) Section 2 – Analytical and Written Study (Time allowed: 3 hours) Section 3 – History and Appreciation of Art, Architecture and Design (Time allowed: 3 hours, plus Extended Essay) Part 2 Appreciation of Design for Living Section 4 – Coursework

Table 8.1 The examining boards' titles for areas of study covered in this chapter.

The syllabuses do not include many references to guide you in this section of the examination, but this does not matter. Just remember that the basic principles of study and work which apply to one area of the subject will apply equally to the others. Of course, each practice will also have certain discrete criteria which apply to it.

The more distinctive criteria in textile design usually arise from notions such as:

- function;
- technology;
- social habit;
- climatic conditions;
- political decisions;
- cultural traditions.

This is why historical, contextual and critical studies are so important in your approach. If you do not find out about such influences, and the taboos and traditions which arise from them, then you are working with one hand tied behind your back, no matter how well developed your level of practical skills. As we said at the beginning of this chapter, there is little use in producing work which is excellently crafted if it is poor in design and inappropriate and irrelevant to the needs of the society for which it is planned.

The JMB Craft (Design and Practice) (Advanced) syllabus does expand upon the practice. It reinforces the view that any study of the subject area should be as broad as we have outlined for you. The syllabus even contains a reference to the advantages to be gained by a broad, contextual approach to your studies. It states:

> ***The candidate's interests will naturally promote the development of one study area over other study areas. This in turn will give an emphasis to the complementary craft and historical studies throughout the course, and determine the choice of the controlled test. Whilst this is to be permitted, the studies of other study areas are important in broadening, enriching and complementing this main study area, and in providing a breadth to the understanding of craft.***

This bears out the suggestion that study in breadth leads to understanding in depth.

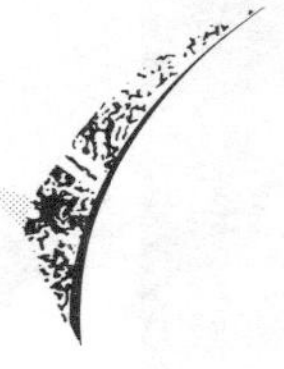

EXAMINATION QUESTIONS, STUDENT ANSWERS AND EXAMINER COMMENTS

Textiles

The questions involving textiles tend to offer you a choice of themes to design from rather than specific purposes to design for. We would suggest that when you get your question paper, if it does not specify what your textile is to be used for, *you* add a purpose to your work. If you do so, you will find that the criteria the specific purpose introduces will enable you to make your decisions on a more rational basis. Of course, never be afraid to be irrational and indulge in flights of fancy in your designs!

Fashion

Garments or furnishings designs of any kind have an intrinsic purpose, which means you will need to try to satisfy the criteria behind the particular purpose. In this section of the examination, when you are producing your own material to use in your garment or furnishing design, make sure that the design of your material complies with the criteria underlying its ultimate purpose.

Stage costume design

Apart from the opportunity to design for a particular type of performance, such as a concert, you are usually asked to design for very specific plays or characters within them. This is implicit in such questions, even if you are allowed to choose your own play. If you have any choice at all of this kind, we propose most strongly that you choose a 'vehicle' to design for which will allow you to be extravagant in your ideas. Take risks!

Producing textile and fashion work

As we have said, it is important that you always bear in mind the specific use your textile is planned for. This means that your work should show most clearly that you recognise the differences of use between, for instance, a dress fabric and an upholstery fabric. Your work should also show that you can control your media and can work according to the accepted standards which aesthetics impose upon your designs.

Your work should be accompanied by investigative studies, design developments and decisions explaining your choice. It should also include your analysis of what you have done, why you have done it and how successful you think it is. Where time and circumstances allow, it should be 'field-tested' and the criticisms of others should contribute to your own analysis.

Not all the candidates' work in the examples which follow covers every point we have made, but the means for it to be attempted exist in each example. Even if the individual candidates still received A grades in their examinations, to have gone the whole way would have prepared them for similar work at degree level in art and design!

Using a theme

In Fig. 8.2 the candidate has used a simple theme as the basis for the work. This theme might be described as 'Sun, sea, land and air'. In the work the candidate has not ended up with too literal a version of the theme. The preparatory studies do contain some fairly straightforward approaches to the subject matter, but they interpret and develop the initial investigations. A number of alternatives are considered and the final designs for the pattern are logical conclusions from the earlier studies.

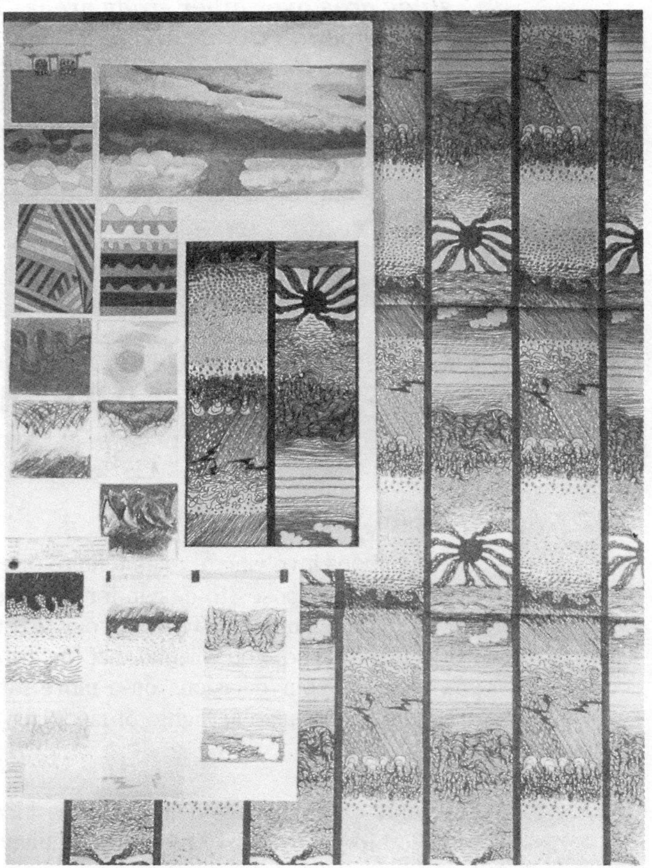

Fig. 8.2

The shape of the single motif which goes to make up the pattern – an upright, exaggerated rectangle – lends itself to the build-up of a repeat pattern. The question you must ask yourself is whether the figurative content of the single motif builds up into a satisfactory repeat pattern? In most textile designs the designer creates an image or pattern in the motif which is complete in itself but is then repeated in all directions to form the length of printed fabric. The success of the design, therefore, depends both on the appearance of a single motif and its repetition across the whole width and along the whole length of the fabric. Fig. 8.3 helps to explain this phenomenon.

One of the dangers you encounter as a repeat pattern unfolds is that unexpected directional lines occur, where an element in the design links up to create diagonals, uprights or horizontals. It is necessary to test for the likelihood of this happening by mass producing the motif in an experimental situation. We suggested earlier that photocopiers might help in this respect. Computers certainly can perform the task for you, almost at the pressing of a key. If you do not have these facilities, you might use tracings or multi-sheet cut-outs, or even make up a small screen print, lino-print or potato-print of your idea. Doing this, you will find that you can also experiment with different colour

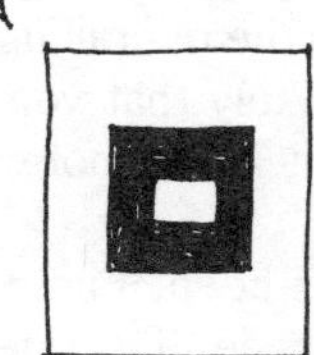

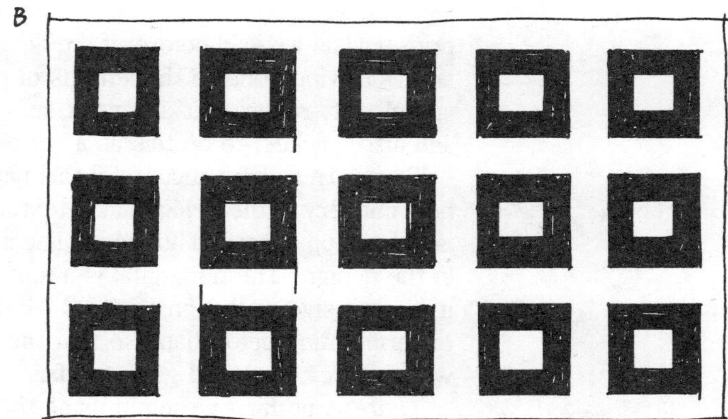

A very simple motif, such as in 'A', can produce a variety of pattern effects.

The motif is a coloured rectangle with a hole in it on a white ground.

In 'B' the regular pattern is very still, but the new network of lines the white ground cause suggests that more could be achieved with the motif. The "half-drop" pattern system in 'C' explores this.

By preparing a pattern grid, as in 'D', a wide variety of further ideas can be quickly investigated. Felt-tips can be used for this. Great accuracy does not matter.

Our point is that DESIGN is central to your work in these practices. No matter how good your motif is, it is equally important to explore its fullest design possibilities.

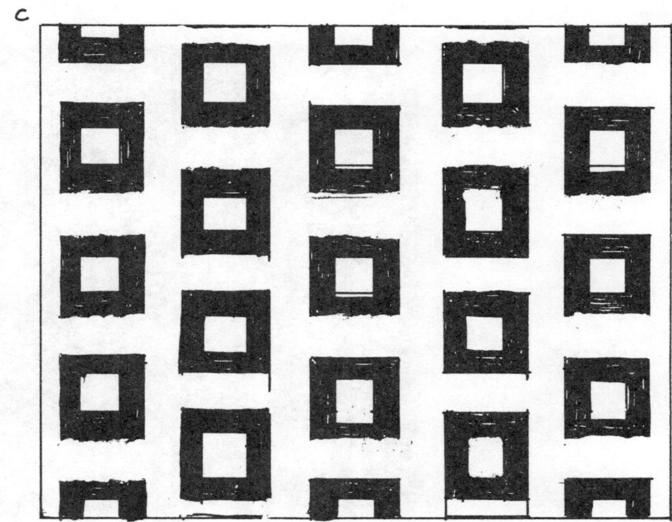

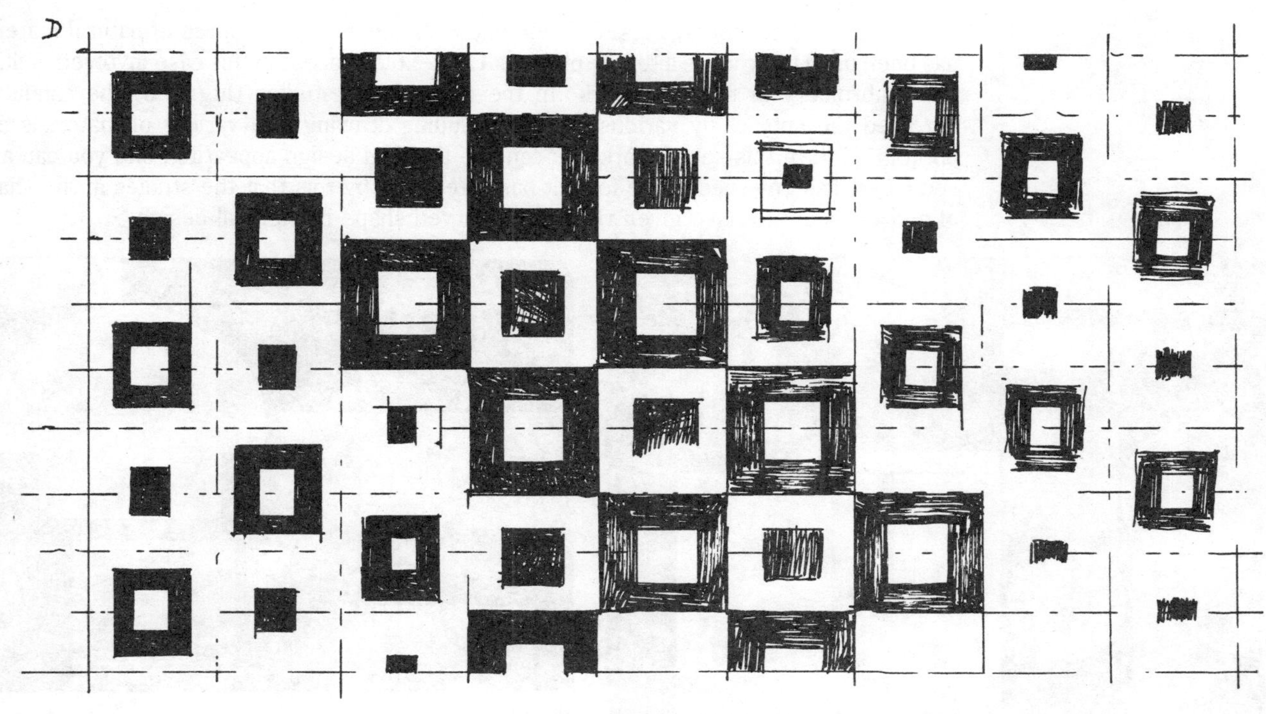

Fig. 8.3

combinations and arrangements. Whatever method you use, you should not design a motif and then go ahead and print it full-size on a length of fabric. You might make a good fabric print but, as we said before, if the design is found wanting, what is the overall use of your work? Having gone to the lengths of printing your fabric, it is unlikely that you will then appraise it, redesign it and print an alternative length. Anyway, it is far more sensible, and also quicker, to do this as a series of experiments.

To return to how successful this particular candidate's work has been, Fig. 8.3 shows how imagery in the design has a textural and semi-realistic appearance. The effect of this is to build up a marked horizontal line in the repeating pattern, half way between the 'suns' in the design. The horizontal is a feature of any landscape. In this instance, do you think it is obtrusive in the final fabric? Might things have been better if time had been spent experimenting beforehand so that the horizontal line in the design could have been dealt with before things had gone too far?

There is nothing wrong in using the textural and the realistic in textile design. This is something the ARTS AND CRAFTS MOVEMENT did quite often, as Fig. 8.4 shows. The design, by WILLIAM MORRIS, is obviously taken from a naturalistic source. Try to decipher the motif, which is repeated time and time again in order to build up the repeat pattern. When you do so, evaluate how it does, or does not, create unexpected lines and forces in the overall textile.

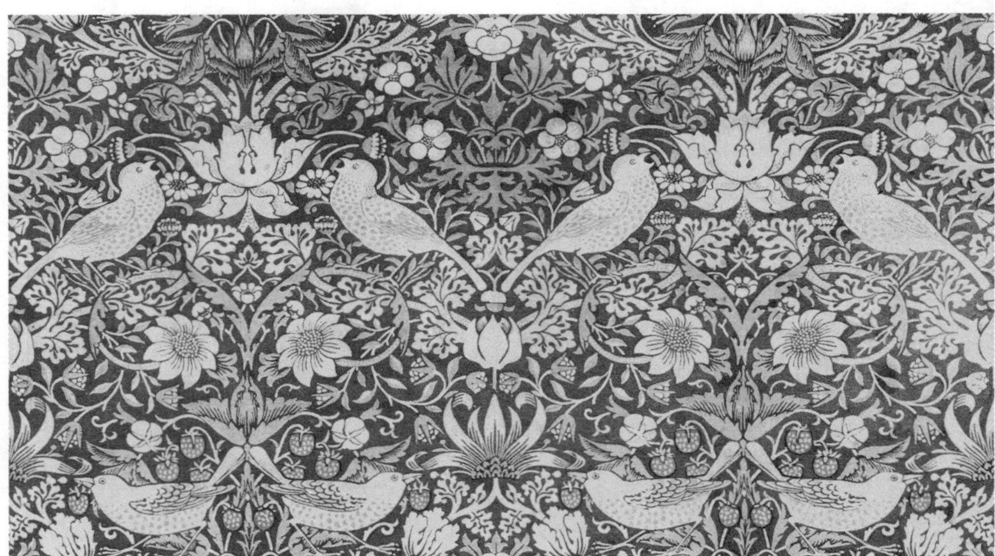

Fig. 8.4 William Morris

The next set of works, Figs. 8.5, 8.6 and 8.7, shows how a source of natural material has been used to produce a textile picture. The textile process in this case involved quilting and embroidery in the final work. In the preparatory studies (Fig. 8.5) the candidate explored the subject by various means, including drawing in a variety of materials and photography. In this set of work you can see the final design appearing, and you can also see *why* it has emerged in the form it has. We mean by this that the studies in the shape of a circle seem to have given rise to the curved shape in the final design.

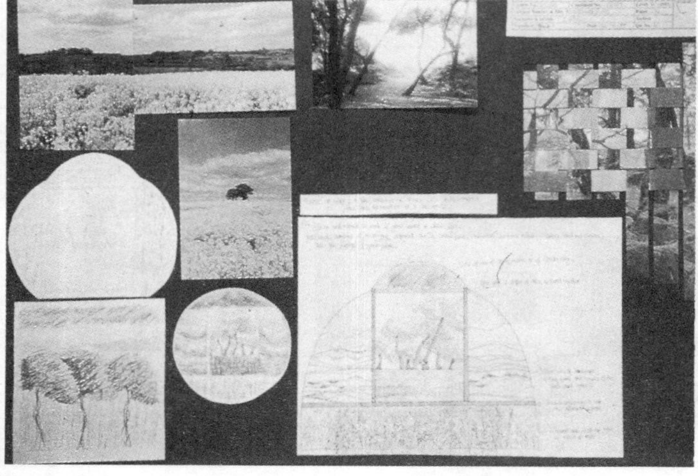

Fig. 8.5

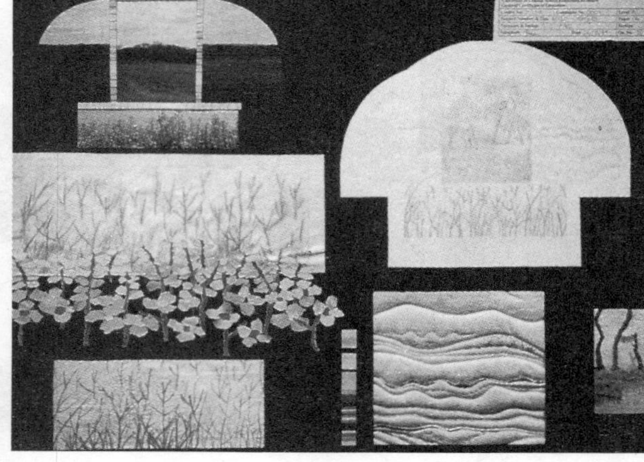

Fig. 8.6

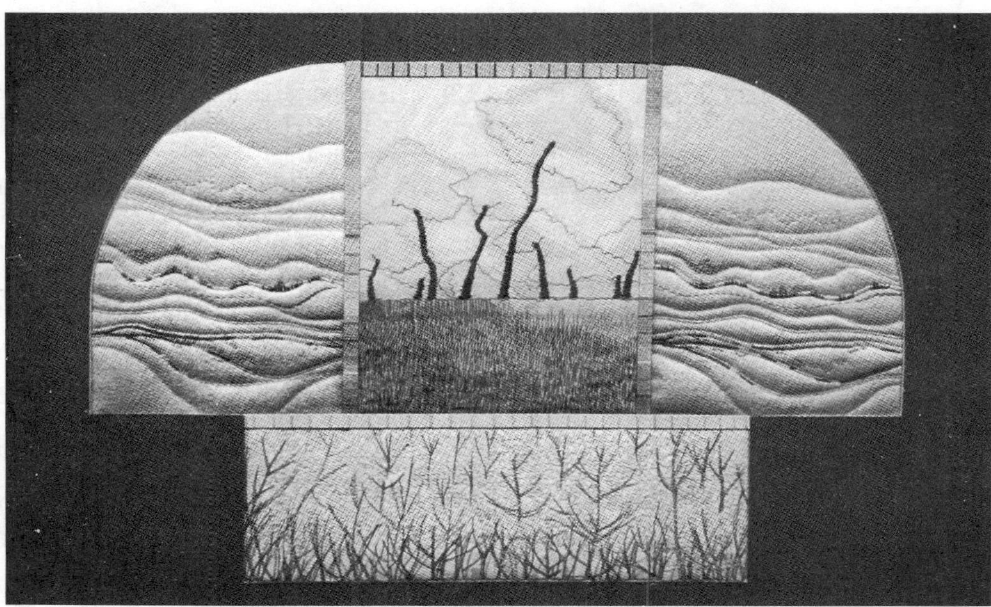

Fig. 8.7

In the further preparatory work (Fig. 8.6) we can see the idea developing, as well as some experiments in textiles materials and techniques. However, as far as the final detail of the end piece of work is concerned, while it is becoming inevitable now, it has still not been tackled in full. This pleasure is put off until the final piece of examination work (Fig. 8.7). The result is interesting, made all the more credible by the way in which the preparatory studies explain and justify the final detail so well.

The shape of the picture in this work is unusual, accustomed as we are to pictures being rectangular in shape. However, there is no need for this to be so. In Fig. 8.8 the work of PIERO DELLA FRANCESCA (*c.*1410 – 92) is in a shape very similar to that of the candidate's embroidered work. At one time painting was done on walls in buildings, particularly churches, and on occasions artists followed the curves of the building. In Fig. 8.9, 'The Last of England', the artist, FORD MADOX BROWN (1821 – 93) has done his painting in the shape of a circle.

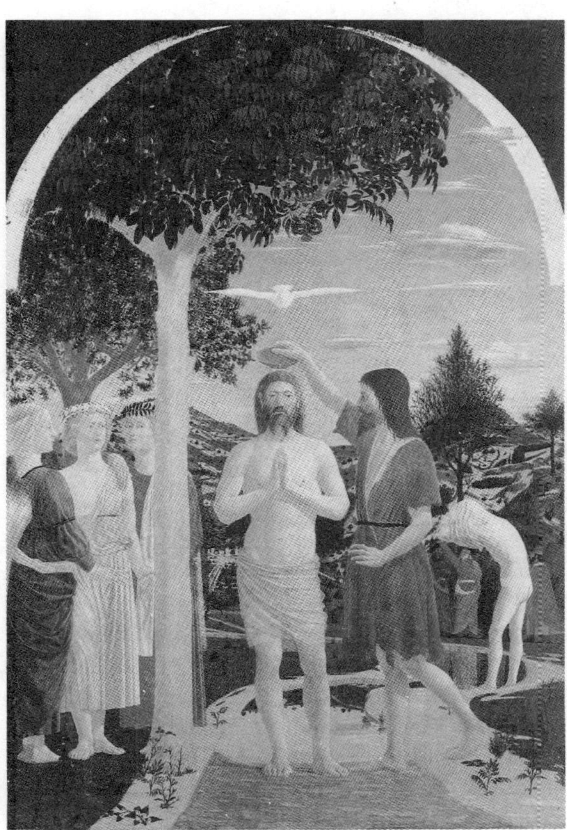

Fig. 8.8 'The Baptism of Christ', Piero della Francesca (reproduced by permission of the Trustees of the National Gallery, London).

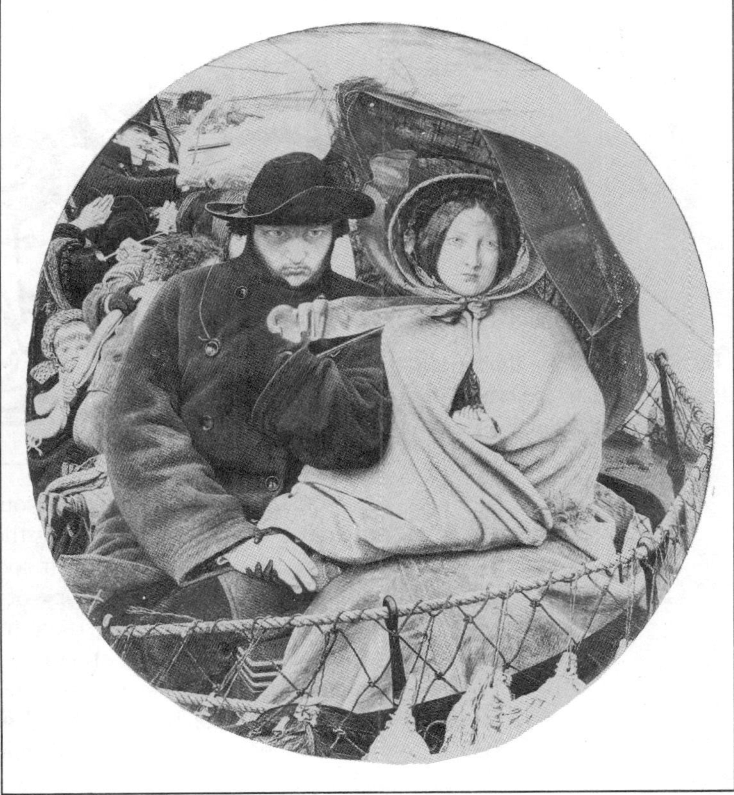

Fig. 8.9 'The Last of England', Ford Madox Brown (reproduced by permission of the Birmingham City Art Gallery).

Using cultural and historical sources

Figs. 8.10 and 8.11 show a strong cultural source, taken from either the Mayas or the Aztecs (Fig. 8.12). The cultural imagery and patterns from these peoples have been studied and used as the basis of that candidate's work. This gives it an identity and a direction. The danger is that, largely because of the power of the original source material, the candidate's work becomes little more than a pastiche of the original. We believe that this danger has been avoided here. What do you think? To begin to answer this question you need to research the Mayas and the Aztecs, finding out about their history, their social organisation, their cultural beliefs, their artefacts and the imagery they used. Without this you will not be certain as to how much interpretation is involved in the various studies present in the candidate's work.

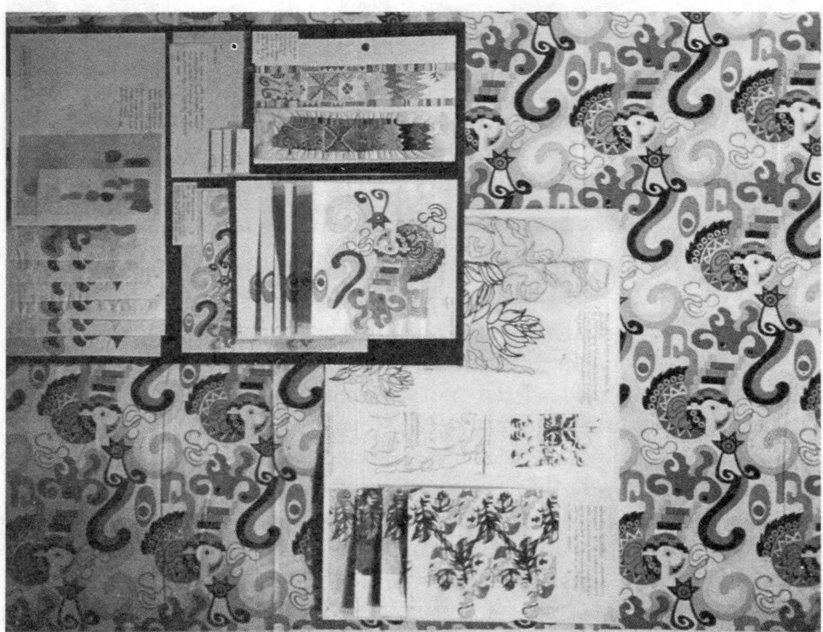

Fig. 8.10

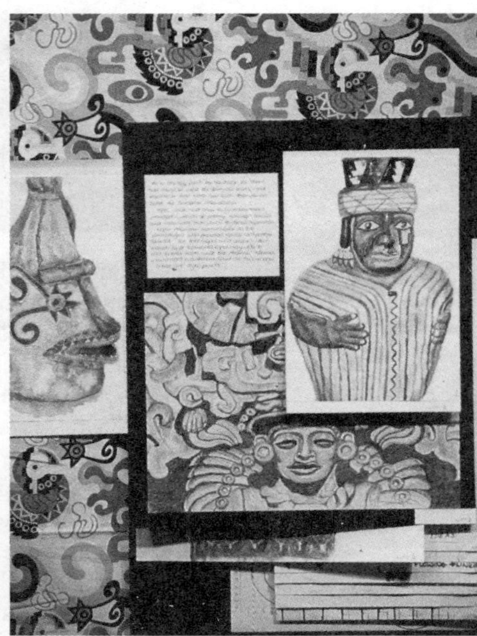

Fig. 8.11

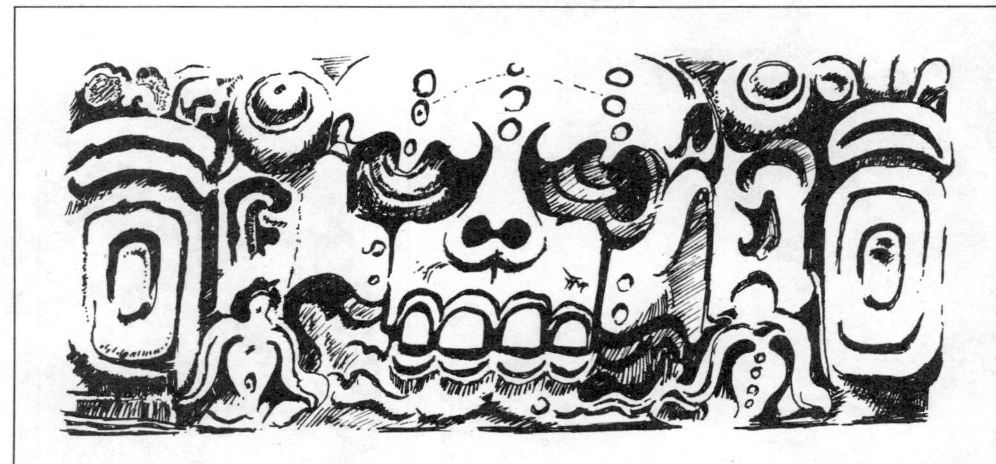

Fig. 8.12 Head of the Death God, from a Mayan altar (reproduced by permission of the British Museum, London).

If you *do* study the original source material you could become aware how well the **natural** content of the work of the Mayas and the Aztecs has been transformed into a series of consistent patterns. If so, you might then make a connection between that and another incident in the history of art and design which is not apparently linked. The Symbolists, such as PAUL GAUGUIN, MAURICE DENIS (1870 – 1943) and EMILE BERNARD (1868 – 1941), created a style of painting which translated the real, observed world into a composition of flat shapes and colours which were drawn and coloured according to the demands of the picture itself and not real-life reality. Fig. 8.13 gives you an example of what we mean by this. In it Gauguin has flattened forms and pushed their boundaries into each other, until he has created what is to him a satisfactory composition. Remember, a satisfactory composition is not just a matter of the shapes within it but involves the colours, textures, patterns and spatial relationships between them all.

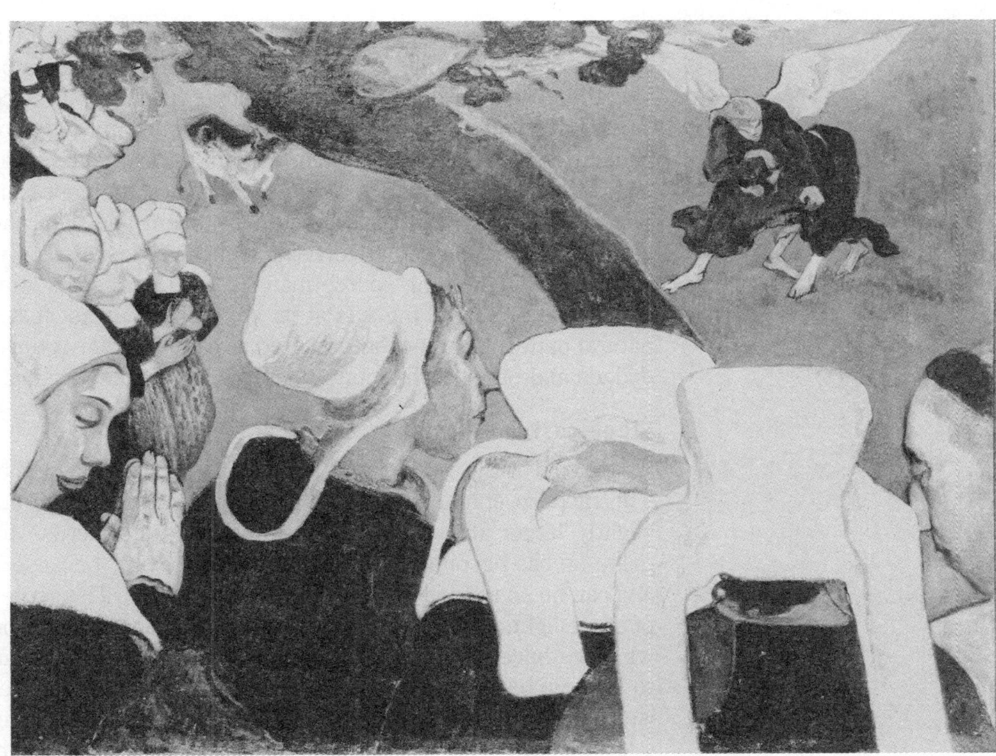

Fig. 8.13 Paul Gauguin 'Vision after the Sermon' (reproduced by permission of the National Galleries of Scotland)

Textiles for specific purposes

When designing for a specific purpose it is vital that you show you have considered your textile design in its intended situation and use. To do this, we have suggested that you might use a small doll to achieve a full three-dimensional effect in your work. However, you could also model small pieces of furniture if you were designing a furnishing fabric, and print your design on paper again and fix it *in situ* on the model. Otherwise you could show by the aid of drawings how your design would look in its intended situation.

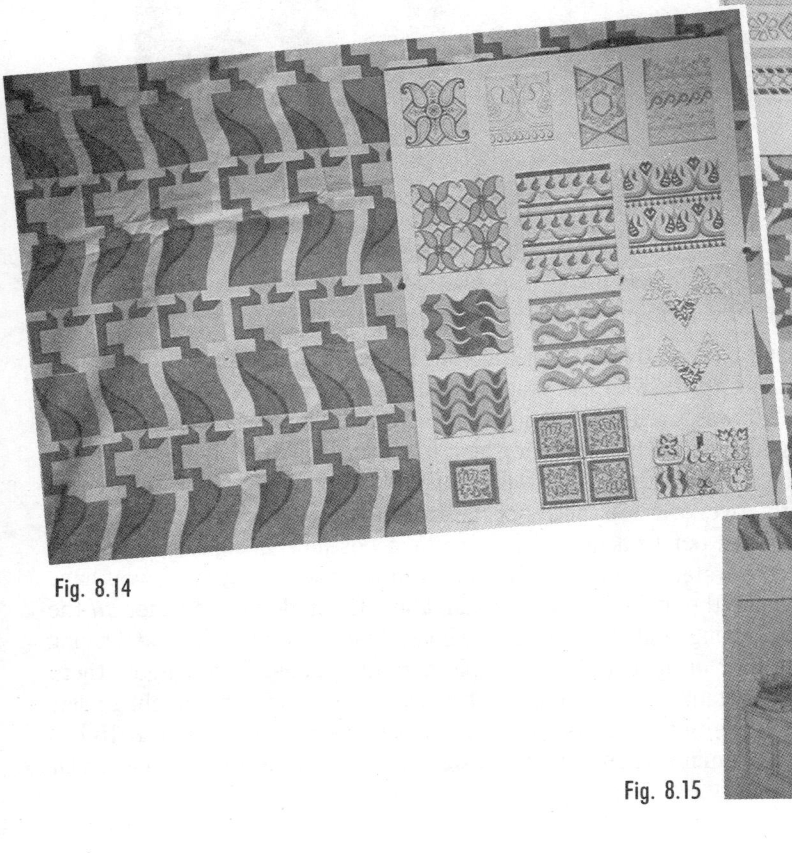

Fig. 8.14

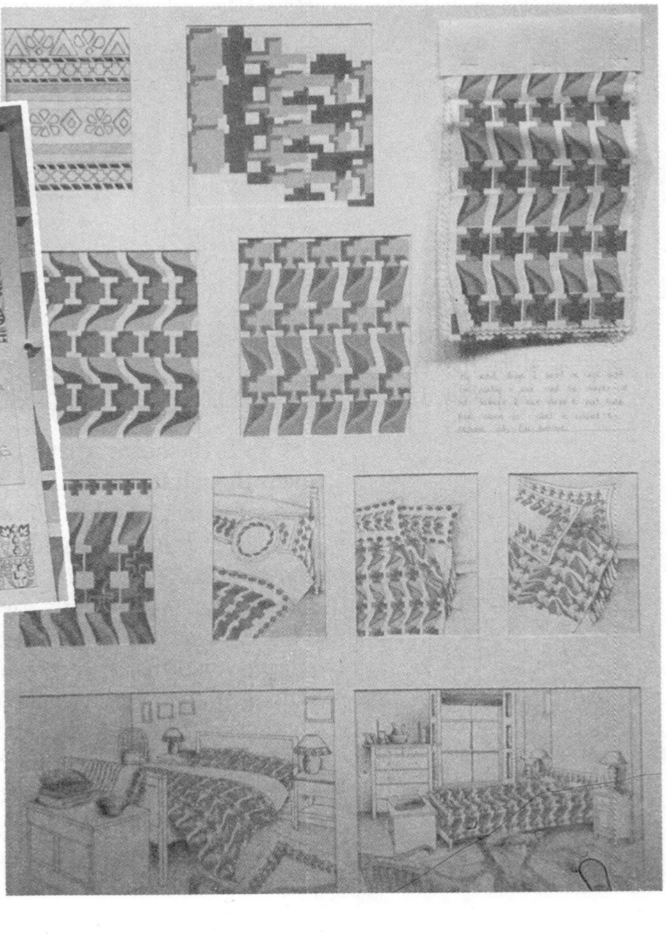

Fig. 8.15

The candidate whose work is illustrated in Figs. 8.14 and 8.15 has taken this latter course. Not only is the textile shown as a bed cover on a bed, but the bed itself has been situated in an environment. The candidate has made an excellent move here. By including an environment you could further display your knowledge of aesthetics and your ability to handle them. You could show how your textile would look in the appropriately coloured environment. If you do so, this must enhance the appearance of your textile. Of course, you could even model the whole environment and then photograph your work in colour, as would happen in any advertising campaign designed to sell the fabric.

In these studies the source material for the designs is not completely apparent, but it is possible to hazard a guess at it. We would suggest that it is derived from examples of natural pattern, perhaps interpreted already in other artefacts, such as door arches, tiles, dadoes and other architectural features. What do you think?

Stage costume design

As we said at the beginning, your work in this area should be bold and even **flamboyant**. The modern stage, despite all its sophisticated lighting and other devices, still needs a slightly larger than life feel to get its message across to the audience. The fact that make-up has become more subtle is possible only because stage lighting is now so strong and can be controlled so accurately by computer. This larger than life intensity and control of stage lighting enables other elements in stage work to be slightly understated, despite what we have just said. The thing is, you need to be aware of all the contingencies and to strike a balance between them. Nevertheless, if you are producing a stage costume in isolation from an actual production of the play it comes from, then you *need* to overemphasise the statements in your design, because they will not be subject to the modifications exercised in a full-stage production.

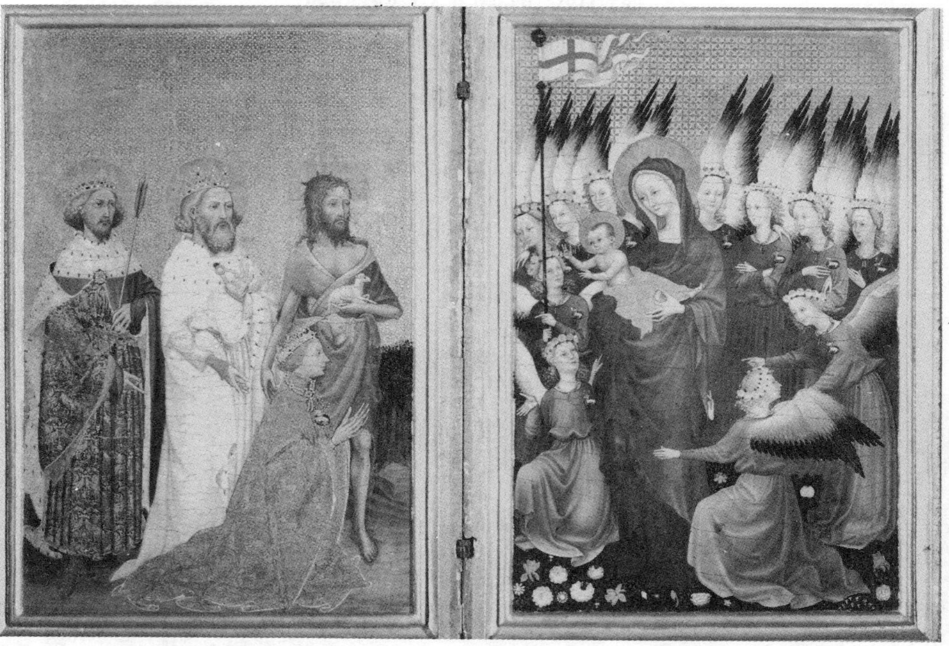

Fig. 8.16 'The Wilton Diptych', *c.* 1400 (reproduced by permission of the Trustees of the National Gallery, London).

Fig. 8.16 shows what we mean by emphasising your message in your costume design, even though it has nothing to do with the stage. Or does it? It is part of a **diptych**, a two-part, hinged panel. It was used to commemorate events or in private devotions. In a sense, it *is* like a staged production, but everything is static. However, in this work the composition of the whole – the angels, the background decoration and the flowers in the foreground – is slightly 'over the top' but is orchestrated into an **harmonious unity**. This is what you should set out to achieve in your stage costume designs. But always bear in mind that if you overstate the minor characters in the play in any way, you have little or nothing left to make the major characters stand out. If you do not consider *all* the characters from the beginning and as a unified whole, your costume for the leading character could easily either disappear or be completely outrageous. The danger, then, is that we are all very reluctant to revise our 'best' work, even though we might realise how inappropriate it is in the final analysis. So, study the messages which Fig. 8.16 can give you, and bear them in mind when you are designing your costumes for a particular play.

When you are given the play to be costumed, or choose it for yourself, the first thing you *must* do is read it thoroughly and carefully, making notes as you go about the personality of each character as the playwright has built them up. Then read the play again, emphasising the points *you* wish to make about each character. To be able to do this effectively, you must know the story of the play well and your characters thoroughly. Otherwise you will end up not designing for a particular play, or a specific set of characters, but just producing a number of ideas which reflect your own interests, beliefs or even prejudices.

The candidate whose work is shown in Figs 8.17, 8.18 and 8.19 must have studied the play in question and the characters in it deeply. The work displays an awareness of the individual characters, and a sensitive appreciation of their relationship with each other and within the whole play.

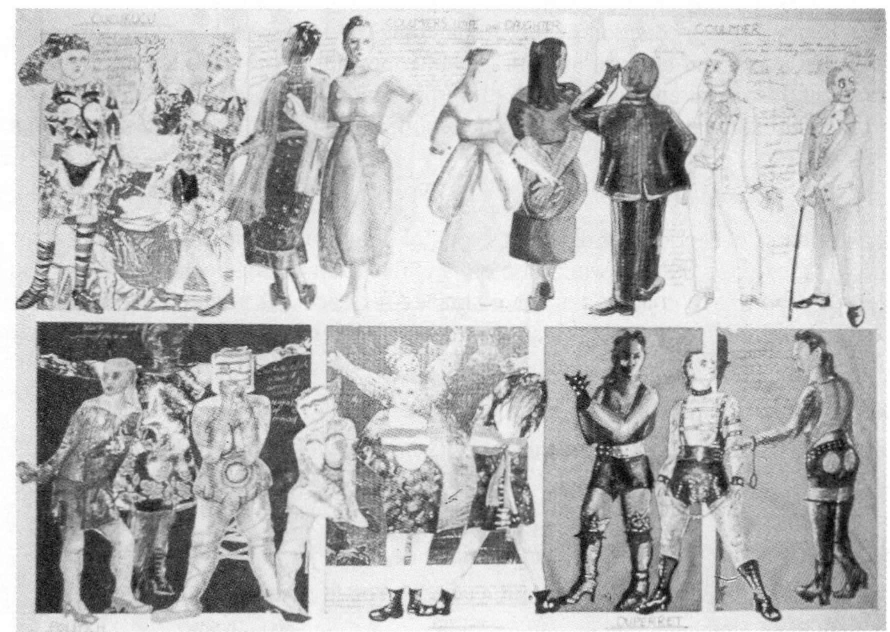

Fig. 8.17

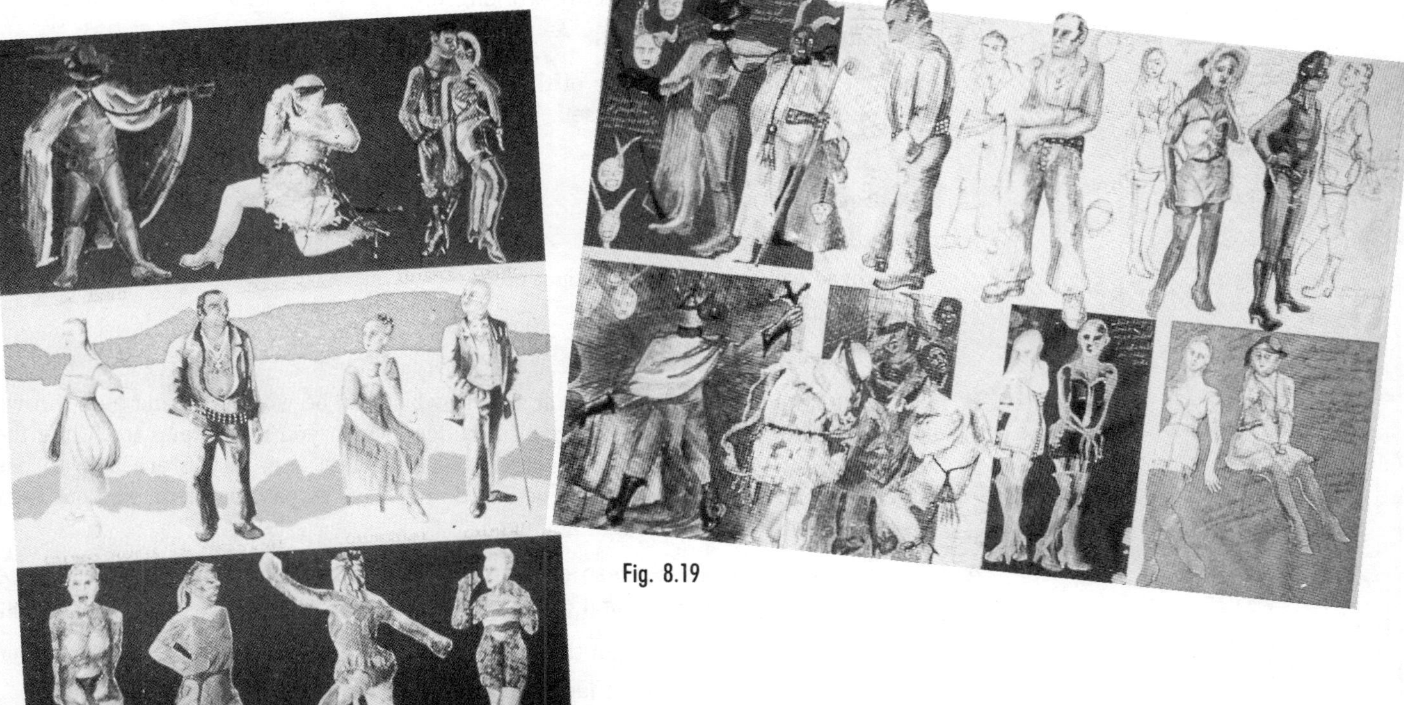

Fig. 8.19

Fig. 8.18

The work contains a number of references to the history of art and design. There is obviously the inclusion of 'The Death of Marat' by JACQUES LOUIS DAVID (1748 – 1825), but it is also possible to identify references to the work of artists such as ALLEN JONES (1937 –) and HENRI TOULOUSE-LAUTREC, as well as comic-books. Of course, the candidate may not have been consciously using these sources, but they do seem to be present in the work.

Above all, however, the candidate has produced a flamboyant set of designs which state emphatically the candidate's personal and creative interpretation of the playwright's original, creative piece of work.

The essence of high grades in the assessment of these practices lies not in gaining technical proficiency in the processes and materials associated with the activities alone but in producing well-founded designs which serve appropriately the specified purpose they are designed for.

This necessitates a study of the historical and contextual circumstances which in the past have surrounded the production of the items concerned, as well as an awareness of the contemporary social and cultural influences which pertain in the production of similar items today. This historical and contextual study need not – indeed, should not – be restricted to actual examples of the items in question, but should involve a whole series of related phenomena.

EXERCISES

1 Makes a series of collections of different types of source materials by means of your own photographs. Use the following themes, and make up albums for each theme. Do not stop when you have collected a few examples for each but keep alert throughout your course, and add to the albums as you recognise further examples around you. The themes are:

- pattern of natural phenomena in architecture;
- repeating patterns made from the repetition of single items stacked or built together;
- pattern made by broken objects;
- pattern made by the effect of wind, rain, tide or snow;
- pattern made by the close-up studies of textures in objects;
- pattern made by reflection;
- pattern made by the effect of working with tools or machines upon materials;
- pattern made by shadows.

2 Find out all you can about one of the following themes. Design a textile to be used for a purpose you specify yourself. The themes are:

- Greek vases;
- Egyptian tomb paintings;
- Russian icons;
- Music hall, boxing or wrestling posters;
- Television interference;
- Computer-graphic images.

3 Design an item of clothing to wear at a party which can be worn once and then thrown away. Before you start, give yourself a budget which you must keep to. Make the actual amount you can spend a realistic but economic one. If you are able to use materials from your school or college and do not have to pay for them, find out their cost and debit your budget that amount.

4 Choose a set of Shakespearean characters, such as Bottom and his friends from *A Midsummer's Night Dream*, and design three sets of costumes for them, as follows;

- in historical costume from the period of Shakespeare;
- in costume based upon a Japanese culture of any period;
- in modern costume based upon your own society and culture.

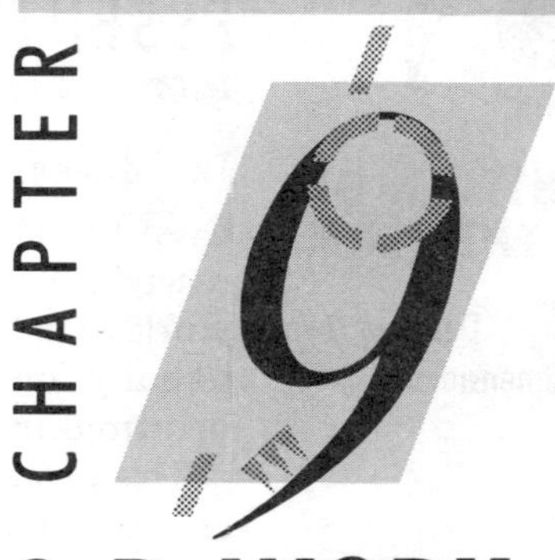

3-D WORK, STAGE DESIGN AND INTERIOR DESIGN

GETTING STARTED

In this chapter we will cover a number of activities which can be broadly described as three-dimensional. What we have to say will not necessarily refer to activities by name, but it will be generally applicable. You can readily translate what we point to as essential for one activity to the particular area of study you are taking for your examination. Thus what we say about ceramics, for instance, will be just as applicable to jewellery or metalwork.

While our main concern here is three-dimensional work, we will also look at stage design and interior design. Before we define 'three-dimensional', as the term is used most often in art and design in contrast to 'two-dimensional', it is useful to define 'two-dimensional' as well.

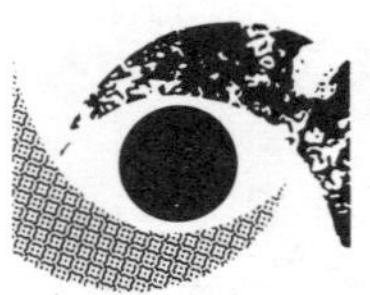

ESSENTIAL PRINCIPLES

DEFINITION OF THE TERM

"Defining 'two dimensional'."

Two-dimensional

Even though two-dimensional work in art and design often portrays three-dimensional reality and often sets out to achieve a three-dimensional effect, it can be taken to mean: **work in art and design which has only width and height; it is 'flat', carried out usually on paper, cardboard, board or canvas, using any graphic, paint, printmaking, photographic or collage material in its creation**.

This defines two-dimensional work in art and design, but it does not exclude the use of any of the materials listed above in three-dimensional work. Even two-dimensional work, such as a photographic print mounted on a sheet of card, can be constructed into a three-dimensional form or object by folding, cutting and joining the card in a variety of ways. We shall return to this later.

"Defining 'three dimensional'."

As to the definition of three-dimensional, the main consideration is that **in art and design, three-dimensional work has width, height and depth**.

That three-dimensional work has **depth** makes it different from two-dimensional work. For the purposes of this book and even the examinations, it does not matter if the depth is only slight, as in a piece of **relief** sculptural work or something as small and restricted in depth as an earring in jewellery. In contrast to the definition of two-dimensional work in art and design, we shall consider all such work to be three dimensional.

Having introduced the term 'relief', we will now define that. It is **a method of carving or building up forms, shapes and textures so as to project physically from an otherwise flat background**.

We are regarding relief as just one point along a spectrum from two-dimensional work at one end to three-dimensional work at the other. So, we might have a pencil drawing done on white cartridge paper at one end of the scale, which passes through work done in relief, via something such as a brooch to a life-sized, realistic sculpture of an elephant at the other end.

The question remains, does the term three-dimensional require any further definition? As we introduced the aspect of materials in defining two-dimensional, it might help here if we add a similar remark to our initial definition of three-dimensional. **In art and design, any work which has width, height and depth to it is three dimensional; the degree of width, or height, or depth is immaterial; it can be created and constructed using any of the materials associated with art or design, or even those which do not traditionally come from the history of art and design but facilitate the work in hand at any time**.

All that remains now, having pointed out to you how broad we regard the definition of three-dimensional work to be, is to emphasise that in three-dimensional work it is not necessary that *all* the work should be three-dimensional. That is to say, the ideas and design of your three-dimensional work can be expressed in a mixture of two- and three-dimensional activities.

Stage design

Stage design is concerned with the local environments and effects in which individual plays are produced and performed. That is to say, your work will hardly ever be associated with designing the architecture of a theatre, but with the circumstances which each play is performed in. Thus the definition of stage design for our purposes is: **the control and design of the physical appearance of the environment in which plays are performed**.

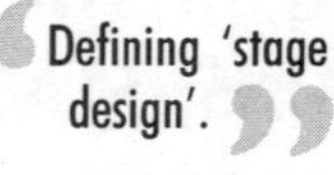

"Defining 'stage design'."

Although we mentioned theatres above, it is not necessary for a play to be performed in a purpose-built building of that kind. Some plays are performed in open-air theatres, which are little more than open 'shells' for the actors to operate in, or even totally natural settings such as gardens, parks, cliff tops and so on. Remembering this in your work is as important as realising that not all plays in theatres are performed behind proscenium arches with curtains which draw to and fro. There are open stages, thrust stages, theatres in the round and so on.

Interior design

Interior design is concerned with the design and appearance of interiors for specified purposes. Again, this differentiates between the work you might do as an interior designer and as an architect. The architect designs and creates a 'space', whereas the interior designer translates that space into a particular environment, designed to carry out a defined function. Thus interior design could be concerned as much with the design and appearance of living spaces as with shop interiors, hotel foyers, the insides of bingo halls and so on.

"Defining 'interior design'."

With this in mind, we shall define interior design as **the control and design of the physical and decorative appearance of internal environments for specified purposes**.

AESTHETIC CONSIDERATIONS

It will now be evident that aesthetic principles are fundamental in anything you might do in response to these areas of your examination. A lot of three-dimensional work is a form of fine art, and this depends upon appropriate aesthetic principles for its success. Stage design and interior design are to do with the physical dimensions and appearance of environments, and the successful organisation and visual effect of the environment depends upon appropriate aesthetic principles. The same argument would apply to any other aspect of the areas and activities covered by this chapter. For instance, jewellery is concerned with the selection of subject matter, the organisation of pattern, decoration and colour, the composition of shapes and so on, and these matters are dependent upon the use of appropriate aesthetic principles for their successful interrelationship.

What seems to distinguish the activities covered in this chapter from two-dimensional work in art and design is that the results of designing, and the work which is the product of the designs concerned, are always seen in relation to another three- dimensional environment or background.

So, while we can study a picture, or any other two-dimensional piece of work, by isolating it from the environment we are in at the time, we cannot easily do the same with anything which has its own three-dimensional reality in the real three-dimensional world. One of the ways much two-dimensional work is isolated is by means of the rectangular shape it often exists within, or the frame which surrounds it. This cannot be achieved in three-dimensional work, not even in the case of the proscenium-arch stage production. The proscenium arch appears to isolate the stage and its physical reality, but the whole is still an emphatic part of the theatre at large.

Because of this it is necessary to consider the wider aesthetic complications of the total environment in which most three-dimensional work is to exist, although in fine art activities such as sculpture, aesthetic decisions about the object which constitutes the sculpture would take priority above all else.

MATERIALS, TOOLS AND EQUIPMENT CONSIDERATIONS

As we have already said, there is no apparent limit on what you might choose to use as materials in your three-dimensional work. Each material will have its own tools and equipment for working it, so you must take into account your ability either to use these tools, or to spare the time to learn how to use them, when choosing what to do in your work.

Much three-dimensional work is dependent upon the mixing of more than one set of materials and the traditions associated with them. For instance, if you have ever been to London and arrived via Euston Station, you are likely to have seen the sculpture by EDUARDO PAOLOZZI (1924 –) which stands just outside the main station entrance. This is a metal sculpture, and was conceived and designed as such by Paolozzi, but it went through various stages in its design and production. It is likely that it existed as:

"Stages in a particular metal sculpture."

- a commission by the client, presumably British Rail;
- an idea in the artist's head;
- a site survey, including plans, measurements and flow diagrams of people and road vehicles;
- some designs and drawings;
- a maquette (preliminary model) in clay or plaster;
- a full-size and worked-up version in clay or some other material suitable for mould-making;
- the mould;
- the casting we see now at Euston Station.

This is what we mean by a mixture of materials and the traditions associated with their use. Paolozzi's sculpture is likely to depend upon his knowledge of the way similar sculptures have been produced throughout history, his expertise at handling materials appropriately and his aesthetic appreciation of the site and the task as much as it does upon his original idea for the work.

CRAFTSMANSHIP

It is an almost inescapable fact that if you make a piece of pottery, people who see it will pick it up and turn it over. If they know anything about the production of pottery they will be judging its weight to size ratio, and looking to see how you finished the base of the work. So, if for no other reason than this, you can see how essential it is that you attend to the basic standards of craftsmanship in your work.

Whatever you are doing, because you are producing a three-dimensional item to exist in a real three-dimensional world, you need to pay attention to the standards of production in your work. This is regardless of what you are actually doing and the aesthetic decisions involved. You cannot expect that if your stage set falls apart after one night's use nobody will complain! If you design the interior decoration for a room, it is no use blaming those who construct and decorate it if they find your plans and designs impossible to understand and follow. Anyone wearing a brooch you designed and made will not expect it to scratch and injure either themselves or others who get too near them.

Even so, it is no use displaying the best standards of craftsmanship if your designs were not worth carrying out in the first place. This all-embracing meaning of the term 'craftsmanship' is what is so important in the advice we give you. For instance, craftsmanship is what Paolozzi displayed in his sculpture for Euston Station. As we have already said, however, this depends on the satisfactory blend of many things and not just the standards of production in your work. Do not lose sight of this in anything you do.

HISTORICAL FACTORS

Each of the activities covered in this chapter is rich in history. You have only to visit any museum or gallery, or read any number of books, or go to a theatre, or study your local architecture, to find a range of excellent examples of work relevant to the activities you are doing for your examination.

" Art Deco as a case study. "

The important thing to remember is that you should not concentrate upon the outstanding and historically important examples alone. Visit an elderly relative. With any luck you will be likely to find a piece of pottery which will be an example of **Art Deco**. This might be only a chipped saucer, kept but long forgotten in the back of a cupboard. It might well have been bought originally in a store such as Woolworth's, where it was made especially for them, to sell in large quantities to the general public. To help you in a quest such as this, you will be looking for something made and purchased in the 1930s. In their day, the products of Art Deco were often looked upon as modern. Nowadays many people might describe them as 'jazzy'. In fact they are very much the outcome of a mass-production system, using a variety of materials in a mechanised way. Their pattern and decoration are usually geometric, and their colours bright and important to the overall appearance.

It will be useful to stick with Art Deco for a while, as it elucidates much of what we have been talking about so far in this chapter. The style included architecture, and many of the buildings erected in the 1930s reflect the aesthetic principles of the style, not least the cinemas of that era. In the case of buildings such as cinemas and hotels, the interiors were also designed to fit the total environment represented. In turn, this was reinforced by the choice of carpets, textiles and furnishing contained. Where people were eating and sleeping in the buildings, the lights, the ornaments, the bedlinen, the crockery, the cutlery and so on all came under the umbrella of the overall aesthetic values associated with the style.

Continuing our theme that you do not have to explore only the outstanding examples of a period or style, consider a room you are familiar with. It might be a room in your own house. Analyse how it has been decorated and furnished – that is, presented as a piece of interior design. Most of us have to make use of the furniture we already have and most of the fittings we already possess when we redecorate a room in our own home. It is sensible, therefore, to take these items into account when we plan the colour scheme and types of materials we are going to use. But how often do we? We would suggest that it is more usual to plan the interior design of the room deliberately ignoring the furnishings and fittings which will have to be put back into it. When the decoration of the room is finished, *then* we put everything back. Are we able to see the overall effect this creates, or do we manage to see the new decoration in isolation from all that has gone back into it? What we are trying to stress is that you should learn how to critically analyse and evaluate what it is you actually see around you. Examples in museums, displays and so on do offer you a benchmark to use when looking at other, possibly less successful, examples you may find, but they are not the only things to study.

Similarly, if you go to a local amateur dramatic production in a church hall and the stage set is poor, it is usual to excuse it on the grounds that those who made it did their best. This suggests that the practical standards of craftsmanship are wanting. Maybe that is true, but if the original designs were good, and took into account the full range of considerations we have emphasised throughout this chapter, the practical standards of craftsmanship would not matter very much. After all, in the play itself we do not blame the playwright if his or her words are delivered badly, saying that the script was rubbish. We can differentiate between the aesthetics of the text, the person speaking the words and the overall direction the cast received. If we were unable to do so, we might see the same play by Shakespeare performed in a variety of situations and by a variety of companies of actors and be forced to say that the same words were sometimes very good and sometimes very bad – a patent impossibility. The aesthetics of Shakespeare's writings stand up, no matter who performs them. What we are claiming is that if the designs for the stage sets are well produced, according to certain standards of aesthetics, then they will stand up on this score, even if they fall down physically on the night! If this is so, then you *can* learn from an amateur production in the same way that you can from a performance at the National Theatre. Again, it is *how* you analyse and critically evaluate what you see that will lead to good, practical work of your own.

CONTEXTUAL INVESTIGATIONS

What we have said so far emphasises that almost all three-dimensional work has to be planned and produced, as well as seen, with its contextual surroundings in mind. However, once more, if you do study the history associated with your area of activity, you will be able to uncover much contextual information that you can translate into a meaning for the way you work yourself. For instance, in the example above, referring to Art Deco, there are many contextual factors which could lead you to understand not only why the products of the style looked the way they did, but also *why* they came about in the first place. The reasons why are instrumental in many ways to the appearance of items associated with the style.

We have mentioned already that the style was, in part, the product of the ability to mass produce items. But it was not just that items could be produced in large numbers. Instead the style was partly the product of a determination to add quality to quantity as far as machine mass produced items were concerned. Part of the aesthetic principle behind the style was a willingness to use aspects of the designs of machinery in its own imagery. So we can see the effect of the design of ocean-going liners in architecture, or cogs and wheels in the fine art products associated with the style, as well as shapes similar to the bows of yachts or the wing-tips of aeroplanes in textile designs and so on. In addition, the style also associated with a marked readiness to pick up and use the new materials of the age, such as plastic and chrome. From all this you can see how the contextual circumstances of the Art Deco period were not only influential upon the style in a covert manner; they were actually taken up and used by the artists, designers and craftspersons in a most overt way. In this respect, the contextual circumstances can certainly be said to have helped to account for the aesthetic appearance of the style. If you remember, we have stressed continuously that materials and they ways of being worked have very strong effects upon what they are used for, and upon what the products they are used for look like. Art Deco is an excellent example of this if you study the style closely.

What is important is that you should see how, in this example, contextual circumstances affected Art Deco – and vice versa, of course – and then look to see where the modern counterparts lie. This might lead you to consider how the use of things such as computer graphics, the modern development of plastics, the aesthetics of things such as space shuttles or the molecular models of chemicals and so on, and their effects, can affect your work. It is this constant interplay between the history of art and design and its contextual circumstances that is so vital to your own original and creative practical work.

3-D WORK; STAGE DESIGN AND INTERIOR DESIGN

What the examination syllabuses say

Perhaps it is because three-dimensional activities such as ceramics, sculpture, jewellery and so on have such a strong craft element in the processes associated with them that the examination papers do not give you a lot of criteria to follow. Maybe it is felt that the traditions of these processes and the materials involved, develop their own criteria and

EXAMINING BOARD	SYLLABUS/TITLE OF AREA OF STUDY
AEB	ART AND CRAFTS/605 Paper 1 – Design and Practice of a Craft 605/1 (Time allowed: 15 hours) Option 08: Pottery Option 12: Sculpture Paper 3 – Part of Coursework 605/3 CRAFTS – POTTERY/663 Paper 1 – Design and Practice 663/1 (Time allowed: Up to 15 hours) Paper 2 – History and Technique 663/2 (Time allowed: 3 hours) Paper 3 – Coursework 663/3
JMB	CRAFT (DESIGN AND PRACTICE) (ADVANCED) Subject Group C: THREE-DIMENSIONAL STUDIES Study Areas i) Ceramics: any form of making any type of functional or decorative pottery ii) Sculpture: any form of construction, modelling, carving, casting, utilising any materials or processes iii) Theatre Studies: realisation of specific theatrical texts or dramatic performances within specified theatrical venues iv) Jewellery: the use of any materials and construction techniques *[These areas cover your Coursework Studies and your Controlled Test]* Controlled Test (Time allowed: up to 15 hours) The Written Paper (Time allowed: 3 hours) Craft Study (Done during your Coursework, and assessed by your teachers)
NISEC	SYLLABUS A Paper IV: Design for a Craft (Time allowed: 3 hours) pottery, metalwork, stage decor SYLLABUS B Section 1 – Main Study (Time allowed: 15 hours) 3. Three-dimensional Studies a) Ceramics b) Jewellery c) Silversmithing and beaten metalwork d) Constructions e) Sculptures f) Plastics g) Furniture h) Interior Design i) Stage decor Section 2 – Analytical and Written Study (Time allowed: 3 hours) Section 3 – History and Appreciation of Art, Architecture and Design (Time allowed: 3 hours plus Extended Essay) Part 1 History of Architecture and Sculpture Part 2 Appreciation of Design for Living Section 4 – Coursework
OXFORD	ART WITH ART HISTORY/9894 Paper 1 History of Art (Time allowed: 3 hours) Section I History of Architecture Section III Visual History Paper 5 Imaginative Work in Three-dimensional Media (Time allowed: extended period)

Table 9.1 The examining boards' titles for areas of study covered in this chapter.

control over what it is you do. If this is so, then there is even more reason for you to develop your **designing skills**. In the final analysis it is the quality of your design, combined with the quality of your productive skills, which will gain you the highest grades in the examination. We return to our initial contention that it is no use making something skilfully if it was not worth making in the first place. We mean by 'worth making' that your work should be well designed and relevant to the context which surrounds its existence.

Table 9.1 outlines the established syllabuses which make explicit reference to the practices covered in this chapter. What we say in this chapter is still relevant to you if your syllabus is not mentioned here.

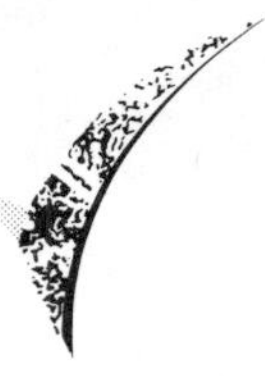

EXAMINATION QUESTIONS, STUDENT ANSWERS AND EXAMINER COMMENTS

In all the activities in these sections of your examination you are most likely to be given a specific theme, problem or play to work from. Of course, you will have a certain amount of choice between a number of questions each time, but it is unlikely that you will be invited to do anything you like. Even where you may be allowed to choose your own theme, problem or play, your work will be expected to contain somewhere within it a statement specifying which theme, problem or play you are responding to. As a result, you will always have a number of *external* requirements to fulfil in your work, no matter what the original and creative decisions you may yourself take and what the personal criteria which surround those decisions are.

THREE-DIMENSIONAL WORK

Ceramics

Most of the work done in the three-dimensional sections of the A-level and related examinations fall under the general umbrella of ceramics, or pottery. In fact, a lot of the sculpture will also be made in clay and include ceramic decoration.

Working in clay, which is the basis of all ceramic work and pottery, demands that you get to know the qualities of the medium well. To do this there can be no substitute for handling clay. If you are going to approach each problem you tackle by getting an idea, exploring it by means of photographs and drawings, doing designs in two-dimensional media and only *then* making your design in clay, you will be very much restricted in your knowledge of clay as a plastic and ductile material. We suggest instead that you get used to 'thinking in clay' right from the very beginning of your course. What we mean by this is:

- if you have an idea, model and shape it in clay, no matter how crudely;
- when you explore the imagery you want to use, in addition to drawings, get used to recording some aspects of it in clay; we suggest that, as you have a drawing and painting sketchbook, so keep a clay sketchbook, using slabs of clay to create relief 'drawings' of what you can see, or paintings in ceramic colours and oxides;
- get into the habit of making a clay maquette of your intentions in your designs at a very early stage in your work;
- practise making clay forms, using a variety of processes and techniques, without a design problem in mind, and then make your problem the aesthetic one of composing the forms you have into either a decorative or functional designed object.

It is unfortunate, but in the examples of ceramic work in this chapter we have no way of knowing whether the candidates worked in this way throughout their course. However, we would suggest that they did not, because had they done so, their use of clay would have been more free and relaxed. Nothing should stop you working in the way we propose.

To take this point up more strongly, let us begin by studying the work in Figs. 9.1, 9.2 and 9.3. This is a good set of work. Fig. 9.1 shows a range of explorations of the subject matter, an orange, all obviously done from direct observation. The work in Fig. 9.2 shows, by means of photographs, how the image of the orange gave birth to the aesthetic design decision for the ceramic work. The ceramic work is also documented by means of

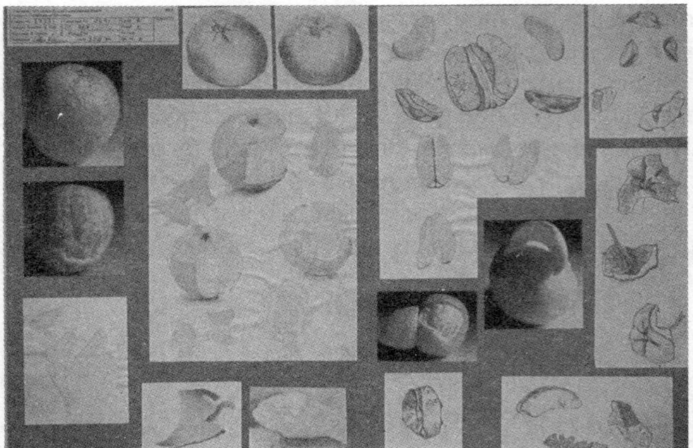

Fig. 9.1

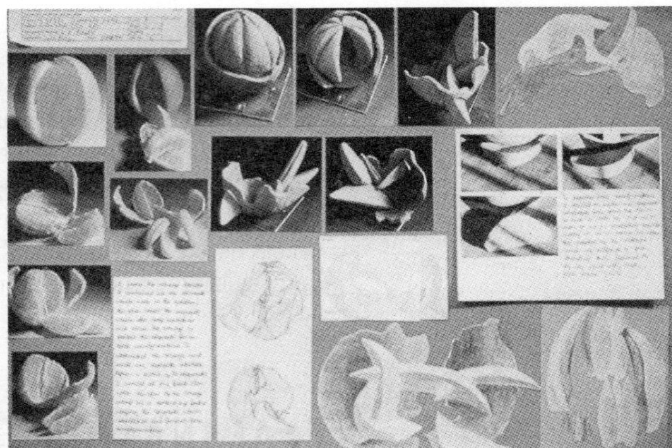

Fig. 9.2

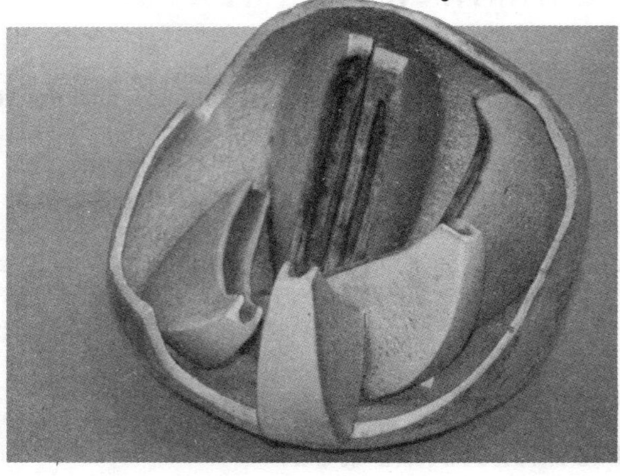

Fig. 9.3

photographs, showing some alternative ideas for the eventual design. The painted images pick up some of the directions which began to emerge, documenting them, but also developing them in terms of the work at large. Nowhere, however, is there any evidence of the use of clay, until the final design was being worked out.

There are photographs of an orange being peeled in Fig. 9.1 which we would have loved to 'draw' in clay, in order to investigate just what it was we thought we were observing. In turn, the painted work in Fig. 9.2 could have been made in clay, with the segments of the orange and the pith made separately. Then these 'units' could have been played with, rather like children's building bricks, and each design could have been photographed as it occurred. The result, in about the same time as it took to do the paintings, could have been innumerable images of design thoughts. There is a fine pedigree for this. A German educationalist, Friedrich Froebel, designed a set of building blocks for use as educational toys. An architect as important as FRANK LLOYD WRIGHT acknowledged the part they played in his development. The blocks, or a version of them, were also used in the Foundation Studies course at the BAUHAUS in Germany during the early part of this century, when design students and craftspersons used them in their three-dimensional studies.

However, the final result by this particular A-level candidate (Fig. 9.3) is interesting and sound. We would ask, though, what set of principles and criteria accounted for this final design decision? In our opinion the preliminary work does *not* lead logically to this result. As a consequence the final work looks like a collection of different ideas. In fact, it seems to reflect the variations in the preliminary studies, as if the candidate had established insufficient criteria during the work to allow a decision to arise which illustrated exactly which principles were responsible for its outcome. In this respect the result is not a very convincing design, although it is undoubtedly a satisfactory enough piece of work.

In the next set of work Fig. 9.4 shows a vigorous, well-presented collection of ideas. The whole page of work suggests an excitement which is, unfortunately, not carried into the final result (Fig. 9.6). In many respects this candidate has a level of ability in handling the two-dimensional media and work which is not always reached by those who choose to do three-dimensional studies in their examination. All too often, it seems, the three-dimensional aspects of the work are used almost as an excuse to avoid the problems of drawing. Yet, as we have pointed out so far, drawing in three-dimensional media in ceramics is more or less ignored!

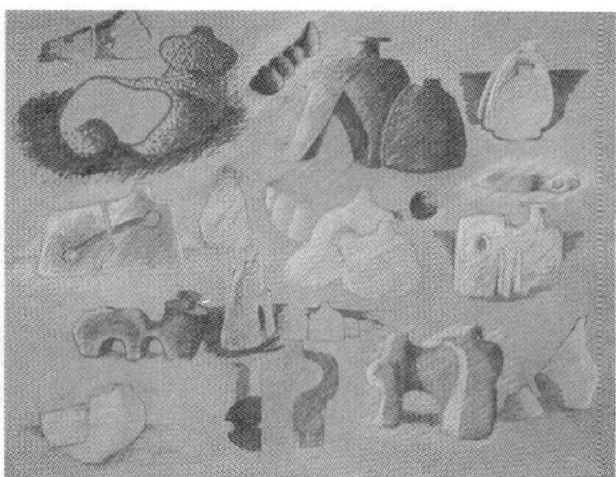

Fig. 9.4

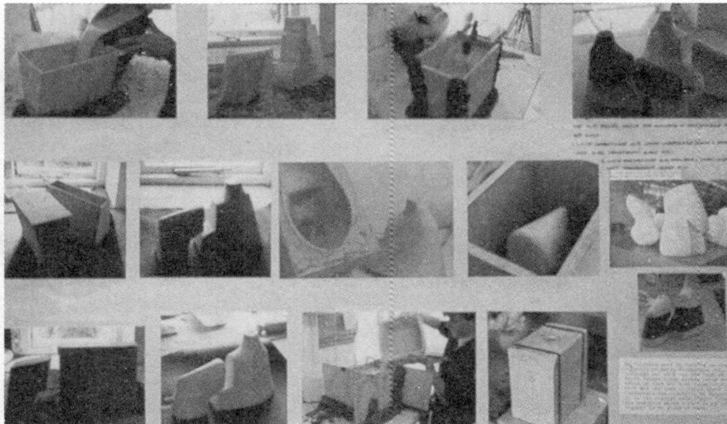

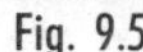

Fig. 9.5

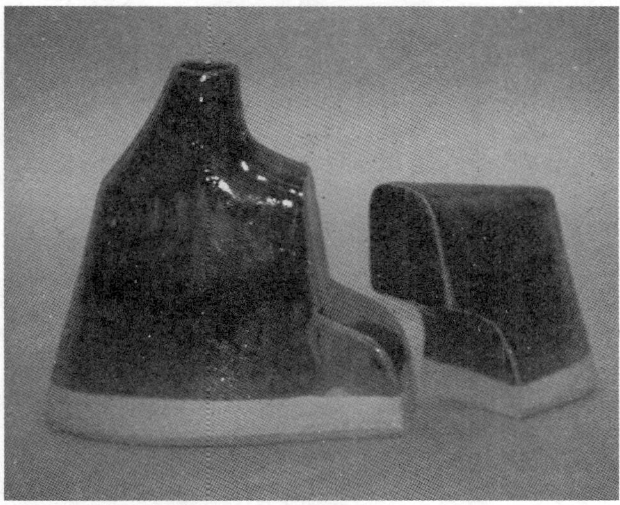

Fig. 9.6

To return to Fig. 9.6, in the final piece of ceramic work the candidate appears to have concentrated on the technical aspects of the work, to the detriment of aesthetic appearance. While we stress that the technical side of your work *is* very important, we also emphasise that you should be looking for a constant balance between that and the aesthetic. In this case, we almost seem to have *two* different candidates working, first on the preparatory studies and then the piece of craft work.

One positive thing this candidate does offer us is the very clear documentation of the working process, contained in Fig. 9.5. A photographic and written account such as this sheet conveys to others your level of understanding and decision-making. This cannot be conveyed in full in your final piece of work, or by the drawings of your ideas.

Whatever you do in your final piece of work and the drawings of your ideas, there are a lot of gaps which your teachers and examiners *will see* and have to *guess* at. Instead of allowing this to happen, it is very much in your interest in your examination to make clear to others *everything* you have done. This includes not just your drawings and your ceramic products but also what you rejected – with an explanation of why you rejected it and how you came to your decisions. If you want a comparison, think how in mathematics you get marks for showing your workings-out, even if the result to the problem is incorrect. Well, the same applies in art and design; perhaps even more so. Because there are no absolute rights or wrongs in art and design, it is highly important that you make it clear which rules you were playing to in coming to your conclusion at any time.

In the same way that we remarked upon the type and quality of the 'ideas' drawings for the work in Figs. 9.4, 9.5 and 9.6, other 'types' of drawings are valuable in your work. When you throw a ceramic shape on a wheel, or coil it, or make it from slabs of clay for that matter, one of the essential aspects of the form you make are the 'walls' of the form. Using this aspect in your drawings conveys to others part of your understanding of what it is you are doing. If you throw a shape on the wheel and then cut it from top to bottom with a wire, you will see the 'wall' drawing of what it is you have done. Using this form of imagery in your drawings in ceramics lets you show your intentions and planning in a way that the whole outside shape of the form does not. You can show, for instance, how you will make a lip to support a lid, how the lid will fit within the neck of the form so that it does not fall out if the form is tipped, how a spout will be fitted to the body of a pot and so on. These aspects are shown well in Fig. 9.8.

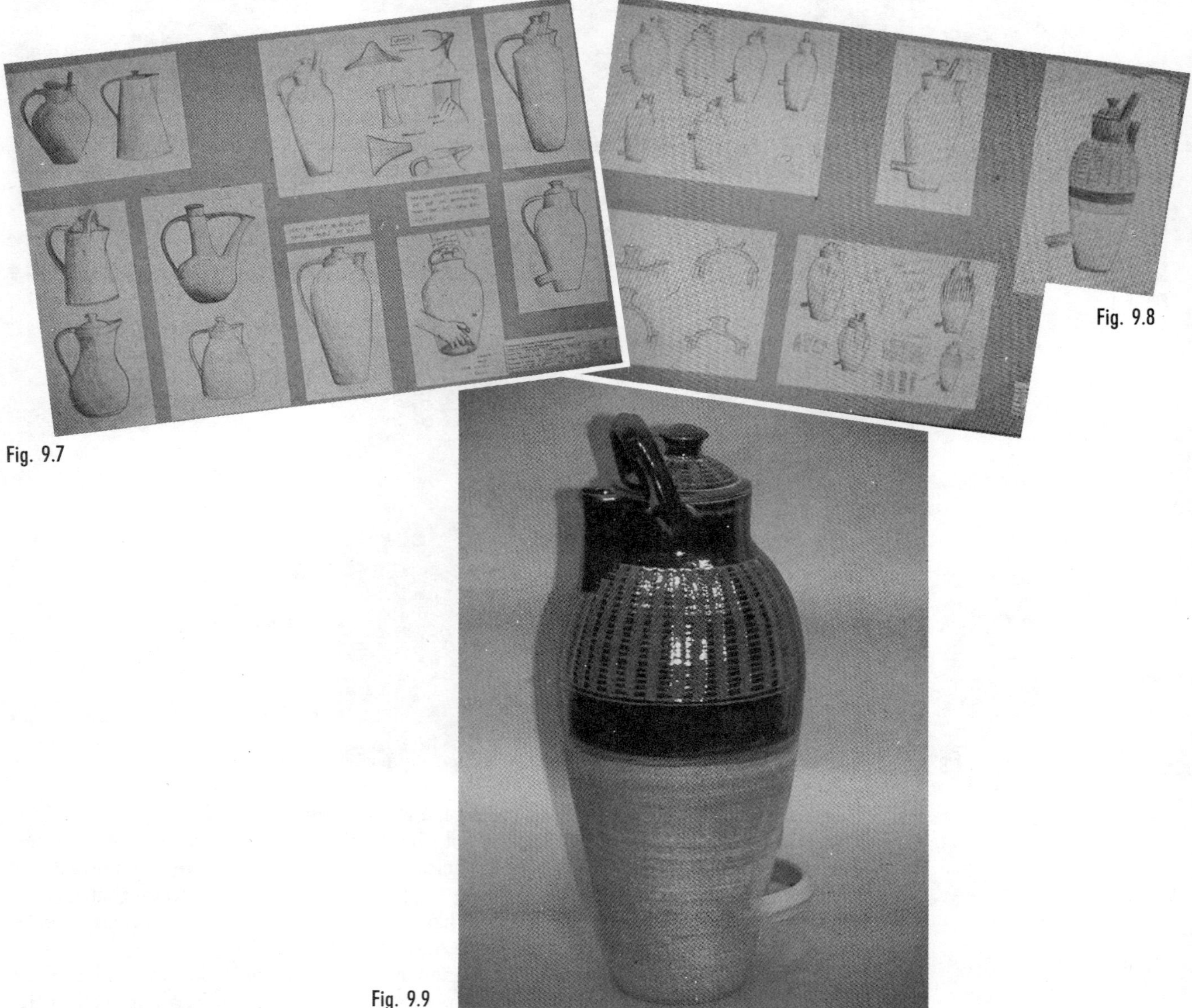

Fig. 9.7

Fig. 9.8

Fig. 9.9

There are other ways to 'draw' in this more technical way, in contrast to the visual impression way which is so well done in Fig. 9.4. This more technical type of drawing would logically follow the visual impressions of your ideas coming about when you are beginning to harden up the idea you will probably work on. It is not clear in either Fig. 9.7 or Fig. 9.8 if this candidate used such a process, but when you are drawing a form which has an identical profile either all the way round or on each side, you would be well advised to use a template. You could draw the profile first on a piece of cardboard, cut it out and then use it to draw both sides of the form in question. Or you could draw one side of the form on paper and then trace it, reverse it and transfer it to create the other side of your drawing. This not only saves much time in the long run but creates the uniformity you should be looking for. In a similar way, you could save time if you took a piece of sugar paper the colour of the clay you intend to use, drew one profile on it, folded the paper at the correct place and cut round the profile. This would give you the whole form when you unfolded it. This could then be stuck down on another sheet of paper – say strong white cartridge – and you could then show your plans for decorating the pot you then have by using other pieces of collage which you stick on the surface of your 'sugar-paper pot'. You have got to be inventive in your work, and this is one of the advantages which suitable experiments in the earlier stages of your course provides you with. One of the benefits this particular method gives you is that you have an almost infinite number of 'sugar-paper pots' to experiment with, as Fig. 9.10 shows.

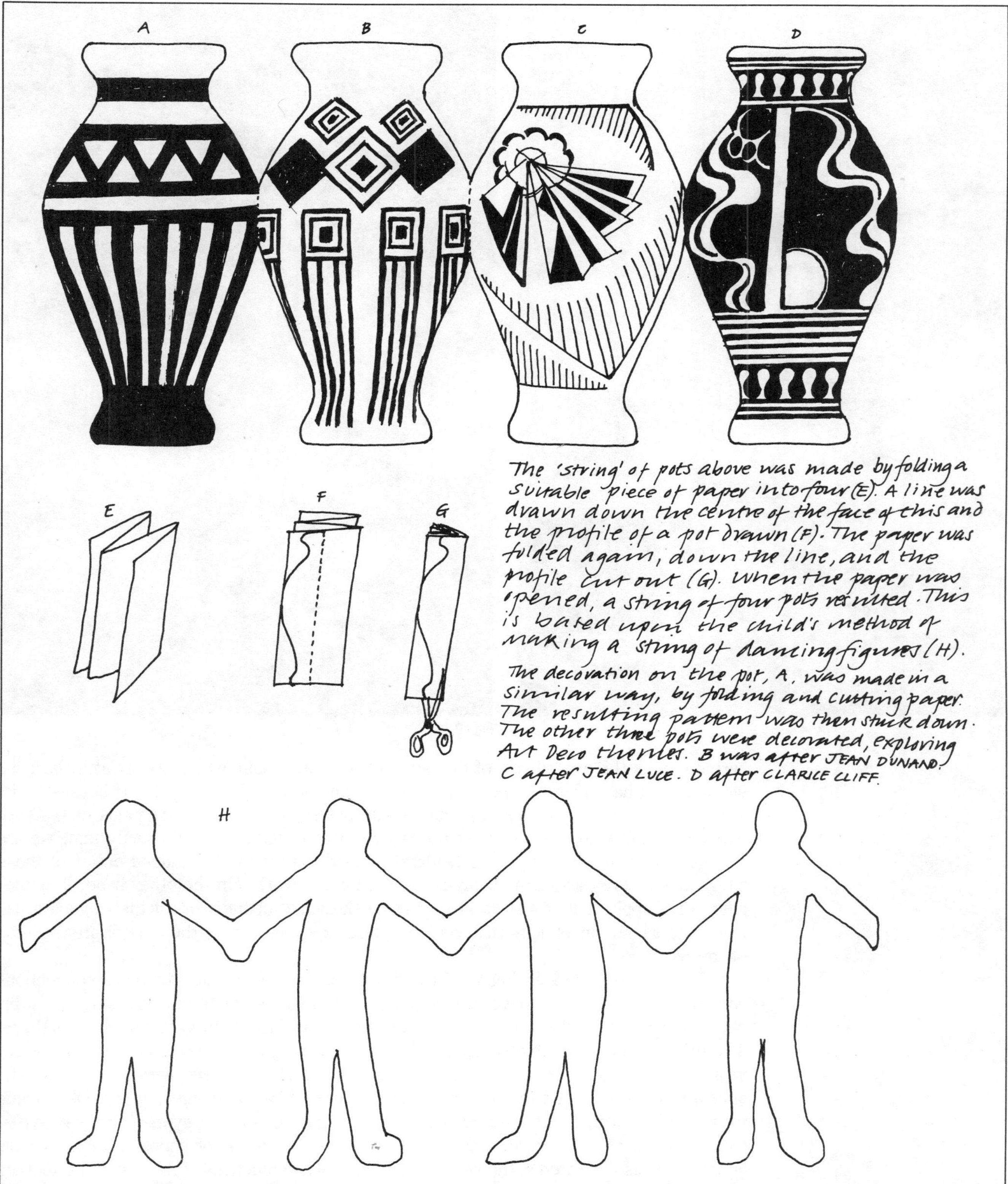

Fig. 9.10

The drawings of alternative pots in Fig. 9.7 are not very well or very excitingly portrayed. Apart from this, they do not indicate where the ideas for the alternatives came from. After all, it is a safe bet that you could find similar pots in a shop on your high street and on a visit to a museum. If you have studied other pots, acknowledge them in your work. Rather than causing examiners to restrict your marks, it will encourage them to add marks as a reward for the amount of work you have done.

One of the reasons it is important to acknowledge your sources of information and inspiration is apparent in this work. The final pot, in Fig. 9.9 has a lot to commend it. It appears to be well made. The handles are strong, bold and aesthetically in keeping with the overall form of the pot. The lid is large enough to form a positive element of the pot and its overall shape and appearance. The proportion of glazed decoration is in suitable

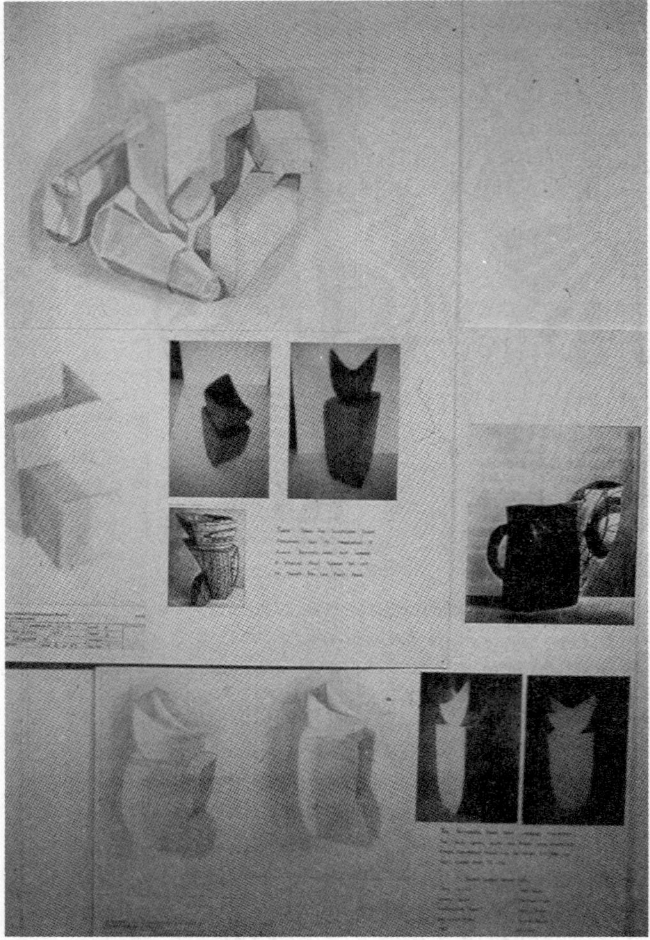

Fig. 9.11

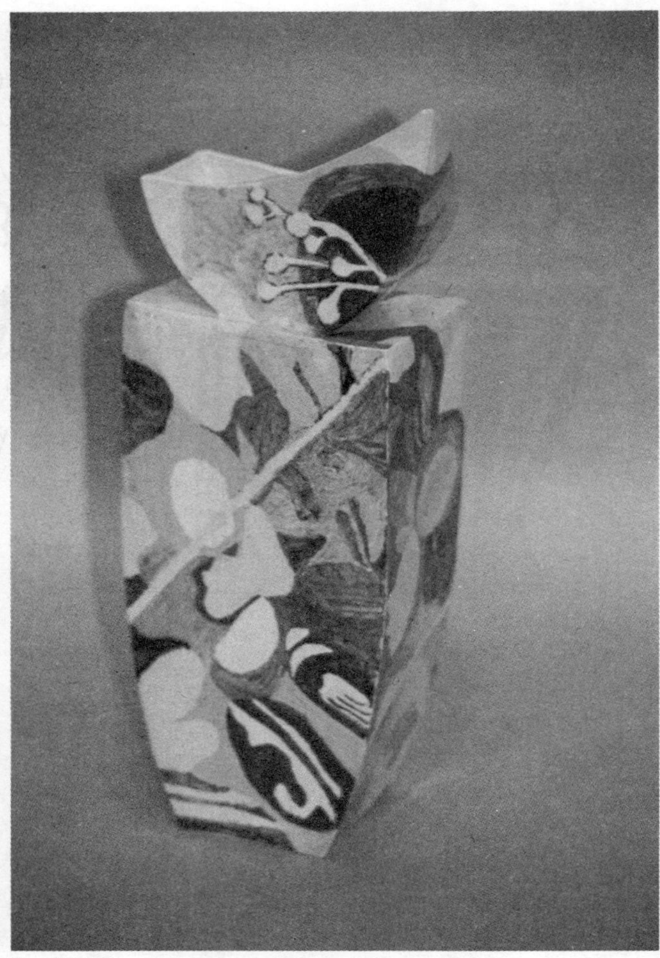

Fig. 9.12

harmony with the overall size of the pot. Yet we feel uneasy when looking at it, because we believe it has strong connections with African sources. Whether this is because it is, in fact, part of the traditions of some African pottery or because it reminds us of those African women who elongate their necks by means of bangles fixed round them, we are not sure. It would benefit this candidate to clarify the matter, if indeed either of these alternatives were part of the source material for the work. On the other hand, if neither alternative applied, it would greatly enhance the value of the work if the candidate had made the same connections that we have, and explained this in the overall presentation of the work.

We include the work in Figs. 9.11 and 9.12 because it has strong visual connections with Art Deco, which we have used as a thread to make some of our points so far in this chapter. To be fair, the work in Fig. 9.11 offers very little explanation of the pot there. The drawn study of geometric shapes in Fig. 9.11, might be various packages arranged in a still life. If you recall, we said that geometric shapes were part of the aesthetic appearance of some Art Deco work. Other sources of visual imagery in Art Deco came from African tribal art, Aztec and Mayan architecture, Egyptian art, FAUVISM, CONSTRUCTIVISM and CUBISM, among others. Stylised versions of young women, animals and flowers also featured in the work of Art Deco. The influences of these various sources were not restricted to the decoration of the products of Art Deco but also accounted for the shape and form of those products. In this respect, the shape of the pot in Fig. 9.12 causes us to suggest it has a resemblance to Art Deco.

While the decoration on this particular pot is a conglomeration of visual ideas, each of which reflects the style of Art Deco, they deny the principle of **clarity** in that style. To understand Art Deco it is vital to study Art Nouveau as well, because the former was in part a reaction against the latter. Whereas Art Nouveau had relied heavily on floral motifs, sinuously intertwining to create patterns and decorations, Art Deco was a definite move to the purity and clarity of MODERNISM. It was a style that was influenced by the possible precision and formality which could be achieved by machines.

Despite all this, somehow the pot in Fig. 9.12 has a feeling which is reminiscent of Art Deco. If historical and contextual study had been part of this candidate's approach, the examination work would most likely have been all the stronger. For instance, such studies might had led the candidate to the realisation that a connection could be made between the intentions emerging in the work and the style of Art Deco. This would have been to the advantage of the work and the candidate's ultimate examination grade.

Sculpture

As we have said, in our opinion three-dimensional work is a spectrum between two-dimensional work on the one hand and real-life, three-dimensional reality on the other. Sometimes the point along this spectrum employs two-dimensional work, turning it into three-dimensional work which has very little of the dimension of depth in it. Fig. 9.13 is an example of this.

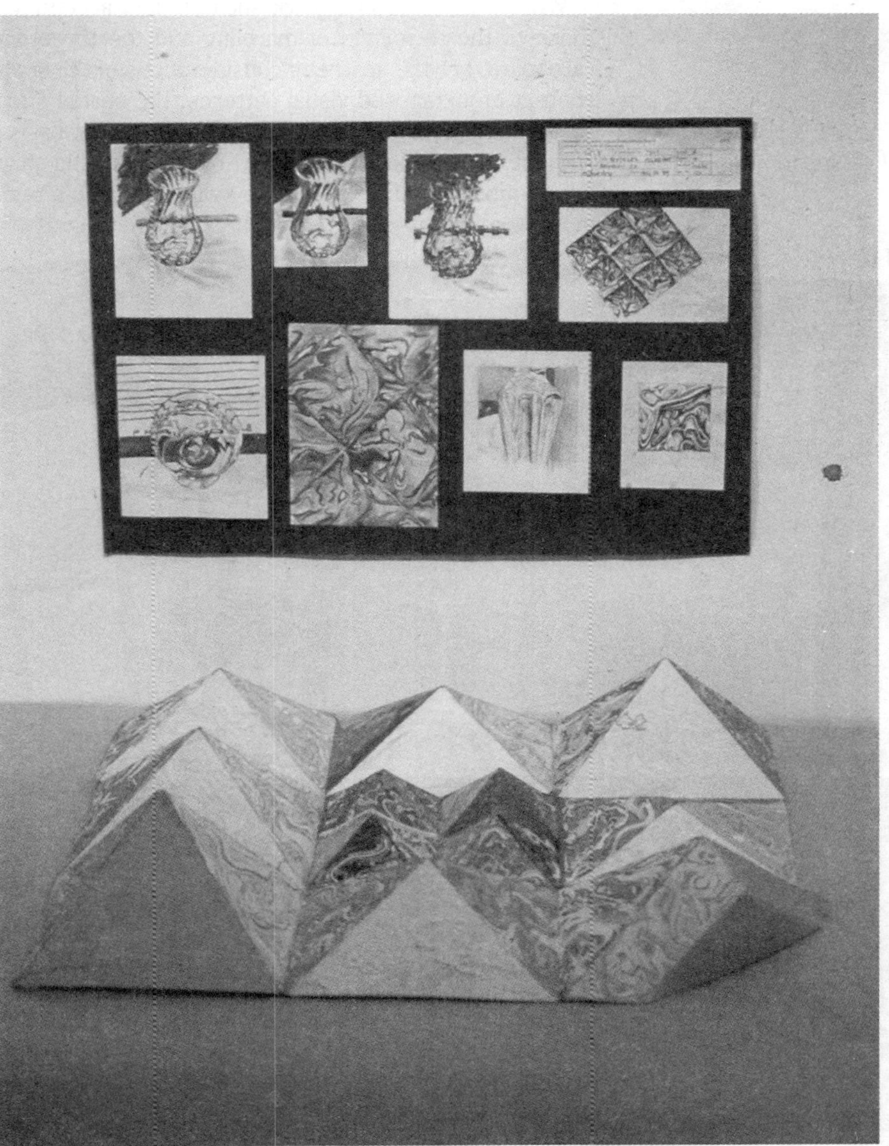

Fig. 9.13

Sculpture does not have to be representational – it is not only forms representing soldiers on horseback or two figures locked in a kiss. EDUARDO PAOLOZZI'S work at Euston Station is not representational in this sense, although it is very emphatically at the three-dimensional end of the spectrum we suggest. Neither is the work in Fig. 9.13 representational in this sense. It appears to have come about, following some form of visual inquiry no doubt, by first marbling sheets of paper. Marbling, as you may well know, is a process which involves floating drops of oil-based colour on water and then passing a sheet of paper over the surface of the water. The floating oil paint adheres to the paper, being pulled after it in streaks as the paper passes across the surface of the water and is then lifted off. When the paper is dry you will have a piece of paper permanently patterned in the colours dropped on to the surface of the water. In the past this technique was often used to decorate the end-papers in books. It has been revived to cover notebooks in more recent times.

In the work in Fig. 9.13 these marbled papers seem to have been stuck over cardboard constructed into a series of linked pyramids. If we look down on to these from directly above, the three-dimensional quality of the work may be not be very apparent, but when we look across the surfaces of the pyramids, as we can in the illustration, the three-dimensional aspect is clearer. However, again in this work, the reasons for what has been done are left unsaid and consequently unexplained. To have introduced something about the historical significance of marbled papers in the bookbinding trade, or to have explained how the marble effect perhaps made the candidate connect its appearance with the swirls of the sea, or the effect of the tide upon the mud on the banks of an estuary, or the appearance of the landscape from the sky, would have given the work much more value than it has as it stands.

What is at stake in a work such as this, accepting that it had no other influences than those of the technique of marbling and the three-dimensional construction of shapes in cardboard, are the aesthetic considerations of the spatial relationship of colours, the spatial context of juxtaposed visual patterns, the spatial effect of light and dark areas and so on. As it stands, the work must be evaluated on the basis of aesthetic and technical principles, without the added advantage of surrounding historical and contextual study and information. Because it sinks or swims on such a restricted set of criteria, it needs to be most excellent to achieve a high examination grade. Where would you place it?

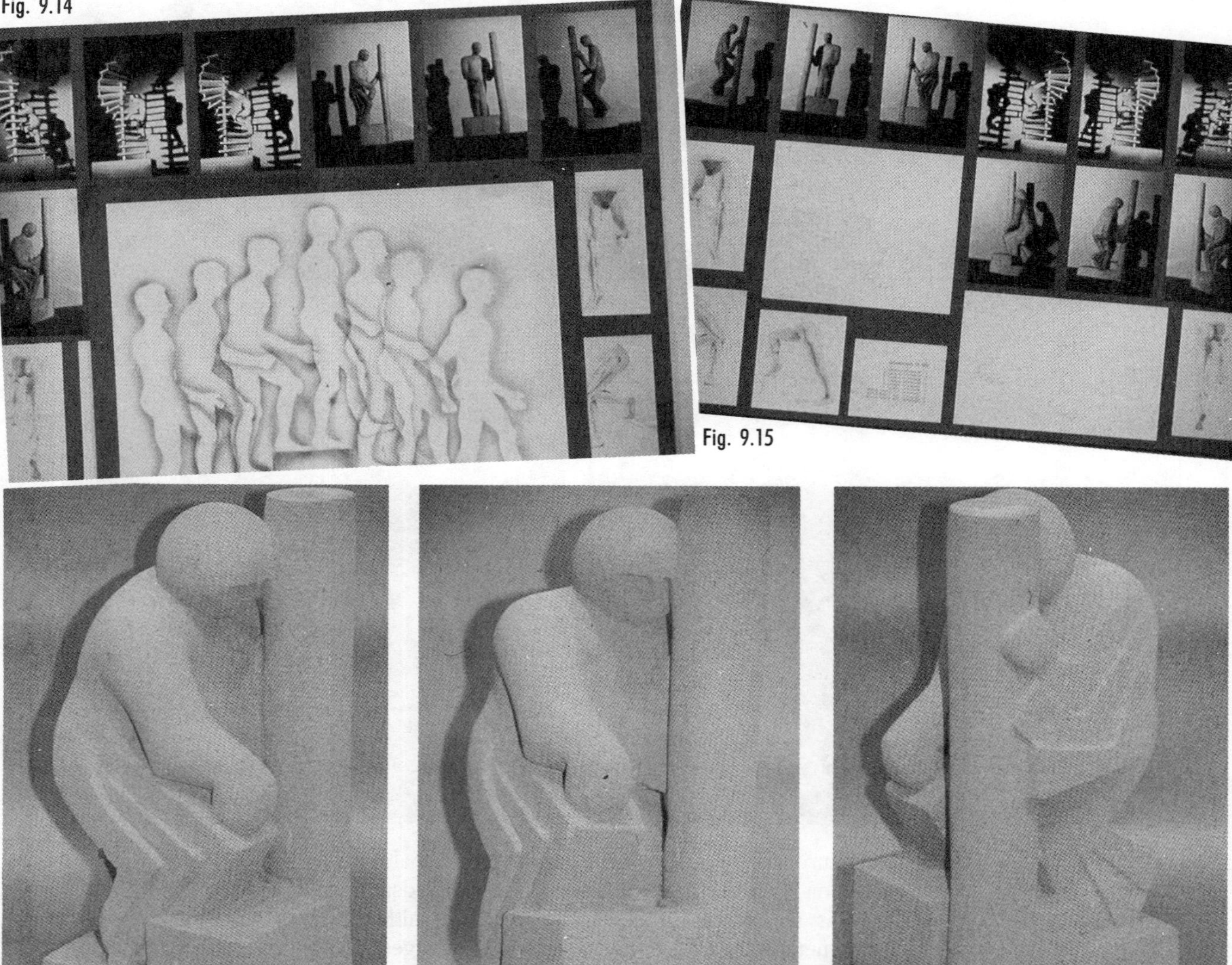

Fig. 9.14

Fig. 9.15

Fig. 9.16

Fig. 9.17

Fig. 9.18

Figs. 9.14 to 9.18 show a set of works which are at the furthest three-dimensional end of the spectrum we have built up. It does not matter that the finished work was no more than 300 millimetres high, it still comes within the notion of a 'full, three-dimensional sculpture'. The preparatory studies show work which could have had obvious connections with the work of artists and movements in art such as:

- MARCEL DUCHAMP (1876 – 1918) and his work 'Nude Descending a Staircase', in which we see a figure which is composed of what we would call 'multi-exposures' in photography; the overlay of these exposures creates a strong sense of movement, as if the figure is descending the stairs.
- From this connection, consideration of the Italian FUTURIST MOVEMENT might have come about; a group of artists, among other things, tried to show the movement of people, animals and transport; the work by GINO SEVERINI (1883 – 1966) called 'Suburban Train Arriving in Paris' probably best exemplifies this connecting similarity with Duchamp's work.
- The idea of movement could then have been taken up with the consideration of 'flick-books', zoetropes and kaleidoscopes.
- The study of movement might then have been explored further within the notion of **kinetic sculpture**, in which sculptural works are made to move, sometimes by motors, sometimes by more natural methods such as gravity or rising hot air. Sculptors such as ALEXANDER CALDER (1898 – 1976), LYNN CHADWICK (1914) and NAUM GABO (1890 – 1977), as well as BRYAN WYNTER (1915 – 75), POL BURY (1922 –) and JULIO LE PARC (1928 –), have all done work which falls within this notion, and might be studied to good advantage.

Of course, while it is likely, though it is not said, that the candidate was aware of the Duchamp work, none of the other elements is explored and absorbed into the work. Nor has the very obvious visual connection that the work has with the CONSTRUCTIVIST MOVEMENT been explored.

This Movement was primarily based in Russia, at the time of the Revolution. It had only a short life, embracing not only painting and sculpture but also furniture design, stage work, typography and architecture. The roots of Constructivism had had considerable influence upon what we now think of as the INTERNATIONAL STYLE in architecture. It is the candidate's photographs of the staircase constructions, in Figs. 9.14 and 9.15, which strike this visual chord with Constructivism. These photographs are very reminiscent of the stage designs of such as ALEXANDER VESNIN, (1883 – 1959) and LYUBOV POPOVA, as well as the constructions of VLADIMIR TATLIN (1885 – 1953). These leads could have been followed up by the candidate; the work would have benefited.

When a 'full' sculpture such as this is produced, it is essential that it is viewed from all sides. The photographs we have taken of the work, and include here, begin the investigation form all angles but, of course, it is easy enough to lift and turn this particular sculpture round in order to see it from the side and the back. This is due to its size. What the photographs here, in Figs. 9.16, 9.17 and 9.18, signify for your own work is that it would be very sensible to take a series of your own photographs from all around your work *as it proceeds*. This would allow your examiner to see the types of decisions you took as the work evolved, as well as documenting not only your progress but also your changes of mind and direction.

Stage design

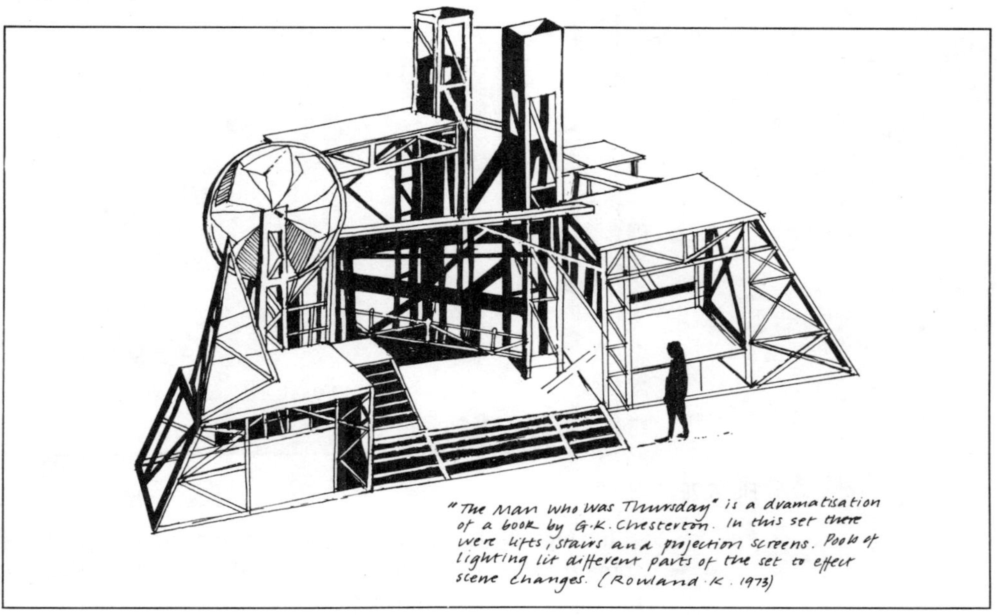

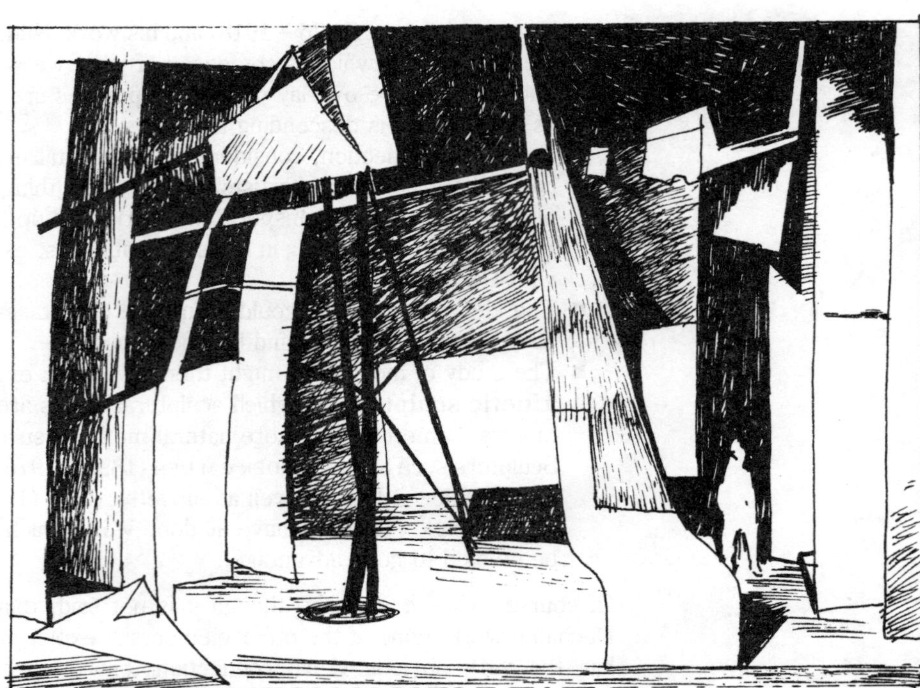

VLADIMIR TATLIN's design for "Sangezi" – 1923
To understand this design more fully, apart from reading the text of the play, you should study Tatlin's 'Relief' sculptures and his "Monument to the Third International" (Tatlin's Tower), as well as the work of other Russian artists and designers during the 1920's.

Fig. 9.19

We have mentioned the stage designs of the Constructivist Movement: Fig. 9.19 shows some examples. They demonstrate that you do not have to either paint a naturalistic background for a staged play or to create a scene by means of pieces of furniture. You can design a set which captures the mood of the play rather than the detail. Sets such as these seem to have influenced the approach of one of the major scenic designers in the United Kingdom, SEAN KENNY. His work in the 1950s and 1960s, on productions such as *Oliver*! and *Blitz*, revolutionised design on the British stage. Since then, companies such as the RSC and the National Theatre continue to use some of the aesthetic principles that were present in Kenny's work.

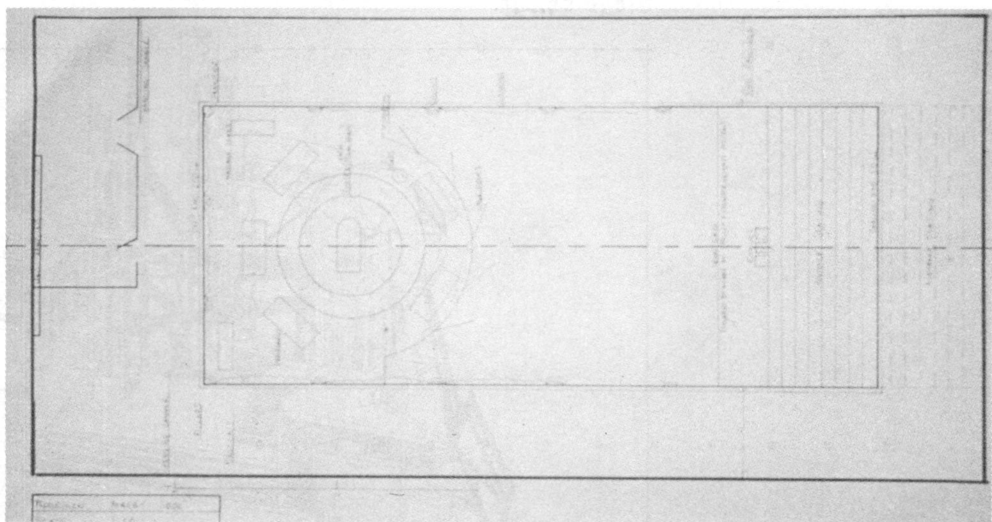

Fig. 9.20

In stage design, above all else, it seems important that you work in a way which reflects some of the excitement, mystery and magic of the theatre. When you have a design ready to stage, a thorough plan is necessary, so that you and others can see exactly how it fits the stage, how it should be constructed and how it will 'work' during production. Fig. 9.20 is a good example of what we mean by this. A plan is a formal and exact drawing, conveying very little of the designer's 'handwriting'. By handwriting we mean the drawing style each of us develops as we work in art and design. Of course, with designers, this style or handwriting changes very deliberately from time to time, to fit the demands of a particular design problem.

Figs. 9.21 and 9.22 do reflect the excitement, mystery and magic of the theatre. This due to the handwriting the candidate has employed, which is to a large part due to the materials used in these drawings, the qualities the materials have contributed to each drawing and the overall collation and presentation of the sheets.

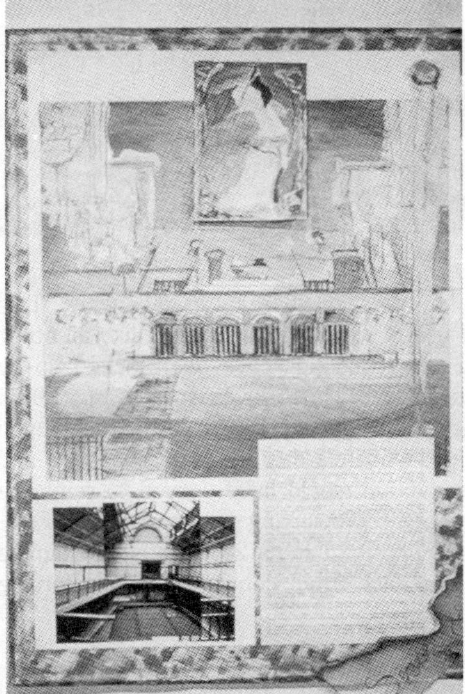

Fig. 9.21

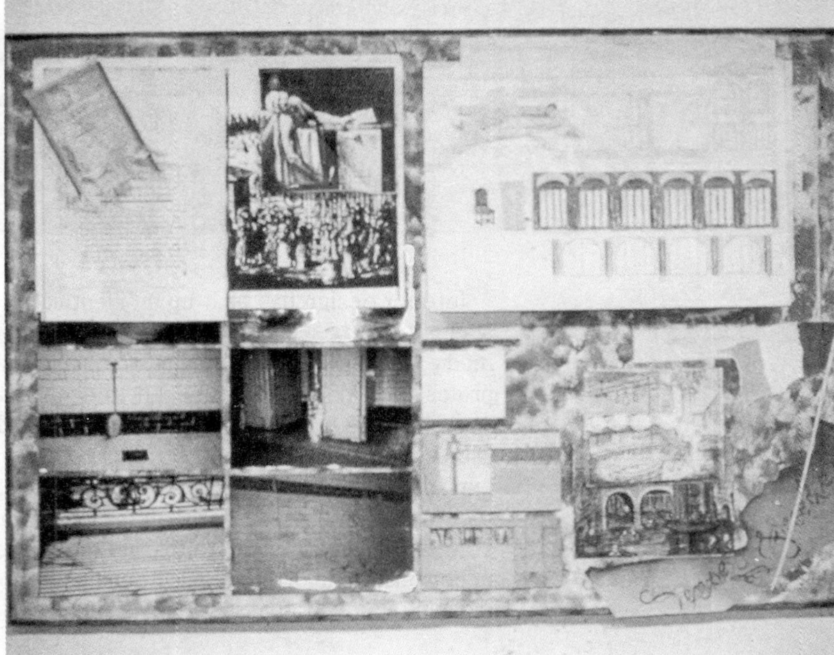

Fig. 9.22

In the work of the A-level candidate illustrated in Figs. 9.21 and 9.22 it is a great pity that there is no indication of a three-dimensional interpretation of the design. Plays take place in a three-dimensional environment, no matter if it is an empty stage, theatre in the round, or an open space such as is used for *Son-et-Lumiere* productions. Therefore, it is essential that you explore the three-dimensional reality of your designs. Apart from building them on the actual stage where the play is to take place, which is an expensive way to discover any shortcomings the designs may have, the obvious way to manage this is to construct a model.

A model of your designs is important for more than one reason. It certainly should not be constructed when your design is complete, as another form and image of your work. Instead, it should accompany *all* your designing work, allowing you to get ideas and try them out in the model by making little objects to represent your ideas. This allows you to move them around, change their appearance and size, or scrap them altogether. You handle your ideas three-dimensionally within the model in the same way that you handle them two-dimensionally in your drawings and plans.

This was the essence of the model in Vesnin's set in Fig. 9.19. When you see it in use in the same illustration, you can see how it works at full size with actors using it. Without the model Vesnin would have been taking a chance with its aesthetic appearance, its efficiency for the actors and the cost of making something full size which had then to be scrapped because it was unworkable!

Of course, nowadays there is a fast way of exploring some aspects of your three-dimensional ideas. This is with the aid of a computer. There are programs which will allow you to feed your two-dimensional drawings into it and they will then project these in three dimensions from any angle or eye level you choose. This is an excellent aid to three-dimensional designing but even so, it does not replace the physical model altogether. The qualities of the two – the computer and the physical model – are different and produce different images and forms. Once more, they complement rather than replace each other.

Interior design

What has been said about the importance of a model in stage design applies just as much to interior design. Again, you are involved in a real three-dimensional design problem, even if your designs will probably not get created at full size. Therefore, you should explore your ideas three-dimensionally as well as two-dimensionally.

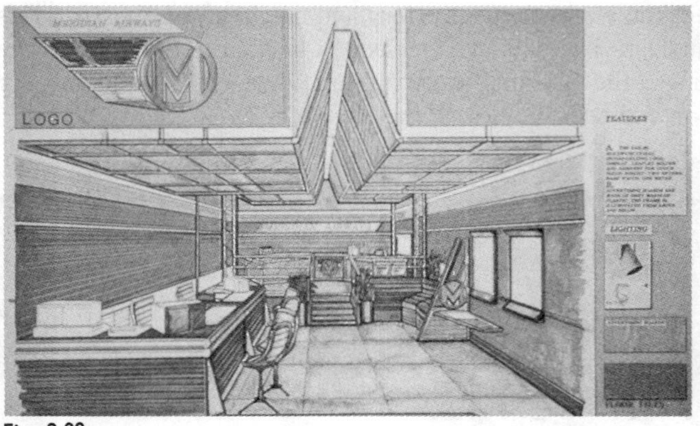

Fig. 9.23

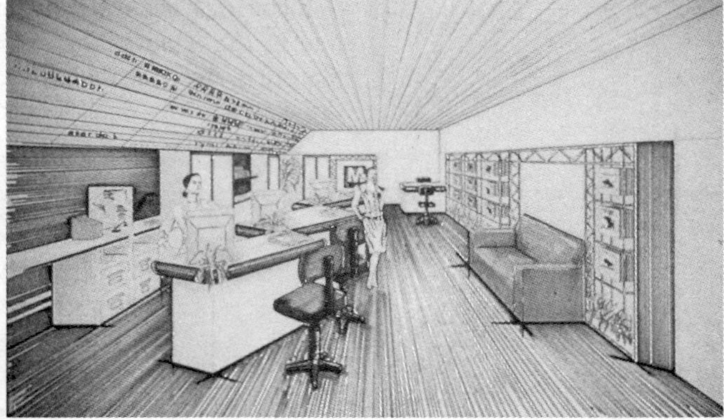

Fig. 9.24

Interior design has built up an identifiable style professionally in its graphic work. This seems to be based most often upon the expert use of felt tip pens. These, like all other media, have their own particular qualities and these qualities have been picked up by professional designers and used to excellent advantage. The A-level work in Figs. 9.23 and 9.24 has used this medium in a sound graphic style which is clearly based upon professional work. Both illustrations convey the candidate's designs in an attractive and explanatory manner. To have used a model in addition would have served to reinforce their achievements, rather than remedy a lack. The accompanying design sheets in Figs. 9.25, 9.26 and 9.27 help to explain the images in Figs. 9.23 and 9.24. This is an example of how plans and orthographic drawings complement each other, conveying and reinforcing meaning in a way that just one or the other fails to.

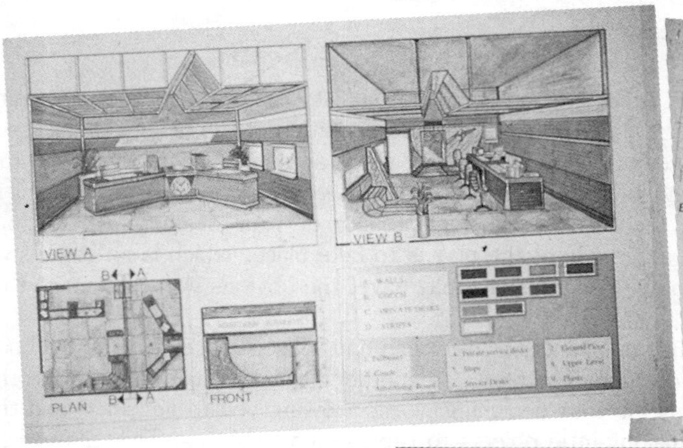

Fig. 9.25

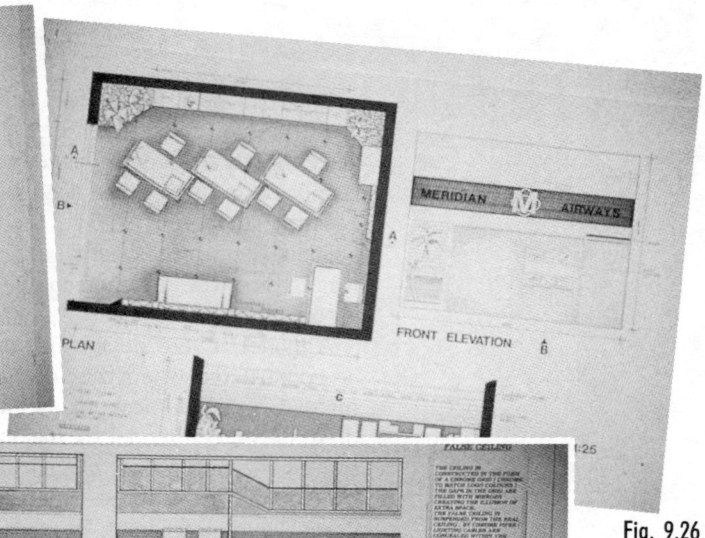

Fig. 9.26

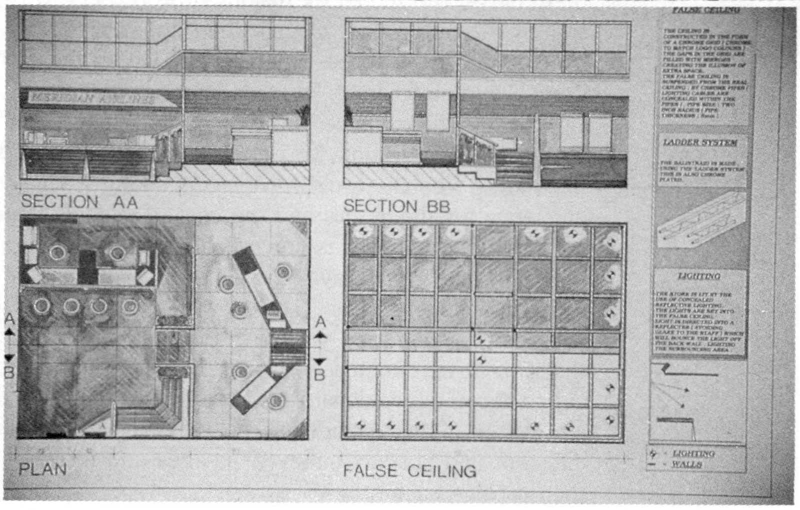

Fig. 9.27

The only criticism we have of this otherwise excellent set of work is that nowhere can we see how the designs came about. The drawings and mistakes which have been 'cleaned out' of the work would have shown this. We appreciate that you have a dilemma at the time of your examination. You wish to show yourself in the best light. This is only natural – after all it is the essence of examinations. As a result you tend to preserve only the most technically expert and the most aesthetically successful pieces of your work for the examination. In doing this, you must safeguard against failing to include pieces of work which show the extent and sensitivity of the value judgements you have made.

If all your value judgements remain interwoven into your finished and presented set of work without showing any of your 'working-out', the danger is that the examiners are left to guess at these qualities in your work. We think it better that you find a way of pointing *everything* out at the time of your examination.

In the case of this candidate, even the work in Fig. 9.28 continues this tendency to present only that which shows the final achievement. This is certainly the correct way to present your designs to a client, but an examiner is not a client. He or she is someone who needs to be helped to see the full extent of your explorations and achievements, not just how well it all turned out.

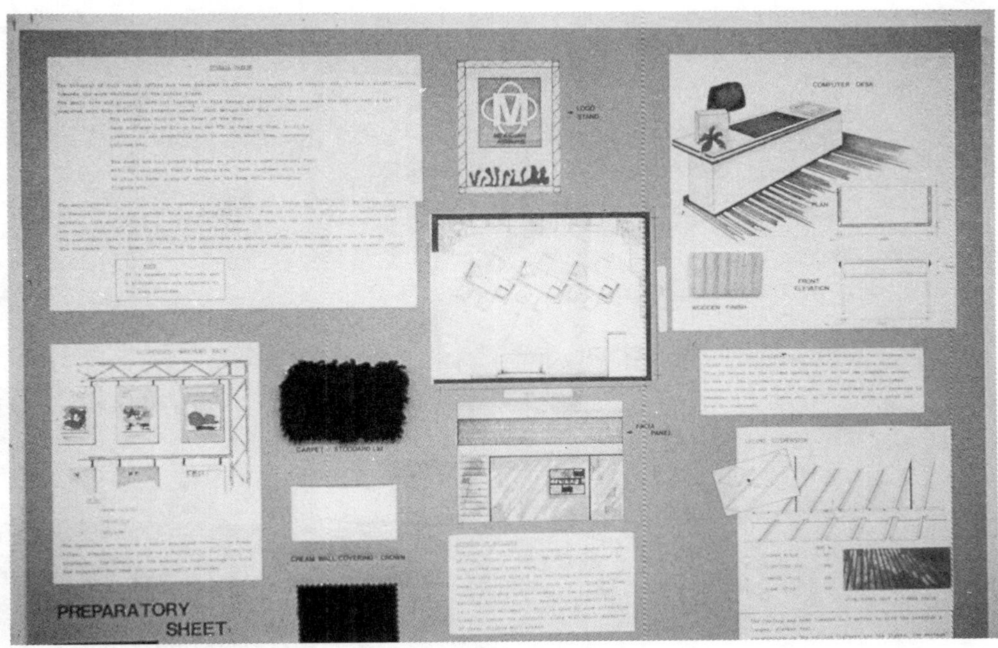

Fig. 9.28

We mentioned above the style associated with the use of felttip pens. Of course, these are not the only materials professional designers use, nor is the style we identified the only one to come out of their work. Professional designers use professional materials, such as transfer lettering and transfer colour sheets and texture sheets, as well as computer-aided graphics in their work. Materials and equipment like this are expensive, and all too often we do not see much of their use in schools and colleges, which is a pity. It can mean that when you use other materials to try and obtain effects similar to those which the expensive materials produce, your work suffers in comparison. Nevertheless, you should study how professional designers set about obtaining certain effects and how they convey their messages and meanings in their work.

Figs. 9.29 to 9.32 show this well. Using water colour in thin washes, the candidate achieves effects in Figs. 9.29 and 9.30 which are similar to transfer colour and texture sheets. In turn, the work in Fig. 9.31 conveys the candidate's explorations and intentions in ways similar to sophisticated colour photocopying from detailed specification samples of a variety of interior design phenomena. In Fig. 9.30 the candidate has attempted a very difficult projection of the design in a highly commendable way. In Fig. 9.32 the candidate seems to explore this in an alternative manner. In this the 'levels' of the floors are built up like layers in a biscuit, using corrugated cardboard. This is a fine example of what we mean by showing how your ideas have come about. We do not know if the projection in Fig. 9.30 or the model in Fig. 9.32 was done first, but one complements the other well. The model is nowhere near as expert in finish and presentation as the rest of the work is, but this does not matter. As we have pointed out before, we are looking for further explanations of the candidate's ideas and working habits.

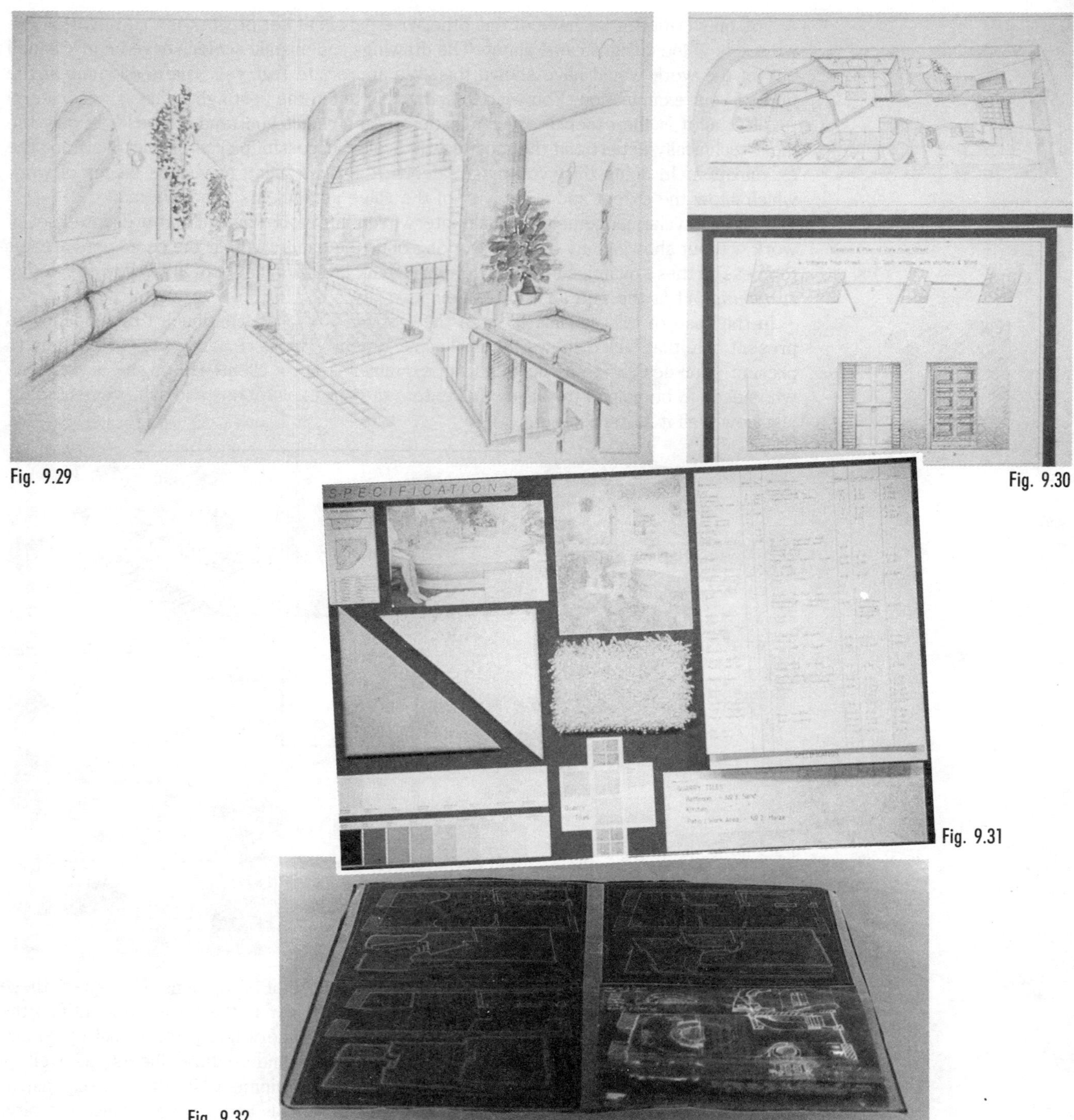

Fig. 9.29

Fig. 9.30

Fig. 9.31

Fig. 9.32

Working in three dimensions does not mean that you do not have to develop skills in two-dimensional materials. Two-dimensional materials often form part of a three-dimensional object, but they are also essential in allowing you to express your ideas and test your intentions.

Nevertheless, you should avoid separating your materials on the basis of using only two-dimensional for your preparatory studies in any problem. Using three-dimensional materials to express your ideas and test your intentions creates a beneficial and necessary link between your preparatory studies and your final design and work.

Never fail to look for historical connections with what you have in mind. The knowledge which arises from such investigations informs you and equips you with some of the criteria necessary to produce really successful work.

Always acknowledge your sources of information and inspiration. You are in a learning situation and in your examination one of the things you must do is demonstrate the breadth and depth of your learning and understanding, not just produce art and design items which measure up to acceptable technical and aesthetic standards, although these are fundamental aspects of your examination.

EXERCISES

1 Collect together a number of each of about six different proportioned rectangular blocks. These can be cut from wood or made from clay. Colour them white. With these blocks, using as many as you wish each time, create three-dimensional constructions on the following themes:

- reaching up;
- spreading out;
- twisting and turning;
- the ins and the outs;
- light and dark;
- enclosed space;
- tenuous links;
- outward-looking;
- inward-looking;
- collapse.

In your work at all time pay attention to the aesthetic decisions in what you do. Each time you think an arrangement is satisfactory, photograph the result from a number of angles and eye levels.

2 Make an alternative set of arrangements for the themes in 1. and photograph your results again. Compare the two results for each theme. Mount the photographs side by side in a notebook in each case and write your own critical appraisal of the results next to them.

3 Rearrange your blocks into your solution to one of the themes. 'Draw' what you see in clay. You *must* walk around the arrangement quite often or have it on a board so that you can turn the arrangement around from time to time.

4 Set up a person or an object you would like to work from. Mount a large sheet of white cartridge paper on to a drawing board, preferably by stretching it, using brown sticky tape. Start in one position, using a coloured felttip pen to draw with, and make a study in line only of what you can see. Give yourself about five to ten minutes to do this. The move about 45 degrees to your right. Using a different coloured felttip pen, draw what you can see now, in outline again, but *on top* of your first drawing, to the same scale and positioning on the paper. After about ten minutes move on another 45 degrees and draw again to the same rules, but with another coloured felttip pen. Repeat this until you are back where you started.

5 Repeat the exercise in 4 only this time use your felttip pens to 'block in' masses as well as for drawing in outline. Use the same subject for this set of drawings, but cut your time down to about three minutes for each drawing.

6 From the two drawings you have from 4 and 5 using any material or combination of materials you wish, construct a three-dimensional object which looks like the two drawings combined and *not* like the original subject matter. That is to say, try to simulate the imagery in your drawings and not your memory of the original person or object.

7 Produce preparatory studies and a finished three-dimensional work, either in ceramics, sculpture, stage design or interior design, for both the following themes:

- inferno;
- cold blasts.

These are deliberately contrasting concepts. In your work you should reflect this quality of contrast.

CHAPTER

THE REVISED SYLLABUSES

UNIVERSITY OF CAMBRIDGE LOCAL EXAMINATION SYNDICATE (UCLES)

JOINT MATRICULATION BOARD (JMB)

OXFORD AND CAMBRIDGE SCHOOLS EXAMINATION BOARD (OX/CAM)

SCOTTISH EXAMINING BOARD (SEB)

UNIVERSITY OF LONDON SCHOOLS EXAMINATION BOARD (ULSEB)

WELSH JOINT EDUCATION COMMITTEE (WJEC)

GETTING STARTED

Chapter 3 outlined the various **established** syllabuses – that is, those which tend to divide what you can do during your studies and for your examination into different art and design practices. Chapters 4 to 9 dealt separately with these various practices, all of which are relevant to your work in art and design, no matter which syllabus you are studying.

In this chapter we look in detail at the various **revised** syllabuses, which take into account more explicitly the recent changes in GCSE and Scottish Standard examinations. Although you will be particularly interested in your own examination board, do look at the material presented for other examination boards, especially the sample student work and illustrative material under the heading 'Work requirements and practices'. Many themes and practices overlap the various boards and contain much that is relevant to you.

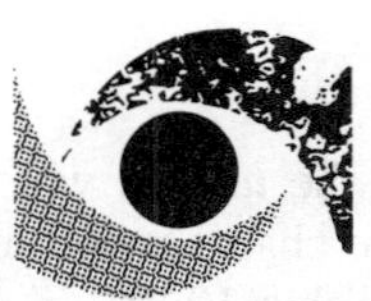

ESSENTIAL PRINCIPLES

UNIVERSITY OF CAMBRIDGE LOCAL EXAMINATIONS SYNDICATE (UCLES)

A-LEVEL AND AS ART AND DESIGN

The UCLES A-level syllabus was examined for the first time in June 1990 and, like all the 'new' Art and Design syllabuses mentioned in the book, it is intended to follow on naturally from GCSE Art and Design examinations. The Syndicate states that it is desirable but not essential that candidates have previously reached GCSE grade C standard. It will obviously help if you achieved a high grade at GCSE, but do not be too concerned if you did not. As long as you develop the study skills and methods of working discussed earlier, you should be able to meet all the requirements of the examination.

We have mentioned already that it is most important for you to understand the **values** the syllabus is concerned with. If you can tease out the spirit or philosophy of the syllabus, you will be well placed to interpret more fully what the examiners are looking for in your work.

For example, the introduction to the syllabus expresses something about the intended *outcomes* of studying an A-level course in Art and Design. It is hoped that the student will develop 'sensitivity, powers of observation, analytical abilities, aesthetic pleasure' – among other things. You can see from statements like this that the examiners are concerned about much more than the basic skills of painting a picture or making a pot.

Aims

The Aims of the syllabus provide an idealised view about what might be achieved by successfully following the syllabus. They outline the range of qualities that someone who has completed the course should possess but do not specify particular examination requirements.

Assessment objectives

The Assessment Objectives *do* specify what you must achieve in order to do well in the examination. They define a range of qualities and skills that you must demonstrate in order to achieve an award.

PERSONAL QUALITIES	Candidates will be expected to demonstrate the ability to: i) show an individual, sensitive and creative response to a stimulus, i.e. an idea, theme or subject; ii) show independence in concept and execution;
Manipulative Skills	iii) select and control materials, processes and ideas in an informed and disciplined way appropriate to any brief given; iv) recognise and use as appropriate; contour, surface, shape, colour, tone texture, pattern, structure and the relationships of forms in space; v) record analytically from direct observation and personal experience;
Knowledge and Understanding	vi) analyse an idea, theme or subject and select, research, communicate and evaluate in a systematic way; vii) sustain a chosen study from conception to realisation;
Analytical and Aesthetic Qualities	viii) make critical judgements and show aesthetic awareness; ix) organise ideas and images.

Table 10.1 Assessment objectives (reproduced by permission of the UCLES).

The Syndicate has grouped the objectives under four headings (Table 10.1). This allows you to focus on the key requirements of the syllabus and separate out the skills and qualities you will need. The various components of the examination will stress some objectives more than others, but your work will need to take all the objectives into account if you are to achieve a high grade.

Scheme of assessment

The Scheme of Assessment is the means by which the examination tests whether you have met the assessment criteria and, perhaps more importantly, the *level* at which the criteria have been met. We will explain how this is done later in the chapter, but first let us look at exactly what you need to do by the end of the course (Table 10.2).

COMPONENT	TITLE	WEIGHTING OF MARKS	TIME ALLOWED
1	Controlled Test	30%	10 hours max. (3 hours min. to run consecutively)
2	Coursework	40%	–
3	Personal Study	30%	Title to be submitted by 31 October in year before the examination

Component 1 will be externally marked.
Components 2 and 3 will be internally marked and sent to the syndicate for external moderation.
All three papers will be viewed as a whole by teams of two or three chief examiners.

Table 10.2 Scheme of assessment.

WORK REQUIREMENTS AND PRACTICES

To help you make a start on the work required for the examination we will deal with each component in turn. We will not cover all the practices mentioned in the syllabus, but you will find reference to them elsewhere in the book – even if they are referred to in another board's syllabus.

This will not harm your chances of success with the UCLES examination because there is close agreement between all boards and their examiners about what **good practice** is. You can be confident that the guidance given elsewhere in the book will be appropriate to your work for the UCLES examination.

COURSEWORK SUBMISSION

Your coursework submission must include a folder of work and up to three coursework pieces, maximum size for any work to be A1.

Folder of work

The folder should contain a *selection* of work from the full period of the course. This means that it is your responsibility to select work which will reveal the full extent of your abilities and preoccupations. The examiners will be looking for evidence of specific qualities and skills in the folder of work, so it is important that you understand exactly what they are looking for. When making your final choice, you should discuss your work with your teacher so that the right balance of work is included.

The syllabus indicates that the folder should show evidence of your investigation, recording, development, realisation and critical evaluation.

If you have read Chapter 1 carefully, you should now be familiar with these terms and will perhaps recognise the similarity between them and what we have described as **study contexts** and **study skills**. These will be appropriate regardless of the area(s) of study you choose for your work.

These headings are generally accepted by teachers and examiners as representing the main stages of most art and design activity. This does not mean that they always follow the same sequence or that they must all be apparent in *every* unit of work you do. However, they are a useful way of describing the nature of the activity as a whole. Later in the chapter, under the 'Assessment' headings you will see how these qualities are expressed in more detail and how the examination actually awards marks for each of them.

Your folder should contain a *range* of source material and there should be evidence of both **primary** and **secondary** sources of information. The recording and development of your ideas should take into account the **historical, cultural** and **technical** contexts of your chosen ideas (see Chapters 1 and 2).

The folder may contain material which does not lead to a final artefact or product, but it must contain the supporting material for your three coursework pieces.

Coursework pieces

Your three coursework pieces can be chosen from any of the areas of study listed below:

- textiles;
- environmental and interior design;
- painting and mixed media;
- sculpture;
- ceramics;
- graphic design;
- printmaking;
- industrial design;
- theatre design;
- photography;
- film and video;
- thematic studies.

Obviously, for a number of reasons, some of these practices may not be available to you. Perhaps your school does not have film or video equipment or anywhere suitable for processing film for photography. Do not worry if you have only a limited range of study areas in your school. This will not make it more difficult for you to do well in the examination. In fact, it is sometimes an advantage to concentrate your study on one particular practice.

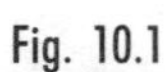

Fig. 10.1

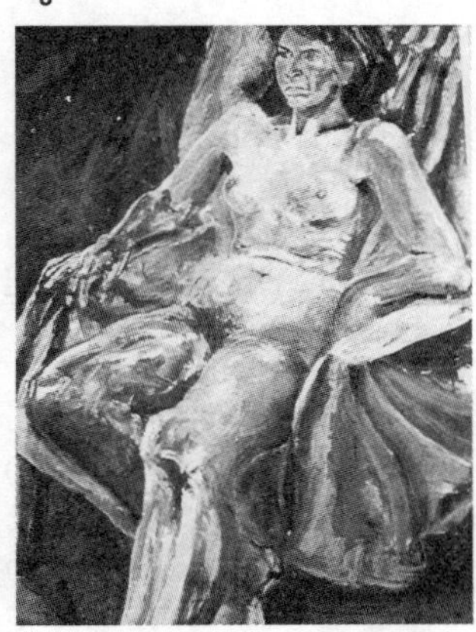

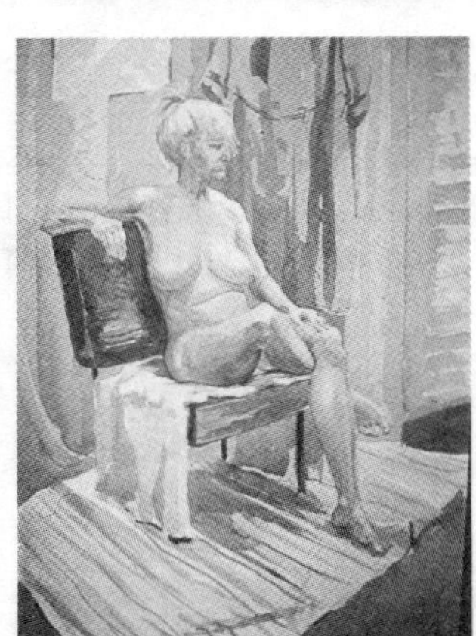

What is more important is that the **structure** of your course is appropriate to your needs and aptitudes, and this is largely determined by your art and design teacher. Your teacher should be able to match these to the school's resources, and also to their own skills and expertise. After all, no individual can be expected to be accomplished in all the practices listed.

Your three coursework pieces should demonstrate a range of approaches to your work, even if the work is undertaken within one area of study. To show how this is possible, we will give three examples in Table 10.3 and in Fig. 10.1 of ways in which you can pursue ideas within the 'Painting and Mixed Media' area of study.

Table 10.3 Ideas for 'Painting and Mixed Media' area of study.

	MEDIUM	PROCESSES AND BASIC ELEMENTS
Example 1	Drawing, Painting	Visual analysis, observation, recording, investigation
Example 2a	Drawing	Composition, line, tone, mood
Example 2b	Painting	Composition, colour, observation, balance, proportion
Example 3	Painting	Thematic inquiry, expressive response, critical appraisal, experimentation

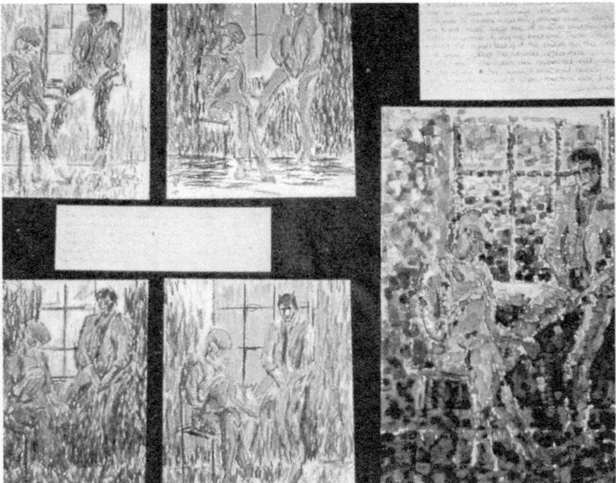

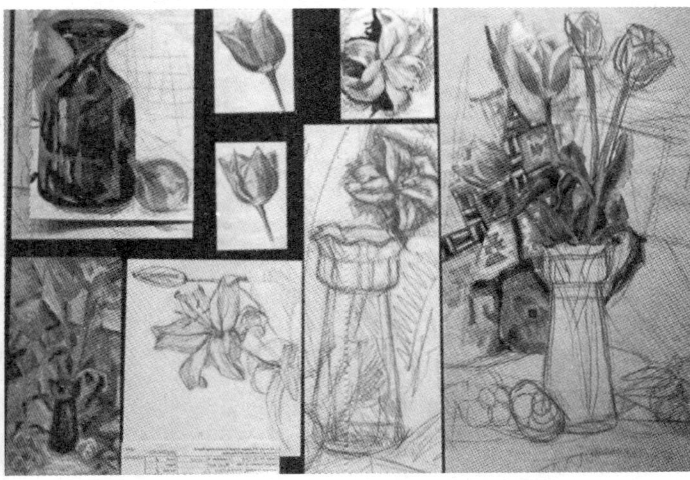

DOMAINS	RESPONSE TO ASSESSMENT OBJECTIVES	MAXIMUM MARK
Personal Qualities	i), ii) Scope and vitality of personal ideas, subjects and themes. Degree of imagination and inventiveness. Experimentation.	25
Manipulative and Analytical Skills	iii), iv) Use of media, processes and techniques to explore and investigate intentions.	25
Aesthetic Qualities	v) Composition and the use of chosen elements to emphasise and communicate intention.	25
Knowledge and Critical Understanding	vi), vii) Selection and evaluation of information as a means of developing intentions. Critical appraisal of the work of others; evidence of awareness of other cultural influences as displayed in Work Folder.	25
	TOTAL (Max.100)	

Table 10.4 Assessment criteria for Coursework submission (reproduced by permission of the UCLES).

PERSONAL STUDY

The Personal Study is worth 30 per cent of the total marks available for the examination and therefore forms a very important element in your final submission. You are required to make a detailed study of any aspect of the visual arts which interests you.

Submission requirements

Your submission can take one of two forms: *either* an illustrated report of 3,000–5,000 words *or* a carefully structured sequence of labelled or annotated drawings, paintings, photographs, prints or three-dimensional objects. A slide/tape or video presentation is also acceptable. Your teacher is allowed to guide you in your choice of study and to give help with the presentation of your proposal.

Assessment criteria for the personal study

To give you a guide as to how your study will be assessed we have reproduced the Syndicate's assessment criteria in Table 10.5. Both your teacher and the external moderators will use this scheme to assess your work, so it is important for you to ensure that each criterion has been met to the best of your ability.

DOMAINS	RESPONSE TO ASSESSMENT OBJECTIVES	MAXIMUM MARK
Personal Qualities	i), ii) The relevance of the study as an aid to personal development; and the ability to articulate personal views and reasoned judgements with supportive material.	25
Manipulative and Analytical Skills	iii), iv) Research and the use of media, processes and techniques and their appropriateness to the study.	25
Aesthetic Qualities	v) Composition and the appropriate use of visual/written elements to emphasise and communicate ideas and intentions.	25
Knowledge and Critical Understanding	vi), vii) Systematic use and evaluation of information to inform personal view and articulate judgements in the context of the candidate and his or her culture. Comparison with other cultures where appropriate.	25
	TOTAL (Max.100)	

NB Due to the complementary nature of these objectives, assessors should guide against applying a rigid definition of the boundaries between each of these domains.

Table 10.5 Assessment criteria for the Personal Study (reproduced by permission of the UCLES).

Study plan

The best way to ensure that the assessment criteria are met is to work out a study plan before you start work. You may well have had some experience of this with other subjects you are doing and the skills required are much the same. We believe that the following broad approach should be suitable, regardless of the title or subject matter you have chosen.

- Provide a statement of the subject matter to be investigated, giving reasons for selecting the subject. List the problem(s) to be considered and make clear the parameters set for the study.
- State how the investigation will proceed.
- Identify and collect the information.
- Select, prepare and present the information – including written material and, where appropriate, drawings, photographs, explanatory diagrams, plans, annotated sketches, etc.
- Draw inferences from the study and state conclusions reached.

Choosing a topic

While the choice of topic is left to you, it is most important that you consult fully with your teacher about the appropriateness of what you have chosen. For example, you must ensure that you have the resources to pursue the study to a successful conclusion. Also, there is little point in choosing a topic which is either too broad or too narrow in content, because you will either have too much information or too little to handle.

Your teacher should ensure that the study can be pursued *in depth*. This is most important, because of the proportion of marks allocated to this component of the examination. If your study is superficial, it is highly unlikely that you will meet the assessment criteria satisfactorily and as a consequence you will not score highly on any of the criteria. Do remember that the proposal has to be approved by the moderator before you start. This should act as a safeguard, ensuring that inappropriate proposals are weeded out.

Possible titles

The syllabus indicates a range of possible topics for study, but bear in mind that these are only examples and are not intended to restrict you in any way. Your choice need not be related to the work you are doing in the other parts of the course but can come from any aspect of art and design which interests you.

The following is a sample of the type of topics the Syndicate might consider suitable:

A A study of four works (four portraits, four landscapes or four religious subjects, etc.) from the Italian Renaissance that are available to the candidate in a local gallery or collection, tracing their relationship to other works of this period and showing in which ways they are influenced by the ideas and aspirations of the Renaissance. [A similar type of approach could be adopted for other periods, schools of painting or sculpture, or 'isms' or indeed for the work of a single artist.]

B A study of the use of sculpture in the candidate's locality [this could be public sculpture, memorial sculpture or decorative sculpture, depending on the resources available], making a comparison with similar works elsewhere, with an attempt to trace the influence of major sculptors on local work and of the ideas and fashions of the period in which the work was created.

C A study of the ideas and work of the artists, designers and craftsmen associated with the Bauhaus and tracing the influence of their work in the design and appearance of buildings and objects that the candidate sees and uses daily in his/her immediate environment. [A similar approach could be made to other groups such as the ARTS AND CRAFTS MOVEMENT and to the influence of specific designers or to the design of specific objects such as cars, buildings or clothing.]

D A study of nineteenth- or early twentieth-century public building or church in the candidate's locality, tracing the various original designs that influence the architecture and how these features have been adapted to new functions. [A similar approach could be made to other architectural revivals, etc., or could be adapted to the study of an ancient building.]

E A study of a local street [estate, town centre, block of flats, etc.], involving research into the origins of the design and those involved in its execution. There could well be comparisons with similar areas elsewhere and a discussion of the ideas, fashions and original function that influenced the design. This could lead to the candidate making some suggestions as to how the original character of the area could be preserved whilst the use is adapted to modern requirements.

F A study of the contents of a photographic archive or collection with reference to the historical development of the technical aspect of photography and to the ideas and attitudes that have influenced photographers at various times. Such a study might lead to a discussion of the relationship between photography and the other visual arts.

(Reproduced by permission of UCLES)

CONTROLLED TEST

The Controlled Test contributes 30 per cent of the total marks for the examination as a whole. You are allowed a maximum of ten hours to complete your work, which must be done between 30 April and 14 May in the year of the examination. You will be given the question paper three weeks in advance of the examination so that you can complete the necessary preparatory/supporting work. This should be taken into the examination room and must be submitted with your final work. Not more than two sheets, maximum size A1, are allowed. The Controlled Test will normally be completed in two-dimensional form only.

Purpose of the controlled test

This component of the examination is intended to monitor your ability to **observe, record, analyse** and **develop** ideas based upon a task or brief set by the Syndicate. We have discussed these skills and qualities in detail elsewhere in the book so it is not intended to cover them in detail here, but the syllabus does provide some useful pointers to indicate where the emphasis of your work should be directed.

For example, it states that you should **investigate** the theme or topic chosen rather than merely **reproduce** it. This is a strong indication that you should be seeking to achieve more than just an accurate record of, say, a scene or object. Recording is only part of what you are asked to do. A series of studies showing the development of your ideas is envisaged, with the emphasis on the **process** paramount. In a sense you are being asked to provide **evidence** of your thinking through the visual images and ideas you produce.

Assessment criteria for the controlled test

Perhaps the most useful way of indicating what the examiners will be looking for is to show you how the assessment criteria will be applied to your work and how the marks will be distributed (Table 10.6).

Areas of study

The themes set will be broad and flexible, with elements of:

- the landscape;
- individual objects;
- interiors;
- the human figure;
- light and colour;
- reflective material;
- movement.

This list is not intended to be either prescriptive or comprehensive. You can decide, as far as is practicable, where and how you wish to work within the limits of the subjects set. Supervision of your work outside or in any other unusual location must be sufficient to enable your teacher to certify that the work submitted is entirely your own. Alternatively, you may bring source material of your own choice into the examination room. Your teacher may be consulted as to the choice of objects but you must arrange these objects yourself.

DOMAINS	RESPONSE TO ASSESSMENT OBJECTIVES	MAXIMUM MARK
Personal Qualities	i) Individual, sensitive and creative response to stimulus. ii) Independence and confidence in concept and execution.	25
Manipulative and Analytical Skills	iii) Selection and control of media, processes and techniques. iv) Analysis from direct observation and personal experience.	25
Aesthetic Qualities	v) The recognition of contour, surface, shape, colour/tone, texture, pattern, structure, form and the relationships of forms in space, and their appropriate use.	25
Knowledge and Critical Understanding	vi) Analysis of the idea, subject or theme chosen; suitability of selection and ability to evaluate and communicate in a systematic way. vii) Critical judgement and cultural awareness and appreciation.	25
	TOTAL (Max.100)	

Table 10.6 Assessment criteria for the Controlled Test (reproduced by permission of the UCLES).

SPECIMEN QUESTIONS

Component I (10 hours maximum)

Choose *one* of the following stimuli, analyse and develop your ideas from it. Aids such as lenses, microscopes, slide and overhead projectors may be used.

1 Light across a variety of surfaces.
2 Smooth and rough forms.
3 Figure or figures in movement.
4 Gaps and openings.
5 Chairs.
6 Machinery and landscape.
7 Changing forms.
8 Destructive process.
9 Coloured objects in coloured lights.
10 Mechanical movement.

(Reproduced by permission of UCLES)

Example of response to the controlled test

We have chosen an example of a response to 3; namely Figure or figures in movement. Bear in mind that the Controlled Test is intended to test your ability to observe, record, analyse and develop ideas, so these should be evident from your total submission. This is particularly important as the work is externally marked and there will be no opportunity for you to *explain* your intentions to the examiner.

It is evident from the sheets of preparatory/supporting work (Fig. 10.2) that the student has made good use of the preparatory period of three weeks. The theme has been **investigated** through direct observation in a café. Detailed **observations** have been made of individual figures as well as the general scene. Other studies show how compositional issues have been analysed and developed.

The final work (Fig. 10.3) has been completed in paint and has followed closely what appears to be the final sketch done in pencil on one of the preparatory sheets. This is not always necessarily a good idea, because a slavish copying of a predetermined composition can sometimes create a rather sterile, rigid, final image. However, in this case there is a certain vitality about the final work which allows it to avoid this pitfall.

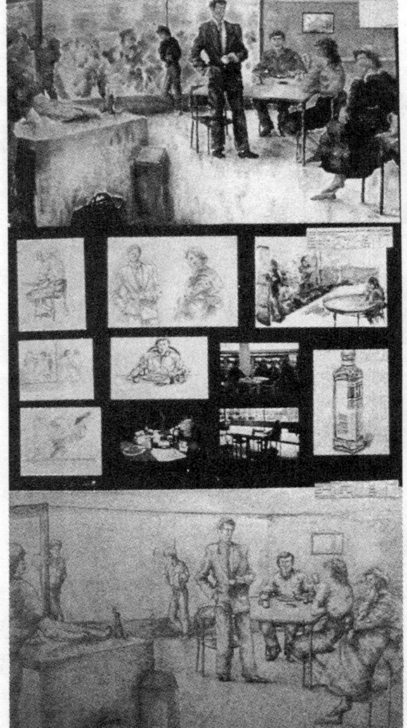

Fig. 10.2 Preparatory/supporting work.

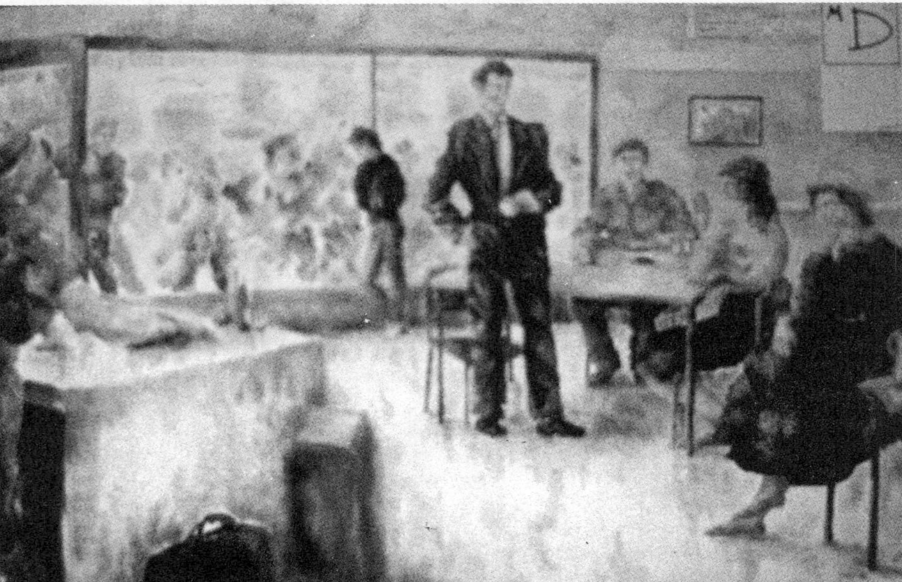

Fig. 10.3 Final work.

You might find it useful to apply the assessment criteria mentioned earlier to this example. Perhaps you can do this with your fellow students and generate discussion about how you have interpreted the criteria. In this way you should begin to relate the criteria to your own work. No doubt at some stage in your course you will have a trial run or mock examination. This would be a valuable opportunity for you to ensure that you meet the assessment criteria as fully as possible.

ADVANCED SUPPLEMENTARY SYLLABUS

The UCLES AS syllabus is closely linked with the A-level offered by the Syndicate. It shares the same syllabus content and assessment criteria as the A-level but the amount of work required is different. Instead of three components only two are required.

Scheme of assessment

You must take Component 2, then *either* Component 1 or Component 3.

COMPONENT	TITLE	WEIGHTING OF MARKS	TIME ALLOWED
1	Controlled Test	40%	10 hours max.
2	Coursework	60%	–
3	Personal Study	40%	–

The personal study should *not* exceed 3,000 words in the case of a written study or considerably less in the case of a visual presentation.
Your work will be viewed as a whole by teams of three chief examiners at the Syndicate.
Component 1 will be externally marked by Syndicate examiners at the Syndicate.
Components 2 and 3 will be internally marked by your teacher(s) and moderated by teams of three moderators at the Syndicate.

Table 10.7 Scheme of assessment: AS-level.

You should be aware of the differences between AS-level and A-level, as these differences may have a bearing on your decision about which examination to take. For example, AS is intended to require half the study time of A-level and while the grade standards are related to A-level, AS is worth half an A-level.

To help you decide whether the AS is the right examination for you the Syndicate provides the following information.

It is envisaged that the Advanced Supplementary (AS) syllabus will encourage the development of suitably well-balanced courses that combine this breadth and depth of study with the freedom of choice necessary to accommodate a wide range of abilities and material resources.

It will provide an appropriate continuation for those candidates who have previously followed any endorsed GCSE syllabus as well as for those who have followed a more generalised course of study for an unendorsed GCSE syllabus. The syllabus will be suitable for those candidates who, in search of a broader education, wish to combine Art and Design with another subject at this level, and also for mature students wishing to embark on a part-time course of study leading to a qualification in Art and Design.

JOINT MATRICULATION BOARD (JMB)

A-LEVEL AND AS ART AND DESIGN

The JMB A-level Art and Design syllabus was examined for the first time in June 1990. The board also offers a Craft (Design and Practice) A-level, which has been discussed already (Chapter 3). If you are entering both examinations you are not allowed to submit the same work for both.

If you have studied for the Northern Examining Association (NEA) GCSE examination in art and design you should be well placed to tackle the A-level examination, as both syllabuses have much in common. In fact all art and design GCSE examinations will provide a suitable foundation for this A-level, so you should not have difficulty in recognising the similarities between your own GCSE course and the JMB A-level.

We strongly recommend that you have your own copy of the syllabus, which you can get from your teacher or by contacting the board. By becoming thoroughly familiar with the requirements of the syllabus, you should be able to recognise whether you are developing the skills, knowledge and understanding necessary for success.

We have stressed throughout this book the importance of recognising and understanding the **spirit** or **philosophy** of the syllabus and examination. If you understand the beliefs and intentions of those responsible for drafting the syllabus, you should be well placed to respond in the best possible way in your own work.

Aims

It is normally in the Aims that the philosophy of the syllabus is expressed. They will provide generalised statements about what the examiners believe art and design can contribute to a person's educational development. Bear in mind that this idealised view is expressed as a kind of **ultimate goal** and for most people this will be impossible to achieve. After all, many artists spend a lifetime in pursuit of these ideals.

It is not our intention to reproduce the aims here, but we do recommend that you read them and discuss them with your teacher and fellow students.

Assessment objectives

The Assessment Objectives specify what you must achieve in order to do well in the examination. They define a range of qualities and skills which you must demonstrate in order to achieve an award.

Obviously, it is most important for you to be aware of what is required here. Generally, you must meet *all* the assessment objectives specified, but it is the *way* in which you meet them that determines the grade you are likely to achieve. That is, the *quality* of your work is the important factor in determining how well you do. We have reproduced the assessment objectives below to indicate what is required.

OBJECTIVES OF THE EXAMINATION

Candidates will be expected to demonstrate the ability to:

a) conceive, organise, develop and evaluate various elements in a continuum to produce a coherent visual statement;
b) identify, analyse and explore design problems, using appropriate strategies, techniques and materials;
c) use with understanding formal elements such as line, tone, colour, pattern, texture, shape, form, space, rhythm, harmony, composition, balance, symmetry, decoration, volume, structure;
d) show evidence of a personal response to an idea, theme or subject;
e) work from any observed phenomenon as an aid to the development of ideas or for its own sake;

f) organise and present evidence of research from both primary and secondary sources as a means of communicating ideas and concepts;
g) understand and define the relevant aesthetic, historical and social developments in fine art, architecture or design within the areas and periods specified by the candidate by means of the written word, supported by diagrams, drawings, photographs, video, film, computer disc;
h) produce a critical appreciation of works of artists, architects or designers and to make and support value judgements.

(Reproduced by permission of JMB)

The various components of the examination will stress some objectives more than others and we will refer to this in detail later, but first let us look at what you actually have to do by the end of the course (Table 10.8).

	COMPONENT	WEIGHTING OF MARKS	TIME ALLOWED
1	Coursework	45%	–
2	Personal Study	30%	–
3	Assignment	25%	15 hours (max.) (first 3 hours continuous)

Table 10.8 Scheme of assessment.

Scheme of assessment

To achieve a pass in the subject you must reach a minimum specified mark in all three components. This means that you cannot afford to neglect any aspect of your work, for you might risk failing the examination altogether, even if you have done well in one or two components. The minimum pass mark for the coursework and the assignment is 24 (out of 100) and the minimum pass mark for the Personal Study is 25 (out of 100).

OBJECTIVES	COURSEWORK	EXTERNALLY ASSESSED ASSIGNMENT	PERSONAL STUDY
a)	*	*	*
b)	*	*	
c)	*	*	
d)	*	*	*
e)	*	*	
f)	*	*	*
g)			*
h)			*
(Allocation of marks)	45%	25%	30%

Table 10.9 Allocation of the 'Assessment Objectives' to each component (reproduced by permission of the JMB).

We mentioned earlier that some components well stress some assessment objectives more than others. It can be very useful for you to check the objectives against the work you do in each component, to ensure that they have been dealt with to the best of your ability. In Table 10.9 we show how the objectives relate to each component. From this you can see, for example, that objectives a), d) and f) are dealt with in all three components, whereas objectives g) and h) are dealt with solely in the Personal Study.

The course

Unlike most boards the JMB does not list a range of practices to describe the course, but suggests discrete **processes** which should be included in a course determined by the school or college. This means that your teacher(s) will have the task of deciding how your course proceeds within the framework determined by the board, and taking into account the resources available in your school or college. Your course must include all of the following:

1 Visual perception and perceptual relationships: e.g. tactile qualities; figure and ground relationships; picture plane; recession; horizontal and vertical phenomena; the interrelationships which constitute the basic concepts of a visual language – line, tone, shape, form, colour, texture, rhythm, harmony, composition, balance, symmetry, space, pattern, decoration, volume, structure.
2 Image making; the interpretation, in a variety of media, of personal observation and/or imaginative intention through expressive two- and/or three-dimensional forms.
3 Exploring a range and variety of media to realise their main characteristics and their potential contribution to artistic form and responses to design problems. Some experience and exploration of colour must be present.
4 The delineation and expression of form through an understanding of drawing and draughtsmanship.
5 The use of materials for model-making, maquettes and 'mock-ups' in conceiving and analysing in designing.
6 The initiation, development and realisation of sustained pieces of work to produce a unified whole.
7 The study of the forms of art and design and how they are affected by human needs, aspirations, materials and techniques. This need not be only of Western Europe but may also embrace any other culture.

(Reproduced by permission of the JMB)

There are many different ways in which your work might develop. Bear in mind that the examples we have given throughout this book should be appropriate for your JMB course as there is general agreement between examiners and teachers from all boards about what is meant by **good practice**. Do not be concerned if your school or college can offer only a limited range of practices, since this need not limit your chances of success in the examination. The course structure is designed to allow you to demonstrate a wide range of approaches to your work and this is quite possible *within* one or a small number of practices.

WORK REQUIREMENTS AND PRACTICES

To help you to make a start on the work required for the examination we will deal with each component in turn, explaining the basic requirements for each and, where appropriate, giving examples.

COURSEWORK SUBMISSION

In mid-May in the year of the examination, you will be expected to mount an exhibition of work, produced during the course. This will be internally marked by your teacher(s) and externally moderated by a board-appointed moderator. It is the moderator's responsibility to ensure that your teacher's assessment is in line with the standards agreed for the examination as a whole.

The work you display needs to demonstrate your ability to research, organise, develop and evaluate ideas in a variety of ways in order to produce coherent final statements. You should also present work which shows visual investigation arising from direct observation and stimulus.

Example: graphic design

The example we have chosen is based upon a design brief set as part of the course. This brief was closely specified, but work of this kind can be developed from a much broader stimulus, without a predetermined outcome. See Fig. 10.4.

The brief required a number of illustrations for a series of magazine articles on government departments and the ministers responsible for them. The 'treatment' or style of illustration was left to the student, but the integration of text and visual material was considered to be important.

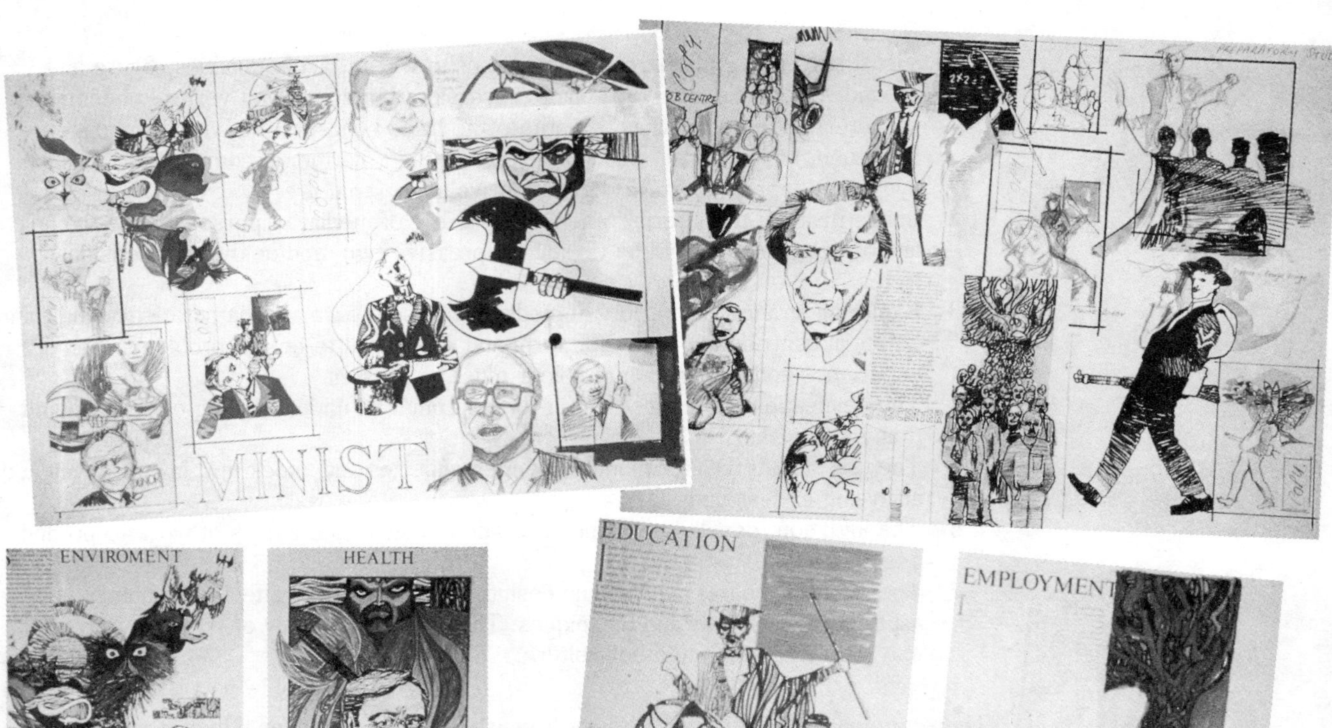

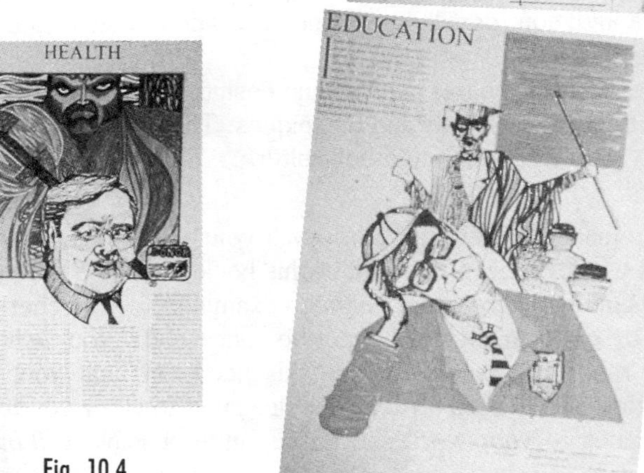

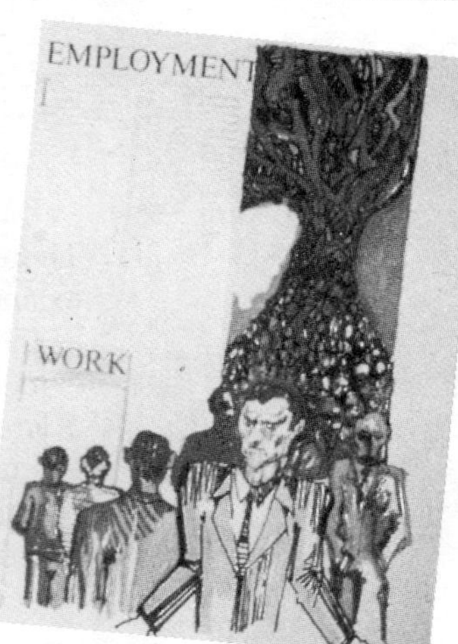

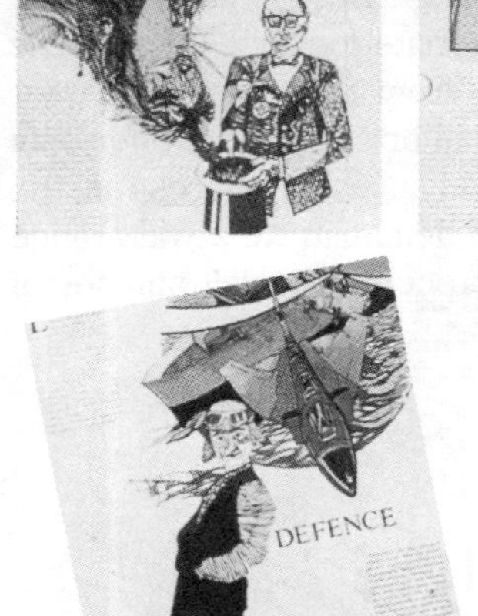

Fig. 10.4

In our view the total presentation is extremely successful, it is well researched and developed and arrives at a satisfactory conclusion. We mentioned earlier that it would be very useful to relate the assessment objectives to your own work to ensure that they had been properly covered. Try to do so with this example. You can see from Table 10.9 that objectives a) to f) are allocated to the coursework component. Do you think that they have all been dealt with satisfactorily in this example or could further work have been done?

Sometimes it is easier to look at and evaluate the work of others than to be critical of our own efforts. The difficulty is in being objective about work with which you have become deeply involved. By looking at other people's work in this way, you should be able to make the task of assessing your own work that much easier.

If you concentrate your studies in one particular area or medium, you must show evidence of supportive and exploratory work in a variety of media. The board does not specify how much work you should present, but you are allowed to consult your teacher to ensure that what you do submit best meets the assessment criteria.

By now, you should be familiar with the terms used here and should see how they relate to the **study contexts** and **study skills** described in Chapter 1. The terms are intended to represent or describe what is most recognisable about art and design activity *as a whole*. They do not necessarily always follow the same sequence and need not be demonstrated in every unit of work you produce, but they must be evident in your total submission if you are to do well in the examination.

Your exhibition of work will almost certainly be a *selection* of the work you have done throughout the course and should reveal your particular interests and preoccupations. Remember that the examiners will be looking for evidence of how you have met the assessment objectives in the total submission, so it is most important that your selection gives a *balanced* view of your work as a whole.

Scale of Work

Because your work does not have to be sent to the board you are able to work on a scale and with materials which would not be suitable for sending in the post. This can be to your advantage if, for example, you tend to work on a large scale or with heavy materials. Most of the examples of student's work you see in this book are of a size suitable for sending to the board, but do not rule out projects which might involve working directly in the community. For example, you might wish to produce a sculpture or relief for the local church or shopping centre; you might wish to work with your fellow students on a mural for a community centre or underpass (see Fig. 10.5). Such large-scale projects can be very exciting but they do require careful planning and resourcing. If the work is to form part of your examination submission, your own contribution must be clearly identifiable for assessment purposes – which might not be easy to ensure. We recommend that you discuss this thoroughly with all concerned and, if there is any doubt at all, the board should be consulted before going ahead with the project.

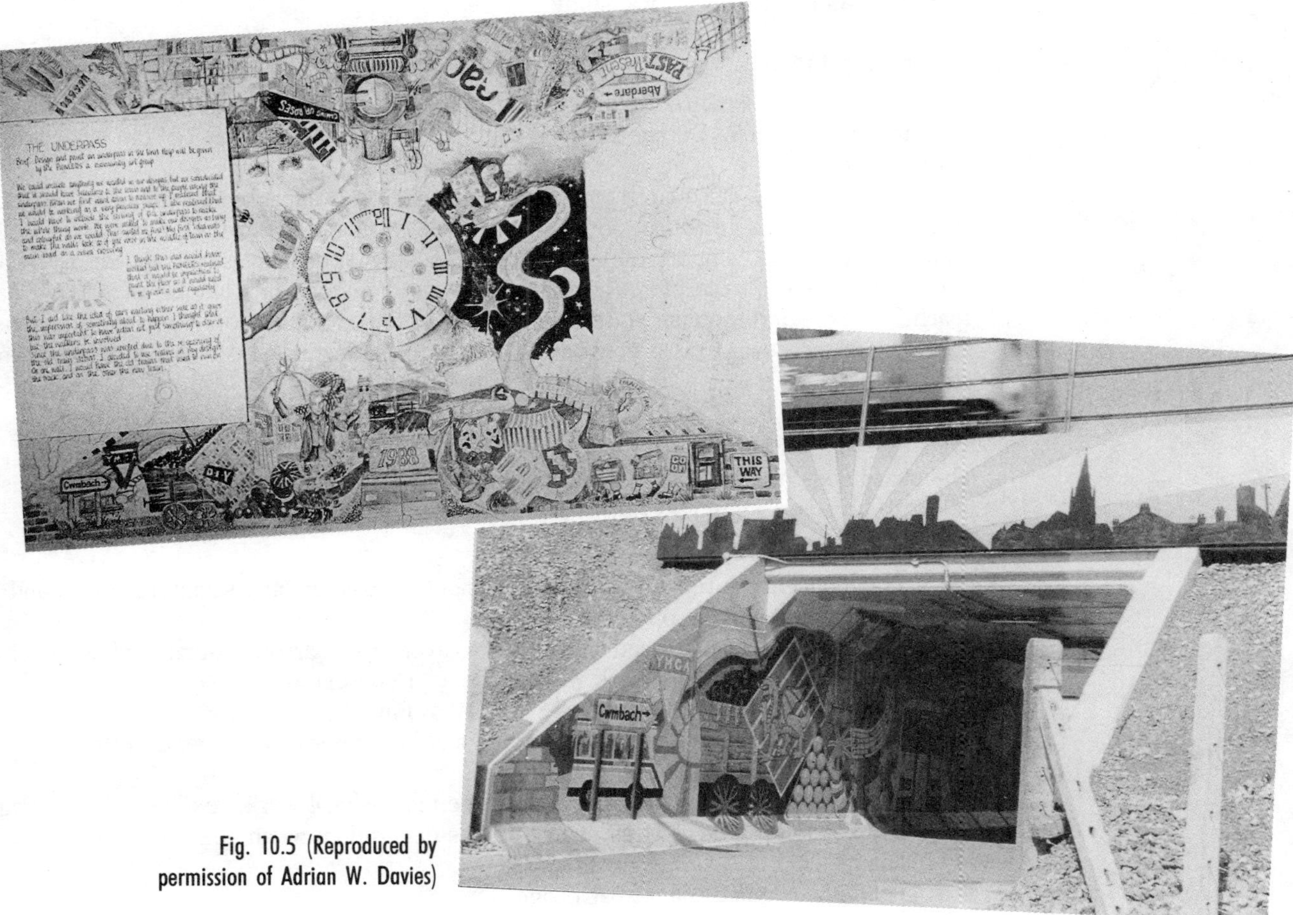

Fig. 10.5 (Reproduced by permission of Adrian W. Davies)

PERSONAL STUDY

Your Personal Study is intended to arise out of a **taught course** in Critical and Historical Studies in Art and Design. The work is assessed by your teacher(s) and externally moderated by a board-appointed moderator.

You must submit a topic to the board for approval before you start work. This can be done at any time between 1 April and 1 December in the year before the examination. The study must be completed by 5 April in the year of the examination.

These are the basic requirements of the Personal Study. To help you to tackle this in the best possible way, we will deal with each aspect of the study in turn.

Taught course

The board does not specify what the **content** of the course should be, so this will largely be the responsibility of your teacher(s). However, the board does require that the study be submitted under *one* of the following headings:

- FINE ART – aspects of painting, drawing, sculpture and fine printmaking; its history and development; its methods and material; artists in context; schools, styles, major subject areas – landscape, portrait; art reflecting human history and aspirations;

- ARCHITECTURE – religious, domestic and institutional, polite and vernacular, industrial, prefabricated and high tech, and could also include aspects of exterior and interior design, aspects of landscape design, exhibition design and structure with related graphics;
- DESIGN – advertising, graphic and communication design, fashion and stage costume, interior design, theatrical design, illustration, glass, ceramics, textiles, the domestic environment, industrial design, body adornment, folk art, transport design.

(Reproduced by permission of the JMB)

It may well be that your teacher(s) decides to concentrate on only one of these areas, or perhaps chooses to cover all three. It is most likely that the decision will be based upon the kind of practical course you are following, so that there is a link between your practical work and your critical/historical study.

Choosing a topic

You will probably follow the critical and historical course for several months before you need to choose a topic. During this time you may discover some aspect of the work which interests you.

Perhaps you have discovered an artist with similar preoccupations to yours, or perhaps there is a particular historical period with which you have sympathy. What you should bear in mind is that your topic must be able to sustain your interest for almost a year of concentrated study, therefore trivial or superficial material should be avoided. Your teacher is expected to guide you in your choice of topic and the board's moderator must approve the proposal before you begin, so it is unlikely that you will make the wrong choice.

Examples of topics

The board does provide some examples of suitable topics and we have reproduced these below to give you some idea of the variety of approaches.

FINE ART

1 Traditional areas related to National Schools of painting and sculpture. Local and regional Fine Art resources.
2 Topics which deal with individual artists, avoiding a narrow biographical approach and setting the artist's work within a broader context.
3 Colour. Its form and function in a variety of Fine Arts.
4 The changing presentation of the artist and his or her environment, both in a European context and in other cultures.
5 The use made of painting, drawing, three-dimensional work, textiles, printmaking as a communicator of ideas. Their role as decoration, as an educator and as illustration.
6 The influence and role of patronage.
   Personal : Commercial : Religious
   The visual characteristics of differing historical eras as reflected in the Fine Arts.
   Renaissance : Baroque : Romanticism
   A study of aspects of the Modern Movement.
   Surrealism : Cubism : Expressionism
7 The influence of science on any of the Fine Arts e.g. Photography : Anatomy : Colour Theory
8 A study of the nature of artists' materials, methods and techniques used in the full range of the Fine Arts, historical and contemporary.

ARCHITECTURE

The selected topic should be concerned with an approach to architecture related to the critical appraisal or comparative analysis of building in the following areas.

1 Significant building types with particular regard to the way in which their function and social use has affected the resulting building (cathedrals, churches, chapels, castles, country houses).
2 The periodic change in the design of local buildings for community use (schools, hospitals, colleges, civic and other institutional buildings).
3 Buildings designed for use in industry, business or commerce (market-halls, shopping centres or malls, offices, hotels, factories, foundries, harbours, docks, ports, mills and warehouses).

4 Buildings associated with transport (motorways, railways, airports, rivers and canals).
5 Vernacular architectural styles associated with the needs of the domestic, cottage industry and agricultural aspects of building.
6 Town centre development or re-development considering the way in which changing patterns of commerce, transport or social use have been accommodated and solved.
7 Buildings designed for the pursuit of leisure recreation and entertainment (theatres, cinemas, leisure centres, swimming baths, clubhouses, pavilions, museums and art galleries).

DESIGN

1 A study in a chosen area of industrial design: e.g. camera design since 1950. Functions, aesthetics, the work of individual designers, new technologies.
2 A study considering an aspect of communication media: e.g. advertising and packaging of chocolate since 1900, and a critical appraisal of selected contemporary examples as a comparison.
3 A critical appraisal of shop display methods in a chosen area, street or shopping centre.
4 A study of a selected period (or periods) of costume or fashion history based upon examples seen in local or national museums, shops or market-stalls, together with a consideration of 'revivals' or earlier styles in recent fashion design.
5 A study of a particular local tradition in the design and production of furniture.
6 A critical review of furniture as found in a varied selection of local retail outlets, with further examples from the candidates' own home.
7 Clothes and accessories as influenced by the cinema.
8 A study of jewellery, its history, current designers and their materials, appraisal of examples seen in craft-shops, exhibitions or studios.
9 A critical review of the work of a particular designer in a field such as fashion, interior, product or graphic design e.g. Armani, Guigiaro, Laura Ashley, Terence Fitch.
10 Icons and imagery in TV advertising – analysis and appraisal of the visual content of selected advertisements with a view to understanding the methods and techniques being employed.

(Reproduced by permission of the JMB)

Study plan

It is a requirement of the syllabus that once your topic has been approved you must produce a study plan or outline of the proposed topic. This outline should include:

- a statement of the topic to be covered;
- the matters to be investigated:
- the point of view to be developed;
- the kind of evidence available and its source;
- methods of research;
- a time chart/programme for the study.

Study format

The board requires that the study should be submitted in a manila file cover A4 size. The study must be written, with a maximum of 3,500 words, supported by illustrations, drawings, diagrams and photographs as appropriate. Bear in mind that it is highly unlikely that a written submission alone will be satisfactory. Video, film and computer disc are also acceptable, but only in support of the written text. Although each study will have its own character, the board will normally expect to see:

- a series of chapters or sections with appropriate headings;
- a summary;
- a conclusion which attempts to analyse how successful the study has been in meeting the study plan and which states what further work might be necessary to provide a more satisfactory conclusion.

There are other, more detailed requirements for the presentation of the study, but these will be dealt with by your teacher at the appropriate time. We have tried here to give you an understanding of the essence of the study so that you can tackle it systematically, without being daunted by the complexity of the requirements.

EXTERNALLY ASSESSED ASSIGNMENT

The externally assessed assignment is essentially a unit of unaided coursework chosen by the student and completed at the end of the course.

There is an initial three-hour session, followed by not more than twelve hours' additional supervised time. An outline of the proposal must be submitted to the board for approval between 1 December and 31 January in the year of the examination. Your teacher is permitted to guide you in your choice of topic. Your assignment is initially assessed by your teacher(s) and then sent to the board for final assessment.

Suggested topics for the externally assessed assignment

It is stressed that you should come up with your own proposals for externally assessed assignments in consultation with your teacher. The examples given below indicate types of submissions *only*, and are meant to be a *guide*.

1 As part of your assignment produce a number of preparatory drawings/colour studies and/or maquettes which are derived from *one* of the subjects listed below:
   a) an object;
   b) a plant;
   c) a landscape;
   d) a self-portrait;
   e) an interior.

   Observe the chosen subject under different lighting conditions and/or from a variety of angles, situations, etc. Work might include: tonal analysis, linear analysis, colour analysis, analysis of form and structure, etc.

   Your initial studies should show evidence of the elements you found most stimulating. They could be developed into the areas of graphics, textiles, three-dimensional design or fine art.

2 Design a sign-posting and direction-finding system for your school or another public building to which you can obtain access (e.g. museum, arts centre, etc.).

   Your approach should be based on active research into existing examples of such systems, and the research material produced should be presented as part of your submitted work.

3 Using the human figure as a starting point consider any *one* of the following:
   a) design and make a structure you can wear and which can be used to entertain others.
   b) 'People in relation to their environment'. Produce a considered response.
   c) A study of jewellery or body adornment of current designers and their materials may lead you to design a series of your own. Submit at least two completed pieces, together with your design ideas.

4 Study and critically appraise the supporting material and merchandise associated with a film or television programme. Offer alternative designs for a real example with which you are familiar. You might consider book-covers, video-cassette sleeves, badges, T-shirts and games as possible vehicles for your designs.

5 Modern sculptors and designers have used a variety of constructional methods in the production of functional and non-functional objects. Develop a sculpture or design object based on a considered constructional method which emphasises your own observations and research.

6 Design and produce by screen-printing either of the following:
   a) A printed fabric suitable for making up into beachwear. It should be based on your observations of the external and internal structure of a fruit or vegetable.
   b) A cardboard package intended to securely contain a small domestic appliance. Research into existing examples is essential and should be submitted with your final designs.

7 There is much interesting visual data in the local environment. It can be seen in back streets, derelict spaces, allotments, markets, shopping centres, supermarkets,

building sites, scrapyards, farmland, machines and waterways, etc. From such an observation produce a visual response in a medium or media of your own choice.

8 Design and produce, using photography and other relevant media, a story-board for a 30-second TV advert. You should produce not less than 12 images.
Select *one* of the following subjects:
i) hair-care products for men or women,
ii) a breakfast cereal,
iii) publication information campaign (anti-smoking, safety in the house, etc.).
Your own view of advertising should be considered and appraised in order to develop strategies in this project.

(Reproduced by permission of the JMB)

Examples of responses

Fig 10.6 shows the student's solution to Question 1 d). Only the final study is shown.

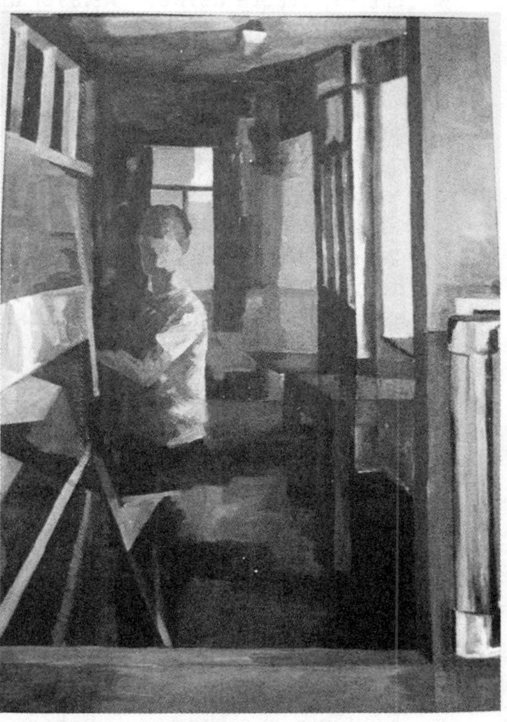

Fig. 10.6 Self-portrait (Reproduced by permission of Adrian W. Davies)

However, it is evident from this that the various forms of analysis required by the question have been dealt with. The result is a study with mood and presence.

Fig. 10.7 shows the work of a student who designed a storyboard in response to question 8. This is a typical storyboard using a preprinted format. The key to all storyboard illustrations is the need to indicate narrative, sequence and coherent development of the idea. Graphic skills need be sufficient only to convey the information clearly. The storyboard is a **working document** and not an end in itself.

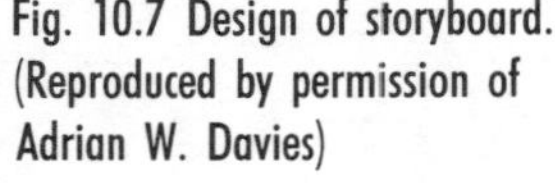

Fig. 10.7 Design of storyboard. (Reproduced by permission of Adrian W. Davies)

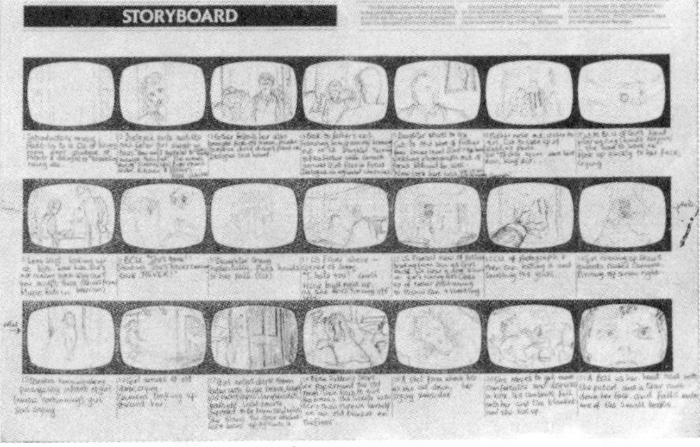

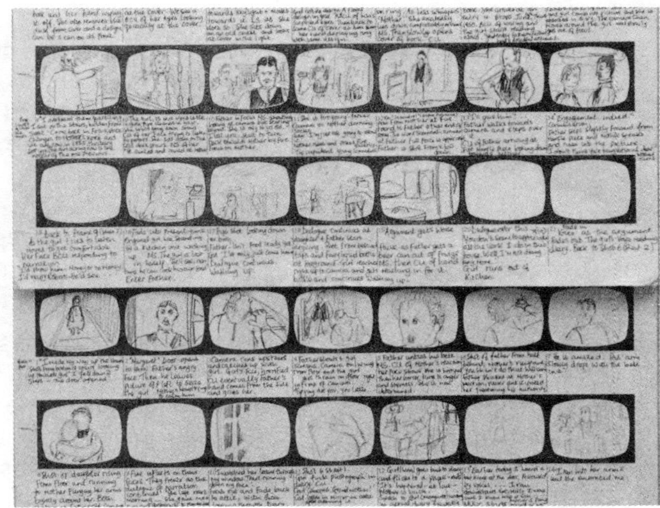

Assessment of the externally assessed assignment

The same Assessment Objectives apply to both the coursework and the assignment and they are listed in order of importance. By referring to the 'Assessment' section of this chapter you should gain a clear idea of what is required.

ADVANCED SUPPLEMENTARY SYLLABUS

The JMB AS syllabus has the same aims and assessment criteria as the A-level syllabus. The only major difference is that the Personal Study is replaced by an Extended Essay of three hours' duration. In the AS syllabus coursework should consist of at least two pieces of work. The allocation of marks, assessment objectives and relative weightings of marks are the same for both syllabuses.

The difference between A-level and AS

Having read the paragraph above, you may be wondering whether there is any point in taking an AS examination when the requirements are so similar. However, genuine differences exist between the two examinations and you should be aware of this as it may have bearing on which examination you choose to take.

The AS examination requires *half* the study time of A-level. The grade standards are related to A-level, so the AS is 'worth' half an A-level for the purpose of gaining entry to college or university. AS is intended to *broaden* the sixth-form curriculum and allow students to pursue subjects which would not normally be available to them. You can see from this that your choice will have a great deal to do with your career aspirations. For example, if you want a career in art and design or some closely related field, then you should almost certainly take the A-level examination. If you have always enjoyed art and design but do not consider it relevant to your future career, then an AS in art and design would be an appropriate means of broadening your sixth-form studies.

The extended essay

The Extended Essay is a timed, three-hour examination which will take place in June in the final year of the course. It is intended that this examination will follow the same taught course as the A-level and will deal with the same broad areas of study, namely:

- fine art;
- architecture;
- design.

Ten topics in each area of study are given by the board so that you can research and collect resource material appropriate to your chosen topic. This material can be taken into the examination but all sources must be acknowledged. A maximum of ten illustrations, *relevant to the text*, may be included with the essay (maximum size A4).

At least one question will be set on each of the ten topics in the three areas of study listed below:

A Fine Art
1 The representation of the human figure
2 Landscape
3 Colour as a form of expression
4 American painting and sculpture since 1940
5 Impressionism and Post-Impressionism
6 Open-air sculpture
7 Art as decoration
8 The impact of non-European cultures on European art
9 The systems of representing space in painting and sculpture
10 The methods and materials used in the production of fine art

B Architecture
1 The Romanesque style from the 7th to 12th centuries
2 Form and function in the Gothic world
3 The Baroque style in Western Europe
4 The architecture of Islam
5 A traditional local style of building
6 Relation of decoration and structure in architecture

7 Industrial and commercial architecture 1850 – 1900
8 The architecture, theory and practice of the Bauhaus
9 The contribution of the individual architect to the modern movement in architecture, based on a study of one of the following:
Charles Rennie Mackintosh; Frank Lloyd Wright; Charles-Edouard Jeanneret; Le Corbusier
10 Contemporary public architecture of the last twenty years

C Design
1 Packaging design and shop display
2 Graphics in magazines, posters, record sleeves, etc.
3 Industrial design and designers in the twentieth century
4 Domestic interiors, both past and present
5 Footwear, historic, fashion, utility and sportswear
6 Exhibitions, collections and museums, as found in the student's locality
7 The media and new technology
8 Aspects of men's and women's fashions
9 Jewellery and personal adornment, hair, make-up and accessories
10 Photography, the cinema and television

(Reproduced by permission of the JMB)

OXFORD AND CAMBRIDGE SCHOOLS EXAMINATIONS BOARD (OX/CAM)

A-LEVEL ART AND DESIGN

This syllabus is examined for the first time in June 1991. If you have studied for a GCSE Art and Design examination offered by any of the GCSE groups, you will recognise considerable common ground, both with syllabus content and the Scheme of Assessment.

The board states that the syllabus will meet the needs of the following types of candidates:

- those intending to pursue further study in art and design;
- those who will study subjects or seek employment for which an art and design background is relevant;
- those with an interest and aptitude in art and design for its own sake.

You may recognise yourself in one or more of the above categories, but do not be too concerned if you are still undecided about your future career. By now you should at least be aware of your own interest and ability in the subject, otherwise you are unlikely to be reading this book! As you progress through the course, you should be able to recognise whether your skills and interests are developing sufficiently to suggest that a career in the subject is a realistic possibility. We would suggest that even if you are firmly within the third category listed above, there is much that is rewarding and much to be gained from studying the subject at this level. You can expect to work in much greater *depth* than was possible in your GCSE course and the subject matter is as *broad* as you wish to make it.

As teachers and examiners of art and design we believe that you should try to understand the *essence* of the syllabus you are studying, so that, in a sense, you try to 'read between the lines' of the bare requirements of the examination and interpret what the examiners are thinking. We are talking about the **educational philosophy** which underpins the syllabus and scheme of examination. For example, it would be a very limited philosophy which believed only that 'all students should be able to paint a bowl of fruit', or that 'all students should be able to shade with a 6B pencil'.

Most syllabuses attempt to state what it is believed will be the **educational outcomes** of pursuing a course of study to a satisfactory conclusion. Bear in mind that this is not the same thing as stating what the examination intends to measure or **assess.** *The former is usually set out in the Aims and the latter is usually explained in the Assessment Objectives.*

Aims

As indicated above, the Aims are expressed in wider and more general terms than the Assessment Objectives. They include some qualities and attributes which cannot or should not be assessed in the examination but which are considered important in the study of art and design in general. The OX/CAM aims are noted below and we strongly recommend that you spend some time trying to get to grips with them.

Within the context of a general education at Advanced Level, the aims of this Art and Design syllabus are to stimulate, encourage and develop:

1 special aptitudes and interests of the individual so as to increase confidence, enthusiasm and a sense of achievement;
2 ability to perceive, understand and express concepts and feelings in visual and tactile form;
3 ability to record from direct observation and personal experience;
4 ability to form, compose and communicate in two or three dimensions by the use of appropriate materials in a systematic and disciplined way;
5 technical competence and manipulative skills which will enable individuals to realise their creative intentions;
6 experimentation and innovation through the inventive and imaginative use of materials, new technologies and techniques;
7 ability to identify, research and solve problems in visual and tactile form through design processes;
8 ability to organise and relate abstract ideas to practical outcomes;
9 acquisition of a working vocabulary relevant to the subject;
10 understanding of economic considerations which could be limiting factors in the design process;
11 critical and analytical faculties;
12 an appreciation of the richness of human expression through the visual arts which recognises and utilises the cultural diversity of contemporary society;
13 awareness and appreciation of the relationship between Art and Design and the individual with historical, social and environmental context.

(Reproduced by permission of OX/CAM)

Assessment objectives

As we mentioned earlier, the Assessment Objectives show what you are expected to do in the course and provide the basis for the examination of your work. They may seem rather daunting, but if you take time to read them you will recognise what we have described in the early chapters of this book as a **sound working habit**.

Bear in mind that you must meet *all* the 'Assessment Objectives' if you are to do well in the examination. This will be accomplished through the different **components** of examination. We will explain how this is to be done later; for the moment it is sufficient to know broadly how your final grade will be assessed.

Your work is measured against the appropriate assessment objective and it is the **qualitative judgement** of your assessors which determines the grade awarded. If you look at the assessment objectives below, you will perhaps realise that with such a range of qualities and attributes to assess, it is not sufficient to be 'good at art' or 'able to draw'. You must show a much wider range of abilities if you are to do well in the examination.

Candidates will be expected to show evidence of:

1 a personal, individual, creative, coherent response (showing appreciation of multicultural and/or historical context where appropriate) to an idea, brief, theme or subject;
2 ability to work from observed phenomena and personal experience;
3 ability to select, control and use appropriate technologies, techniques, materials and processes in an informed and disciplined way, taking account of economic consideration where appropriate;
4 understanding of and ability to use the formal elements of visual and tactile language (line, tone, colour, pattern, texture, shape, form, space);
5 understanding of and ability to use the language of visual symbols, gestures and expressions to construct coherent statements and to develop ideas;
6 ability to identify and analyse an idea, theme, subject, design problem or brief;
7 ability to organise and evaluate ideas and images including where appropriate multicultural and/or historical context and to select and develop a chosen realisation;
8 ability to work independently and to sustain a response from brief to realisation;
9 aesthetic awareness and understanding of art and design problems, and ability to make critical judgements on the work of other artists and designers in multicultural and historical context where appropriate;
10 critical appreciation of works of an historical, cultural and personal nature and ability to communicate this appreciation.

(Reproduced by permission of OX/CAM)

Scheme of assessment

There are three components of the Scheme of Assessment (Table 10.10). Candidates are required to attempt Components 1, 2 and 3. Table 10.11 shows the relationship between the assessment objectives and the examination components.

COMPONENT	WEIGHTING	MAXIMUM MARK	DURATION
1 Controlled Brief	30%	60	15 hours
2 Coursework Folio	50%	100	–
3 Related Study	20%	40	–

Table 10.10 Scheme of assessment.

ASSESSMENT OBJECTIVES	COMPONENT 1	COMPONENT 2	COMPONENT 3
1	*	*	
2	*	*	
3	*	*	
4	*	*	
5	*	*	
6		*	*
7	*	*	
8		*	*
9		*	*
10		*	*

Assessment objectives carry equal intended weighting within each component.
An asterisk * indicates that the objectives will be assessed in that component.

Table 10.11 Relationship between assessment objectives and examination components (reproduced by permission of the OX/CAM).

WORK REQUIREMENTS AND PRACTICES

To help you make a start on your work we will deal with each component of the examination in turn, giving examples where appropriate. We do not intend to cover all the practices mentioned in the syllabus. These can be found elsewhere in the book even if they are mentioned in another board's syllabus. Bear in mind that there is a high level of agreement between examiners and teachers about what is meant by **good practice**, so you can be confident that the examples given elsewhere in the book will be appropriate for your OX/CAM course.

The course

Before we deal with each component, it might be helpful to explain briefly what the board considers an appropriate range of activities to make up the course. It might include:

- drawing and painting;
- sculpture;
- printmaking;
- ceramics;
- theatre design;
- graphic design (including advertising design, packaging design, illustration);
- textiles.

It is not necessary for you to tackle all these **practices** during your course. In fact, it is highly unlikely that your school or college would be able to offer all of them. Your choice will be limited by the **resources** available and the **expertise** of your teacher(s).

Don't be alarmed if your particular school is able to offer only a limited range of activities. Your teacher(s) will be able to structure the course to ensure that you satisfy the requirements of the examination – after all, that is their professional responsibility. You will be able to demonstrate a wide range of approaches to your work even within a narrow range of practices. Bear in mind also that there has to be an appropriate balance between **breadth** and **depth** in your course and that covering a wide range of practices might not be desirable anyway.

In our view, what is most exciting about art and design, as opposed to many other subjects, is that the **content** of the course can be determined by you and is limited only by your imagination and skill.

COURSEWORK FOLIO

You must submit no less than three and no more than five pieces of work, with supporting studies, selected from the work done during the course. Your teacher can help with this selection. The work is marked by your teacher and externally moderated by moderators appointed by the board.

The **selection** of work for submission is very important because you need to reveal a wide range of qualities and characteristics if you are to meet all the assessment objectives. You might imagine that all you need to do is to choose your 'best' work for submission, but this may be of little value if, for example, you submit four figure drawings, all in the same medium and scale. You could then reasonably claim to have met Assessment Objective 2, the 'ability to work from observed phenomena and personal experience'. But what about the other nine assessment objectives? This is why it is very important for your teacher to help with the choice of work for the folio.

The syllabus indicates that you must show evidence of:

- research and investigation;
- formation and development of ideas;
- realisation of ideas;
- critical evaluation.

The ten assessment objectives can be grouped under these headings and teachers and examiners generally accept that they represent the main stages in most art and design activity. These stages need not be represented in every piece of work you do and they do not necessarily follow the sequence indicated above, but your *total* submission should ensure that they are fully represented.

If you refer back to Chapter 1, you should be able to recognise how these terms relate to what we have described as **study contexts** and **study skills**. If your work is developing in this way, you should have little difficulty in producing appropriate material for the folio. For the purpose of assessment the assessment objectives are grouped under these headings and marks are awarded accordingly, so it is useful for you to consider your work in these terms.

THE RELATED STUDY

The Related Study is a critical/historical/contextual study done in connection with your practical coursework. It is intended to help you to see the **context** in which your practical work is produced and to direct your interest beyond your immediate environment. This experience will hopefully feed back to help you develop your own work and appreciate the work of others. The basic material for the study should be conducted, *concurrently* with your practice work, over the full period of the course.

The board provides useful guidance on the kind of work which would be an appropriate foundation for the final submission of the Related Study:

> Throughout the two-year course of study of Art and Design, the keeping of research note books (or equivalent) should be encouraged. This work should be a genuine record of discovery and collection. Also involved should be interpretation and evaluation of visual material and aesthetic and technical principles and might include drawings from observation and experience, photographs taken, ideas noted, interview notes, etc. Investigative work forms an integral part of understanding procedures, practices, techniques and ideas of artists, designers, historians and critics in a context that enhances and broadens the candidate's own work. Resources may be gathered from visits to galleries, museums, libraries, studios and workshops and consideration should be given to availability and access to information from a variety of sources to ensure the originality and depth of personal research.

(Reproduced by permission of OX/CAM)

The form of the study

The presentation of the study for assessment may take one of three forms:

- practical work investigating visual ideas, techniques or processes relating to a chosen topic, supported by written work where necessary;
- an illustrated paper, not exceeding 3,000 words, critically analysing and appraising a chosen topic;
- a video of approximately ten minutes' duration. This should be accompanied by a design brief of not more than 1,000 words.

Examples of topics for the related study

To give you some indication of the variety of possible topics for the Related Study the board has provided the following list. Like all such lists it is not meant to be exhaustive and there is no requirement that these topics must be chosen.

1 The use and relevance of materials in the 20th century.
2 The techniques of drawing in the Renaissance.
3 The development of serigraphy in the work of contemporary artists.
4 The geometric designs of Islamic art more usually found in ceramics, textiles and architecture might be considered by a candidate primarily interested in painting.
5 Work of a named theatre designer.
6 The development of stage construction and technology.
7 The use of lustre.
8 Decorative ceramics of women in the Arts and Crafts Movement.
9 Techniques of West African potters.
10 Techniques of stump work in the 17th century.
11 Dress designs of Mary Quant.
12 Patterns of ethnic batik printing.
13 The tapestries of Andreas Pirot.
14 The influence of politics on visual communication.
15 The graven image in illustration.
16 Computer graphics in advertising.
17 The work of a contemporary artist or designer.
18 The historical development of a technique – e.g. bronze casting, etching.
19 The development of a means of communication – e.g. the poster in the late 19th century
20 The study of different treatments of subject matter – e.g. the tree in 20th century painting.
21 The study of an aesthetic movement in a narrow period – e.g. ceramic sculpture in the 1960s.
22 The study of Art as symbol and icon – e.g. African sculpture of North Africa.
23 Transcriptions or copies of Art and Design objects.
24 Analytical study of Art and Design objects.

Examples of responses

The example we have chosen (Fig. 10.8) shows part of a study which uses computer-generated images to develop the theme of 'The face in art through the ages'. What is interesting about this study is the way in which the manipulation of the image has created qualities which the student has been able to relate to different periods in the history of art. For example, the **texture** in images 1 and 2 has suggested the kind of **surface** created by medieval tapestry. In image 5 a greater degree of colour separation has created associations with pointillism, a technique of applying paint used by some artists in the nineteenth century. In image 11 the repeated screen-printed images of Andy Warhol are suggested.

Obviously, all these themes need to be developed further if a study of substance is to be produced, but the example does illustrate how the student's own work can be related to the work of other artists and designers.

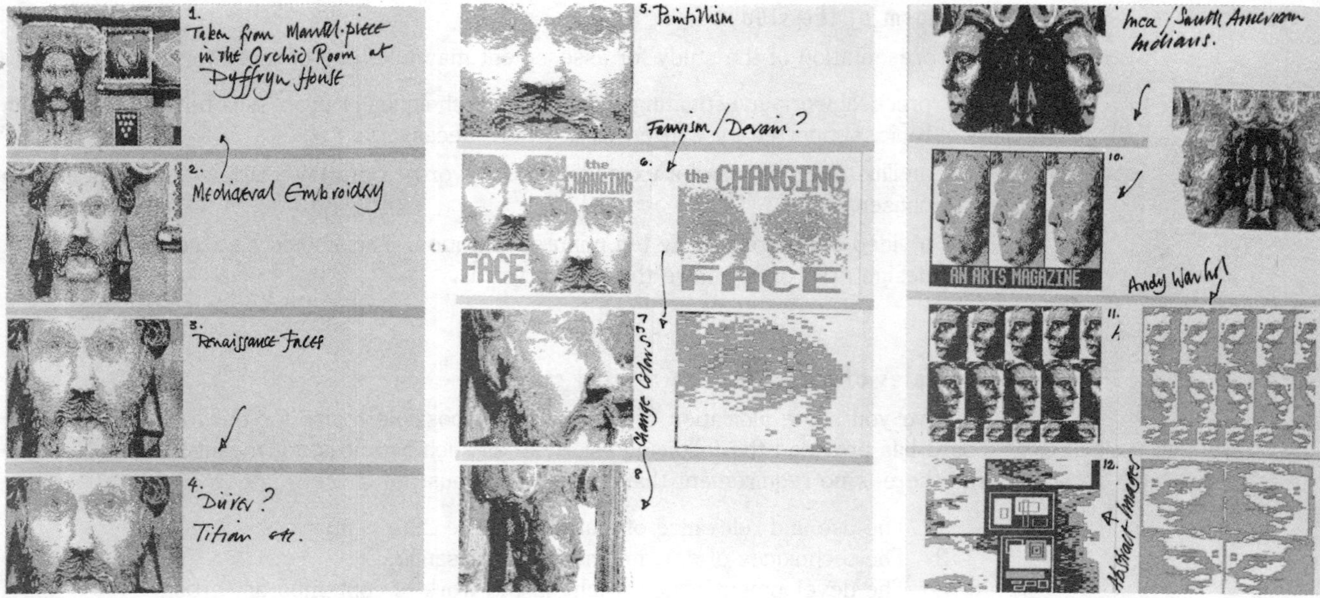

Fig. 10.8

CONTROLLED BRIEF

The Controlled Brief is a timed paper (maximum fifteen hours) set by the board and completed at the end of the course. The paper is given to you four weeks before the date set for the examination to allow you time to develop preparatory/supporting work. You must answer *one* question only and can work to any size and in any medium (unless otherwise stated in the question). Your teacher may advise you during the preparatory period but the work you do during the fifteen hour period must be your own unaided work. Up to two sheets of supporting/preparatory work (A1 size) should be submitted with the final work. The Controlled Brief is marked by your teacher(s) and externally moderated by the board's moderator.

Purpose of the controlled brief

This component of the examination is intended to test your ability to identify and solve a problem within a set period of time under controlled conditions. The preparatory work and the final piece should demonstrate your ability to:

- research and investigate phenomena related to the chosen question;
- originate and develop ideas from the material assembled/collected;
- realise these ideas into a final statement in an appropriate form.

If you have read and understood Chapter 1, you should be able to recognise the skills which will be required to accomplish the Controlled Brief satisfactorily. It is not sufficient simply to reproduce material related to the chosen question. You must clearly show how your ideas have **developed** from your original research to the final form. In a sense you are being asked to provide **evidence** of your thinking through the visual images and ideas you produce.

Specimen questions

The board provides a large number of specimen questions. These are intended to be starting points from which your ideas should develop and are not meant to be restrictive. They provide a context or set the scene for your work, but seek to control your response only in terms of the time constraint indicated.

1 Local landscape.
2 Inside a greenhouse or conservatory.
3 Decaying.
4 Against the light.
5 Figure or figures in an enclosed space.
6 Reflections.
7 Organic forms.

8 The self.
9 A point of view.
10 Childhood memorabilia.
11 Design and make a container for pouring liquid.
12 Design and make a relief or sculpture where repeated modules play a major part.
13 Using a close study of mechanisms produce a three-dimensional moving form.
14 Design and make a sculpture based on the story of Icarus.
15 Design and make a set of tiles for a swimming pool.
16 Design and make a model of a revolving stage set for the musical 'Oliver'.
17 Design and make a model of a fixed stage set for a production of 'Equus' where the audience will be in the round.
18 For one scene of your choice from any Shakespeare play design and make a model of a set for either an open or proscenium stage.
19 Design a book jacket for T.S. Eliot's 'The Wasteland'
20 Make two illustrations for the children's book 'The Emperor's New Clothes', integrating text and drawings.
21 Illustrate 'A House is a Machine for Living In' for the cover of the 'Architectural Review'.
22 Design a logo for a timber merchants. The logo should be presented in a range of applications from stationery to transport.
23 Design a poster for an antiques fair.
24 Design the opening title sequence (one minute in duration) for a TV series 'The Story of Jazz'. Presentation may be in the form of a sequence of 'stills' and may include videotape.
25 Design and make a container for take-away pizzas.
26 Design and make a free-standing counter display for a new book on 'Gothic Architecture'. The display should hold a number of copies of the book.
27 Design and produce the packaging for a board game where the shape of the package is related to the moves required to play the game.
28 Design a wall hanging suitable for a refreshment area in a museum of ethnology. Make a sample area.
29 Contrasts of light against dark inspire a design for a dramatic item of clothing. Make a garment.
30 Design and make a textile based on geometric patterns and shapes.
31 Design and print a length of fabric suitable for the blinds of a fast-food fish restaurant.

Maximum 60 marks

(Reproduced by permission of OX/CAM)

Examples of responses

The response to Question 5 (Fig. 10.9) is concerned as much with mood and atmosphere as it is with the depiction of the figure, while the response to Question 8 (Fig. 10.10) created pictures within the picture – a device with a long art-historical pedigree. Both examples display interesting variations on the theme of figure painting and both show the development of the ideas through the preparatory studies.

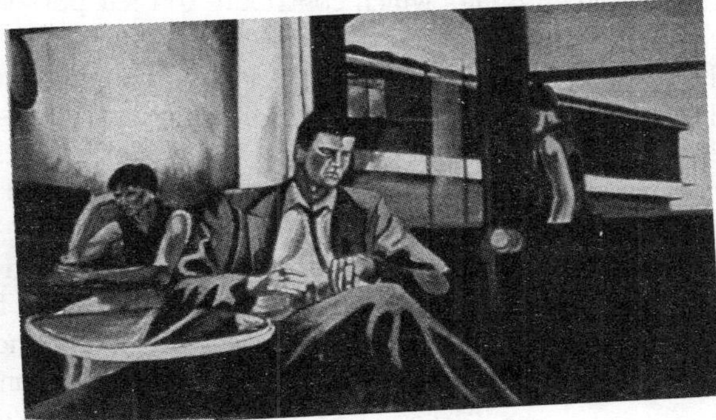

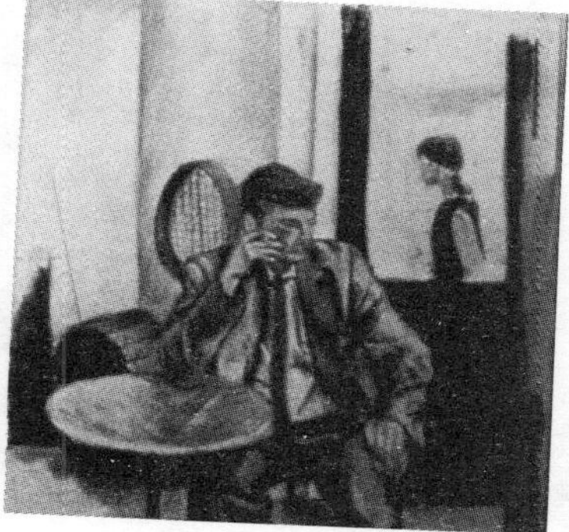

Fig. 10.9

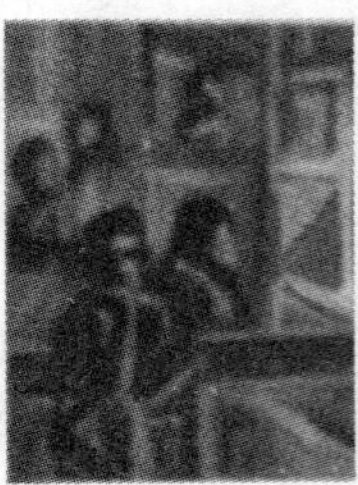
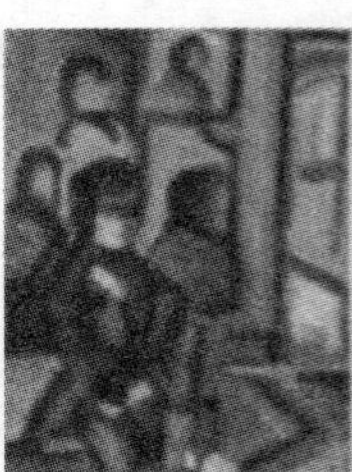
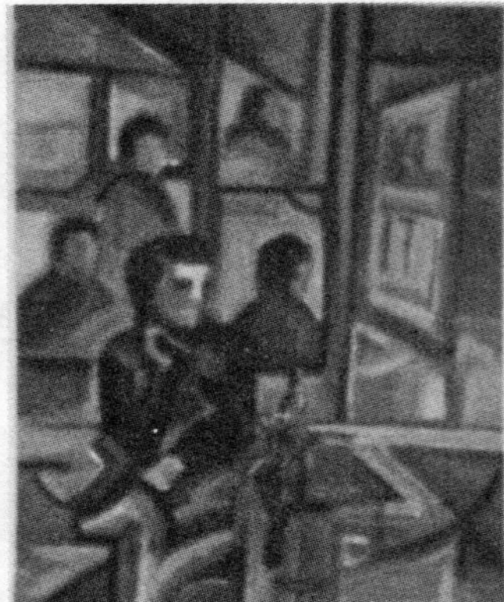
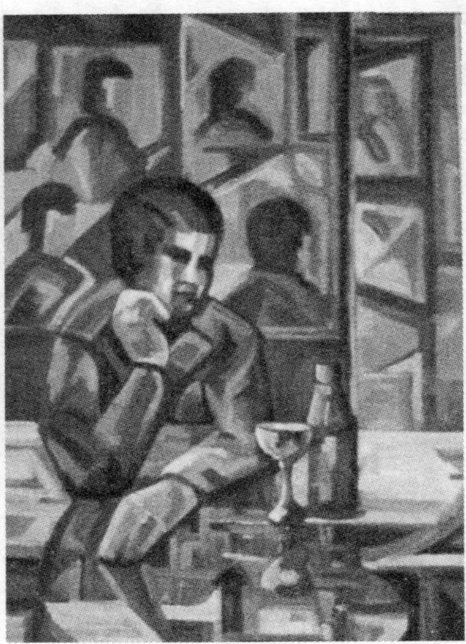

Fig. 10.10

SCOTTISH CERTIFICATE OF EDUCATION HIGHER GRADE IN ART AND DESIGN (SEB)

This is a revised syllabus, examined for the first time in June 1990. The Higher Grade Certificate in Art and Design leads naturally from the Standard Grade examination, so if you have successfully completed a Standard Grade course you will be well placed to begin work at the Higher Grade.

You will be expected to demonstrate the same skills and qualities as before but your level of performance and understanding will need to be of a higher order. To help you understand the requirements of the examination to the full, we strongly recommend that you have your own copy of the syllabus, which can be obtained from your teacher or by contacting the SEB directly, because it is obviously beyond the scope of this book to reproduce *all* the information in the syllabus.

Rationale

What is very helpful about the syllabus is that there is a clear statement at the beginning about the philosophy or **rationale** of the examination. This seeks to explain exactly what the syllabus and examination are intended to achieve and it provides a clear indication of the **values** of those involved with setting and marking the examination. For example, the key components of the syllabus are explained and justified in terms of their contribution to a **balanced** art and design education. We do not intend to discuss it here but we strongly recommend that you read this section in detail.

Aims of the course

The Aims are the formal statement about the nature and purpose of the course. They separate out the key qualities and skills which it is hoped can be developed by following a course in art and design. These are not necessarily attributes which can or should be examined, and to some extent they present a rather idealised view of what can be achieved. So do not be too concerned if you feel you might not be capable of such accomplishments.

The principal aims identified for a Higher Grade course in Art and Design are to provide opportunities for candidates to develop:

interests and aptitudes which contribute to their personal, intellectual, emotional and social development;
ability to express and communicate ideas, thoughts and feelings in visual terms;
ability to identify and seek imaginative solutions to design problems;
ability to make informed, substantiated judgements based on knowledge and understanding of the work of artists and designers and the ideas, beliefs, events and conditions of their times;
capacity for discrimination, appreciation and criticism in relation to their environment;
ability to investigate, select and interpret information from a variety of sources;
appropriate skills in the use of materials, equipment and procedures necessary to the communication and expression of information, ideas and imagery.

(Reproduced by permission of SEB)

The course

The course is separated into three distinct components. Each one is seen to have equal importance in terms of educational value and together they are intended to be taught in an integrated way. Your course will consist of:

- expressive activity;
- design activity;
- critical evaluation and historical studies.

To help your teacher(s) provide an appropriate structure for the course, the board recommends that the above activities are set in the following contexts;

- the environment (human, man-made and natural);
- communication and the media;
- cultural, social and historical factors.

By structuring your course in this way your teacher(s) should be able to provide stimulus and sources of study and to highlight the relevance of the subject to your own life. In particular, the critical and historical study is meant to be directly linked to your practical work and not taught in an abstract, 'academic' way.

Summary of the scheme of assessment

- EXPRESSIVE ACTIVITY (110 marks) – a practical, externally set examination of ten hours over two days;
- DESIGN ACTIVITY (110 marks) – a selection of coursework submitted to the board, consisting of five A2 sheets of appropriate work;
- CRITICAL EVALUATION AND HISTORICAL STUDIES (80 marks) – a two-hour written paper in two sections:
  Section A, Critical Evaluation (40 marks)
  Section B, Historical Studies (40 marks).

WORK REQUIREMENTS AND PRACTICES

To help you make a start on your work, we will deal with each component in turn and discuss how best to ensure that all the assessment objectives are met in the most appropriate way. Bear in mind that there are sections of the book which, although they deal with other board's syllabuses in detail, contain information which will be helpful to you. There is considerable agreement between teachers and examiners about **good practice** in art and design, so examples we have chosen elsewhere should also be of relevance to your work for the Higher Grade Certificate.

EXPRESSIVE ACTIVITY

Requirements of the examination

The examination is of ten hours duration, based upon an externally set paper containing stimuli for study. You are given the stimulus paper in March prior to the examination to allow you time for preparatory work. This will consist of:

- one A2 sheet containing analytical drawings;
- one A2 sheet containing a selection of research material in the form of sketches, notes, photographs, etc.

You are not allowed to take any other two-dimensional material into the examination room, although three-dimensional research materials and models are allowed. The ten hours are spread over two days. Your examination work should consist of either one A2 sheet (two-dimensional work) or maximum 30 cm in any dimension (three-dimensional work).

After the examination you are allowed thirty minutes to assemble your work ready for assessment. Your two preparatory sheets and your examination work are sent to the board for external examination.

Questions will be set based upon the following practices:

- drawing;
- painting;
- sculpture;
- printmaking (*not* graphics);
- fabric craft;
- three-dimensional work;
- still photography.

You can work in any medium *except* oil paint.

The SEB has produced a specimen paper containing a range of stimuli for the Expressive Activity and we have reproduced some of them below. You must respond to *one* stimulus only.

1 Organic growth
2 'Dust, grime, smell, smoke,
Stains, iron steel,
Rust corroding the pipes,
Stains, boilers and machines,
Gear boxes, regulators, registers, thermometers'.
3 Time and tide
4 Seeing is believing
5 'Everywhere I walked, I was confronted by gripping contrasts: the brilliance of the sun – the cerulean depths of the shadows; the familiarity of a homeland – the strangeness of another culture . . . .'

(Reproduced by permission of the SEB)

Assessment criteria for the expressive activity

To ensure that you produce work which is appropriate for this component, it is important for you to be aware of the criteria which the examiners will use when assessing your work. You can use the criteria almost like a check list, which will allow you to structure your response to your chosen question.

Assessment of expressive examination work will be based on:

a) ability to interpret stimulus material, producing evidence of research which contains analytical drawing studies and other investigative preliminary work;
b) development work which demonstrates
selection and investigation of the research material;
sensitivity and competence in the exploration of expressive possibilities;
skill in the selection and use of a range of media;
c) an expressive outcome, resulting from development work, which demonstrates
expression of ideas, thoughts and feelings;
use of the elements of visual language;
skill in the selection and use of the chosen media.

(Reproduced by permission of the SEB)

Example of response

The example we have chosen is an interpretation of Question 4 using the medium of silk-screen printing for the final image. (Fig. 10.11). The student has made good use of the preparatory period to photograph the striking images of the power cables and insulators, and to relate these to the jagged shapes of the lightning. The final image is well carried out in two forms, thus exploiting the medium's capacity to repeat an image with ease.

To some extent we are left to guess at the origin of the idea and it would probably have helped if this had been clearly stated on the preparatory sheets. There is also little evidence of real experimentation or 'exploration of expressive possibilities', as mentioned in the assessment criteria above.

You might find it helpful to apply the assessment criteria to this example yourself. In this way you should develop the awareness needed to appraise your own work critically. It is always very difficult to be objective about work you have been deeply involved with and experience of analysing the work of others should help to make this task easier.

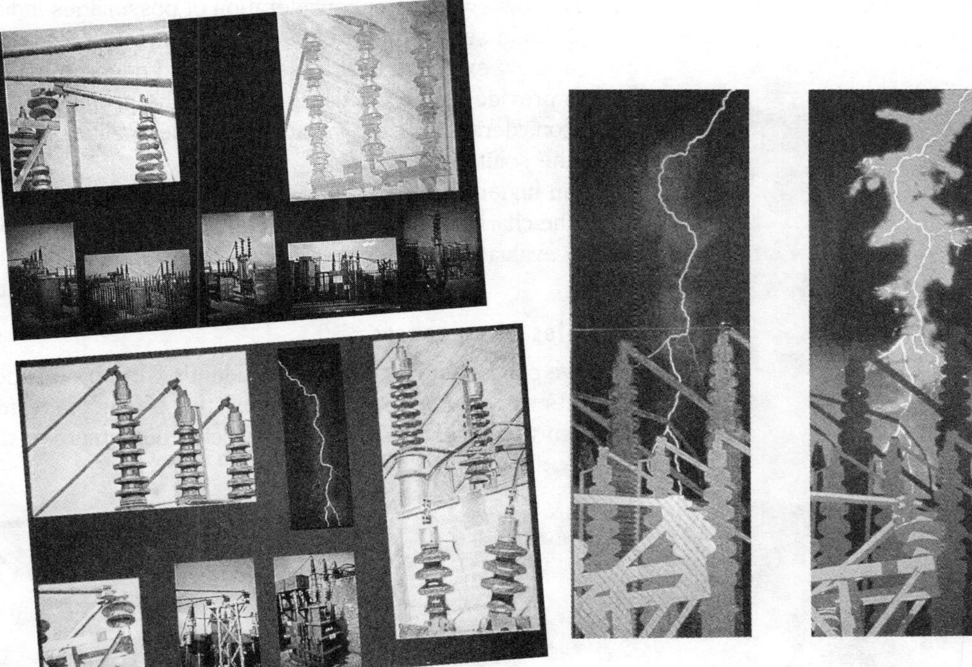

Fig. 10.11

DESIGN ACTIVITY

Requirements of the examination

You must submit to the board a selection of coursework based upon *one* of the following aspects of design:

- interior;
- fashion;
- visual communication (including film and video);
- textile/fabric;
- product;
- three-dimensional;
- environmental.

Your submission should consist of:

two A2 sheets demonstrating research and investigation;
two A2 sheets showing consideration of the problem and development of a solution (where three-dimensional work has been undertaken, photographs of the work should be submitted instead of the actual work);
one A2 sheet or finished model (30 cm in greatest dimension) which shows the solution to the problem;
a completed Evaluation Form (provided by the Board) detailing the brief undertaken and the candidate's evaluation of the solution to the problem.

Photographic prints only, *and not the actual work*, should be submitted for the following:

i) two-dimensional work in excess of A2 size;
ii) three-dimensional work in excess of 30 cm in greatest dimension;
iii) work using valuable or expensive material;
iv) work which cannot be moved.

(Reproduced by permission of the SEB)

Assessment criteria for the design activity

The principles relating to the assessment criteria for the Expressive Activity are equally valid here. The appropriate criteria for the Design Activity are listed below.

Assessment of Design classwork will be based on ability:
to show evidence of research and investigation of the brief;

to show evidence of consideration of possibilities indicating approaches to solving the problem set by the brief;
to show evidence of final selection and decision making;
to provide a solution which satisfies the problem set by the brief demonstrating
 consideration of the visual and textile qualities relevant to the form and function of the solution;
 an understanding of properties, process and techniques;
 the character, form and structure of the artefact through choice and use of materials.
to evaluate the effectiveness of the solution against the intention of the brief.

(Reproduced by permission of the SEB)

Examples of responses

We have chosen four examples of student's work based upon *product analysis* (Fig. 10.12). Students were asked to analyse an existing product in terms of its function and appearance and then to suggest modifications which would improve the product.

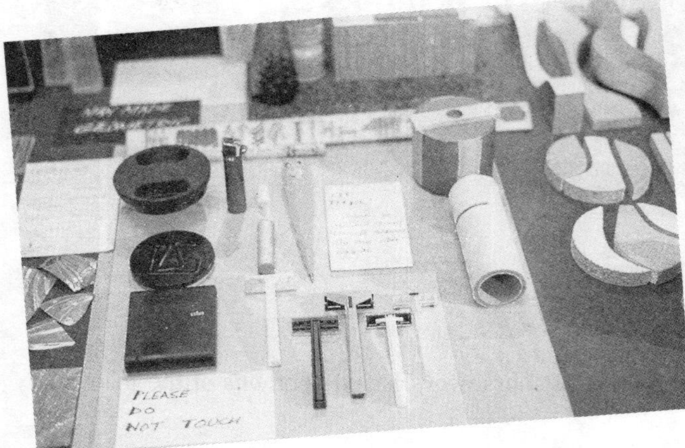

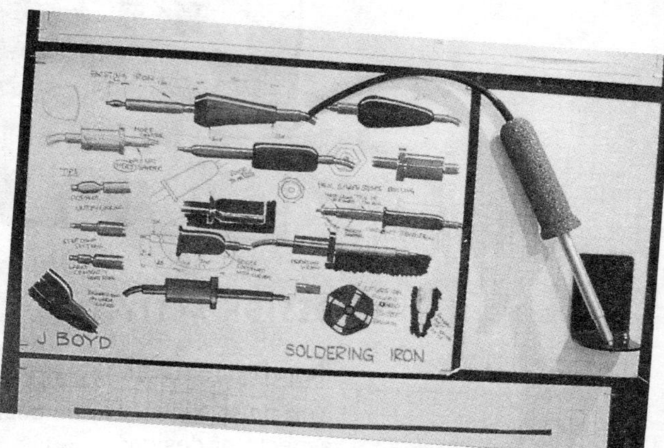

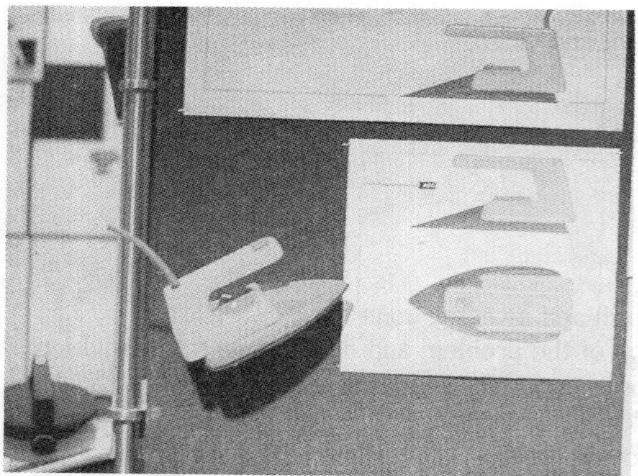

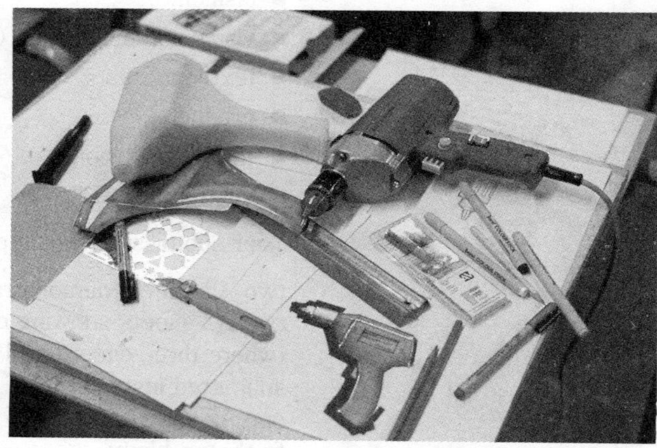

Fig. 10.12

This particular project was devised by the teacher to ensure that all the assessment criteria would be met. Not all the work of each student is shown but you should be able to see the methods of approach which are being used.

What is very helpful about this approach is that the experience of analysing artefacts or systems can be used for your Critical Evaluation section of the written paper. As we mentioned in earlier chapters of this book, a critical vocabulary is essential if you want to make the most of your art and design course.

CRITICAL EVALUATION AND HISTORICAL STUDIES

Requirements of the Examination

Assessment will be by an external examination paper of 2 hours' duration. The paper will be in two sections, A and B, and will be based on the Visual Arts, Design and Architecture from 1750 to the present day.

80 marks will be allocated to this question paper.

Section A – Critical Evaluation (40 marks)
This section will deal with the critical evaluation of works of art, design and architecture.

There will be three questions, one set on the Visual Arts, one on Design and one on Architecture. You will be required to answer all three questions.

You will be required to interpret and analyse visual images of two-dimensional or three-dimensional work presented in the paper under the headings of Visual Arts, Design and Architecture.

This section is concerned with eliciting your reactions and personal responses to works of art, architecture and design which are dependent upon your ability to understand and interpret the language of artists and designers. Acquired knowledge of artists, designers, architects and their work in social and historical terms will not be assessed in this section of the paper.

Assessment of Critical Evaluation will be based on ability to comment on examples of the Visual Arts, Design and Architecture, showing evidence of the following:

interpretation of the content, purpose and effectiveness of examples of visual art, design and architecture;

awareness of the elements of art and design and the uses made of these by artists and designers;

understanding and use of appropriate vocabulary and terms to discuss and support analysis of art and design;

understanding of the materials, media and methods of artists and designers.

(Reproduced by permission of the SEB)

Bear in mind that you are required to answer *all* questions in this section. This indicates that there must be **breadth** in your Critical and Historical Studies course, even if your practical work tends to be rather specialised. No doubt your teacher will ensure that aspects of art, design and architecture will be dealt with, but it is in your own interest to be as widely involved with the subject as possible.

Developing the **critical vocabulary** needed for this paper is not an easy task and is not something that can be learned overnight, so we would strongly recommend that you develop your skills right from the beginning of the course.

Section B – Historical Studies (40 marks)
This section will deal with the social and historical matters from 1750 to the present day, concerning the work of artists and designers and the ideas, beliefs, events and conditions of their times. You will be expected to answer questions in essay form.

Assessment of this section of the paper will be based on:

knowledge and understanding of the aims and intentions of artists and designers, and of their role;

knowledge and understanding of the interaction between artists and designers and the social, historical, environmental and technological factors involved;

informed and substantiated judgements based on interpretation of knowledge and experience.

Eighteen questions will be set in this section, nine in the Visual Arts category and nine in the Design and Architecture category. You must attempt two questions, one from each category. 20 marks will be allocated to each question.

The choice of questions will permit a breadth of response which should enable you to demonstrate knowledge and understanding of skills, concepts and terminology acquired in the critical aspect of the course. The two categories of this section have been further subdivided into key areas for study, with notes on each area describing the content on which questions will be based. Three questions will be set on each of the key areas.

VISUAL ARTS

Within the Visual Arts category the key areas are as follows:

Art and society

This area focuses on the artist in the role of commentator on his or her life and times. Study might include aspects of political, religious, environmental and social comment. Study might focus on, for instance, the artist in a number of highly personal roles, for example, as idealist, philosopher, romantic, visual poet or visionary.

Movements in art

Within this area study should include the origins, influences, character and interrelationships of the major movements and the beliefs, styles and working methods of their exponents.

Themes in art

Study might consider themes which have occurred repeatedly in art and which have interested, inspired and even obsessed artists.

DESIGN AND ARCHITECTURE

Within the Design and Architecture category the key areas are as follows:

Design and the consumer

This area deals with how designers consider human factors in terms of aspirations, tastes, quality of life, economics and function. Studies might include the role of the designer, for example, in communicating information, manipulating thinking or persuading; or the work of the designer when expressing or communicating certain concepts of ideals in, for example, architecture, fashion or styling.

Movements, styles and influences in design

Study of this area should include consideration of the major movements, the sources from which they derived their origins, the form and styling, and the influences that these movements have upon society, and the main exponents involved.

Design and technology

The designer's use and development of the possibilities afforded by technological advancement in, for example, materials, processes and media. Studies might include the impact of these advancements on product design, architecture, engineering and communication.

(Reproduced by permission of the SEB)

UNIVERSITY OF LONDON SCHOOLS EXAMINATION BOARD (ULSEB)

A-LEVEL AND AS ART AND DESIGN

It is important that you understand from the outset exactly what is required of you in terms of the examination or **scheme of assessment**. It is through the scheme of assessment that what is contained in the syllabus is tested or examined. The syllabus contains the skills, knowledge and understanding which you are expected to cover during your course of study.

Your teacher should be able to provide you with a copy of the syllabus but if not, you are strongly advised to contact the board and ask for a copy. It is only by thoroughly understanding what the course is about and how it will be examined that you can expect to succeed. The **sound working habit** discussed in Chapter 1 will be of little value if you fail to produce the material required by the examination.

Aims

Having said this, it is helpful if you are able to identify the **spirit** or **philosophy** of the examination – that is, the broad intention of the examiners who originally drafted the syllabus. You could say that the spirit of the examination concerns beliefs and values of those responsible for it. It will have something to do with their feelings about art and design and about art and design as part of a person's educational development. In most syllabuses the obvious place to identify this is in the Aims which almost always come at the beginning.

The ULSEB syllabus has two sets of aims – General Aims and Syllabus Aims. These set out an almost idealised view of what can be achieved by studying art and design. Do not be alarmed if you feel that your personality and ability do not match up. There are very few people, if any, who would achieve all of these! It is sufficient at this stage to get a 'feel' for what the examination is about.

Certification

The syllabus has been devised to provide two forms of certification. This means that you can receive one of two kinds of certificate (assuming you are successful!) at the end of the course. If you follow a **general** course without concentrating on a particular **practice** or **specialism**, your certificate will simply state 'Art and Design'. If you follow a more **specialised** course – for example, Graphic Design – then your certificate will state 'Art and Design – Graphic Design'.

The full range of options available are:

TITLE	ENDORSEMENT	SYLLABUS NUMBER
Art and Design	–	020
Art and Design	Fine Art *	021
Art and Design	Three-dimensional Design+	022
Art and Design	Fashion/Textiles	023
Art and Design	Graphic Design	024
Art and Design	Photography	025
Art and Design	Film and Video	026
Art and Design	Critical and Historical Studies	027

* Fine Art includes Painting and Drawing, Sculpture and Printmaking.
\+ Three-dimensional Design includes Ceramics, Theatre, Interior and Product Design.

If you enter the general Art and Design examination 020 you can answer questions from any of the endorsed options for your externally set examination. However, your choice must be stated at the time of entry and it should relate to the kind of work you have been doing throughout your course.

It is important to realise that both forms of certification are examined at the same standard and that the specialised or **endorsed** award is not better or more important than the general art and design certificate.

Why endorsed and unendorsed certificates?

Both forms of certification are provided to meet a specific need. For example, consider the student who successfully completed a GCSE course in art and design and really enjoyed the subject but did not want to make a career in art and design. A general art and design A-level might be very appropriate for their chosen career or college entrance requirements. Alternatively, a student might have achieved a high GCSE grade in Art and Design – Textiles and decided that they wanted a career in the fashion/textiles field. In this case it would make a great deal of sense for that student to follow the endorsed course. In both cases, however, it is important to have a broad understanding of the nature of the subject and this can be gained only through developing the **sound working habit** mentioned in Chapter 1.

If you feel that you do not fall readily into either of these categories, then all is not lost! Perhaps you are undecided about whether to follow a career in art and design or to look to another field? In this case it might be better to follow a general approach in your lower-sixth year and then discuss matters with your teacher. Your final decision is not required for entry purposes until February or March in the year of the examination, so this allows you some time to make up your mind. However, you should note that the ULSEB externally set paper is sent out at the beginning of the spring term and that papers are sent to the school or college on the basis of estimated entries sent to the board in November.

The key to making the right decision about which form of certification to go for is to clarify in your own mind where your strengths and weaknesses lie and to ask yourself what it is you want to get out of the subject by the end of the course. You will need to speak to your art and design teacher, your careers teacher and even your fellow students, but most important of all, you will need to be honest with yourself about your own abilities and commitment to the subject.

The examination

The ULSEB examination requires that you submit:

- a minimum of three units of 'practical' coursework;
- a personal, critical or historical study done as part of the coursework but *in addition* to the first requirement above;

- an externally set paper;
- preparatory/supporting work for the externally set paper.

There is no individual weighting for these elements. The *total* of all your work is given a mark out of 100 by your teacher and then the work is sent to the board for external moderation, to ensure consistent standards throughout the examination. It is therefore very important to take your work seriously right from the outset of the course.

WORK REQUIREMENTS AND PRACTICES

To help you make a start on the work required we will cover each **component** of the examination through the 'eyes' of a typical student following a two-year course leading up to the unendorsed certificate in art and design. Many of the **practices** will not be covered here, but these can be found elsewhere in the book, often referred to under another board's syllabus. Remember that there is a high level of agreement between examiners and teachers from all boards about what constitutes **good practice**. You can be confident that as long as you are familiar with the flavour or spirit of your own examination, the advice given elsewhere in the book will be appropriate for you.

PRACTICAL COURSEWORK

The examination requires that you submit a *minimum* of three units of practical coursework presented on *no more than* three sheets or mounts of maximum size A1. This does *not* mean that you need only produce three pieces of work in two years! You should select your best and most representative work for examination so that the examiners are aware of all your qualities related to art and design. To do this you will need to produce work which is within the syllabus and which meets the assessment criteria. These are the rules or principles upon which your work is assessed and, in the case of the ULSEB syllabus, your teacher will apply these criteria to each unit of work you submit. How this works in practice will be discussed later in the chapter, but for the moment it is important to realise that the work you finally submit for examination must be **selected** by you (with your teacher's help) to ensure that the assessment criteria are fully met.

The course

For most A-level art and design students, the **structure** of their course will be largely determined by their art and design teacher. After all, this is part of the teacher's professional responsibility and such a responsibility includes decisions about which examination syllabus to follow. What is interesting about art and design as opposed to many other subjects is that the **content** of the course is often determined by the student's own interests and aptitudes. If you have successfully followed a GCSE art and design course, you should by now have a reasonable idea of what your interests and aptitudes are. In reality you will almost certainly be building upon these as you embark upon your A-level course.

Syllabus framework

If you studied for the London and East Anglian Group (LEAG) GCSE in art and design, you will immediately recognise the similarities with the A-level syllabus. Both syllabuses offer a **framework** from which a course can be constructed. This will have been used by your teacher to provide the structure of the course. Do not worry if your GCSE work was undertaken with another examining board because the same basic principles apply to all GCSE art and design examinations.

The syllabus framework represents the **possible options** open to you. There is no requirement that each, or even a specified number, of the Processes and Procedures and the Practices should be included in any specific course of study.

The framework is presented in a way which places an emphasis on the processes by which work is produced rather than just the artefacts themselves. For the purpose of clarity the Processes and Procedures have been listed separately, but in practice they overlap and are interdependent. It is hard to imagine any work which would not involve, for example visual research and critical appraisal.

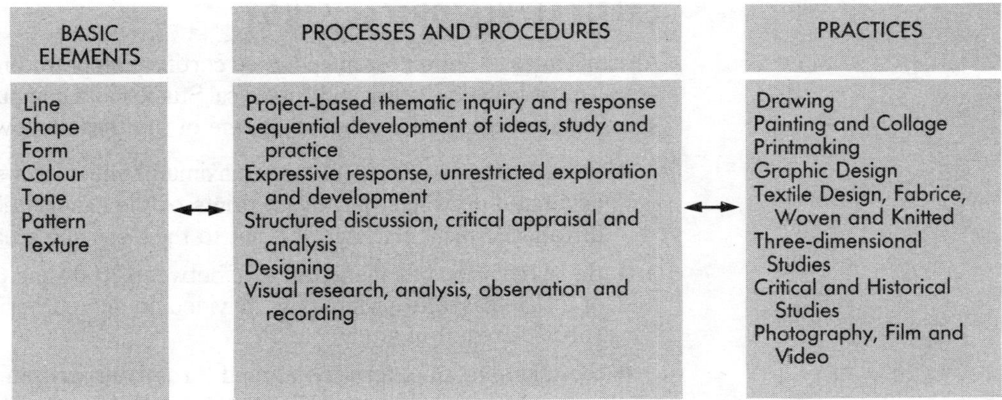

To demonstrate how this works in practice we will use the following example, but bear in mind that to a large extent this framework should be based upon your own interests and aptitudes. This will require careful discussion and consultation with your teacher, who will be trying to ensure that your work fits in with the overall course structure.

The central column, dealing with Processes and Procedures, is the link between the others. It provides focal points for studies which explore the complex relationship between formal language, content and a range of particular practices. For example, a study mainly based on the sequential development of ideas, study and practice, might explore only shape, colour and pattern, while concentrating on drawing and painting.

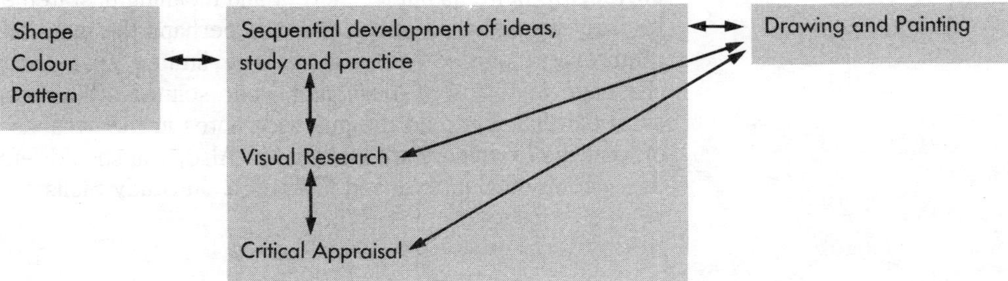

Shape, colour and pattern are, of course, fundamental elements in art and design. They can be studied for their own sake, in isolation, or they can be considered in conjunction with almost all art and design activity. The example (Fig. 10.13) we have chosen shows the development of an original still-life study into a more abstract form, which becomes less concerned with the representation of objects originally observed and more concerned with the dynamic relationship of shape, colour and pattern. The distinction between the objects and the background disappears and each study progresses towards a more satisfactory composition until the student decides that a 'final' statement can be made.

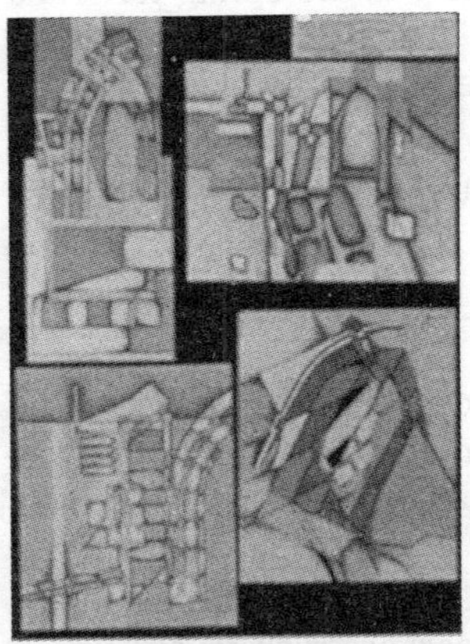

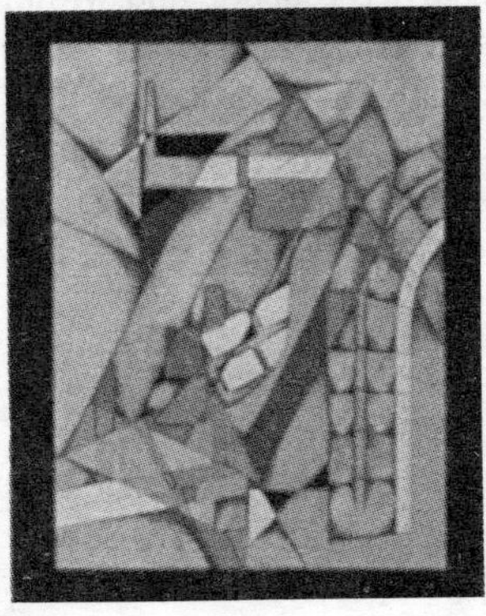

Fig. 10.13

Before the twentieth century it was the rule rather than the exception to see the difference between object and background inpaintings However, from the early years of this century, movements such as FUTURISM and CUBISM deliberately avoided this distinction. Images were fragmented, with multiple viewpoints, typified by the work of PABLO PICASSO and GEORGES BRAQUE. Instead of simply arranging recognisable **objects** within the picture's rectangle, the concern was for the arrangement of **shapes**, with the **subject matter** playing a secondary role.

The reduction of things to their basic geometric shapes has been a feature of art and design for centuries, but usually this was done to aid drawing or to train students. In the twentieth century many artists have been concerned with shapes *in their own right*, without the need to represent things seen. It is within this context that this example should be viewed. The **visual research** and **critical appraisal** are evident through the way in which the studies have developed, but it may have benefited the student, for assessment purposes, if reference had been made to source material.

This is but one way in which you might proceed through your course of study. It may well be worth referring back to the section on **study contexts** in Chapter 1 to remind yourself of the **breadth** of activities which are available to you. If you have chosen an endorsed option for your examination, there will be a greater expectation of **depth** in your work, but this must not be at the expense of a broadly based concern with the nature of art and design.

CRITICAL/HISTORICAL STUDY

All candidates, whether for unendorsed certification or for one of the six practical endorsed areas, must include Critical and Historical Studies as a compulsory element of their course. The requirement can be satisfied by one of the three following options:

- the submission of one A1 size (maximum) sheet or a sketchbook notebook of annotated drawings, paintings, prints or the candidate's own photographs, of historical/critical material relevant to their specific area(s) of study;
- the submission of a dissertation of between 3,000 and 6,000 words or the production of a slide/cassette programme or video on an appropriate topic relevant to the the specific area(s) of study:
- the taking of an externally marked three-hour written examination on one of the prescribed periods in the History of Art and Design (this option is not available to candidates entering for the endorsed practical papers, who must take the externally set paper of their chosen endorsement).

You can see from the range of possible options that you should be able to choose one which suits your particular interests and abilities. It is important that whichever approach you choose, the work should be of **substance** – that is, the work you do must show evidence of your knowledge and understanding of your chosen topic.

A1 sheet sketchbook/notebook

If, for example, you choose to submit the A1-size sheet, it should not be simply a **collection** of items but a coherent and meaningful statement or comment about the topic. In many ways the A1-sheet option is perhaps the most difficult with which to satisfy this requirement of the examination. The limited space at your disposal presents a real challenge in terms of 'designing' your solution. Whichever approach you choose, it is essential that you read the guidance notes in the syllabus to gain the best understanding of what the examiners are looking for. Also, you should refer back to Chapter 1 and review the section on Contexts and Chapter 2 on Study Skills.

EXTERNALLY SET PAPER

The externally set paper will be available to you at the beginning of the spring term and your work must reach the board by the second week in June. This may seem like a very long period of time, but bear in mind that you will probably have many other requirements then, not least revising for your other A-level subjects.

You will have a range of questions to choose from but the requirement is that you tackle one only, spending between 15 and 20 hours on the final work.

Preparatory/supporting work

During the preparatory period you are advised to select a source for ideas relevant to the question you have chosen to answer. The examiners are interested as much in the way your ideas develop as in the final work, so your preparatory studies are extremely important.

Any suitable methods and media may be used in working out your ideas but you should discuss your ideas with your teacher to ensure that your proposals are realistic and within the resources available to you. You must show as clearly as possible how your ideas progressed to the final solution. This may be done in many different ways and it is important that you discuss this with your teacher too. Preparatory work may be taken into the examination room and your submission should consist of the main work with not more than two mounts of preparatory/supporting studies directly related to the chosen question.

Choosing a question

You now know what the bare requirements are for your externally set paper. All that remains for you to do is to choose an appropriate question and begin work. Unfortunately, this is often the most difficult stage for many students, so it is perhaps worth considering carefully just what is needed at this stage. Let us refer again to our 'typical' student following the unendorsed course. The majority of the student's coursework has been painting and drawing, so it would be unwise at this stage to opt for anything other than the fine art paper. The questions are provided to allow responses by painters, sculptors and printmakers, but we can assume that our typical student will be unlikely to respond as a sculptor or printmaker.

The paper is divided into three sections, with a number of questions in each section. The sections are structured to allow responses which are mainly concerned with:

- the human figure;
- still life;
- composition from a theme.

However, these are broad categories and it is not intended that they should be restrictive. The questions in each section are meant to be *starting points* from which ideas should be developed. They set the scene or provide a context but are not seeking a standard response.

Having understood this, our typical student has read the question paper several times and discussed a number of options with the art and design teacher. This is a very important stage in coming to a decision about which question to tackle, because your teacher will be aware of your strengths and weaknesses and should be able to offer guidance on the most appropriate area of study.

Having taken these factors into account our student has chosen the question shown below. This has been taken from the ULSEB specimen paper for Fine Art (021) and comes from Section 3 – Themes.

> Through wear and tear and the gradual disintegration of posters on walls, fences advertising hoardings and shop windows, we can perceive underlying layers of imagery stretching back over a period of time.
>
> This accidental tearing and decay creates strange and unexpected configurations of colour and form, and the accumulated accretion of shapes and incidents suggests new possibilities which stimulate the imagination.
>
> A closer consideration of these developing structures can add much to our understanding of the nature of pictorial space.
>
> Go out and research information; use these chance relationships as a starting point to develop a work abstract or figurative, which allows you to employ your growing interest in the involvement with visual and/or tactile language.
>
> (Reproduced by permission of the ULSEB

Let us consider what factors have led our student to this choice of question, which in turn might help you to come to a decision at the appropriate time.

- the question is clear and unambiguous about what is required: 'Go out and research information – develop a work abstract or figurative';
- the **context** is closely defined: ' . . . .posters on walls, fences, advertising hoardings, shop windows . . . .'
- the **source material** is easily accessible;
- the **basic elements** and **processes** are clearly defined ' . . . configurations of colour and form . . . accretion of shapes . . . stimulate the imagination . . . the nature of pictorial space . . . visual language . . . .'
- there are precedents for this kind of work in the history of art, with PABLO PICASSO, GEORGES BRAQUE, HENRI MATISSE and the AFFICHISTES for example.

Tackling the question (preparatory/supporting studies)

Timing your preparatory studies It is vital that you have some kind of work schedule for your preparatory/supporting work. There is no point in gathering together lots of interesting material if you do not allow yourself the time to make full use of it. To some extent your work schedule will be dictated by external factors over which you have no control, such as the school timetable, fixed holidays and the pressures of your other subjects. This means that you should discuss things fully with your teacher before embarking upon the work. Set yourself a timetable and try to keep to it.

Gathering information In Chapter 1 we explained what is meant by study contexts and suggested that there were a number of study skills which would help you to produce good practical work.

These were described as the skills of:

- researching;
- using primary sources of information;
- using secondary sources of information;
- selecting;
- organising.

These are skills which are appropriate to most subjects, not just to art and design, but, as we emphasised in Chapter 2, they are essential to a **sound working habit**. At this stage you should keep an open mind about the possible outcome(s) of your work and should concentrate on gathering as much information as possible about the theme itself.

Our student will, no doubt, have researched the **historical context** of the theme and will be familiar with artists and artistic movements associated with this kind of work. For example, books on the history of art (secondary sources) will have indicated that Picasso, Braque and Matisse were key figures in the use of **collage** and that Picasso and Braque were founders of what became known as SYNTHETIC CUBISM, in which pieces of newspaper and other materials were stuck on to canvas and combined with drawing and oil painting. In the 1950s the French artists and photographers RAYMOND HAINS (1926) and JACQUES DE LA VILLEGLÉ (1926) devised a technique of making collages from fragments of torn-down posters. This technique was known as *de collage*.

This information in itself is of little value unless our student understands the **cultural context** of these activities. For example, Hains was obsessed with what he called the 'aesthetic bankruptcy' of the advertising world of the 1950s and his work was a kind of **critique** of this.

Our student would also need to have information about the **technical context** of these practices and might research into the printing of posters using screenprinting (serigraphy), lithography and photography.

Galleries might be visited to see works by these or other artists and printing works or studios might be visited to see how posters are printed (**primary sources**). The most obvious primary sources are the posters and advertising hoardings themselves. Our student would almost certainly take photographs and do drawings of these.

Developing your ideas The very act of gathering information often suggests ways in which your ideas might develop. Perhaps our student's photographs of real torn posters might in turn be torn themselves – to create a **photomontage**, for example. The important thing is to remain open-minded about, and receptive to, the ideas and images which confront you.

It is worthwhile at this stage to reconsider the chosen question to see how our original perception has changed in the light of all the informtion gathered. It is almost certain that if we have kept an open mind about the outcome(s) our view will be different.

To help with this process our student has listed some **key phrases** from the question which might help:

- develop a work abstract or figurative;
- configurations of colour, form, shape;
- stimulate imagination;
- pictorial space;
- visual language.

Note that in the question there has been no mention of the **medium** which might be used in the final work. The emphasis has been firmly placed on the **formal language** of art and design, with a great deal being left to the discretion of the student. It is, therefore, possible to pursue a wide range of approaches – photography, collage, de collage, photomontage, drawing, painting or any combination of these.

The decision to develop the work in an abstract or figurative way may be a conscious choice based upon the student's experience or lack of experience of one or the other. In the case of our student, the decision favoured a more abstract approach (Fig. 10.14). However, the choice might equally have been determined by the research material available.

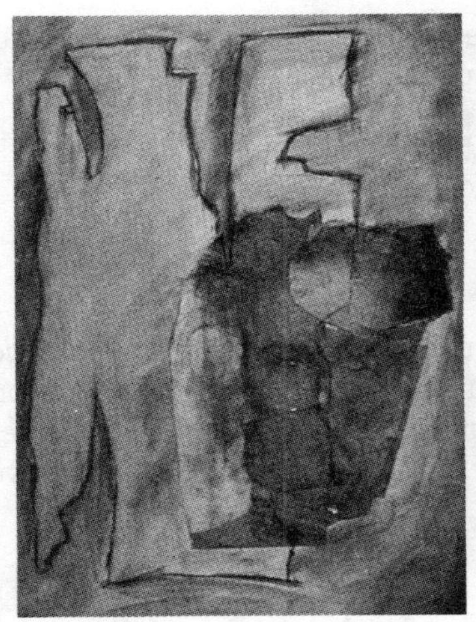

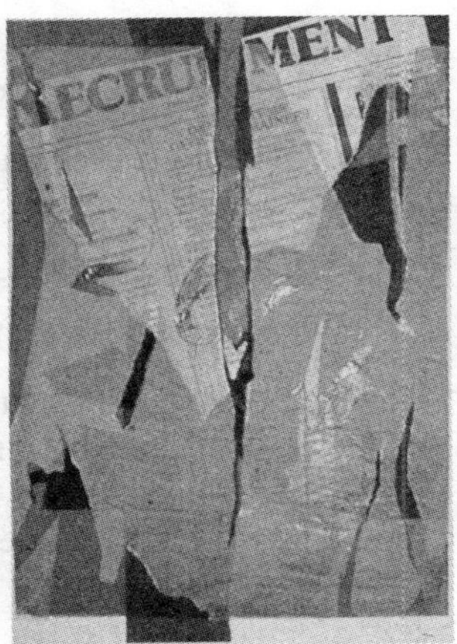

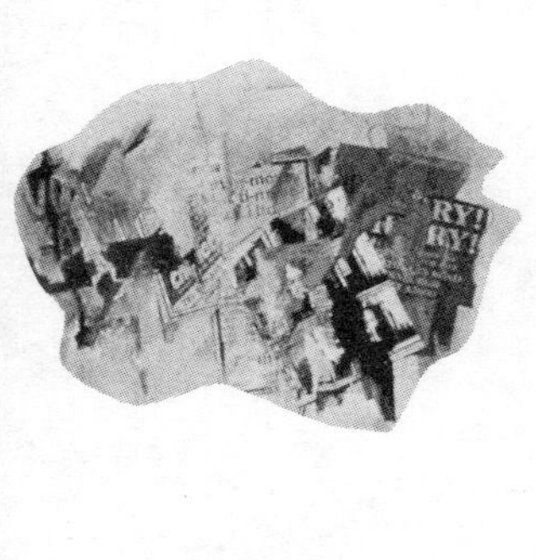

Fig. 10.14

ASSESSMENT

The scheme of assessment in the ULSEB syllabus is relatively straightforward compared with many other A-level syllabuses, because your total submission is assessed as a whole, without separate weightings being given to any components.

Your total work is awarded a mark out of 100, according to the scale shown below. Your art and design teacher provides the initial assessment, then the work is sent to the board for external moderation. The purpose of moderation is to ensure that your teacher's assessment is in line with assessment for the examination as a whole. This is very important as it ensures the **fairness** of the examination for all candidates by trying to maintain a consistent **standard** of work for each grade awarded.

GRADES	MARK RANGE
A	80–100
B	70–79
C	60–69
D	50–59
E	40–49
N	30–39
U	Below 30

Assessment objectives

It is important to understand that you must meet *all* the assessment objectives if you are to do well in the examination. The objectives list what it is you are expected to do during your course. Your total submission at the end of the course should demonstrate that all the objectives have been met.

This is really less daunting than it sounds and if you refer to the assessment section of the syllabus you will see that the nine assessment objectives refer to what we have described throughout the book as a **sound working habit**. The way in which grades are determined is through the **qualitative judgements** of your teacher(s) and the external moderator(s). They make judgements about the quality of your work set against each objective in turn. It is not sufficient to be 'good at art' in the traditional sense of the phrase. Being 'able to draw' is important, but on its own is not enough to allow you to do well in an examination which is concerned with a much wider range of qualities and skills.

Grade descriptions

To help your teacher and the external moderator apply the assessment objectives to your work, the syllabus provides grade descriptions for Grades A, B and E. These give an **idealised model** for each grade, but bear in mind that it is highly unlikely that any student will match these descriptions consistently in all of their work. For example, a student who finally achieves a Grade B may well demonstrate Grade A and Grade C qualities in some aspects of their work while being predominantly Grade B in character.

To make the grade descriptions easier to understand and apply, the assessment objectives have been grouped into four main headings:

- Visual Research and Investigation;
- Formation and Development of Ideas;
- Realisation of Ideas;
- Context and Evaluation.

These headings are meant to describe in a shorthand way the main stages of art and design activity. This does not mean that the stages always apply or that they always occur in the sequence shown here, but they are characteristic of the activity as a whole and are recognised as such by teachers and examiners. No doubt you will recognise these stages in much of your work.

Assessment matrix

The syllabus provides a detailed breakdown of Grades A, B and E under these four headings. This shows how each assessment objective can be explained in grade terms. You are strongly advised to read this and try to apply these descriptions to a sample of your own work. Perhaps your teacher can be persuaded to do this with the whole group. By discussion and by using the descriptions, you will be in a strong position to evaluate your own work.

The syllabus also provides an **assessment matrix** which summarises the grade descriptions under the four headings. You may well find this easier to use and, to assist you, it is reproduced in full in Table 10.12.

NATURE OF ACTIVITY	ATTRIBUTES OF PERFORMANCE		
	GRADE A	GRADE B	GRADE E
Visual Research and Investigation Objectives:	A high level of visual enquiry. Ideas will be well researched. An ability to observe and record material relevant to the main task. Clear evidence of aesthetic awareness.	Candidates will understand the purpose of visual research and will respond to stimuli in an exciting way. Candidates will be able to observe and record in a lively way. Aspects of visual language will be understood and if second-hand images are used they will be imaginatively developed.	Some visual research but disproportionate reliance on second-hand material. Some ability to observe and record but little development beyond uninformative discrete images. Aspects of visual language will be used but not exploited.
Formation and Development of Ideas Objectives:	A meaningful development of ideas where the emergence of ideas is nourished. A high level of understanding of the formal elements. Ability to manipulate components in terms of fitness for purpose.	There will be a tendency to reiterate rather than develop ideas. An appreciation of the media, its strengths and its limitations. There will be well constructed solutions but ideas will not always lead to exciting conclusions.	Ideas will be minimal, lack sublety and are likely to be obvious and literal. Development will be frustrated by limited technical competence. Images might be abandoned early. There will be some evidence of being able to manipulate ideas.
Realisation of Ideas Objectives:	A sustained and high level of personal response. A sustained control of technique and a feel for the organic or formal whole. An understanding of the effect of the media with the ability to manipulate imagery.	Confident awareness of problems but might lack authoritative handling. There might be some pedestrian imagery but it will be well crafted with a command of technique. The imagery might not be consistent throughout.	There will be some interest but insufficient knowledge to demonstrate originality. Visual language will be partially understood but with little appreciation of its abstract dimensions. Images are likely to be unresolved with an inconsistency of style. A minimal knowledge of the medium will be evident but not exploited.

ATTRIBUTES OF PERFORMANCE			
	GRADE A	GRADE B	GRADE C
Context and Evaluation Objectives:	Complete and systematic evaluation. A full recognition of the context in which the work was produced. The work will reflect a high level of understanding of Art and Design issues/concerns. Critical/historical material will reflect the candidates ability to present a convincing and informative view demonstrating a full command of critical vocabulary.	A coherent evaluation of the candidates work and/or the work of others. The work will have sufficient personal identity to reflect an understanding of Art and Design issues/preoccupations which have confronted other artists/designers. The context and historical continuum of Art and Design will be recognised and understood. Judgements will be well founded but will lack the fluency found in the higher grade.	Some evidence of evaluation but this will be fragmentary. Limited recognition of the context of own work. Some understanding of the preoccupations of other artists/ designers but this will not be exploited beyond the obvious and literal. Research into historical/ contextual aspects will be evident. Personal views constrained by limited critical vocabulary.

Table 10.12 Assessment matrix (reproduced by permission of the ULSEB).

ADVANCED SUPPLEMENTARY SYLLABUS

The ULSEB Advanced Supplementary syllabus is being revised by the board at the time of going to press but the present syllabus will be examined until June 1991. The new syllabus will be examined in June 1992.

There are only minor differences between the old and new syllabuses and these are in the scheme of assessment rather than in syllabus content. In *both* syllabuses there is a strong link with the A-level offered by the board and the guidance offered for the A-level is equally relevant to AS. For both the old and new AS syllabuses the end of course paper will have common questions to the A-level.

We shall outline the basic requirements for each syllabus below, but first it is important to recognise the *differences* between A-level and AS.

- AS is intended to require half the study time of A-level;
- The grades awarded will be related to grade standards at A-level but, for entrance requirement purposes, will be worth half an A-level grade;
- AS is intended to **broaden** the sixth-form curriculum and allow students to pursue subjects which would not normally be available to them.

The principle of **breadth** is central to the philosophy of the ULSEB syllabus and, for this reason, endorsed certificates are not available at AS. Breadth does *not* mean you must cover a wide range of media and practices; instead it is concerned with a broad understanding of the subject, even if all your work is in one medium. If you are in any doubt about this, refer back to the section of the 'Syllabus Framework' at the beginning of the chapter.

AS examination until 1991

The examination consists of three components weighted 60 per cent for a) plus b), and 40 per cent for c). All components will be externally marked but, for the guidance of the examiners, your teacher will be required to give an order of merit for the coursework.

In the case of all papers other than Papers 6 and 7, you will receive the question papers in advance of the examination so that preparatory work can be carried out.

Components:

a) *A piece of work produced at the end of the course selected from questions which are related to the Advanced-level examination end of course papers.*
You may also choose either the written History of Architecture paper or the History of Painting paper as the end of course test (see below). Marks will be awarded in accordance with the mark scheme appropriate to these papers. If you take one of these written papers you will not be required to submit preparatory work as in b) below, but must include preparatory work with at least one of the practical coursework pieces.

b) *Preparatory work applied and relevant to the above.*
c) *A minimum of three pieces of coursework.*

Papers 1 to 5 (14 hours) – see note i) below
Paper 1: Painting and Drawing:
A Human Figure
B Still Life and Natural Forms
C Composition from a Theme
Paper 2: Sculpture and Ceramics
Paper 3: Graphics
Paper 4: Textiles
Paper 5: Design in three Dimensions

Papers 6 to 7 (2½ hours) see note ii) below
Paper 6: History of Architecture
Paper 7: History of Painting

Note i)
In Papers 1 to 5 you must submit one major work and not more that two mounts of preparatory studies. The preparatory studies must be carried out in answering the examination paper. They are to be directly related to the question answered and can include preparation and working designs and work done in search of information.

Preparatory studies are obligatory and you must ensure that you have submitted sufficient evidence for an accurate assessment to be made. These studies are important in that they provide the examiners with an indication of your intentions when the depth of understanding is not always visible in the final work, especially where the final work falls short of your original intentions. Preparatory studies are meant to be a trace of your thinking and are thus concerned with **process**. It follows that preliminary work, made up of discrete studies of a repetitive nature will have no particular relevance, and that studies executed subsequent to the final work are a contradiction in terms, easily recognised as such, and detrimental to your chances of success. The two sheets of designs and sketches allowed may be carried out during the period prior to the examination or during the examination itself. The **presentation** of finished work, rough work and working details should be regarded as important.

Note ii)
The question papers for Papers 6 and 7 are identical to those for Advanced-level written papers except that you will be required to answer *one* question from the general section (Part 1) of the paper and *two* questions from any *one* section of Part 2. The time allocated for the examination is reduced to 2½ hours.

Coursework

You are required to submit a *minimum* of three pieces of work. These should be representative of the range of work you have undertaken during the course. The submission should consist of not more than three sheets or mounts.

A piece of work is defined as:

A finished painting or artefact; a set of studies showing the development of a project or theme; written and/or visual material produced as part of a critical or historical study (Note: the study or studies need not be restricted to the specific content of the History of Architecture or History of Painting syllabuses but could relate to any aspect of art and design covered during the course); graphic or photographic material developed in accordance with the requirement of the syllabus.

In the case of three-dimensional work, photographic evidence of finished pieces is acceptable so long as a scale is indicated. A *coursework submission consisting solely of photographs or solely of written material or a combination of both is not acceptable.*

While you may wish to concentrate your studies in the specialist areas indicated by the syllabus, *it is expected that the coursework submitted will reflect a broadly based concern with the nature of art and design.* It is equally acceptable to work *across* the specialist areas of the syllabus where this is felt to be appropriate. In such cases the examiners will have regard to your breadth of understanding in terms of syllabus content.

Coursework is to be accompanied by a certificate, signed by you and countersigned by your teacher, stating that the work has been produced without external assistance beyond the normal support provided by a teacher in accordance with the regulations.

You are responsible for selecting your submission but your teacher may give guidance if requested.

Coursework will be assessed by the application of the same criteria as those applied to the other papers. Your teacher, in establishing the order of merit, will be asked to apply the same criteria.

AS examination from 1992

The examination will consist of three components;

- coursework (including a critical and historical study);
- externally set paper;
- preparatory/supporting work for the externally set paper.

All three components will be assessed by your teacher and an order of merit established. The work is then sent to the board for external moderation.

Your work is assessed as a whole, with no weighting of separate elements. However, in order to encourage a balanced response across all three components, when viewed separately the coursework, the externally set paper and the preparatory studies should each be sufficiently substantial in quantity and quality to merit a third of the marks available for the examination as a whole.

A grade will *not* be awarded if you fail to produce the required work in all three areas of the examination.

Practical coursework The examiners consider that coursework has a central role in the syllabus and scheme of examination and they list what they see as some of the benefits of coursework for teaching, learning and assessment:

- it can facilitate active learning on the part of the student;
- it can allow more emphasis to be placed on 'process' as well as product;
- it allows students to develop their ideas without the pressure of a timed examination;
- assessment can be based upon a broader range of characteristics than is possible with a timed external examination alone;
- assessment can be negotiated between teacher and student.

You must submit *one* unit of work. This should be representative of the kind of work you have done during the course. The submission should consist of not more than three sheets or mounts, maximum size A1. As an alternative to one of the A1-size sheets, you may submit a sketchbook no larger than A3 in size.

A unit of work is defined as:

> A finished painting or artefact with appropriate development work; a set of studies showing the development of a project or theme; graphic or photographic material developed in accordance with the requirements of the syllabus.

In the case of three-dimensional work, photographic evidence of finished pieces is acceptable so long as a scale is indicated. *A coursework submission consisting solely of photographs or solely of written material or a combination of both is not acceptable.*

While you may wish to concentrate your studies in the specialist areas indicated by the syllabus, *it is expected that the coursework submitted will reflect a broadly based concern with the nature of art and design*. It is equally acceptable for you to work *across* the specialist areas of the syllabus where this is felt to be appropriate. In such cases the examiners will have regard to your breadth of understanding in terms of syllabus content.

Coursework is to be accompanied by a statement, signed by you and countersigned by your teacher, stating that the work has been produced with no external assistance beyond the normal support provided by a teacher in accordance with the regulations.

You are responsible for selecting your submission but your teacher may give guidance if requested.

Critical/historical study This compulsory part of the course gives you two options. You can either submit a sketchbook/notebook of annotated drawings, paintings, prints or your own photographs, of historical/critical material relevant to your specific area of study. Or you can submit a dissertation of between 2,000 and 3,000 words or produce a slide/cassette programme or video on an appropriate topic relevant to your specific area(s) of study.

Externally set paper The paper will be directly related to the areas of study listed for the A-level syllabus and you will be required to answer *one* question from *one* area of study. Exactly the same requirements apply for both A-level and AS (see beginning of chapter).

Preparatory/supporting work You must submit not more than *two* mounts (maximum size A1) of preparatory/supporting studies. The requirements are identical to the A-level requirements mentioned earlier in the chapter.

WELSH JOINT EDUCATION COMMITTEE (WJEC)

A-LEVEL AND AS ART AND DESIGN

If you are studying for the WJEC A-level examination in art and design, you will almost certainly be living in Wales and it is highly likely that you will have studied for the WJEC Art and Design GCSE. If this is the case, you should be well prepared for your A-level course as there is a high degree of continuity between syllabuses. You will find, for example, that the assessment objectives are identical for both syllabuses. This means that for all practical pruposes the *same* qualities and skills will be examined, although, as you would expect, the **level** of performance is expected to be higher at Advanced-level.

The WJEC syllabus is also extremely helpful in that it provides, right at the beginning of the document, detailed information about the **context** and **rationale** for the subject and the examination. As we have stressed elsewhere in this book, it is vital that you become familiar with the intentions of the syllabus as soon as possible and time spent studying these sections will not be wasted. By doing this you will begin to understand the **spirit** or **philosophy** of the syllabus and examination. That is, you will begin to understand the beliefs and intentions of those responsible for drafting the syllabus in terms of the educational value of following an Advanced-level course in art and design

Aims

These values are expressed more formally in the Aims, which present an almost idealised view of what can be achieved by studying art and design. You must bear in mind that his view is, for most people, an impossible goal and is perhaps what many artists spend a lifetime trying to achieve.

Assessment objectives

However, the Assessment Objectives *do* specify what you must achieve in order to do well in the examination and it is with an understanding of these that you will be best placed to tackle your work. Your final submission will need to meet these objectives through the various components of the examination. Each component will stress some objectives more than others, but your *total* submission will need to have regard to all of them. Remember that your art and design teacher will be on hand to advise you, and to ensure that the various objectives are covered during the course and that the externally set tests are designed in such a way that some objectives will be dealt with in detail.

For example, the WJEC stresses that the Investigative Study is primarily concerned with teaching and learning experiences in the critical/contextual domain of art and design. Although, for example, drawing and/or design work may form part of the study, it should be remembered that these are abilities which can be more fully demonstrated in other parts of the examination submission. If the study is to be presented mainly in visual form, it must be accompanied by verbal and/or written material which explains and supports the visual evidence. It is not intended that the Investigative Study should duplicate evidence of learning which can be more appropriately assessed in other sections of the examination scheme.

Scheme of assessment

These matters will be discussed in more detail later, but for the moment let us look at what is actually required of you by the end of the course (Table 10.13).

To satisfy the requirements of the examination each candidate will need to submit the following:

- three coursework units comprising:
  Personal Record
  Two other units
- controlled practical test in drawing and painting;

	ASSESSMENT COMPONENTS	MARKS	ADMINSTRATIVE PROCEDURES
Coursework	**Coursework units** a) Personal Record and b) Two Units of Work	25	Selected from work undertaken over a substantial period of the course Selected from the course of study
Controlled Tests	**Drawing and Painting** Analytical/Observational/ Compositional study	25	Subjects will be issued early in March with completion date at end of May. Date specified for first 3 hours. Record of time spent on actual test to be included with submission
	Design and Practice Design problem	25	As above
Controlled Test or Coursework	**Critical Studies** *Either* a) Written examination *or* b) Investigative Study	25	3-hour written examination on specified date *or* A study which should be conducted over a sub- stantial period of time and which would follow on from a taught course. It may follow as suggested format and is to be submitted by mid-June
	TOTAL	100	

Table 10.13 Scheme of assessment (reproduced by permission of the WJEC).

- controlled practical test in Design and Practice;
- *either* written Examination in Critical Studies;
- *or* an Investigative Study in Critical studies completed as coursework.

WORK REQUIREMENTS AND PRACTICES

To help you to make a start on the work required for the examination we will cover each component through the 'eyes' of a typical student following a two-year course leading up to the final examination or Controlled Tests. We will not cover all the **practices** which are outlined in the syllabus content, but many of these can be found elsewhere in the book, even if they are referred to in another board's syllabus.

Remember that there is a high level of agreement between examiners and teachers from all boards about what constitutes **good practice**. You can be confident that as long as you understand the basic requirements of your own examination, the advice given elsewhere in the book will be of help to you.

COURSEWORK SUBMISSION

Your coursework submission must consist of three units of work, one of which is to be a Personal Record. The other two units of work must be selected from one or more of the following areas:

- Drawing and Painting;
- Graphics;
- Textiles;
- Three-dimensional Studies;
- Critical Studies;
- Inter-disciplinary Studies.

Additionally, you have the option of meeting the Critical Studies requirement of the syllabus through an Investigative Study treated as part of your coursework. This is done instead of the three-hour written examination, but we shall come to this later in the chapter.

The course

Before we discuss the three units of work in detail it is perhaps worth considering what the course actually consists of. For example, because the examination requires three units of work, this does *not* mean that you need only produce three pieces of work in two years! In you have accepted the idea of **working in depth** mentioned in Chapters 1 and 2, this will be obvious to you by now. Having developed a **sound working habit**, you should have a substantial body of work from which to select your examination submission.

For most A-level art and design students the **structure** of their course will largely be determined by their art and design teacher. After all, this is part of the teacher's professional responsibility and such a responsibility includes decisions about which examination syllabus to follow. What is interesting about art and design as opposed to many other subjects is that the **content** of the course is often determined by the student's own interests and aptitudes. If you have successfully followed a GCSE art and design course, you should by now have a reasonable idea of what these interests and aptitudes are. In reality you will almost certainly be building upon these as you embark upon your A-level course.

The art and design **practice(s)** you pursue will largely be determined by the resources available in your school or college and the expertise of your teacher(s). You could hardly expect one individual to be accomplished in all six areas of the syllabus, so it is likely that your choice will be limited to some extent. In some schools and colleges you may be taught by more than one teacher and this may well widen your choice. However, do not be misled into believing that a limited range of practices will limit your chances of success in the examination. This is just not so. The total coursework submission is designed to allow you to demonstrate a wide range of approaches to your work and this is quite possible *within* one practice, or a small number of them. If you refer to the ULSEB A-level 'Syllabus Framework' section, you should be able to see how a wide range of processes and procedures can be accomplished within any one of the practices.

The WJEC's Teachers' Guide explains the significance of coursework relative to the Controlled Tests and describes the potential scope of the work.

> Whatever form the coursework takes, it is important that it should provide clear evidence of learning experiences which are not easily undertaken within the controlled tests, so that the whole examination submission should address the full range of assessment objectives. it is not intended that the coursework should replicate the kind of work undertaken for the controlled tests. It is expected that full advantage will be taken of the opportunities presented in coursework to explore a range of innovatory approaches to teaching and learning. The integrative character of the subject area should be fully utilised and, where appropriate, interdisciplinary and cross-curricular work may extend into related areas of the curriculum.
>
> Coursework also provides an opportunity for candidates to investigate the important role played by the subject area in community life and within the field of industry and commerce.

You can see from this that your teacher has been given considerable freedom to devise a **course structure** to satisfy these requirements and no doubt this will be discussed with you as the course progresses.

PERSONAL RECORD

The Personal Record is intended to demonstrate your response to the environment and can take the form of a visual diary, two or three sketchbooks, design notebooks or other appropriate recording method. The record should be maintained throughout the course and you should interpret 'the environment' in the widest possible sense. The board states that:

> . . . candidates are well advised to maximise on the richness of direct, first-hand source material which surrounds us. It is a complete resource for gathering information which may trigger off an idea for further development within a particular discipline.

In a sense, the Personal Record will represent what is most uniquely yours in terms of art and design work. It can show your obsessions and your preoccupations with the world around you. It can represent a narrow focus of interest or a wide-ranging exploration of ideas and feelings.

Whichever approach you decide to follow, it is important that the study should be structured and sustained and not simply a collection of random notes and sketches. This will require you to consider very carefully *why* you are pursuing this kind of work. We would strongly advise you to discuss this with your teacher before you start, so that you feel confident about the approach you are taking.

Many if not most artists and designers have kept personal records in the form of sketchbooks or notebooks, illustrated diaries or journals. These are often much more revealing about their ideas and concerns than the 'finished' works displayed in galleries and museums.

For example, the studies from the sketchbooks of HENRY MOORE (1898 – 1986) (Fig. 10.15) show very clearly how he struggled to resolve the problems of **form** in his sculptures through the medium of drawing.

The Personal Record can be both a means of **recording** information and a **source** for **developing** ideas. It can act as a unique database for your own work and can serve to communicate your ideas to others, including the examiners. As a record of your everyday experience over two years, it gives an important insight into your outlook and lifestyle. This is why it has such an important role as part of your examination submission.

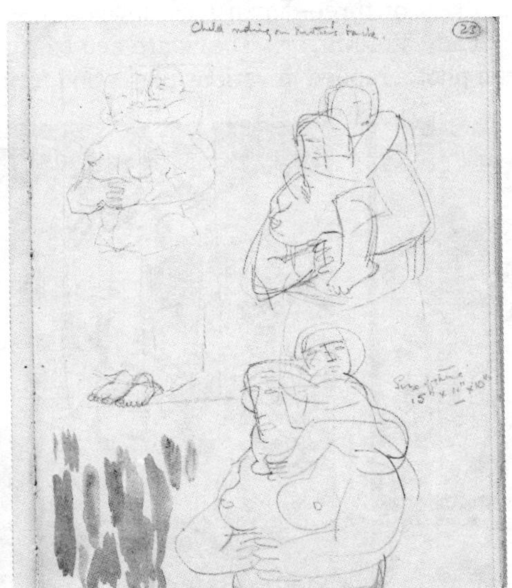

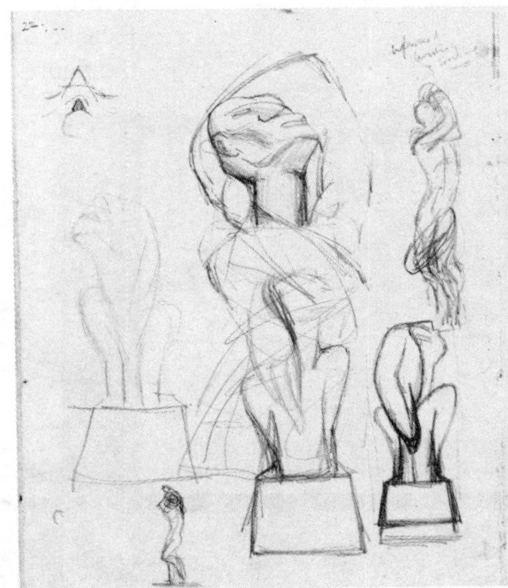

Fig. 10.15 Studies from Henry Moore's sketchbooks. (c. Henry Moore Foundation (1990) Reproduced by kind permission of the Henry Moore Foundation)

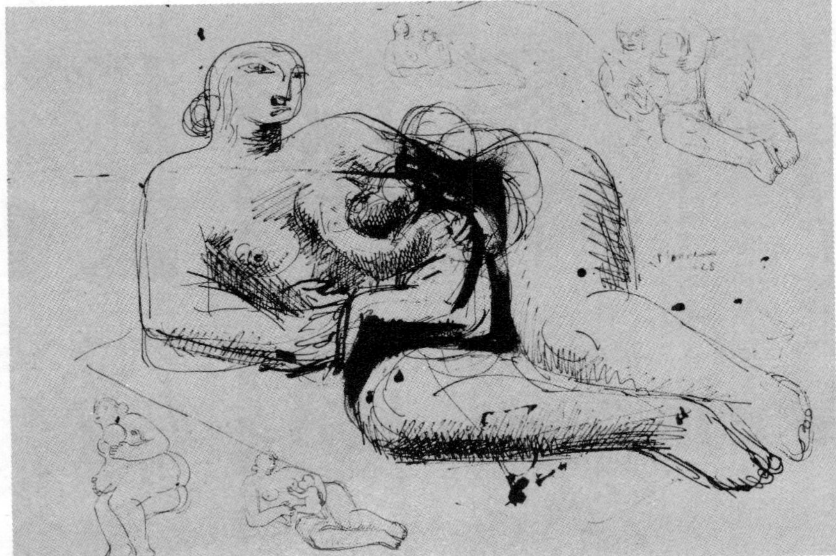

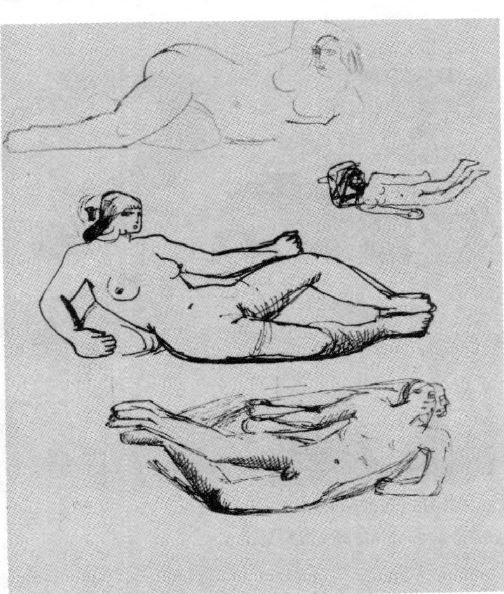

TWO UNITS OF WORK

For the purposes of the examination, your two units of work are selected from the work you have undertaken during the whole course. You should discuss this with your teacher(s) at the appropriate time as they will be in the best position to advise you about the suitability of your work relative to the assessment requirements of the examination.

For example, if you are determined to produce an **expressive response** to the Design and Practice Controlled Test at the end of the course, then you must provide evidence of your ability to work to a specific design brief in one of your units of coursework.

Each unit of work should consist of a minimum of two and a maximum of four mounted sheets not exceeding 520 mm × 635 mm in size. Three-dimensional work should be submitted in the form of photographs.

Other forms of submission are acceptable, such as videos and computer-generated images, but the board should be consulted if specialist equipment will be needed to view the work.

We mentioned earlier that one of the purposes of the coursework submission was that it could provide evidence of learning experiences which are not easily undertaken in the Controlled Tests. The example we have chosen is very firmly within this category. Our 'typical' student has been working within the Drawing and Painting area of the syllabus and is particularly interested in developing an idea which combines the work of other artists, styles and periods and which transforms the original work into a unique personal statement.

Having researched the work of PABLO PICASSO (1881 – 1973), PAUL SIGNAC (1863 – 1935) and other artists our student has explored a number of possibilities through sketches, notes and colour studies. The final expression of the idea is produced in the form shown in Fig. 10.16. A series of three-dimensional images are produced, loosely based upon Picasso's painting 'Lady at a Mirror'. The figure and background have been painted, then the figure has been photographed in various poses and from various angles and distances.

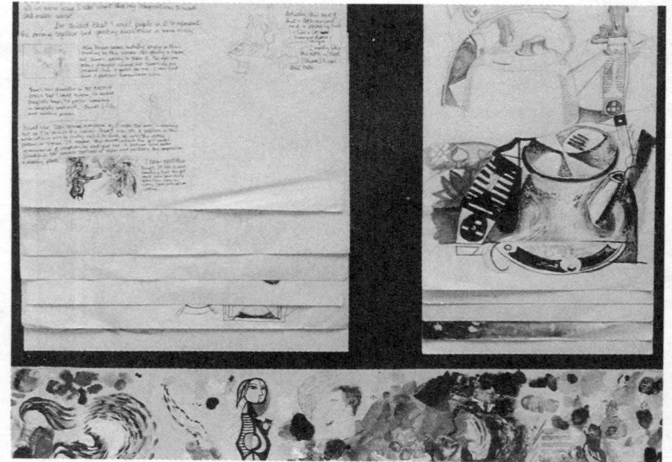

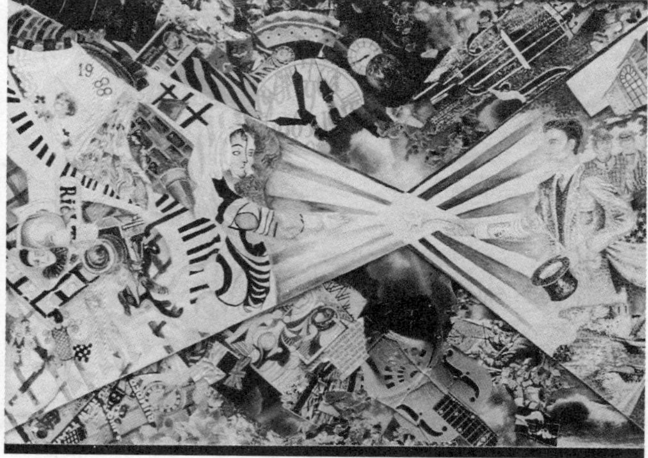

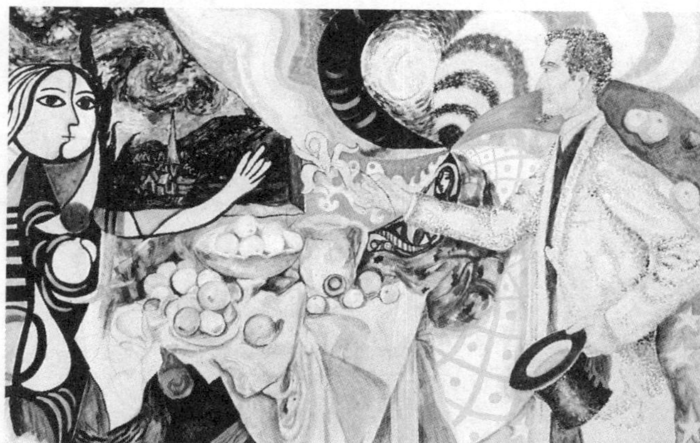

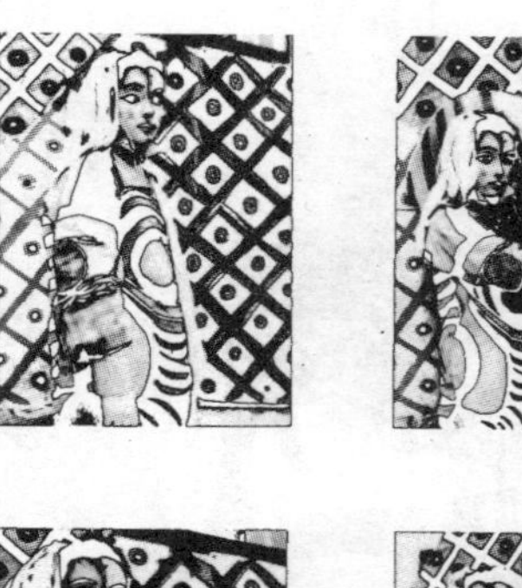

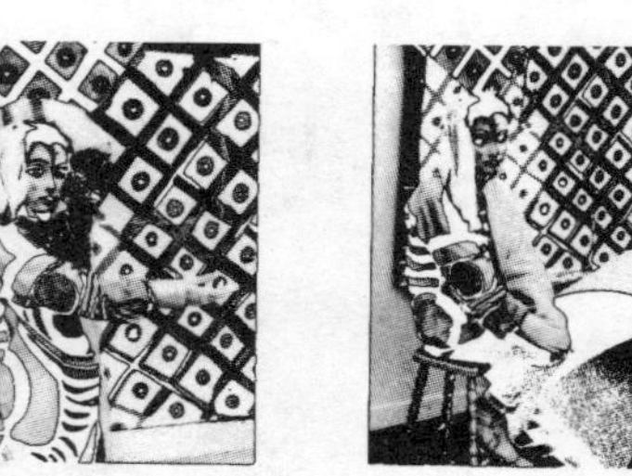

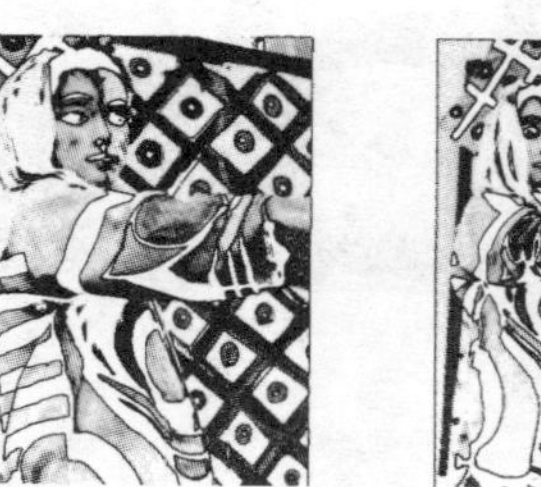

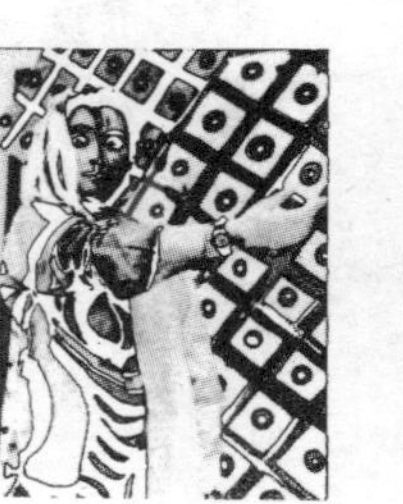

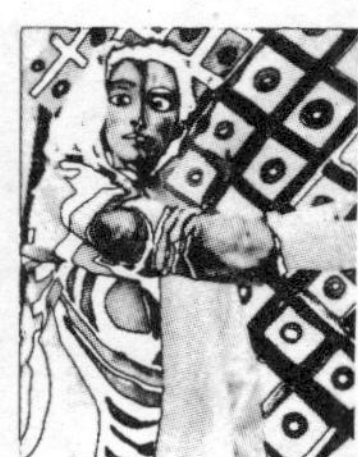

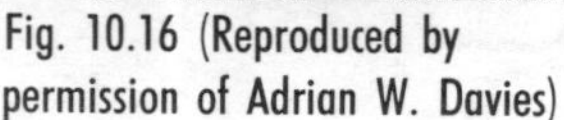

Fig. 10.16 (Reproduced by permission of Adrian W. Davies)

The work differs from the more conventional approach to 'making art' through the representation of three-dimensional forms on a two-dimensional surface. We are presented with the possibility of combining the visual and performing arts, something which Picasso himself did with his costumes and sets for Diaghilev and the Ballet Russe in the early 1920s.

As we mentioned earlier, the **content** of your coursework submission is largely for you to decide, supported and guided by your teacher. We hope that the range and scope of the examples shown throughout this book will encourage you to take a positive and open-minded attitude to what is possible during your course.

CONTROLLED TEST

Drawing and painting

The Drawing and Painting controlled test is designed to test your ability through observation, analysis or composition in the medium or media of your choice.

The board will issue an examination paper in early March and will specify a date for the first three hours of the examination. There is no limit to the time you can take to complete your work but you must keep a record of the time spent.

You must answer *one* question selected from the following four sections:

- Man-made and Natural Objects;
- Environmental Subjects;
- The Human Figure;
- Themes for Composition.

Within these sections topics will be set which are intended to relate to your experience and environment as well as providing stimulus for imaginative and expressive work. Your supporting work must be included with your submission.

No doubt you will have done work within some, if not all, of these sections in the past, even if they have not been expressed in these terms to you before. They represent traditional and long-standing concerns of artists of all kinds and there is a wealth of information available for you to research.

To indicate the wide range of options open to you we have reproduced the WJEC Specimen Paper for the Drawing and Painting Controlled Test in full below.

DRAWING and PAINTING

Candidates are required to answer *one* question from the following.

1 Assemble a collection of items from *one* or more of the groups below:
a) Natural things and man-made things.
b) Equipment used in pot-holing or rock climbing.
c) Stuffed birds or animals.
d) Make-up paraphernalia.

Study the objects carefully, then, using any medium or combination of media:
either build up several sheets of analytical studies based on your investigations,
or where appropriate set up a formal still-life group from these objects and make a composition based on your studies.

2 Select from *one* of the following subjects:
a) Allotments
b) Scrap yard
c) Churchyard
d) Stationary vehicles.

Study the subjects carefully, then using any medium or combination of media:
either build up several sheets of analytical studies based on your investigations,
or make a finished statement on your chosen topic, supported by preparatory study sheets.

3 Study the figure posed for you as follows:
A seated figure, dressed in denims and leather jacket, holding a crash helmet.
Using any medium or combination of media:
either make a single study of the figure,
or make a study of the model's face,
or build up several sheets of analytical study of parts or the whole of the figure viewed from different positions, distances and lighting conditions.

4 After researching the subject fully and compiling relevant preparatory study, all of which will be part of the submitted work, make a composition in any medium or combination of media to illustrate *one* of the following subjects:
   a) Façades
   b) Chiaroscuro
   c) Trying on hats
   d) Crisis
   e) Close-up
   f) Demonstration
   g) A composition based on the whole or part of the following quotation:

> At last she collapsed in the bitter earth. Her hands touched something hard and cold. When she cleared away the leaves she found the iron ring of a trap door. For sometime there had been silence, as though the soldiers had lost her; but now again she heard them crashing through the undergrowth, close behind her. She tugged at the ring with all her strength but it would not give. A shadow fell across the fallen leaves. She closed her eyes, expecting everything to explode inside her head. Then she looked up into the frightened face of a small boy.
>
> 'The White Hotel' by D. M. THOMAS
>
> (Reproduced by permission of the WJEC)

Like all other Advanced-level art and design syllabuses the WJEC examination stresses the importance of the role of drawing and painting in underpinning the whole range of activities which can be undertaken within the subject. In the Controlled Test the examiners will be looking for accuracy of observation, analysis and recording, but of equal importance will be your ability to demonstrate through the preparatory/supporting work your understanding of structure, form and compositional issues. In fact, you should begin to recognise that these qualities are achievable only with practice exercised through working in depth. Experienced teachers and examiners are well able to identify in students' work whether or not they have studied with **serious intent**. Such work demonstrates vitality, a willingness to take risks and sometimes to 'fail', but above all the work will show signs of struggle and real visual inquiry, which seeks to get at the **essence** of the subject matter which is being observed.

Design and practice

Exactly the same requirements apply to this component as to the Drawing and Painting Controlled Test in terms of the length of time and the amount of work allowed.

You must answer *one* question chosen from one of the following headings;

- Graphics;
- Textiles;
- Three-dimensional Design.

You can choose to respond in an expressive way to this component, but if you do, one of your coursework units must be done in answer to a specific design brief.

There are a wide range of practices which you can carry out under the three headings. The one you choose to some extent would depend on what you have been doing during the course, so you should discuss this with your teacher when you see the question paper.

Under the Graphics heading there will be questions relating to:

- advertising design;
- packaging design;
- computer graphics;
- printmaking;
- illustration;
- letterforms;
- photography;
- film and video.

Under the Textiles heading is:

- knitted textiles;
- embroidery;
- printed textiles;
- fashion and costume.

Under the Three-dimensional Design heading is:

- sculpture;
- jewellery;
- ceramics;
- product and industrial design;
- theatre design.

UNDERSTANDING THE BRIEF

Whichever question you choose the key to success is to thoroughly understand the brief and to understand the requirements which you will have to meet in order to provide a satisfactory solution. To help you tackle this problem, it is often very useful to simply **list** the requirements to ensure that each one is covered as you proceed through your research. We mentioned earlier in the book the value of brainstorming or listing and grouping ideas around a central theme before you actually start work. This is particularly useful when tackling a design brief because it gives you the **range** of activities which might be possible and a **range** of ideas which you can select from and experiment with as you tackle the central problem.

Gradually, you should be able to refine your range of ideas down to the one which is most suitable in answering the brief. Do not worry too much at this stage about the quality of your drawings but be more concerned about the range of ideas you are able to consider. For example, you may be noting ideas which involve the use of words, diagrams, illustrations, annotated drawings, colour sketches and any suitable means of recording and communicating your ideas.

Remember that the examiners are as much concerned about *how* your ideas develop as they are with the final work itself, so these recordings, notes and sketches are extremely important in letting you convey to the examiner how you reached your final work.

Three-dimensional design (Product design)

To illustrate this method of approach our 'typical' student has chosen a question from the Three-dimensional Design section of the Controlled Test. Our student is particularly interested in Product Design and has chosen a question from this section.

> An art and craft enterprise workshop has been set up in your locality and you have been asked to design a range of small decorative containers which are to be produced using fairly basic equipment. Produce design sheets, which include an indication of production methods, and make a prototype or prototypes of the containers.

TACKLING THE QUESTION (PREPARATORY/SUPPORTING STUDIES)

Timing your Preparatory Studies

It is very important to plan your work or provide a work schedule for your preparatory supporting studies. There is no point in gathering lots of information and material if you do not allow yourself time to make full use of them. Bear in mind that some factors will be dictated to you and you will have little control over them, such as the school timetable, holidays and the need to complete projects in other subject areas. You should discuss this matter with your teacher before embarking upon your work so that you can set yourself a timetable and try to stick to it.

Analysing the Design Brief

It is very important at this stage to understand exactly what the brief requires you to do.

This particular brief is quite open-ended in its requirements. You are asked to produce a small range of decorative containers, but the brief does not say what these containers should actually contain, so presumably this is left to your discretion. The brief does say that the containers must be decorative and you will have to determine your own form of decoration.

You are asked to produce design sheets which indicate the way the containers will be made and you are also asked to produce a prototype or model of one, or a number of the containers. It is probably helpful to divide the problem into two specific areas. That is a) the design of the container and b) the decorative form that the container should take. However, it is most important that you do not treat the two aspects of the problem in isolation. There should be integration between the design of the container and the decorative form applied to it or included as part of it.

Designs for the container

Having decided that because the workshop has only basic equipment the container needs to be relatively simple, our student decides that they should be basic geometric shapes – that is, cylinders and cubes of various sizes. Her research showed that these shapes were readily available in the form of cardboard packaging of one kind or another and this led her to the decision that the final object should be made from cardboard.

Forms of decoration

During the early part of the course our student had studied a unit concerned with the idea of rhythms and forces. She was particularly interested in the way growth was represented in the form of grain in wood or strata in rocks, or the way in which grasses, waves and currents in water could be represented by drawing in a linear way. As part of the research for this work she had discovered the early work of the Dutch artist PIET MONDRIAN (1872 – 1944). Mondrian's later work was very formal, geometric and abstract (Fig. 10.17) but early work, particularly paintings of trees (Fig. 10.18) had a rhythmic quality which our student was very interested in. Using these studies she developed series of sketches and drawings which were gradually refined until a range of possible solutions was

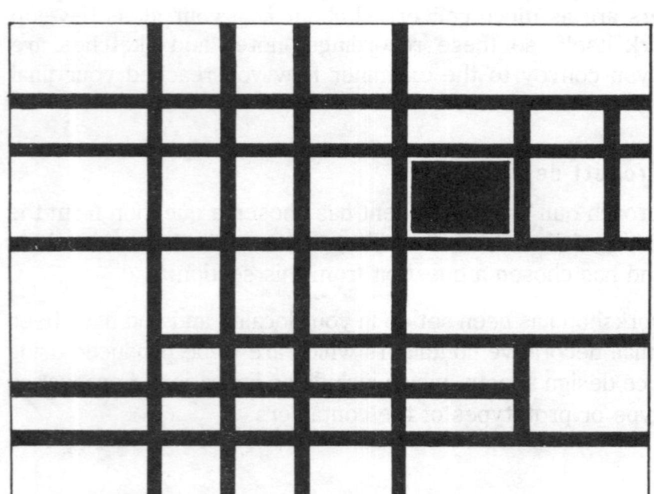

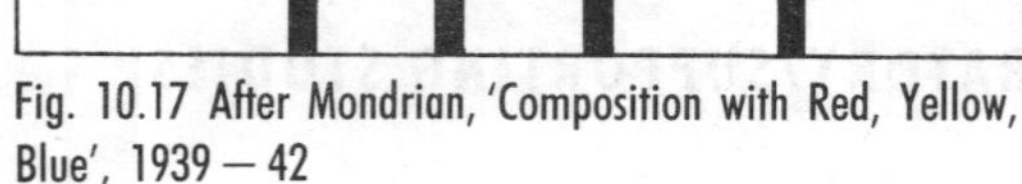

Fig. 10.17 After Mondrian, 'Composition with Red, Yellow, Blue', 1939 – 42

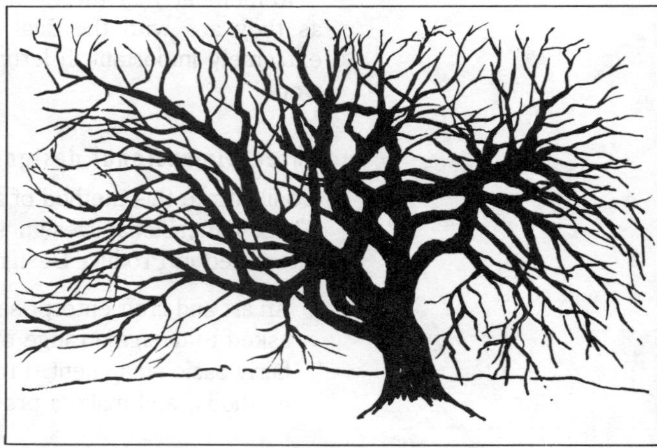

Fig. 10.18 After Mondrian, 'The Red Tree', 1909 – 10

presented (Fig 10.19). Having recognised the decorative qualities of Mondrian's later work, based largely on geometric grids bounded by black lines, our student decided to produce a series of similar studies (Fig. 10.20). These studies suggested that there was potential for different methods of approach in terms of producing the containers. For example, wooden containers could be made using a circular saw, with straight cuts used to decorate the surface. Decorative circles could be produced by simply drilling holes of different sizes. This effect could also be achieved by cutting and drilling acrylic sheet, commonly known as perspex, which has interesting decorative qualities of its own. These materials also have the additional advantage of being relatively cheap and easy to work (see Fig. 10.21)

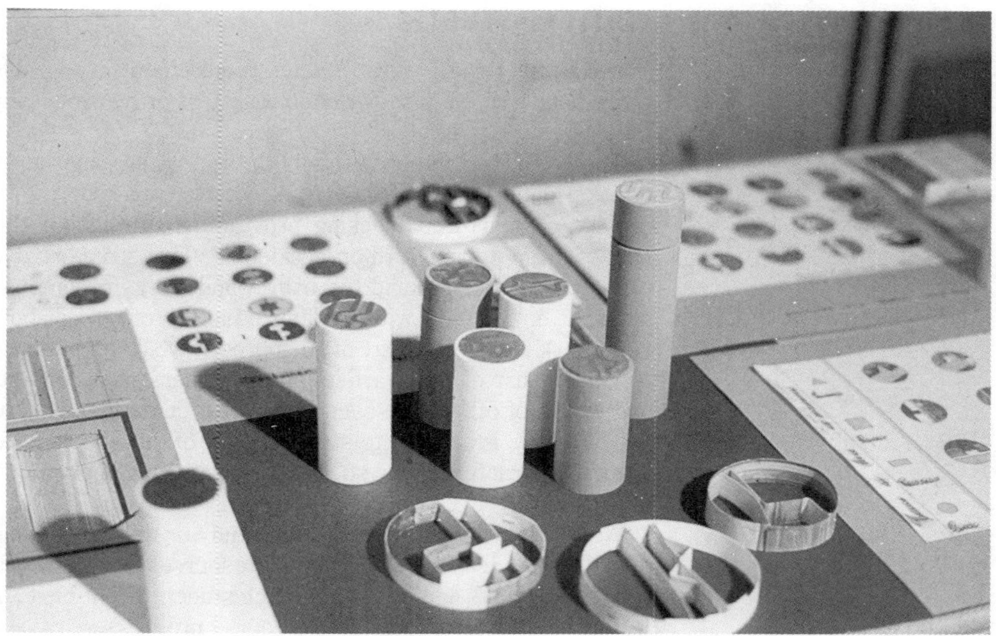

Fig. 10.19

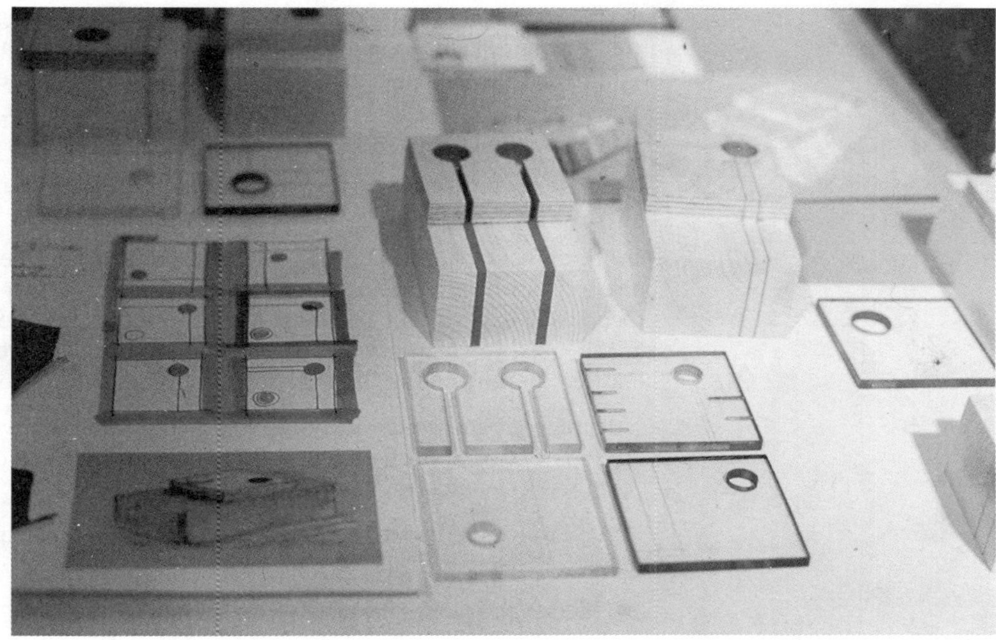

Fig. 10.20

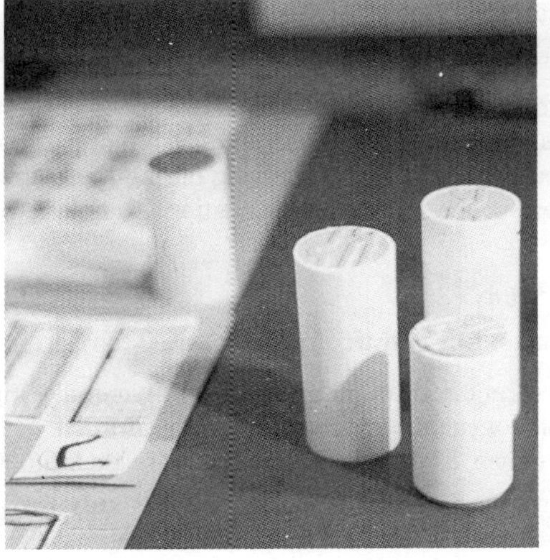

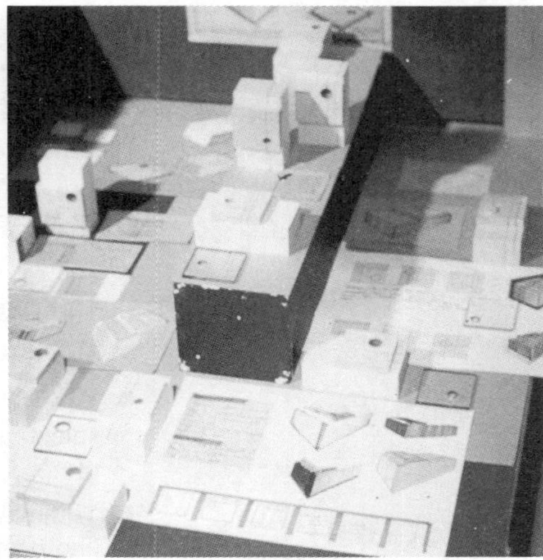

Fig. 10.21

CRITICAL STUDIES

You can meet the Critical Studies requirement in two different ways, either through a three-hour written paper or controlled test or by producing coursework in the form of an Investigative Study.

The WJEC recommends that both the written paper and the Investigative Study should develop out of a **taught course**. This means that the board expects your teacher to provide a structured teaching programme throughout the course so that your critical studies are not haphazard or 'accidental'. This structure does not mean that you will need to learn lots of dates and the names and works of famous artists in chronological order, as might be the case with traditional history of art syllabuses. The 'historical' element of your work is only one part of an approach which might include criticism (of both your own work and that of other artists and designers) and contextual studies, where your work and works of others are seen in a social, cultural and economic context.

The WJEC is at pains to stress that all of this should be **integrated** with your practical work in a structured way so that the relationship between the two is both meaningful and interesting.

Whether you do an Investigative Study or the written paper will depend upon a number of factors, such as the availability of resources, timetable allocation, the size of your group and the interests and aspirations each student might have. You will no doubt discuss these factors with your teacher as the course progresses.

The board recommends that an Introductory or General Study Course of between twelve and fourteen weeks at the beginning of the sixth form will help to 'set the scene' for your studies and allow you to consider the scope or range of alternatives open to you. From this introduction you may develop ideas or themes in greater depth and these may well provide the basis for the Investigative Study or for the period(s) you choose for the written paper. With this approach it may well be possible for you and your teacher to 'tailor' a programme of work most suited to your needs.

Controlled Test

The three-hour paper is divided into two parts. Part One allows you to put forward a personal viewpoint or idea on historical or contemporary issues relating to your own practice and experience. You must answer one question from this section and take about an hour to write your answer. To give you some idea of the kinds of questions you might be asked, here is one of the questions from the WJEC Specimen Paper.

> All art, craft and design work belongs to the culture in which it was produced. Discuss this in relation to work which you have actually seen and consider how it applies to your own work, using sketches where appropriate.

Part Two of the paper requires that you answer three questions from one or more of the following sections:

- Medieval Britain (including Celtic culture);
- Renaissance Europe;
- Baroque and Rococo (Holland, France and Spain);
- The Nineteenth Century (Britain and France);
- The Modern World.

You should take about forty minutes to answer each of the three questions in this section.

Whether you choose to answer questions from one or more sections depends upon the period or periods you have been studying during the course. However, the paper should provide sufficient scope for all three questions to be answered from one section.

Investigative Study

The basic **submission requirements** of the study are as follows:

- You will be required to undertake a first-hand investigation of a chosen subject, selected in consultation with the teacher. If it is mainly in written form, it should be of not less than 2,000 words and not more than 5,000 words.
- You may use any method of illustration that **substantially** contributes to the study; photocopies should not be used indiscriminately.

- The study should amount to no more than thirty sides of written and/or illustrative material, including title page, contents page and bibliography.
- You must submit an outline of your proposal to the WJEC for approval.

Bear in mind that your study should satisfy the assessment objectives of the syllabus which are appropriate to the Critical Study component. The study should demonstrate your ability to:

- show a personal response to a stimulus;
- sustain your study from conception to realisation;
- work independently;
- analyse an idea, theme, subject or concept;
- identify and solve problems;
- show a critical appreciation of artefacts of an historical, cultural or personal nature and communicate this appreciation by suitable means.

Structure of study

To ensure that the assessment objectives are met the board suggests the following outline structure for the study, regardless of the title chosen.

A Statement of the subject to be investigated. Reasons for selecting the subject for study. Statement of the problem(s) to be considered. Reference to the parameters set for the study.
B Process of the investigation. Identifying and collecting the information.
C Selection, preparation and presentation of information – which should include written material and some of the following: drawings, photographs, explanatory diagrams, plans, annotated sketches, etc.
D Inferences drawn from the study and conclusions reached.

Your teacher will want to monitor your study as it progresses and will no doubt give you guidance on the structure as set out above.

Choice of topic or theme

We have already mentioned how the structure of your Critical Studies Course might suggest possible topics or themes for your Investigative Study. But regardless of this, you must ensure that you have the resources available to carry out the study to a successful conclusion. There is little point in choosing a topic which is either too broad or too narrow in content, because if you do, you will have either too much information or too little to handle.

You may well have your own views about suitable areas for research but the WJEC does provide some examples of possible titles. Bear in mind that the most important factor in coming to a decision is that the topic chosen should lend itself to **first-hand personal investigation**. You can see from the example chosen that first-hand personal investigation should not be difficult for a student who lives in such a town.

Title: 'Shopfronts in the Main Street of a South Wales Valley Town'.

A

Statement of the problem:
The study will seek to illustrate that the present commercial developments have taken place mainly at Ground Floor level, and that the historical/architectural influences of the original design have remained unchanged at Upper Floor levels.
Stated more succinctly, the problem may be posed as follows; Why are the Upper Floors of the shops in this town different from those at street level?
Reasons for selecting the subject:
To investigate the influence of commercial enterprise on the street architecture of a local community.
To examine the visual evidence in relation to the historical development.
To consider the influence of building materials and techniques now and in the past.

B
Survey of the locality, to include:

i) Number and type of present buildings and the purposes they serve. Design of shopfronts, uniformity and diversity of style, historical architectural influences. 'House' styles, logos, symbols, graphic images.
ii) Collection of information.
Observational drawing, photographs, interviews. Reference material – old photographs, prints, plans, annotated sketches of shopfronts.

C
Selection, organisation and presentation of information to illustrate the various aspects of the subject, which may include classification of architectural details, roots of stylistic influences and relationships between marketing image and shopfront design.
The format of presentation could range from a study which contains mainly written material with supportive illustrative evidence, to a study which presents the major part of its evidence in visual form supported by explanatory written information.

D
Inferences which may be drawn from the evidence of the investigation.
Conclusions reached in respect of the stated problem.
Bibliography and References.
All references are to be duly acknowledged and a bibliography included where appropriate.

(Reproduced by permission of the WJEC)

ADVANCED SUPPLEMENTARY SYLLABUS

The WJEC AS syllabus is identical to the A-level syllabus. The differences occur in the scheme of assessment, so you can feel confident that any guidance given for the A-level will be appropriate to AS.

However, you should understand that there are differences between A-level and AS. For example, AS is intended to require half the study time of A-level. The grades awarded will be related to grade standards at A-level but, for entrance requirement purposes, will be worth half an A-level grade.

AS is intended to **broaden** the sixth-form curriculum and allow students to pursue subjects which would not normally be available to them.

The principle of **breadth** is central to the philosophy of the syllabus. However, breadth does not mean, for example, that you must do a print, a painting, a piece of sculpture, etc. Instead, it is concerned with a broad understanding of the subject, even if all your work is in one medium. If this is not clear to you it is important that you discuss the matter with your teacher.

Scheme of assessment

The scheme of assessment outlined in Table 10.14 indicates the requirements for the examination. The principle is that the requirements are half that of the A-level and you will note that the marks available for each component reflect the different emphasis at AS.

	ASSESSMENT COMPONENTS	MARKS	ADMINSTRATIVE PROCEDURES
Controlled Test	*One* test selected from *either* Drawing and Painting *or* Design and Practice **Drawing and Painting** Analytical/Observational/ Compositional Study **Design and Practice** Design Problem	30	Subjects will be issued early in March with completion date at end of May. Date specified for first 3 hours. Record of time spent on actual test to be included with submission

	ASSESSMENT COMPONENTS	MARKS	ADMINSTRATIVE PROCEDURES
Controlled Test *or* Coursework	**Critical Studies** *Either* a) Written Examination *or* b) Investigative Study	25	1-hour written examination on specified date *or* A study which should be conducted over a substantial period of time and which would follow on from a taught course. It may follow a suggested format and is to be submitted by mid-June
Coursework	**Coursework Units** a) Personal Record and b) Two Units of Work	45	Selected from work undertaken over a substantial period of the course *and* Selected from the course of study

Table 10.14 Scheme of assessment AS-level.

To satisfy the requirements of the examination you will therefore need to submit the following:

- a controlled practical test in *either* Drawing and Painting *or* in Design and Practice;
- *either* a written examination in Critical Studies;
- *or* an Investigative Study in Critical Studies completed as coursework;
- three coursework units comprising:
  Personal Record
  Two other units.

ART HISTORY SYLLABUSES

PICKING AND MIXING

MULTI-DIMENSIONAL STUDIES

INDIVIDUAL STUDY OR DISSERTATION

'QUESTION AND ANSWER' PAPERS

BEING CRITICAL

EXERCISES

GETTING STARTED

Some exam boards have syllabuses in Art History alone, in addition to their syllabuses for practical Art and Design (which may, of course, include Art History options).

Not all the syllabuses which are the basis of this chapter are called 'Art History'. What they are called, and which boards run these syllabuses, is shown in Table 11.1

EXAMINING BOARD	NAME OF SYLLABUS
AEB	History of Art 606
Brief description Paper 1: six options, grouping periods and movements in art and design; you choose *one* to study and answer questions from. (Time allowed 3 hours.) Paper 2: three parts; your questions must cover all three parts. (Time allowed: 3 hours.) Each paper carries equal marks; Part one of Paper 2 carries 40 per cent of the marks for that paper. You must take both papers in your examination. *There are no restrictions upon you taking this syllabus with any of the AEB practical A-level examinations in Art and Design.*	
Cambridge	Historical and Critical 9311
Brief description There are three parts to the examination. Papers 3 and 4 are compulsory; you have a choice between Papers 1 and 2. Paper 1 and Paper 2: these papers between them cover art and design from the earliest times to the year 1900, as well as across a wide range of cultures. (Time allowed: 3 hours for each.) Paper 3: Western Art, Architecture and Design since 1900. (Time allowed: 3 hours.) Paper 4: individual study. A 3,000–4,000-word extended essay carried out during your course of study. Each Paper carries equal marks. *There are no restrictions upon you taking this syllabus with the Cambridge Art and Design A-level examination.*	
Oxford	History of Art 9893
Brief description There are three compulsory papers. Paper 1: general paper. (Time allowed: 3 hours.) Paper 2: topics paper. (Time allowed: 3 hours.) Paper 3: personal study. 3,000-word work carried out during course of study. Each paper carries equal marks. *There are no restrictions upon you taking this syllabus with the Oxford A-level practical exam, 'Art with Art History'.*	
Ox/Cam	History and Appreciation of Art
Brief description *Current syllabus* There are two compulsory papers. Paper I: Section I History of Architecture and Sculpture; Section II History of Painting. Two questions from each section must be attempted. (Time allowed: 3 hours.) Paper II: Art and Design in Everyday Life. Four questions must be attempted. (Time allowed: 3 hours.)	

EXAMINING BOARD	NAME OF SYLLABUS
	Draft revised syllabus Two papers and a personal study are intended. Personal study – 20 per cent of the total marks for the examination. Approximately 3,000 words on an appropriate art and design topic chosen by you. Paper 1 – 40 per cent of the total marks for the examination. The paper will cover the twentieth century theme. It will contain three sections, one question to be attempted from each. A fourth question must be selected from any of the three sections. (Time allowed: 3 hours.) Paper 2 – 40 per cent of the total marks for the examination. Six themes will cover the history of art and design up to the twentieth century. You must answer four questions, taken from two sections only. (Time allowed: 3 hours.) *This paper, in its original or its planned revised form, can be taken with the examining board's practical Art and Design examinations.*
ULSEB	History of Art 026 *Brief description* There are three compulsory papers. Paper 1: Prescribed Topics in the History of British Art. (Time allowed: 3 hours.) Paper 2: Prescribed Topics in the History of Western Art. (Time allowed: 3 hours.) Paper 3: 5,000-word Dissertation carried out during course of study. *This syllabus cannot be taken with the ULSEB-endorsed Syllabus 027, Art and Design – Critical and Historical Studies.*

Table 11.1

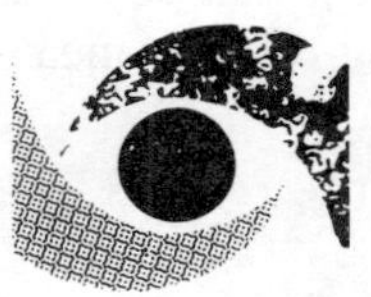

ESSENTIAL PRINCIPLES

PICKING AND MIXING

There are few restrictions on your ability to choose to do both an A-level History of Art and a practical A-level examination in Art and Design in the same year of examination. No matter which examining board you may be using, if they also offer a History of Art A-level examination, you can devise a way of mixing their different types of syllabus in the same year.

Where there *are* restrictions however, they are rather irksome. As we have pointed out all along in this book, we believe that it is most beneficial to accompany your practical work and studies with historical and contextual investigations, even if you are not intending to take an exam option which involves a form of Art History. However, it might be advisable to select such an option where available, as your practical work will benefit as a result of the more extended historical and contextual studies enforced by the Art History syllabus.

This suggestion, that your practical work benefits from the accompanying critical and historical studies, presents a 'chicken and egg' consideration. It seems impossible to say whether it is your personal practical work which allows you to understand more about the history and context of art and design, or whether it is your historical and contextual studies which cause your practical work to improve and develop. Which comes first, the chicken or the egg, is immaterial. The evidence shows that studying on the broad front necessitated when you take both a practical and a historical and contextual examination helps to create a more informed approach to the subject and develop a higher level of skills in *all aspects* of the subject.

This is why we advocate that you should adopt this overall approach in any practical A-level Art and Design examination you may be doing. At the same time, we recommend carrying out some practical work in Art and Design of your own to benefit your Art History studies. This is not to say that you should, or must, sit a practical examination in Art and Design as well as your Art History A-level, but rather that your study in the latter should be 'multi-dimensional'.

MULTI-DIMENSIONAL STUDIES

It is natural to suppose that your studies in Art History will involve:

- reading
- writing
- speaking
- listening

We suggest that they should also include *looking* at:

- videos
- films
- actual works of art
- actual buildings
- actual objects.

This will involve going out to visit museums, galleries, local buildings, shopping arcades and precincts, industries and so on, as well as keeping your eyes and ears open at home and at school.

The benefits of this will be that when you read, you will be able to digest information, just as you can when you listen. When you write, or speak, you can then demonstrate the level of your understanding of the information concerned – but in these instances, the information and the means of communication are bound up in *words*. If this is all that is involved in your studies, then those studies are one-dimensional only, the dimension being that of 'words'.

On the other hand, if you go out 'looking' at the types of information we list above, then the information you obtain is in the form of *visual images, shapes, forms, objects, buildings, environments, colours, textures*, and so on. Even though you might then use words to describe what it is you see and understand, your studies are now more than 'one- dimensional'. To make studies 'multi-dimensional', we suggest that you record and communicate the information you obtain, and your understanding of it, in means other than words alone. That is to say, you might:

- draw
- photograph
- paint
- model

what it is you see. You will then be using the formal aesthetic elements of Art and Design in your own work. As these elements are fundamental to your understanding of the forms and images which are at the centre of your studies, this can only be beneficial to you. Using them as part off your own *means* of study and communication should lead you towards a greater understanding of their presence and effect in the subject matter you are studying for your examination.

This is borne out, we believe, by a central thrust increasingly evident in most of the Art History examinations. Learning history can be done quite adaquately by means of 'words' alone. You can also learn something about critical appreciation by studying the written and spoken criticisms of others, and repeating them yourself. This is quite often done in subjects other than Art History, as well as Art History itself. The question is whether this is what is expected of you here. We think not. We believe that what *is* expected of you is best achieved by introducing a multi-dimensional approach to your studies.

INDIVIDUAL STUDY OR DISSERTATION

Individual Study or Dissertation is central to the type of work expected of you in an Art History examination. Even where an examining board does not have a specific paper of this type in its syllabus, the other papers are interlaced with qualitative criteria which make it clear that a personal, critical attitude is expected in your studies, and not just the learning and regurgitation of facts. In this type of paper, you can choose your own 'topic'. Given the amount of words you can use in this paper, your topic should clearly be *specific* rather than general. For instance, rather than choosing to study the 'Norwich School of Artists', you would be better taking on a more specific aspect of their work, such as 'The Boat Paintings of the Norwich School of Artists'. Or, rather than choosing 'The Work of Paul Cézanne', you would be better off with 'The Watercolour Still Life Paintings of Cézanne'. Again, rather than a subject as broad as 'Georgian Architecture', you could study, perhaps, 'Domestic Georgian Architecture in my Village'. The popular television programme *Mastermind* gives a good example of how a very broad field of knowledge can be sensibly narrowed down into a single aspect. When the contestants specify their chosen subject, the title is often a selection from something much bigger. By this means competitors are able to concentrate their study of their subject so that they can deal fairly comfortably with the type of questions they are likely to receive in the programme. In this section of your exam you are in the same boat, only in your case you are narrowing down the criteria *you* will work to, or the 'questions' *you* will ask yourself, rather than the range of questions someone else will ask you. Because of this, there will come a time when some of the information you uncover, whilst it might be very interesting, will not be relevant to the criteria you are working to in your Dissertation. When that is the case, you must learn to put that particular line of inquiry on one side; otherwise you will confuse your argument and make it difficult to fulfil your work according to the time limit and number of words allowed.

The reason for narrowing down your area of study in this way is not only that the more specific title for your study restricts the range and scope of your work. Your choice of title can also help you to avoid falling into the trap of simply *describing* what exists in your subject. The number of words allowed for your Dissertation or Individual Study can easily be absorbed in describing the extent of your study, if you are not careful. It is therefore essential that you deliver your personal views on and criticism of the subject you are studying as early as possible. The more specific and tightly focused titles suggested above will help you to do this, because they either contain some specific criteria, or they imply suitable criteria so far as the task at hand is concerned. As we have said, it is the establishing and narrowing down of the criteria you work to which is essential in this section of your examination. Only then will your work demonstrate your ability to discover information, use it in an argument, and arrive at some justifiable conclusions. To help you in deciding the form and nature of your final submission, we propose that you broadly adopt the pattern shown in this section when you come to give an initial shape to your work. Of course, as your work develops, it will take on its own momentum and form. Nevertheless, by bearing these factors in mind from the beginning, you are more likely to end up with a result which will satisfy the most rigorous criteria specified in any of the examinations. Your work can be divided into five areas of study.

DESCRIPTION OF THE SUBJECT OF THE TOPIC – APPROXIMATELY 10 PER CENT OF YOUR STUDY

This is the descriptive preamble to your subject. Here you introduce the generalities of your subject as if the examiner knew nothing about it. This should be factually precise and concise. You can keep it short if you avoid *introducing your own opinions into the work at this stage*

OUTLINE OF YOUR INTENTIONS – APPROXIMATELY 5 PER CENT OF YOUR STUDY

Here you should say precisely, and concisely, what is is you are going to do in your study. You will probably find it best if you write this down in your notebook as an account of what it is you have done, before you begin to draw your study together and write it up. By this means you will see how to begin to order your information and intentions. You will have made this fairly easy to do, as it will have been designed to allow you to use the information you have gathered together to work with in your studies.

When you write your Dissertation you will probably find it necessary then to amend what you wrote as your original outline, in order to take into account what actually happened. This does not matter. The examiner will see only the outline in your Dissertation, not the one which helped you to give *shape to your work and to allow you to begin it in the first place.*

CRITICAL ACCOUNT – APPROXIMATELY 75 PER CENT OF YOUR STUDY

This is the main body of your work. You should use historical and contextual information which you have assembled to back up what you say and believe as a result of your investigations. Do not use a lot of space in paraphrasing the views and comments of others, unless it is primary source information you have gathered yourself. (You might have conducted some research in the form of a questionnaire, for instance, seeking people's views about a new shopping precinct. If this is so, then you would correctly use the comments and their outcomes in your work as extensively as you wished in order to make your point.)

Where you do use the written views of others in your work, try to rephrase them not only so they are in your own words, but in order to incorporate them into a critical argument of your own. Where you want to quote directly from a secondary source of information – perhaps to justify your stance – try to write the quotation into your own argument by using introductory phrases such as, 'as so-and-so says', or 'according to so-and-so'. Above all else, try to avoid reproducing long word-for-word statements form the work of others.

What your 'argument' is should be fairly self-evident if you adopt the principle of stating what it is you have done before you do it, as suggested in the section on 'Outline of your intentions'.

CONCLUSIONS AND POSSIBLE FUTURE DIRECTIONS – APPROXIMATELY 10 PER CENT OF YOUR STUDY

In the work so far you will have been making some propositions, trying to prove their validity, and incorporating a variety of conclusions. In order to make it clear what you believe you have been about, it pays to draw your conclusions together and present them briefly in a formal manner.

You will be likely to have two types of conclusion. The first type covers conclusions which are important to your point of view, and which are largely proven in your work. Present these first, under an appropriate heading.

The second set of conclusions may be of lesser importance but, should still be largely proven in your work. They may have arisen despite your original expectations and intentions. These points in particular will suggest the directions you work might possibly take if it were to be extended further. They also show how aware you are, and they have the advantage of helping to make your work more personal.

APPENDICES AND BIBLIOGRAPHY

Don't take these into account in any word count. You use 'appendices' if you have certain information which is valid in terms of what your Dissertation contains, but which would get in the way of the flow of your work and the argument within it in the main body of your Dissertation. In this way, you can ask the reader to refer to the information in the appropriate appendix at any point in the main body of your work, without disturbing the flow of your argument.

The type of material which might go to make up an appendix is the information you have collected from research questionnaires you have used, or secondary source information gathered from outside agencies, manufacturers, museums, galleries and so on. If you have involved yourself in any correspondence with other people or agencies, you could put copies of your letters and the original replies you received in the appendices.

Don't copy out long tracts from books you have read and include them in your appendices. The contents of books are best left in books, and then full publication details of the book put into a bibliography. If you wish to refer the reader to a *specific* passage in a book, perhaps because you have used it in your work in the main body of your Dissertation, then you should include the page in your reference in the bibliography. On the other hand, if you have read and used the book in a *general* way, just list it in the Bibliography without any particular page reference.

When you list books in the Bibliography, use a consistent and accepted style of recording the details. For instance, if you wanted to include this book, and refer to the information on this page, you could enter it in your Bibliography in this way:

McLean, T. and READ, B. (1990) *A-level Revise Guide: Art and Design.* Longman. Harlow, Essex. p.246.

Don't put books into the bibliography if you have not used them in your work. You may have used some in an indirect way, of course, whereby reading them just contributed towards your personal point of view. If so you can include them in your list.

'QUESTION AND ANSWER' PAPERS

In the other papers in Art History exams, the first thing to bear in mind is that, although different sections of a paper (or each paper itself) might carry different marks towards the overall total, every question within a paper or a section of a paper will carry equal marks. So, when you choose which questions to answer, **choose those which you know most about.**

PICKING THE RIGHT QUESTIONS

When you receive the question paper, jot down the information you have in your head on each question in turn as you read through the paper. We suggest you use a 'brainstorming' diagram to do this, as it easier to see what you have and to make connections between the pieces of knowledge you have. In our opinion *the worst thing you can do is to scan the questions, looking for one which appeals to you*. The dangers in this are that:

- you might not know very much about the subject;
- you might know more about a number of other questions in the paper;
- you might fail to grasp the essence of the question, and then fail to answer the question in the best manner.

It is much better that you read each question carefully, and in turn, trying to grasp exactly what it is asking of you. As you do so, begin your brainstorming diagrams. Then move on to the next question, repeat the exercise, and so on. Doing this will *not* waste your time in the examination.

When you have completed your brainstorms, you will find yourself in a sound position to select the questions which you can answer in order to gain access to the maximum number of marks for the paper. If you have to choose and answer three questions, and they all have equal mark weighting, you will be penalising yourself if you answer only two questions, or attempt to answer four. Pick the right number of questions, using your brainstorms as a guide to your ability to answer them well. When you have selected the questions to answer, you can then begin to build up the brainstorming diagrams for those you have chosen. Rack your brains to see if you know any more about the subject central to each question, and, where it is relevant, transfer the information from your rejected brainstorming diagrams to those you are developing.

When you get down to answering your chosen questions, re-read them each time most carefully, and *be certain you know what is expected of you* in your answer. As you continue to clarify this, you will find that the question contains some essential criteria for you to work to in your answer. For example, if the question asks you to 'compare the contemporary works of Picasso and Braque', the word *compare* offers you essential criteria to work to in your answer. It will be of little use if you just *describe* some of the works of each artist. The examiner will be expecting you to understand something about the way each worked and to arrive at a personal critical comparison in your answer. We would suggest that it does not matter if your decisions were somewhat eccentric. What is more important is that you should show that you can establish and work to credible criteria in your argument.

Remember, in the examination you are trying to convey to other how much you know, how you can read and decode questions and how you can organise your knowledge into a comprehensible and well-argued critical response to the particular question. In this sense, although you will be answering specific questions set to test your knowledge about pre-determined aspects of the history of art and design, it is just as necessary for you to include your own critical point of view in these papers as it is in the Individual Study.

In the question papers set for these sections of your exam, you will find that you may be given photographs of art and design work, or of architecture, to use as the basis for some questions. Most papers also include at least one question which allows you to choose the subject matter of your answer, although in these questions it is *even more important* that you grasp and understand most clearly what is expected of you in your answer. This type of question often asks you to use a local building as the basis of your response to the question.

Questions will be set not only to test your knowledge of the subject, but also to *allow* you to convey what it is you do know in your answers. That is to say, the questions are *not* set to trip you up. The reason you have so many to choose from is that the examiners want to provide you with some certainty that you will know what is necessary to answer at least some of the questions. This being the case, it should be obvious that knowledge of *certain prescribed facts* alone is not regarded as vital in these question-and-answer examinations, but rather how you can *work with and organise* the knowledge you do have into a well-reasoned, critical argument.

The syllabuses divide the History of Art up into little 'parcels of time' for your teachers to choose from in planning your course of study. In reality these 'parcels of time' are a false division of the history of the subject, but they do allow you to focus your studies. Even so, understanding something in one period of time often requires that you need to know what preceded it and the consequences it had later. Your teachers will try to ensure that you study your subject in this way, but it will be up to you to remember to include these aspects of your knowledge in your answers at the time of the examination.

BEING CRITICAL

To be 'critical' in your work does not mean that you should 'knock' everything you choose to study. The idea of criticism concerns a *way of working*, rather than what your conclusions might be, which is why we say that you may arrive at an eccentric point of view but still gain a very high mark for your work.

In your examinations at this level, being critical means that you should have a personal point of view. The danger in this is that, if you are not careful, it could quickly turn into a form of licentious freedom, whereby what you think has little or no connection with any form of reality acceptable to society. For instance, you might know someone who paints pictures in his or her spare time, and you might like their work very much. If, in saying how much you liked it, you were to say that, in your opinion, he or she is the best painter in the world, you would have to set out to *prove* this in some way. What you would be saying in such a case is that the painter concerned is better than Rembrandt! They may be, but you would have to give some concrete reasons for coming to this conclusion.

In such circumstances, the way to work is to choose someone or something as a comparison in order to show how you understand and accept the more socially recognised standards of what goes to make a good painter and good art. You do this by showing how well you understand what makes anyone – say Rembrandt in this instance – an outstanding painter. Then you will begin to spell out some of the suitable *criteria* to describe satisfactory and successful painting. Once you have made these criteria clear, you can begin critical evaluation of the artist you have chosen, using the criteria in question to measure his or her work. By this means, you use general or socially accepted criteria to help to justify your own more *personal* beliefs. This is why we talk above about conducting an argument by justifying your decisions form the *contextual* and *historical* circumstances of Art and Design. This is being critical.

Of course, it is more likely that you will be dealing with a generally accepted artist, designer, object or movement in Art and Design than the example above suggests. Even so, there should be no difference in your approach. You still have to use some accepted standards in Art and Design to establish the criteria by which you are going to evaluate the subject of your work. Once this is done, you then apply those criteria to your subject, working into your work your more personal views about the subject matter.

Some conclusions

Combining practical work and historical and critical studies benefits your work in both syllabuses if you are taking two distinct A-level examinations in Art and Design. Even if you are only taking an examination in the History of Art and Design, it will benefit you to include some practical work in your approaches to the study of the subject.

Whilst it is an essential part of your studies that you should learn and be able to remember facts, it is at least equally important they you should study how to *use* such information, as well as to display your personal responses to what you see in your studies and around you within a critical framework. This means that you should have a personal point of view to express, and be able to justify it according to suitable criteria, including references to the work of others more expert than yourself.

EXERCISES

1 Send to the National Gallery, London, and purchase postcards of:

'The Battle of San Romano' by Paolo Ucello
'Interior Scene' by Pieter de Hooch
'The Avenue, Middelharnis' by Meindert Hobbema.

Study, discuss and compare how each has used linear perspective in their work to convey a sense of depth and space within their pictures. Give your opinions about the success and failure of each in this respect.

2 Open a newspaper colour supplement at any page. Choose one picture on the page. Find out as many facts as you can about:

- who took the photograph:
- the process necessary to print it in the colour supplement:
- the subject which the photograph accompanies:
- aspects of the content of the photograph.

Compose all the information you gather into a discussion about the picture in particular, and colour supplements in general.

3 Construct a game based upon the 'types of building' and 'styles of architecture' used by various establishments, such as:

- banks;
- council offices;
- swimming baths;
- libraries;
- churches;
- supermarkets;
- boutiques;
- travel agents;
- DIY stores.

You might take photographs of examples of such buildings and wipe out all identifying words and items in the photographs as a beginning. Or you might decide upon different elements which are present in each 'style' of building, and design a game which enables the players to 'collect' these in order to 'construct' their building in competition with other players.

4 Choose an everyday object. Collect as many different examples of it as you can. Find out all you can about why each variation exists, the reasons for changes of material in their construction and the effects different materials cause, alterations in their design caused by social and cultural changes, and so on. Arrange your objects into an exhibition with accompanying explanatory material. Prepare and deliver a lecture on your collection to your classmates.

5 Select a well-known photographer whose work you like. Collect as many examples of photographic prints of his or her work as you can. Using a 'book' formation, try to show how the photographer and photography is an important and credible part of the history of Fine Art. Use postcard examples of Fine Art works in your text to help make your points.

6 Find a local environment designed for shopping, such as a modern 'shopping precinct' or an old 'shopping arcade'. Take photographs, make drawings, construct plans and maps, use diagrams showing customer flow paths, and so on, to describe what it is you see. Compare the precinct or the arcade with your local 'High Street', where, perhaps, the shops are strung out on each side of a busy road. Which environment do you think is the most desirable, and why? Present your results in the form of a concertina file and models which can be opened out and stood up on table tops. Accompany your visual material and argument with the minimum of words necessary to make your points. You might keep the words down to simple headings, or questions.

7 Using the material you have gathered together for 6 above, criticise either the precinct or the arcade in terms of its functional success with respect to shopping (to do this you may have to conduct some form of on-the-spot research), its aesthetic success as a design arrangement of the formal elements of architecture, and the use of relevant technology and materials to construct it. Present your work and findings in a way which is appropriate to the information you have gathered together, and to the materials you have used in your work.

BIBLIOGRAPHY

ATTOE, W. (1978) *Architecture and critical imagination.* John Wiley & Sons. Chichester.
BESSET, M. (1976) *The Herbert History of Art and Architecture: The Twentieth Century.* The Herbert Press. London.
BUZAN, T. (1974) *Use Your Head.* BBC. London
CONWAY, H. (ed.) (1987) *Design History: a Student's Handbook.* Allen and Unwin. London.
CULLEN, G. (1968) *Townscape.* The Architectural Press. London.
de BONO, E. (1970) *Lateral Thinking: a textbook of creativity.* Ward Lock Educational. London
GOMBRICH, E.H. (1972) *The Story of Art.* Phaidon. London

HAVILAND, J. (ed.) (1985) *A Pictorial History of Art: Western Art Through the Ages.* Galley Press. Leicester.
HUYGHE, R. (ed.) (1969) *Larousse Encyclopaedia of Modern Art.* Paul Hamlyn. London.
ITTEN, J. (1961) *The Art of Colour* Van Norstrand Reinhold Company, London.
JANSON, H.W. AND D.J. (1957) *The Picture History of Painting.* Thames and Hudson. London.
LAUER, D.A. (1970) *Design Basics.* Holt, Rienhart and Winston. London.
LYNTON, N. (1980) *The Story of Modern Art.* Phaidon Press. Oxford.
MURRAY, P. AND L. (1987) *Dictionary of Art & Artists.* Penguin Books. Harmondsworth, Middlesex.
OSBORNE, H. (ed.) (1988) *The Oxford Companion to Twentieth Century Art.* Oxford University Press. Oxford.
PALMER, F. (1988) *Themes and Projects in Art and Design.* Longman. Harlow, Essex.
PIPER, SIR DAVID (ed.) (1988) *Dictionary of Art & Artists.* Collins. London.
POHRIBNY, A. (1979) *Abstract Painting.* Phaidon Press. Oxford.
POINTON, M. (1980) *History of Art: a Student's Handbook.* Allen and Unwin. London.
READ, B. (1988) *GCSE Art and Design: Longman Revise Guides.* Longman. Harlow, Essex.
(1989) *GCSE Art and Design: Longman Coursework Guides.* Longman Harlow, Essex.
READ, H. (1967) *A Concise History of Modern Painting.* Thames & Hudson. London.
RICKEY, G. (1967) *Constructivism: Origins and Evolution.* Studio Vista. London.
ROWLAND, K. (1966) *Looking and Seeing.* Ginn and Company. London.
(1973) *A History of the Modern Movement: Art, Architecture, Design.* Van Nostrand Reinhold Company. New York.
SAUSMEREZ, M. de (1966) *Basic Design: the Dynamics of Visual Form.* Studio Vista. London.
SEMENZATO, C. (1979) *The World of Art.* Arnoldo Mondadori Editore. Milan.
SPALDING, F. (1986) *British Art Since 1900.* Thames and Hudson. London.
STURT, G. (1923) *The Wheelwright's Shop.* C U P Cambridge
VAN GOGH, V (1958) *The Complete Letters of Vincent Van Gogh.* Graphic Society Books. New York
WOOD, C. (1876) *Victorian Panorama: Paintings of Victorian Life.* Faber and Faber Limited. London

ACKNOWLEDGEMENTS

The fruits of much of our own reading and education have become so interwoven into our own personas and working vocabulary that it is sometimes impossible to pinpoint the sources of our knowledge and information. Nevertheless, we recognise our indebtedness to the following works and would like to acknowledge this fact. We hope that this will encourage you to get into the habit of referring to these sources as you go about your own studies.

Gombrich, E. H., *The Story of Art, Phaidon, London, 1972*
Murray, P. and L.,*The Penguin Dictionary of Art and Artists,* Penguin, Harmondsworth, 1987.
Rowland, K., *A History of the Modern Movement: Art, Architecture and Design*, Van Nostrand Reinhold Company, London, 1973.

The authors are indebted to the following Examination Boards for permission to reproduce specimen and past examination questions and to quote from their syllabuses. Whilst permission has been granted to reproduce their questions, the answers, or hints on answers are solely the responsibility of the authors and have neither been provided nor approved by the Boards.
Associated Examining Board
University of Cambridge Local Examinations Syndicate
Joint Matriculation Board
University of London Schools Examination Board
Northern Ireland Schools Examinations Council
Oxford Delegacy of Local Examinations
Oxford and Cambridge Schools Examination Board
Scottish Examination Board
Welsh Joint Education Committee
The authors are especially grateful to the WJEC and the ULSEB for their help in providing candidates' work.
The authors are grateful to the following for permission to use reproductions of works in their collection:
Castle Museum, Norwich
City of Birmingham Museums and Art Gallery
English Heritage, Iveaugh Bequest, Kenwood
Ipswich Museums and Galleries
National Gallery, London
National Galleries of Scotland
Tate Gallery, London
William Morris Gallery, London

INDEX